Give Peace a Chance

Syracuse Studies on Peace and Conflict Resolution
Harriet Hyman Alonso, Charles Chatfield, and Louis Kriesberg
Series Editors

For
CHARLES DeBENEDETTI
(1943–1987)

Contents

Foreword
    GEORGE McGOVERN   xi
Preface   xv
Abbreviations   xix

PART ONE
Antiwar Movement Strategies and Tactics

Introduction   3
1. The Counterculture and the Antiwar Movement
    DAVID FARBER   7
2. You Don't Need a Weatherman but a Postman Can Be Helpful: Thoughts on the History of SDS and the Antiwar Movement
    MAURICE ISSERMAN   22
3. CALCAV and Religious Opposition to the Vietnam War
    MITCHELL K. HALL   35
4. Pacifists and the Vietnam Antiwar Movement
    DAVID McREYNOLDS   53

5. "May Day" 1971: Civil Disobedience and the
   Vietnam Antiwar Movement
       GEORGE W. HOPKINS   71

PART TWO
The Military and the Antiwar Movement

Introduction   91
6. The GI Movement and the Response
   from the Brass
       TERRY H. ANDERSON   93
7. GI Resistance During the Vietnam War
       DAVID CORTRIGHT   116
8. Vietnam Veterans and War Crimes Hearings
       ELLIOTT L. MEYROWITZ AND KENNETH J. CAMPBELL   129
9. They Moved the Town: Organizing Vietnam
   Veterans Against the War
       WILLIAM F. CRANDELL   141

PART THREE
Women and the Antiwar Movement

Introduction   157
10. "Not My Son, Not Your Son, Not Their Sons":
    Mothers Against the Vietnam Draft
        AMY SWERDLOW   159
11. "Women Power" and Women's Liberation:
    Exploring the Relationship Between the
    Antiwar Movement and the Women's
    Liberation Movement
        ALICE ECHOLS   171
12. The Women Who Left Them Behind
        NINA S. ADAMS   182

PART FOUR
The Antiwar Movement in the Schools

Introduction   199

13. "Look Out Kid, You're Gonna Get Hit!": Kent State and the Vietnam Antiwar Movement
    KENNETH J. HEINEMAN   201

14. Conscience and the Courts: Teachers and Students Against War and Militarism
    CHARLES F. HOWLETT   223

Notes   243
Selected Readings   275
Contributors   283
Index   287

Foreword

The Vietnam War and the unprecedented antiwar movement that it spawned were the transcendent political and moral issues of American public life for at least a decade, from 1965 to 1975. The war itself was the most dramatic demonstration of the Cold War anticommunism that guided American foreign policy for more than four decades after World War II, from 1945 to 1990. The growing domestic dispute over America's involvement in Vietnam divided American society as had no other issue since the Civil War.

Politically, that dispute raged largely inside the Democratic party. It was not a struggle that pitted Democrats against Republicans; rather it was Democrats versus Democrats.

When Democratic Senator Eugene McCarthy challenged incumbent Democratic President Lyndon Johnson in 1968, it was the antiwar movement that nearly carried him to victory in New Hampshire—a prospect that doubtless contributed much to President Johnson's decision not to seek reelection.

When four years later I won the Democratic nomination in a field of more than a dozen serious contenders, it was the antiwar movement that propelled me to an upset victory over better known, more established political figures.

But the antiwar movement cut both ways—as did the war itself. In dividing the Democratic party between "hawks" and "doves," it probably contributed decisively to the election of Republican Richard Nixon in 1968 and his reelection in 1972. In 1968 Democratic doves tended to sit on their hands after the defeat of Senator McCarthy and the assassination of Senator Robert Kennedy, also an antiwar presidential contender. The Democratic nominee, Hubert Humphrey, had a genuinely liberal record on civil rights and social justice, but he was "wrong" on the war and he paid a heavy price in Democratic disaffection in the general election.

Yet four years later I too paid a heavy price as a passionate opponent of the war when hawkish Democrats rallied to the war standard of incumbent Richard Nixon.

Neither the Democratic party nor the cause of liberalism, America's oldest party and its most creative political tradition, have recovered from the traumatic impact of the Vietnam struggle. Aside from the shattering and divisive political impact of the controversy over the war, there were other serious costs. The tremendous financial cost of the war initiated a stubborn inflationary spiral and budget deficits that made it politically and economically difficult to finance a liberal agenda for education, health care, housing, and other concerns.

The Vietnam struggle and the Johnson administration's effort to rationalize it in the face of antiwar dissent led to the "credibility gap" that has plagued our national leadership from that day until the present.

I also believe that the Watergate scandals of the Nixon administrations were outgrowths of the siege mentality and the conspiratorial atmosphere that overtook the Nixon White House in its desire to contain and manage the antiwar challenge to the administration.

My biased conviction is that the antiwar movement finally saved America from a moral, political, and economic disaster. It is said by supporters of the Vietnam War that the war was lost not in Vietnam but in the antiwar movement in America. I hope that is a correct analysis. It would be the highest tribute both to the antiwar movement and to American democracy if it could be firmly established that organized public opinion and political action were responsible for correcting the enormous blunders of the leaders who took us into the jungles of Vietnam.

Patriotism doubtlessly guided many of the soldiers and civilian supporters of the Vietnam War. But I shall always believe that the best grounded patriots were those Americans who had both the insight to know that the war was a terrible mistake and the courage to protest it.

Religious leaders and their communicants, students and professors, business and professional people, women's groups, veterans, editors and writers, and ordinary Americans in all walks of life—plus many of my colleagues in the Congress—all of these composed the American antiwar movement.

Many years ago the great British Conservative Edmund Burke wrote: "A conscientious man would be cautious how he dealt in blood." The participants in the American antiwar movement, and those who have written the chapters that follow, have strengthened Burke's wise admonition.

George McGovern

Preface

The Vietnam antiwar movement was the largest and most important antiwar movement in American history. It affected the policies of Presidents Lyndon B. Johnson and Richard M. Nixon in Southeast Asia, as well as those of the North and South Vietnamese. In addition, the movement's activities directly influenced Johnson's decision not to run for the presidency in 1968 and indirectly influenced Nixon's decision to resign in 1974. Beyond the war, the movement contributed to dramatic changes in the nation's university system, its political parties, and the way its leaders and citizens viewed the media.

Students of the Vietnam antiwar movement must grapple with the fact that no one organization or coalition ever captured the leadership of that amorphous group of millions of Americans from all segments of society who protested against the war. The movement included mobilizations and moratoria, letter-writing campaigns, draft resistance, silent vigils, tax protests, picketing, teach-ins, court cases, electoral politics, petitions and newspaper advertisements, civil disobedience, and even self-immolation.

Although the authors of the fourteen chapters in this collection cover only some of these issues, they offer a rich introduction to the ways the movement's activities affected the lives of most Americans. Almost all of the authors belong to the Vietnam generation. Several served in the military during the era. Others were involved in the movement itself. The opening of new archival collections and the increasing tendency of activists and government officials to talk about their experiences, enabled our authors to explore important questions concerning the organization, strategies and tactics, and successes and failures of the movement.

Our understanding of the antiwar movement has been enhanced significantly by *An American Ordeal: The Antiwar Movement of the Vietnam Era* (1990), by Charles DeBenedetti with the assistance of Charles Chatfield.

Charles DeBenedetti was a member of The University of Toledo's history faculty from 1968 until his death in 1987. In addition to *An American Ordeal*, he wrote *Origins of the Modern American Peace Movement, 1915–1929* (1978) and *The Peace Reform in American History* (1980) and also edited *Peace Heroes in Twentieth Century America* (1986).

In 1982, DeBenedetti drew national attention when he uncovered among papers at the Lyndon Baines Johnson Presidential Library a report from the CIA to President Johnson, previously classified as top secret, indicating that the Agency believed there was no communist control or foreign link to American protests against the Vietnam War. Johnson refused to accept that judgment, DeBenedetti's research showed. So important was his research that just before his death, DeBenedetti received a $70,000 grant from the Social Science Research Council for an oral history entitled "Elite Dissent and U.S. Foreign Policymaking: Vietnam as a Case Study."

DeBenedetti devoted a great deal of effort to the Council on Peace Research in History (CPRH). He was on its executive council from 1973 until his death, served the organization both as secretary-treasurer and president, and in 1984 coedited *Peace and Change*, its journal. He conveyed a personal concern that was genuine and unbounded. As one of his friends in the CPRH remarked, he was a rock of quiet strength. A man of warmth and good humor whose advice and encouragement proved invaluable to scores of colleagues, DeBenedetti was a sustaining force in many lives as well as in the field of history.

Charles DeBenedetti died of a brain tumor on 27 January 1987, his forty-fourth birthday. We his colleagues, the history profession, and the community at large are richer for those forty-four years.

The Vietnam Antiwar Movement Conference, held in Toledo, Ohio, on 4–5 May 1990, was a memorial to Charles DeBenedetti as well as a celebration of the posthumous publication of *An American Ordeal: The Antiwar Movement of the Vietnam Era*. The research he inaugurated in that book fittingly extended to the papers at the conference and the essays in this volume.

Sponsored by The University of Toledo and the Council on Peace Research in History, the conference drew outstanding scholars from throughout the United States and several foreign countries. Those who participated in that exciting event whose papers or comments could not be included in this volume were: David L. Anderson, William Berman, Scott L. Bills, Kenneth J. Bindas, Robert Buzzanco, Charles Chatfield, Skip L. Delano, Michael Gillen, Gerald R. Gioglio, Jonathan Goldstein, Jerry Gordon, Philip A. Grant, Jr., Alexis Greene, George C. Herring, Gary Hess, Howard Jablon, Miriam R. Jackson, Steve Kent, Jeffrey Kimball, Michael Klein, Anne Klejment, James Lafferty, Jeffery Livingston, Ronald Lora, Michael A. Lutzker, Robert J. McMahon, Thomas R. Maddux, Martin J. Murray, Lynn H. Parsons, David S. Patterson, Kimberly L. Phillips, Steve Potts, Roberto Rabel, George E. Reedy, Louis Rose, Kim Salomon, Robert D. Schulzinger, J. David Singer, Geoffrey S. Smith, Thomas Socknat, Sandra Taylor, Barbara L. Tischler, David Turner, Clifford Wilcox, Miles Wolpin and Randall B. Woods.

The editors of this volume are especially grateful to the Ohio Board of Regents for a Program Excellence Grant, which provided financial support, and to Paula Ashton and Louise Celley of The University of Toledo Department of History, who were invaluable in the organization of the conference and the production of this volume. To Anne Burnham, also of the History Department, go many thanks for contributing her considerable editorial skills to polishing the final manuscript. Any royalties generated by this book will be divided equally between the Charles DeBenedetti Scholarship Fund and the Council on Peace Research in History.

Melvin Small
William D. Hoover

11 June 1991

Abbreviations

ACLU	American Civil Liberties Union
AFSC	American Friends Service Committee
APA	Atlanta Peace Alliance
ASU	American Servicemen's Union
AWOL	absent without leave
BUS	Black United Students
CADRE	Chicago Area Draft Resisters
CALC	Clergy and Laity Concerned
CALCAV	Clergy and Laymen Concerned About Vietnam
CCI	Citizens Commission of Inquiry
CNVA	Committee for Nonviolent Action
COM	Concerned Officers Movement
CORE	Congress of Racial Equality
CP	Communist party
CPF	Catholic Peace Fellowship
CPRH	Council on Peace Research in History
ERAP	Economic Research and Action Projects
FBI	Federal Bureau of Investigation
FOR	Fellowship of Reconciliation
HUAC	House Un-American Activities Committee
MACV	Military Assistance Command—Vietnam
MDM	Movement for a Democratic Military

Mobe	National Mobilization to End the War in Vietnam
NAACP	National Association for the Advancement of Colored People
NAG	National Action Group
NCAWRR	National Coalition Against War, Racism, and Repression
NCC	National Council of Churches
NCO	noncommissioned officer
New Mobe	New Mobilization Committee to End the War in Vietnam
NLF	National Liberation Front
NOW	National Organization for Women
NPAC	National Peace Action Coalition
NSA	National Student Association
NVA	North Vietnamese Army
OSU	Ohio State University
PCPJ	People's Coalition for Peace and Justice
PLP	Progressive Labor party
POW	prisoner of war
PTSD	post-traumatic stress disorder
RAW	Rapid American Withdrawal
RCP	Revolutionary Communist party
ROTC	Reserve Officers' Training Corps
RU	Revolutionary Union
RYM	Revolutionary Youth Movement
SANE	National Committee for a Sane Nuclear Policy
SAS	Students' Afro-American Society
SCLC	Southern Christian Leadership Conference
SCP	Student Coalition for Peace
SDS	Students for a Democratic Society
SNCC	Student Non-Violent Coordinating Committee
SP	Socialist party
SWP	Socialist Workers party
UAHC	Union of American Hebrew Congregations
UAW	United Automobile Workers

USSF	United States Servicemen's Fund
VVAW	Vietnam Veterans Against the War
VVAW/WSO	Vietnam Veterans Against the War/ Winter Soldier Organization
WLM	women's liberation movement
WRI	War Resisters International
WRL	War Resisters League
WSI	Winter Soldier Investigation
WSP	Women Strike for Peace
YSA	Young Socialist Alliance

PART ONE

Antiwar Movement Strategies and Tactics

Introduction

The antiwar movement was a massive and often unwieldy coalition of both relatively permanent and temporary, ad hoc organizations opposing U.S. policies in Southeast Asia in a variety of ways. Leaders of those organizations constantly disagreed with one another over the choice of strategies and tactics needed to bring American soldiers home from the war. Liberals argued with radicals, the Old Left with the New Left, and all groups argued among themselves. The issues ranged from narrow tactical ones, such as the sorts of signs that could be carried in parades, to broader strategic ones involving the potential for developing a mass movement to overthrow the capitalist system.

The essays in this section examine five areas of contention in the antiwar movement. In one way or another, all study the many serious problems the doves confronted during the turbulent sixties as they groped for the most effective way to end the war.

In chapter 1, David Farber, a historian of the sixties, tackles the controversial issue of the relationship between the antiwar movement and the counterculture. Movement ideologues were nervous about including often apolitical "hippie" elements in their protests. However, as Farber demonstrates, it became difficult to distinguish between the two groups. From time to time they worked together successfully, despite the fact that their opponents purposefully confused their antiwar position, which was supported by a growing number of middle-class Americans, with the long hair, drugs, and rock music that the same middle class abhorred.

The leadership of the Students for a Democratic Society (SDS) was also suspicious of the seriousness of the counterculture. A student of the Left in America, historian Maurice Isserman examines SDS's relationship to the antiwar movement in chapter 2. Isserman contends that there is much to be learned about that important New Left group from studying rank-and-file activities, or history from the bottom up. The civil rights experiences of SDS members and their cooperation with pacifist groups, he finds, were key determinants of the organization's early approach to the war.

SDS was not interested in attracting adult, mainstream liberal support. Another group organized in the sixties, the Clergy and Laymen Concerned About Vietnam (CALCAV), did target that cohort in its activities. In chapter 3, historian Mitchell K. Hall summarizes findings from his book on CALCAV as he traces its development from 1966 to the end of the war. By studying responses from institutionalized churches and their leaders, Hall reveals the often contentious disputes over tactics and strategies that affected the way influential ministers, priests, and rabbis reacted to the escalation of the war.

Some of the religious opposition was driven by pacifism. Longtime pacifist leader David McReynolds became a leader of the War Resisters League (WRL) during the period of the Vietnam War. In chapter 4, an intensely personal essay on the antiwar movement, McReynolds demonstrates how difficult it was to build a unified coalition and delineates the specific role that traditional pacifist groups played at demonstrations as well as in defining the goals of the movement. McReynolds and other pacifists encouraged the use of civil disobedience as a weapon in the arsenal of antiwar protestors.

Now a historian, George W. Hopkins participated in the May Day activities in Washington in early May 1971. This last major antiwar demonstration exhibited one of the largest experiments in civil disobedience in American history. In chapter 5, Hopkins outlines the background of this unique protest and evaluates its impact on the city and the Nixon administration.

The groups and political tendencies discussed in these five chapters illustrate many of the strengths and weaknesses of the antiwar movement. In order to attract as many people as possible to their banners, antiwar leaders welcomed participation from all sorts of dissenting organizations. This practical, no-enemies-to-the-Left approach, which guaranteed huge turnouts at periodic rallies and marches, nevertheless contributed to bitter factional disputes and drew the media's attention to the most extreme and bizarre protestors. Yet one wonders what other approach could have produced the relatively successful record of the Vietnam antiwar movement.

1

The Counterculture and the Antiwar Movement

DAVID FARBER

In the 1960s and early 1970s, no clear delineations separated the movements that were changing the American body politic. Whether with anger or satisfaction, a good many Americans saw in black activism, antiwar marches, the women's movement, student protests, and counterculture enclaves a broad refiguring of what it meant to be an American and what America should mean in the world. The intertwining of so many answers, so many challenges to the narrow realm of 1950s electoral politics follows no simple script, as many men and women found themselves pulled forward and together by forces that transcend the simple groupings of antiwar movement and counterculture.

College students, in particular, found themselves changed by a mood of rebellion that fits only uneasily into simple categories of analysis. As activist and historian Paul Buhle has said, "There was a continuum between politics and culture at every school. At one end there were these tight assed people whom you suspected of being close to the Communist Party. At the other end you had a lot of burn-outs. . . . In between the flow was tremendous. It's important to stress how thin those barriers were."[1] The Movement, people called it then.

Certainly the enemies of that Movement tended to see as one all the faces of 1960s social change. Mayor Richard J. Daley of Chicago said of the antiwar, antiestablishment forces gathering in his city in August 1968, "We are talking to the hippies, the Yippies, and the flippies and everything else."[2]

Nevertheless, especially in the mid-1960s, many in different branches of what can only loosely be called the Movement found little common ground. Those who staked their lives on a radically different culture, one that depended on the promise of acid dreams (overwhelmingly young people), and those who dedicated themselves primarily to ending the war in Vietnam (people of all ages) found that common ground treacherous.

Some, for reasons political or personal or both, did not want to leap those divides between them. Many others felt it essential to build bridges and create a broad-based movement that could rally around the imperative of stopping American involvement in the war in Vietnam and even contest the understandings that made the war possible in the first place. To some extent, the war and escalating draft calls, the broad strokes of the mass media, the percolations of youth culture and the fury of security forces and prowar politicians blurred the divisions between counterculture and antiwar movement. By the end of the 1960s, an antiwar movement existed in which cultural issues played a less divisive, albeit less important, role.

Still, adherents of the different forms and forces of social change in the 1960s carried with them different logics, different priorities, different trajectories. Fitting those different frames of reference onto one movement to end the war in Vietnam was a tricky business. Understanding that business of coalition building—its successes and failures—tells us something about how outside politics works, how cultural rebels and political activists learn from one another, how different priorities—even in the name of the same immediate goal—forge fundamentally different solutions.

Some in the antiwar movement, with the clear and pressing goal of ending America's role in the war in Vietnam, rightfully saw as dubious allies the counterculturists who wedded themselves to drug use, promiscuity, costumery, and the creation of alternative institutions. And many who saw the future of America hinging on a broad shift in consciousness saw only old debates and narrow thinking driving the antiwar movement. The tension was real and for some unresolvable.

In the mid-1960s, when a mass movement against the war in Vietnam was just beginning, some well-known leaders in the antiwar movement and the nascent counterculture did draw lines. In particular, some in the front ranks of the counterculture, in their general rejection of politics, saw antiwar activism as beside the point—a kind of ping-pong match. As they would have it, they were onto new games.

Acid visionary Ken Kesey, author of *One Flew Over the Cuckoo's Nest* and emblem of the counterculture, saw all politics as a dead end. In 1964 he and the Merry Pranksters, while "flying high" across the country in their psychedelic bus, made a pit stop in Arizona. There they announced their analysis of the 1964 presidential race: "A Vote for Barry is a Vote for Fun." As co-Prankster Gurney Norman recalled many years later, "It's just perfect dopey, dope prankster analysis . . . it shows this total lack of interest in real politics." For the Pranksters and a lot of others inventing the 1960s counterculture, the struggles for civil rights, the antiwar movement, and other political issues of the mid-1960s were simply beside the point. That was the lesson they had taken away from their acid visions—and acid, above all else, set the counterculture off from the tamer thrills and smirks of the early sixties youth culture. Kesey, to the degree that he thought about antiwar activists, felt hostility towards them.[3]

He made his feelings clear the next year at the Vietnam Day teach-in at Berkeley when he showed up in the Pranksters' bus, which was "painted blood red for the occasion and covered with nationalist symbols: swastikas, hammers and sickles, rising suns, stars of David, the Great Seal of the United States, the American eagle." When he spoke and played his harmonica to the crowd of 14,000, Kesey compared the antiwar movement and the military: "You're not gonna stop this war with this rally, by marching . . . look at the war, and turn your backs and say . . . Fuck it." Speaking for many who saw acid consciousness, rather than political critique, as the solution to—or more accurately, a salvation from—Cold War America, Kesey waged war on the forms of everyday life. He saw the antiwar movement as a different political line, but still a line. He saw the leftist politics that determined the antiwar movement in Berkeley as denigrated by nineteenth-century visions of political economy and a narrow concern with the means of production and those in charge.[4] Like others in the counterculture, Kesey wanted to invent a new way of life. As acid apostle Timothy Leary—half Huxley and half huckster—would say, "Turn On, Tune in, Drop Out."[5]

Many in counterculture enclaves that sprang up around the country between 1965 and 1970 tuned in to Kesey's vision. The Diggers, master theorists of the American counterculture who, more than anyone else, tried on a daily basis to keep the Haight-Ashbury on an even keel, felt that the antiwar movement took away from the here-and-now necessity of building community and "making magic on a daily basis." The Diggers saw American intervention in Vietnam as despicable, but only predictably so. To fight the war, they said, you had to fight the mad nightmare of control. Gary Snyder's poem, "A Curse on the Men in Washington, Pentagon," said it all for the Diggers.

> Om a ka ca ta ta ya sa svaha
> As you shoot down the Vietnamese girls and men
> > in their fields
> > Burning and chopping,
> > Poisoning and blighting,
> So surely I hunt the white man down
> > in my heart. . . .
> As I kill the white man,
> > the "American" in me
> And dance out the Ghost Dance;
> To bring back America, the grass and the streams
> To trample your throat in my dreams.
> This magic I work, this loving I give
> > That my children may flourish
> > And yours won't live.

The Diggers printed the poem and passed it around the community. Later they ran it as a part of the *Digger Papers,* the seminal statement of the organized counterculture. In the eyes of the Diggers and in the parlance of the times, marching, rallying, and politics constituted part of an old head.[6]

Many a young antiwar activist found this antipolitical stance infuriating. As one Berkeley politico complained in early 1967, "They're putting us down for doing anything . . . like we have a peace march and they turn up, all upset, saying that marching's not dropping out, marching's a bad bag, marching's not pure."[7]

Looking back, John Sinclair, who was at the center of the counterculture in Detroit, supports the Berkeley activist's viewpoint. In the mid-1960s, Sinclair and his friends "were interested in blowing people's minds, basically . . . We never really felt very comfortable with the protest thing; we came from the point of view that said, 'It doesn't do any good to protest against these people. They're the ones that made it like this. . . . Create an alternative way of life to this, yourself. They aren't going to do it, you've got to do, we've got to do it.'"[8] For a number of those in the antiwar movement the dropout mentality of many counterculturists was regrettable but not a pressing concern. Although in retrospect young people would seem to be the driving force of the antiwar movement until mid-1967, they had a circumscribed leadership role. The countercultural forces that seeped onto college campuses in 1965 and flooded them by 1967 seemed largely beside the point to most antiwar organizers. When Norma Becker reached for the phone to set up the Fifth Avenue Peace Parade Committee in New York, the nascent counterculture was far from her mind. She chose to call, she says, the "existing peace groups—SANE, WRL, WSP, Women's International League for Peace and Freedom."[9] The leadership of the off-campus antiwar movement remained non–youth-oriented, let alone countercultural, from 1965 through mid-1967.

Old Left activists, who played a critical role in organizing antiwar protests, especially the Socialist Workers party (SWP) and its youth affiliate, the Young Socialist Alliance (YSA), showed little sympathy for the counterculture. Their position changed very little over time. As Norma Becker recalled, it was always easy to spot the Socialist Workers cadre: "They were the clean-cut neat ones, with short hair."[10] In a private communiqué, a leader of the YSA summed up the Trotskyist perspective, circa March 1968, on the counterculture as "a sick escapist milieu."[11] The Trotskyites, like Communist party members, wanted to keep their lines open to the American working class. As they saw it, that meant maintaining distance between themselves and the counterculture. Fred Halstead, one of the antiwar movement's best behind-the-scenes organizers, believed it essential to present the antiwar movement as respectable, law-abiding, patriotic. A mass movement could be created only in this way.[12]

For some young people, the essentially political form of the antiwar movement made sense but not its cultural blinders. Carl Oglesby, early SDS leader and one of the most self-conscious of the sixties activists, saw as early as 1965 that fighting against the U.S. role in Vietnam meant limiting in some fundamental ways aspects of personal rebellion and expressiveness. The "do your own thing" otherworldly imperative of the counterculture that prized self-expression above social responsibility had to be reigned in at a time of collective emergency. As Oglesby told a group of poets in Ann Arbor before the first campus teach-in on the war, there is "a moment in the life of the poet, when he has to put poetry itself behind and find some way to use poetry in a world that threatens it."[13] But to put poets to work in a political movement did not mean simply to turn their dancing visions into pragmatic stratagems. Oglesby believed a synergy could be created between a new politics and a new culture, even though he saw that combining political activism with cultural rebellion would force individuals to make personal compromises and could cost the antiwar movement more traditional constituencies. He believed that the organization into which he had been drawn, Students for a Democratic Society (SDS), could thrive on the sort of liberating culture he had in mind.

Oglesby and some, but by no means all, of the early leadership in SDS believed young people could live out what others saw as the contradictions between countercultural otherworldliness and radical political engagement. He rejected the stance of the traditional Left that cultural rebellion was anathema to a serious political commitment. "Rock music and long hair and dope, the damned socialist organizations couldn't stand that stuff," he recalls. "They had no conception at all, it seemed, of the relationship between political and cultural rebellion." SDS organizers did. "Our approach always was to make that connection happen, to bring cultural and political into the most intimate possible interplay." [14] Certainly many an enemy saw SDS in just those terms, most infamously, FBI director J. Edgar Hoover, who reputedly explained his utter contempt for the organization by noting that "its members dress in beatnik style." [15]

Other leaders of the New Left remained far more suspicious of countercultural tendencies. Tom Hayden, the best-known New Leftist in the sixties, had little to no respect for the drug culture. According to a fellow activist, Hayden thought "the counterculture was a joke. He hated grass and rock music. He wore his hair long [in the late 60s] for 'political' reasons." [16] Hayden, less caustically, remembers that he "went to few concerts, owned hardly any albums, rarely danced, and was privately frightened by the loss of control that drug advocates celebrated.... All during the 'cultural revolution' I remained the straight man." [17]

Todd Gitlin, onetime president of SDS, returned from the Christmas 1967 Cultural Congress in Havana hypersensitive to the privileges taken for granted by Americans, whether members of the mainstream culture or the counterculture. In particular, he excoriated the counterculture for its frivolity and lack of engagement in the struggles of Third World people. In a piece widely distributed by the Liberation News Service, he charged, "The love you flaunt... is made possible only by your privilege.... This love is more than luxury, it is founded on a theft.... At some time we shall hopefully be forced to go without some luxuries so that the rest of the world may eat." [18] Through 1967, among both theorists and organizers at the national leadership level, SDS and its founders remained divided about the political meaning of the counterculture. And among those active in the antiwar movement, SDS represented the organization most sympathetic to the counterculture. [19]

Most organizers in the early antiwar movement sided with the traditional Left, their ideological home, in their suspicions about the counterculture. The fact that after the April 1965 antiwar march the national leadership of SDS deliberately disengaged itself from a leadership role in the movement meant that young people who believed in bridging the gap between counterculture and political engagement had no clear representation. Some older members of the antiwar movement, however, had begun to look at the counterculture with more sympathy, if for no other reason than that its size made it hard to ignore.

The April 1967 issue of *Liberation,* a movement journal edited by Dave Dellinger, chairman of the National Mobilization to End the War in Vietnam (Mobe), debated the question of the counterculture. That question had become crucial to Dellinger as he reconsidered which generation had the best ideas on how to protest the war. Henry Anderson laid out the anticounterculture position most vigorously. "I find the drug culture to be, in the end, merely pathetic.... Nothing pleases the keepers of our political-economic zoo more than contented, amiable, unambitious inmates," he argued. Allen Ginsberg, long a one-man band of spiritual enlightenment and cultural rebellion, tried to explain another way of looking at it. He argued that the counterculture represented a fundamental critique that could transcend "the illusions of the political state." Ginsberg, a poet first, believed that the antiwar movement, like the rest of the nation, needed "academies of self awareness, classes in spirituality." He saw the counterculture—with its reliance on drugs, especially acid—as a requisite to right political thinking. On paper, no meeting of minds became apparent, but the antiwar movement had begun to recognize the potential power of a new constituency. [20]

Although it does not show much in his *Liberation* article, by 1967 Ginsberg came to believe that the counterculture and the antiwar movement needed each other. The poet considered the divisions between young activists and hippies harmful. As he told a group of young people in Berkeley at the beginning of 1967, "the hippies have deeper insight into consciousness, the radicals more information about the workings and the nature of consciousness in the world." [21] By mid-1967, Ginsberg's admonition came to be something more and more young people were living out, even as movement leaders debated the parameters of cultural rebellion and the necessity of active engagement in antiwar protests.

In late 1967, for example, when the Chicago Area Draft Resisters (CADRE) organized that city, no clear cultural-political lines were drawn. On the one hand, the group set up a ten-room communal apartment and some of the members commonly used drugs; on the other hand, at the heart of the commune lived a happily married couple who never experimented with drugs. They all got along and worked together against the war through their personal acts of draft resistance and through their GI coffeehouse, Alice's Restaurant. By mid-1967 the political-cultural synergy that Ginsberg advocated was percolating through the antiwar movement. Among young people, such practical coalitions became commonplace at the local level.[22]

By 1967 many young people in the antiwar movement—even those who by no means considered themselves a part of the counterculture—regularly used marijuana and other drugs. Looking back at the 1960s, Carol Brightman, who edited *Viet-Report* and traveled the country speaking out against the war, says that she had nothing to do with what she called "the drug culture." She then noted that she did experiment with acid and smoked lots of dope. For Brightman, as well as many others, she was not by definition a part of the counterculture or drug culture because of her role in the antiwar movement culture.[23] While many younger activists increasingly accepted and practiced drug usage, it remained peripheral to their personal identity and to their political agenda. As they saw it, they had more important things to do than devote themselves to full-time exploring of inner space and setting up enclaves from the corrupt world.

As Paul Buhle noted about the scene in Madison, by 1967 those young people around the country who saw themselves as purely counterculture or purely antiwar represented a decided minority. At the New Brunswick campus of Rutgers University, an alumnus remembers, "The political people and the hippies overlapped a lot." Still, some young people did see themselves as self-conscious representatives of separate forces with divergent views about social change. "I vividly remember a food fight that happened in the Ledge [a student hangout] when 'Revolution' came on the juke box right after 'Street Fighting Man' and this fight broke out between the hippies and the people in SDS.... We were literally throwing food at each other over whether or not a political revolution was appropriate." For this Rutgers student, the difference between SDS members and his hippie friends did not arise over the war in Vietnam; they all abhorred America's role in Vietnam. Rather, they disagreed over what to do about the war and the society that gave shape to the war machine. "Being a hippie," he says, "was all about developing an alternative lifestyle, and the style was really important and the agenda was not."[24]

Still, for most students at times of crisis, a shared opposition to the war in Vietnam overrode day-to-day differences about the relative weight of culture and politics in bringing about social change. In Lawrence, Kansas, home of the University of Kansas, several campus drug dealers and a small group of political heavies hung out at the same bar, where they traded jibes about who influenced students more. But they saw eye-to-eye on stopping the war while living out a new cultural vision. When the campus rose up in May 1970 against the Nixon administration's escalation of the war into Cambodia, the two groups joined together in the most militant protests.[25]

By 1967 the potential of such alliances became obvious to more and more antiwar organizers and members of the counterculture. To some extent, the January 1967 human be-in in San Francisco's Golden Gate Park made a purposeful attempt to link Berkeley activists with counterculture enthusiasts. Allen Cohen, editor of the psychedelic San Francisco *Oracle,* declaimed at a press conference just before the Be-In: "A union of love and activism previously separated by categorical dogma and label mongering will finally occur ecstatically when Berkeley political activists and hip community and San Francisco's spiritual generation and contingents from the emerging revolutionary generation all over California meet for a Gathering of the Tribes for a Human be-in . . . so that a revolution of form can be filled with a Renaissance of compassion, awareness and love."[26] Jerry Rubin, at this point an un–turned-on Vietnam Day Committee stalwart, represented the politicos. He, too, praised the be-in as a way for hippies and radicals to unite in opposition to "napalm, the Pentagon, Governor Reagan and the rat race."[27]

The actual event did not go very far toward uniting the two constituencies. In fact, the issue of the *Oracle* publicizing the be-in carried a long interview with Richard Alpert, acid guru and partner of Timothy Leary, in which he argued: "Like, a lot of the papers that come out—a lot of the hip papers [which have gone political]—I don't want to have in my home because they bring me down. Now you say, 'Well, the world of reality is a bringdown, man.' . . . Well to me . . . that is still horizontal game playing. . . . That isn't the individual human being arising above it all."[28] Few listened to Jerry Rubin when he spoke out at the be-in on behalf of the politicos and tried to be hip about politics. Emmett Grogan put him down: "He seemed about to wet his pants, ecstatic over his getting to speak to so many at once. But he was afraid to begin sounding like the cornball square he is, so he gave up the microphone after a few minutes."[29]

Nevertheless, connections were being forged. In the days preceding the be-in, Rubin and Cohen talked about the war in Vietnam. Cohen had come up with the idea of helping to end the war by exorcising the Pentagon of demons, five-sided buildings traditionally being the repository of such evil beings. Rubin liked the idea.[30] And Jerry Rubin, who had not smoked dope until he was twenty-eight and who had at the time of the be-in dropped acid for the first time at the urging of his new allies, also liked the idea of bringing the color, the excitement, and the allure of the counterculture into the antiwar movement.[31]

Rubin was not the only activist thinking straightforwardly about how to bring more energy and color into the movement. Dave Dellinger, too, hoped to invigorate and nationalize the movement. Identifying Jerry Rubin as one answer to the problem, he asked him to bring West Coast activists into the National Mobilization planning effort for the October 1967 march on Washington. Dellinger recognized in Rubin a thoughtful tactician who had created powerful protests in Berkeley against the war by appealing to young people's imaginations.

Rubin advocated several ideas for the October antiwar protest. Most critically, he recommended that it focus on the Pentagon and not, as some older activists urged, Capitol Hill. Further, he strongly advocated Cohen's idea of staging an exorcism, both as a way of gaining mass-media coverage and as a way of bringing the counterculture into the movement.

Making the most of his ambiguous role as project director, Rubin printed up a wild, radical version of the Mobe's usually staid newsletter, the *Mobilizer*. Zeroing in on the Establishment's cultural underbelly, Rubin wrote, "We live in society which trains its sons to be killers and which channels its immense wealth into the business of suppressing courageous men from Vietnam to Detroit." Half counterculture rhapsody and half New Left rap, Rubin's harangue, which he distributed to the press as well as printed in the *Mobilizer*, infuriated many older leaders of the antiwar movement.[32]

In fact, Sidney Peck, a middle-aged Case Western Reserve professor of sociology, long-time Leftist, and Mobe leader, tried to halt distribution of Rubin's *Mobilizer*. As Nancy Zaroulis and Gerald Sullivan recount in their fine history of the antiwar movement, *Who Spoke Up?*, Peck and several other Mobe organizers feared that Rubin's planned protest and deliberate inclusion of the counterculture would turn off "the middle class types so necessary to give credibility to any antiwar action."[33] Dave Dellinger was not as sure.

Dellinger believed that the Mobe should work harder at including younger people. Moreover, he believed that the antiwar movement needed an infusion of the more radical politics and cultural sensibility represented by the younger activists. The huge number of people that came to the Pentagon protest and the attention that the protest drew convinced Dellinger that he was right to look toward the radical energy of younger activists. As he told Zaroulis and Sullivan: "We had upped the ante from protest to resistance. Women Strike [for Peace], the Socialist Workers had said that we would cut down the numbers. This was one of the most uphill fights I had to make—all the traditional people, the people who had been in the longest, were saying we shouldn't do it and I went the other way with a lot of the younger, newer people. And to get there and find all those people confirmed my feeling that the older people were wrong in their prediction."[34] During the next year, Dellinger consciously tried to move the Mobe into a closer alliance with increasing numbers of young radicals who were using drugs and looking to the counterculture for insights into everyday life and changing consciousness.

Eric Weinberger, Mobe treasurer and mainstay of New York's Fifth Avenue Peace Parade Committee, recalls the difficulty in consummating an alliance. By 1968, "lots of people, the not very militant people, you know, the old line religious groupings, etc., played a decision-making role that ignored the feeling from the young people that there had to be more representation of the young people."[35] Dellinger believed that the antiwar movement needed a radical, confrontational edge and that young people could and would play the part.

Few older leaders of the Mobe, however, were ready to accept the flashy cultural politics Rubin offered the movement. When he showed up at a national Mobe planning meeting in March 1968 with Abbie Hoffman and other advocates of an activist counterculture who called themselves the Yippies, he found himself no longer considered a serious player in antiwar circles. As Hoffman later commented, "We were treated like niggers, you know, like we were irrelevant."[36] Weinberger spoke for many when he said that he feared that Yippie rejection of traditional antiwar marches and rallies and their emphasis on drugs and rock music would at best only water down the movement and would at worst be seen as fundamentally apolitical. A *Chicago Tribune* reporter best captured the Mobe's general rejection of the counterculture: "The meetings were all business and most of those attending wore conventional clothing.... The only one seen wearing beads was a Negro."[37]

If most older antiwar organizers found the intrusion of the counterculture into the movement counterproductive, those who felt themselves a part of the counterculture also voiced great skepticism about Rubin's attempt to co-opt their symbols and sensibility for political protest. The Diggers ridiculed the Yippies and urged freaks to pay no mind to their call for a protest Festival of Life at the 1968 Democratic Convention in Chicago. In Chicago, the local freaks also issued warnings when they determined that Rubin was really promoting a protest in the guise of a festival and not a counterculture be-in. In a style and language redolent of the times, Abe Peck, editor of the underground newspaper the *Seed*, and also for a while Hoffman and Rubin's agent in Chicago, warned the hip community: "Chicago may host a festival of Blood.... But people are still into the Festival flash.... The only way to end the sham is to withdraw our permit request.... There are many reasons to disrupt the Death Gala. If you feel compelled to cavort, then this is action city. There is no reason to wear flowers as masks.... As a group our advice is—Don't come to Chicago if you expect a five-day festival of life, music and love."[38]

A more potent rejection of all that the Yippies stood for came from a new powerhouse, Jann Wenner of *Rolling Stone,* an underground publication that had started in November 1967. If some antiwar organizers feared that a shift toward the counterculture would turn off most Americans, Wenner believed that politicizing the counterculture would turn off most young people. In the 11 May 1968 *Rolling Stone,* Wenner's front-page story blasted Yippie attempts to mix radical politics with a counterculture celebration. He labeled Abbie Hoffman, Jerry Rubin, and their allies "a self-appointed coterie of political 'radicals' without a legitimate constituency," and argued that their planned protest/festival of life was "as corrupt as the political machine it hopes to disrupt." As he saw it, "Rock and roll is the only way in which the vast but formless power of youth is structured." [39] If Hoffman and Rubin had dreams of politicizing the counterculture, especially by using the mass media as an organizing tool, Wenner saw a very different dynamic at work.

Wenner recognized the same phenomenon that had intrigued Dave Dellinger: the counterculture's expansion to the national level. It no longer involved a few intrepid travelers dreaming with the lights on in San Francisco or New York's lower East Side. As acid spread across the country, so, too, did acid rock and a sporting interest in Eastern mysticism. While young people everywhere were turning on to marijuana, the boundaries between youth culture and the counterculture, never clearly drawn in the first place, rapidly disappeared. Wenner recognized that as freaks had become mass-media hippies, so the raw-edged world of the underground was fast becoming just another market sector to be served. Wenner meant to be there, providing the *Life* magazine of the turned-on generation. He did not want radical politics or the antiwar movement playing drum major or pied piper to the parade he intended to help lead. If Rubin's turned-on politics represented one avenue for the counterculture to take, Jann Wenner's hip capitalism represented another, far more likely, route.[40]

Jann Wenner represented one substantial threat to an activist antiwar counterculture; electoral politics represented another lure for young people looking for self-expression. In 1968, a number of long-haired, flower-power students decided not to wear armor in the hair, as Abe Peck advised potential Chicago protesters, but to go "clean for Gene" McCarthy, Minnesota senator and antiwar candidate for the Democratic presidential nomination. Others put their doubts on hold and worked for Robert Kennedy, also running on an antiwar platform. They cut their hair and traded in their blue jeans for sportcoats and dresses. Although the assassination of Kennedy in June and the flameout of the McCarthy campaign frustrated many, the student power that drove the McCarthy campaign quickly flowed into antiwar organizing. On a national level, young politicos moved on to organize the highly successful October 1969 Moratorium.

Many of these young people—like Sam Brown, David Hawk, and Marge Sklencar—lacked interest in fundamental cultural or political critiques. They wanted to reform the system. Accessible to the broad mainstream, their approach over the next three years appealed to Americans of all ages. These young liberals, firmly opposed to the antics of Jerry Rubin and the Yippies, hoped to minimize the countercultural tendencies of the antiwar movement.

But at the margins of the movement, a small group of other young people embraced and took even further the vision of a militant, politicized counterculture that Jerry Rubin and Abbie Hoffman so ably promoted. In New York between 1967 and 1972, the Yippies, the Crazies, and the Up Against the Wall Motherfuckers, all advocated what was called "armed love." In 1968, the provocatively named Motherfuckers slammed home the message: "We must learn to fight as well as seek love. We must take up the gun as well as the joint." [41]

In Detroit, John Sinclair, who had joined forces with the Yippies in Chicago in 1968, created the White Panthers to link rock 'n' roll and revolution. By 1970 the Weather Underground, the breakaway cutting edge of SDS, openly advocated a countercultural revolutionary politics: "LSD and grass, like the herbs and cactus and mushrooms of the American Indians . . . will help us make a future world where it will be possible to live in peace." [42] All of these militantly revolutionary groups participated in antiwar protests. Their form of protest, however, remained a far cry from what Allen Ginsberg had envisioned when he first began promoting links between the counterculture and the antiwar movement. In the words of the Motherfuckers: "We defy law and order with our bricks, bottles, garbage, long hair, filth, obscenity, drugs, games, guns, bikes, fire, fun and fucking." [43] Though few in number, such zealots gave antiwar protests a negative image and provided ammunition to administration supporters struggling to discredit the movement as anti-American.

After the protests at the 1968 Democratic National Convention resulted in violence and public hostility to the movement, most older antiwar organizations moved away from the counterculture, whether it was politicized or not. At a major antiwar conference in Cleveland in early 1969, leaders like Norma Becker, Sid Peck, and Sid Lens joined forces with the young liberal reformers of the Moratorium. The original leaders of the antiwar movement were fast moving toward a common cause with a more mainstream group and away from both the increasingly fanatical politics of SDS and the anarchistic wild-in-the-streets dreams of politicized members of the counterculture. At the same time, the antiwar movement continued to draw on folk and rock music, as it had done since 1965, to lend a sense of generational homage and welcome to young people.

Similarly, as film footage of antiwar protests shows, by 1969 young rallygoers and marchers often wore long hair, jeans, and T-shirts. On college campuses the distance between the counterculture and antiwar activism had become by the late 1960s a distinction without much meaning as young people, comfortable with one form of protest, joined in the other, giving a political sensibility if by no means radical ideology to the vague forms of youth culture. Mainstream styles of appearance for the middle-class young had changed dramatically in the United States between 1960 and 1970, and antiwar protests mirrored that culture as they helped, existentially, to cast the change.[44]

Some young antiwar activists did, however, look to a more pristine form of the counterculture as a way out of the personal and political frustrations endemic to antiwar organizing. The founding members of the Liberation News Service, a critical voice in getting the antiwar message out to campus and underground newspapers around the country, set up a rural commune in Massachusetts in the fall of 1968 and quickly left any real commitment to antiwar work behind.[45] For others, too, the burgeoning communal scene represented a way out after years of organizing work. One New York City antiwar activist, in summing up her 1971 move to an upstate New York commune, said, "What I saw it as was living out my politics. Even though we were not politically active as such, we felt that we were setting this example."[46] Especially after the explosive protests of the spring of 1970 and the de-escalation of American involvement in the war in 1971, many young antiwar organizers who needed to put their lives in order after several years of protesting the war, brought issues of lifestyle and culture to the fore. The counterculture, while pulled into the mainstream on the one hand, in the early 1970s moved toward a rural communalism on the other. This move offered a clear escape from both the radical political fundamentalism of some and the rapprochement with the political mainstream that others sought. It represented a way out, personally, for young people seeking to hold onto the values that had brought them into antiwar work in the first place.[47] In the early 1970s many activists would find sweet pleasures and a sense of meaning in the call of the counterculture—even as that counterculture become less and less well defined.

Antiwar activists never made a simple peace with the counterculture. Over the years, as the counterculture changed from an exotic efflorescence to a mass and mass-mediated phenomenon, antiwar activists, on a personal and political level, wrestled with the implications of drug use, cultural critiques of the mainstream, protest tactics that made best sense to the stoned, mysticism, and antirationalism. Increasingly, as all of these forms of resistance to the standing order became both more commonplace and less threatening, they were incorporated into the antiwar movement, though never easily or smoothly. Most older activists never felt comfortable with counterculture representations. But most antiwar activists could incorporate some of the music and the communitarian sensibility of the counterculture and often utilized it to bind the movement together.

Of the many images that have been used to describe the political and countercultural movement of the 1960s, one stands out—the image of a shaggy-haired young man, a tranquil look on his face, putting a flower into the barrel of a soldier's bayoneted rifle at the Pentagon. This image, and the collective memory it encapsulates, is more myth than history. And this myth—antiwar protesters as stoned hippies—officially promoted by guardians of the standing order, stands alongside the myth of antiwar activists as agents or dupes of the international communist conspiracy. Both die hard in America. Yet another memory, more true, is worth preserving. For many people involved in the antiwar movement, the triple calls of an ideological awakening, a political responsibility, and a cultural creativity, while hard to juggle and often in contradiction, gave their experience and their actions in the 1960s an explosive, liberating, and potent force. As the antiwar movement proceeds from the realm of memory to that of history, we most remember that the fusion of cultural and political rebellion can offer powerful synergy and joyful possibilities.

2

You Don't Need a Weatherman but a Postman Can Be Helpful

Thoughts on the History of SDS and the Antiwar Movement

MAURICE ISSERMAN

"Wait a minute, Mr. Postman, look and see," Motown's Marvelettes sang imploringly in 1961, "Is there a letter, a letter for me?" Historians studying the history of the New Left and the antiwar movement might consider asking the same question. Although the basic organizational history of the New Left—or at least of its largest component, Students for a Democratic Society (SDS)—has been established and developed in a series of recent works, we still know surprisingly little about the thousands of students who were attracted to the movement in the years of its greatest influence. One such student, an Illinois high school junior, wrote to the SDS national office in 1966 asking for information about the organization. Like many others whose letters are preserved in the Wisconsin State Historical Society's collection of the SDS Papers, she decided to explain a little about her own political ideas and values: "I feel so strongly about civil rights, the war on poverty, etc., but I do so little for them.... I listen to Pete Seeger's "We Shall Overcome" album, deck my bedroom with freedom posters and buttons, and argue in my English class. (I am one of two out of twenty-five who is pro–Civil Rights.) ... My mind is torn as to whether we should be in Viet Nam. But I do feel that war is outdated and morally wrong. Knowing that it is my duty to form my opinion, I would like and appreciate your help."[1]

This student's subsequent political involvements, if any, remain obscure. But if she did join SDS when she enrolled in college in 1967, she had plenty of company. SDS had fewer than 15,000 members when she first wrote to the national office; a few years later the number had grown to an estimated 100,000 and that only touched the surface of campus radicalism during her college years. A 1968 Harris poll found 4 percent of college students identifying themselves as "radical or far left"; the number claiming that affiliation had grown to 11 percent by 1970 (approximately 770,000 students out of more than 7 million enrolled in college that year, or more than seven times the membership of SDS at its height in 1968 and 1969).[2]

Historical treatments of the movement have neglected such students of the New Left, in their hundreds of thousands. She—and they—arrived on the scene a little too late. As several critics have commented, recent studies of the politics of the New Left by Todd Gitlin, James Miller and others, including me, have been preoccupied with the doings and sayings of SDS national leaders. These histories have emphasized the positive aspects of the early "good sixties" (when SDS was a small but relatively harmonious organization) while treating the later "bad sixties" (when SDS was, by the standards of the Left and anybody else, a large and extremely disharmonious organization) as a chronicle of what Richard Flacks sees as "dissolution and disillusion, loss and ending." These authors, Flacks contends, do not "deal adequately with the campus milieu within which the day-to-day life of late sixties' student activism was played out. Instead, they focus on the national leadership groups in SDS, whose experience and perspectives were increasingly remote from those shared by most members."[3] The later sixties and its New Left adherents deserve serious consideration in their own right, not just as cautionary examples in a tale of declension. Not everyone could be present at the creation at Port Huron.

How, then, can we do justice to the experience of students of the less organizationally coherent, but far larger, New Left at the end of the decade? In part, it comes down to a question of sources. One of the attractions of viewing the sixties through the prism of SDS national organizational history is that the source material has been ready at hand in the form of *New Left Notes,* the resolutions and working papers presented to SDS national conventions, and the memoirs and memories of SDS's more prominent personalities. In order to apply to the history of the New Left a principle established back in the sixties by New Left historians—that is to say, history from the bottom up—we need to search out, assemble, and interpret new sources. For an example of this perspective, I will draw on the less-official record of SDS to make two main points.

1. Most histories of the sixties agree that the black freedom struggle greatly influenced the antiwar movement. Thomas Powers, for instance, described one early protest march in Washington against Johnson's policies in Vietnam as "essentially a civil rights demonstration which happened to focus on the issue of the war."[4] But the ways in which the two movements were interwoven has yet to be fully explored. I would argue that the civil rights movement offered two rather contradictory lessons to white activists of the New Left in the mid-to-late sixties: one stressing the need for patient, long-term organizing at the grassroots level around issues of political power; the other pointing to the potential for dramatic, media-oriented confrontation around issues of personal morality. Although both approaches served the civil rights movement well in the early sixties, their impact on the campus antiwar movement of the late sixties proved more problematic.

2. SDS represented a more politically diverse movement than is commonly assumed. Several historians have noted the split that grew between the views of the SDS national leadership and those held by the SDS rank and file, but little has been done to explore the latter. The view from the bottom up offers a different perspective on SDS's decline and fall than that provided by the existing top-down accounts, with their near-exclusive focus on the struggle between the Old Guard and Prairie Power, the Revolutionary Youth Movement (RYM) versus the Progressive Labor party (PLP), and so forth. Both at the top and at the bottom, SDSers veered towards greater militancy in tactics and rhetoric in the second half of the 1960s, but not at the same pace or necessarily with the same political emphases. Even at its most revolutionary stage, the SDS rank and file became less infatuated with visions of Marxist-Leninist vanguard politics than did the organization's leaders. A rank-and-file caucus at the 1968 SDS national convention denounced the "careerists, professional radicals and movement spokesmen" who dominated such gatherings. They were "insensitive to chapter needs," as shown by their "grandiose programs based on inaccurate perceptions of the state of SDS. National meetings increasingly reflect, both in attendance and content, an irrelevance to the basic concern of the majority of members: that is, the building of a predominantly campus-based organization.... We [do] not recognize the appropriation of the words 'revolution' and 'revolutionary' by those whose major attributes are the abilities to harangue and quote."[5] At the base of SDS, anarchist, pacifist, and "small d" democratic ideas existed uneasily alongside the various forms of Maoist orthodoxy being promoted from the top. But on the whole, rank-and-file

SDS anarchists, pacifists, and democrats failed to show much interest in SDS's national policies in the later sixties. It was not as much by strength of argument as by default that groups like the Weathermen and the PLP gained the influence they held. The failure of those with alternative political views to contest the power that sectarian extremists had gained within SDS's leadership goes a long way towards explaining the triumph of SDS's worst instincts and its shattering demise in 1969. In the discussion that follows, I will pay particular attention to the extent and limits of pacifist influence within SDS.

• • •

Historians of the civil rights movement have argued that pacifism played an essential role in shaping a broad spectrum of protest movements in the later 1960s. Some on the New Left won their spurs as organizers of the struggle in the South; many more may have had little direct contact with the civil rights movement but were nonetheless inspired by its example. SDS understood its debt, especially to the Student Non-Violent Coordinating Committee (SNCC). As SDS president Carl Oglesby declared in 1965: "I see SNCC as the Nile Valley of the New Left. And I honor SDS to call it part of the delta that SNCC created. . . . At our best, I think, we are SNCC translated to the North."[6]

SDS's first public demonstration against the war, the April 1965 march on Washington, was infused with the imagery and spirit of the civil rights movement. SDS consciously linked the issues in its "Call" for the march: *"What kind of America is it whose response to poverty and oppression in South Vietnam is napalm and defoliation, whose response to poverty and oppression in Mississippi is . . . silence?"*[7] On the day of the demonstration, SDS president Paul Potter told the audience gathered at the Washington Monument that "the reason there are twenty thousand people here today and not a hundred or none at all is because five years ago in the South students began to build a social movement to change the system."[8]

Despite the success of SDS's first antiwar venture, four years would pass before the organization sponsored another national demonstration against the war. Paul Potter attributed the presence of so many antiwar demonstrators in Washington in 1965 to the groundwork laid by the civil rights movement. But it was in part the example set by the civil rights movement that caused SDS national leaders to drop the Vietnam War issue so precipitously in the months that followed. Less than two years before SDS's antiwar march, civil rights supporters had gathered in Washington for the demonstration that culminated in Martin Luther

King's "I Have a Dream" speech. That event had left SNCC activists fuming about the last-minute censoring of the speech by their then-chairman John Lewis. Although they did not go as far as Malcolm X in condemning the march as the "farce on Washington," SNCC leaders concluded that such demonstrations were a wasteful diversion from the far more important task of organizing the black masses of the rural South to stand up for their own interests. Patient, long-term organizing, not one-shot extravaganzas appealing for the solicitude of white liberals, led the way to freedom. [9]

SDS's founding generation agreed. Since the summer of 1964, they had sought to emulate SNCC's example by means of a dozen or so Economic Research and Action Projects (ERAP) in northern slums. Antiwar protests did not fit in with their long-range plans to build an "interracial movement of the poor." The Old Guard opposed the April 1965 march when it was proposed and afterwards insisted that SDS should concentrate on organizing against the "seventh war from now" through a long-term commitment to change the way decisions were made in the United States. Citing the example of the civil rights movement, ERAP organizers Lee Webb and Paul Booth argued in the summer of 1965 that the antiwar movement must "become a movement for domestic social change." Single-issue protests were not enough. Only "old and tired radicals" remained unimaginative enough to believe "that the way to end the war is to organize people on the issue of the war." [10]

This much is a familiar story. Less familiar is the battle fought within SDS over alternative interpretations of the lessons to be drawn from the experience of the civil rights movement. SNCC's commitment to long-term organizing was, after all, only part of the reason for the successes of the civil rights movement in the first half of the sixties. The dramatic, media-conscious campaigns of direct-action protest organized by the Congress of Racial Equality (CORE) and SNCC in the 1961 Freedom Rides, by the Southern Christian Leadership Conference (SCLC) in Birmingham in 1963, and by SCLC and SNCC in Selma in 1965 figured heavily in the collective political memory of young antiwar organizers.

A particularly influential and often-cited model from civil rights days was the brilliant *coup de théâtre* represented by the 1964 Mississippi Freedom Summer Project. Publicized as a community undertaking, the actual organizing the volunteers did represented only a token effort for the most part, a rationale for putting one thousand white college students in Mississippi for the six to eight weeks. It was, as the project's organizers understood, the riskiness of the enterprise, the appealing drama of morally inspired youth arrayed against official and vigilante violence that would draw the attention of the national media and the federal government. What Staughton Lynd later said of the draft resistance movement could be applied to the subsequent history of the campus antiwar movement in general: "We were looking for something white radicals could do which would have the same spirit, ask as much of us, and challenge the system as fundamentally, as had our work in Mississippi." Within SDS the search for the moral equivalent to the Mississippi Summer coexisted uneasily with, and in time came to supplant the notion of, opposing the "7th war from now."[11]

At SDS's national convention in the spring of 1965, a delegate from a small left-wing sect urged passage of a proposal to organize an international brigade of Americans to go to Vietnam to fight alongside the National Liberation Front (NLF). The proposal found few supporters at the convention but remained the topic of at least half-serious discussion within the national office for several weeks afterwards. Paul Booth, then working in the ERAP project in Oakland, made clear his personal lack of enthusiasm for the idea because of "the whole violence question." He was, he wrote, "far from the point of bearing arms in even the NLF's army." Nonetheless, he felt obliged to state the argument for, as well as against, the proposal. The language in which he couched his consideration of the issue contained little hint of the anti-imperialist rhetoric that would characterize SDS internal documents later in the decade. Instead, Booth found the proposal worth considering only to the extent that it evoked memories of the civil rights triumphs. The youth brigade might prove useful if it could "force Americans to confront in personal terms the reality of the war; as Mississippi makes people in civil rights take a measurement of the extent of their commitment, so would this project make people decide whether to shit or get off the pot."[12]

By the fall of 1965, Booth had left Oakland for Chicago to assume the post of SDS national secretary. Soon after he arrived, the international brigade proposal resurfaced in revised form. Writing to Ira Sandperl and Joan Baez in September, Booth argued that in the face of the government's continued escalation of the war in Vietnam, the antiwar movement had to escalate its own commitment to ending the war: "[W]e need something dramatic, yet not at all cranky or far out." Booth asked Baez if she would be willing to join "two to three dozen" volunteers on "a mission to North Vietnam, hopefully to rebuild one of its bombed-out hospitals, to tour the country for three weeks, etc. to draw attention to the effect of the bombing. We'd stay there something in the neighborhood of a month. We're talking about going around 4 months from now at the latest."[13]

He had already discussed the plan with Staughton Lynd and SNCC's Bob Moses, apparently winning their approval. As evident in his earlier letter, the model of the Mississippi Summer Project was much on Booth's mind. In Mississippi, whites had put themselves at risk alongside black civil rights organizers, attracting widespread media attention and pricking the national conscience. In similar fashion, young Americans would now be called on to protest the American war in Vietnam by putting their bodies on the line beneath American bombs. In other words, being convinced that marches were bad—the kind of thing "tired, old radicals" did—did not mean that SDS should avoid Vietnam protests. Radical tactics could be used to reveal radical truths about the war.

Dena Clamage, one of SDS's most indefatigable organizers in the early days of antiwar protest, disagreed. She warned Booth in December against the misapplication of the civil rights model. Advocates of the peace brigade proposal had made the argument "as with the civil rights question, so with the peace question," the link between the two "the idea of laying our bodies on the line and acting outside of the government when the government is obviously wrong." But Clamage did not find the analogy persuasive: "When the civil rights people went down South, they were demonstrating courage in defense of a principle which, at least in the rhetoric of the country and of the Constitution, was considered justified; they were committing themselves to helping *Americans* achieve Constitutional rights which had been denied them. However, in the case of the Peace Brigade, the action would probably be interpreted as aiding an avowed enemy of the U.S. . . . The civil rights struggle and the peace movement are not on the point analogous; we do not have the mass support to make laying our bodies on the line for North Vietnam seem laudable."[14]

There the argument rested for the moment. Booth may have been persuaded by Clamage; in any case, neither of the proposed brigades ever made it off the drawing boards. The battle over the meaning of the civil rights movement was confined, for the moment, to SDS elite circles. Neither SDS's leaders nor its rank and file were yet willing to identify themselves openly with "the other side" in the Vietnam War.[15]

• • •

All that would change, of course, by the late 1960s when imagery of heroic guerrillas brandishing automatic weapons filled *New Left Notes*. By then, SDS national leaders no longer consulted the likes of Joan Baez. Those antiwar protesters who clung to the doctrines of nonviolence that had inspired the civil rights movement in its early days were now scorned as wimpy. In 1968, SDS interorganizational secretary Carl Davidson derided the pacifist tradition of moral witness. "After many high-sounding words," he wrote, the bodies of pacifist resisters to the Vietnam war were "willingly or limply carted off to the clink. . . . A good number of us were deeply moved by these solitary acts, overwhelmed by the small, still voice of conscience resounding loudly over the moral wasteland. But it was not enough. After a few headlines, mailings from 5 Beekman, and a demonstration or two, our righteous anger subsided and the war machine only too readily set aside the prison cells for us and went lumbering on about its business."[16]

In the early sixties, however, SDS leaders had paid more respectful attention to the mailings from 5 Beekman Street, headquarters to the War Resisters League (WRL), *Liberation* magazine, and a host of other New York–based radical pacifist groups. SDS gratefully drew upon the resources, contacts, and literature that the pacifist movement could provide, which by the Left's standards of the time were considerable. Until at least the mid-1960s, pacifists had more of an organized presence nationally than any of the organized Old Left groups vying for the allegiance of young radicals. SDS national officers wrote frequently for pacifist publications like *Liberation* and *Peacemakers,* far more frequently than for any of the available Marxist or social-democratic periodicals. SDS also reprinted articles from the pacifist press under its own imprimatur, including, in 1964, its very first pamphlet on the Vietnam War.[17]

SDS kept its guard up whenever it had to deal with representatives from the Old Left but maintained cordial relations with pacifist leaders like Dave Dellinger. Unlike many Old Left groups, pacifists had no tradition of capturing or boring from within the organizations of erstwhile allies. Moreover, there seemed to be an affinity between pacifist thinking and early New Left ideology, particularly in the two movements' common emphasis on decentralist democracy and their belief that choices regarding personal morality and lifestyle were, at bottom, political issues. And some of SDS's national and chapter leaders were themselves the children of parents who had been conscientious objectors to earlier American wars.[18]

In SDS's flagship chapters, Marxists of varying ideological bents vied for the allegiance of chapter members, and pacifists played a minor role at best. But in reading through the chapter correspondence in the SDS Papers, it becomes clear that—without any concerted organizational effort—pacifism managed to have considerable appeal, especially to rank- and-file SDSers on smaller, more remote, or less politically charged campuses. It would be only a slight exaggeration to say that on some campuses SDS chapters functioned in the mid-1960s as youth affiliates of adult pacifist groups. Consider, for example, the summary of chapter activities that a member of the University of Rhode Island SDS sent to the SDS national office in February 1966:

> *October:* Folk concert and food sale to support member now working with MFDP [Mississippi Freedom Democratic Party]. Silent vigil (in coordination with nationwide protest) to end the war in Vietnam.
>
> *November:* Sponsor Rev. Arthur Lawson, Fellowship of Reconciliation, speaking on visit to Vietnam. Eleven go to Washington to participate in the SANE [National Committee for a Sane Nuclear Policy] demonstration.
>
> *December:* Organized open discussion on the war in Vietnam.
>
> *January:* Sponsored a CNVA [Committee for Nonviolent Action] table and discussion on conscientious objection.
>
> *February 11–13:* Three members to attend conference on International Law and World Order at Sarah Lawrence College.
>
> *February 15:* Tom Cornell, Catholic Worker (burned draft card) to speak.[19]

Without the resources and speakers provided by the Fellowship of Reconciliation (FOR), SANE, the CNVA, and the Catholic Worker Movement, there would have been little SDS activity on campus at the University of Rhode Island that year.

On other campuses, the initiative to organize an SDS chapter sprang directly from the pacifist movement. A student at Albright College in Reading, Pennsylvania, wrote to the national office in July 1967, announcing the establishment of the Rosa Parks Society at his college. Its six founding members sought to affiliate their group with SDS at the suggestion of Ron Young of the FOR. Young, according to this letter, "recommended SDS as a student organization better equipped to handle the wide range of radical student opinion than, the say, WRL or the FOR." As its name suggested, the Rosa Parks Society drew its political language and outlook from its pacifist namesake. Its "declaration of conscience" declared the group's purpose was "to investigate the feasibility of non-violent methods of social change."[20]

The thousands of new members who organized SDS chapters from 1965 through 1968 most often embraced political radicalism because of the war. SDS's campus popularity derived from its availability as a vehicle for antiwar protest. The founder of Ventura College's Free Students For America, wrote in November 1965 seeking to affiliate with SDS because "we feel there is considerably more creative power in the unity of many groups than there is in many separate groups." The Ventura students listed their basic aims as "the removal of all American troops from Vietnam" as well as "the affirmation of the right of any individual not to kill." [21]

Once in the organization, however, local SDSers were often left to their own devices in coming up with ideas and materials to use in opposition to the war. Partly because of the Old Guard's recalcitrance and partly because of the monumental incompetency of the national office in answering correspondence and filling literature orders, SDS had difficulty living up to its image as the nation's leading campus antiwar group. Traditional pacifist groups helped fill the organizational vacuum for local SDSers. When an SDS chapter sponsored a demonstration or a teach-in, they found that they could turn to the pacifist movement to provide literature, speakers, and encouragement. "For the last two days we have been distributing Vietnam and C.O. material on the campus, which we got through the American Friends," a member of the River Falls, Wisconsin, chapter reported to the national office in March 1966. "This morning we held an antiwar demonstration."[22]

Pacifists provided tactics as well as literature to the New Left; their emphasis on exemplary action proved agreeable to SDSers. Even large city SDS chapters, like the one at Columbia, sponsored activities such as vigils and fasts, the basic tools of pacifist moral witness. The discomfort of the fast served not only to establish a symbolic connection between protesters and the victims of the war but also to offer a vicarious sense of risk-taking that seemed more authentic than marching or other conventional tactics. When Wesleyan University SDSers sponsored a fast to protest the war in Vietnam in the spring of 1966, they explained that "unlike mass demonstrations, fasting is a personal sacrifice which will arouse people's sympathy and make it impossible to avoid the point of the action, as well as allowing individuals who are distrustful of marches to participate."[23]

Why then did Che Guevera supplant Rosa Parks in SDS iconography? The ambiguous legacy of both the civil rights and the pacifist movements, as revealed in letters and internal communications preserved in the SDS Papers, offers us some essential clues. Between 1967 and 1968 pacifists found themselves less and less able to speak to, and provide appropriate outlets for, the mood of angry alienation spreading on college campuses. The continued escalation of the war and the embrace of violent rhetoric and tactics by sections of the black freedom movement lent legitimacy to those who argued for a strategy of retaliatory violence. Both factors influenced Steve Halliwell, a graduate student in European history at Columbia and assistant national secretary of SDS, when he wrote to his adviser, Professor Leo Haimson, in the summer of 1967. Having studied the history of the Bolshevik revolution with Haimson the previous year, Halliwell hesitated to describe the current American political situation to his somewhat skeptical mentor as "revolutionary." But he did believe that the moment had arrived when exemplary acts of revolutionary violence could have significant impact: "The USA cannot continue to send black men overseas to learn how to fight in jungles and then bring them home to kill their brothers in the ghettoes—they just won't have an army. . . . Three guys with rifles could stop the Lake Street el every night at rush hour. I'm not suggesting that this is the substance of a revolutionary movement, but it is important that there is a growing reservoir of very militant people that can have real debilitating consequences even in small numbers." [24]

By the following spring, when Halliwell was involved in the Columbia University strike, New Leftists had begun to use the term "revolutionary" without self-consciousness. Columbia established SDS's credentials in the eyes of those whom many white radicals regarded as their most important audience. "I thought up until this stage of the game that white people weren't ready," Students' Afro-American Society (SAS) leader Bill Sales told a crowd of SDSers early on in the Columbia confrontation. "But I saw something today that suggests that maybe this is not true. Maybe you *are* ready. Because when the deal hit the fan, you were there, you were with me." Columbia was "a revolt against the imperialism of a university," Julius Lester, black columnist for the left-wing *Guardian* newspaper wrote approvingly in mid-May. The strike had proven "it is not necessary to go into the black community to act against racism." The strike provided an example of "how revolutions begin." [25]

Much changed in the politics of the New Left from the early to the later sixties, but one constant was the impulse of the white New Left to look to the black movement for direction and validation. Students willing to follow Stokely Carmichael into nonviolent battle with forces of racism in Mississippi in 1964 continued to follow his lead in 1967 when he boasted from a podium in Havana that black revolutionaries in the United States were organizing "groups of urban guerrillas for our defense in the cities." Martin Luther King's assassination in April 1968 stilled the voice of the nation's most eloquent nonviolent revolutionary and lent credence to H. Rap Brown's charge that "violence was as American as apple pie." By 1969, SNCC had dropped the by-then-despised description "non-violent" from its organization's title.[26]

The willingness of young civil rights supporters to risk their personal safety in the Mississippi Summer of 1964, which had a clear strategic rationale, led to dramatic risk-taking for its own sake in the antiwar movement. This tendency had already become visible in 1965 during the first summer of active antiwar protest, when the Oakland SDS cosponsored demonstrations in which participants stood on the tracks to block troop trains rolling into the Oakland Army Base. SDS organizer Steve Weissman, a veteran of Mississippi Summer, commented on what he saw as the success of the demonstration in SDS's *National Vietnam Newsletter:* "Civil disobedience is good when it feels good—not only at the point of disruption, but also as one looks back after the euphoria and the crowds have dispersed. This means—orientation of civil disobedience is more than self-indulgence: creative social dislocation that feels good will enlarge participation and limit the disillusionment and depoliticalization that often follows those grueling days in court."[27]

Some of SDS's Old Guard, like Tom Hayden, accommodated themselves to the new mood of antiwar militancy; others, like Lee Webb, were disturbed by its implications but powerless to stand against it. Webb may have had Weissman's article in mind when he complained in a working paper for the December 1965 SDS national conference that SDS no longer provided its members the "rich internal life" of intellectual debate it had enjoyed in earlier years. Now, in contrast, "SDS influences its membership to become more militant rather than more radical. At the same time as our intellectual life has declined, the calls to fight the draft, stop a troop train, burn a draft card, avoid all forms of liberalism, have become more vocal. Thus commitment, confrontation, martyrdom, anger become the substitute for intellectual analysis and understanding."[28]

The standard of political effectiveness used to measure and justify the campus antiwar movement's embrace of more militant tactics increasingly became the sense of gratification and commitment they provided to participants. There was a seductive exhilaration to being part of a redemptive minority that began to get out of hand. A stance of what might be called "prophetic alienation" had certainly been present during the civil rights era of the early 1960s but had remained subordinate to the larger political purposes of the movement. Now, for some young radicals, violent risk taking, such as heaving a rock through a window of the Bank of America or an ROTC building, could provide a sense of accomplishment, of doing material damage to the war-making state, that the passively absorbed discomfort of a fast or a vigil proved incapable of matching. The pacifist movement, internally divided by the mid-1960s over questions of coalition politics, exclusionary policies, and attitudes towards the Cuban and Vietnamese revolutions, could not provide a clear alternative to SDS's swing towards violence. As Catholic radical pacifist Tom Cornell would later argue: "We are mostly anarchists in our end of the peace movement and we hate authority. Therefore when authority devolves upon our shoulders we don't want it.... We would never speak to the young folk exerting any kind of discipline. It was, 'Do your own thing.'"[29] The demoralization of pacifists and their principled but ultimately self-defeating attachment to decentralist political philosophy made it impossible for them to set forth any serious challenge to the Marxist-Leninist infatuation and intrigues that consumed the national leadership of SDS between 1968 and 1969.

• • •

Tapping new historical sources can add an important dimension to our understanding of the New Left's fatal entanglement with doctrines of violent revolution in the late 1960s. Looking at the organization from the top down, we might conclude simply that SDS turned away from its civil rights and pacifist heritage in those years. Looking at it from the bottom up, we begin to form an impression of how the tactics, values, concerns and motives of both civil rights and pacifism continued to inform or at least interact with SDS's rank and file in the latter part of the decade. The "good sixties" gave way to the "bad sixties," but letters and other evidence preserved in the SDS Papers suggest the two are not totally disconnected. When it comes to writing sixties history—to paraphrase the decade's bard Bob Dylan—you don't need a weatherman ... but a postman can be helpful.

3

CALCAV and Religious Opposition to the Vietnam War

MITCHELL K. HALL

In late January 1967, members of the American religious community gathered for a Washington, D.C., mobilization sponsored by Clergy and Laymen Concerned About Vietnam (CALCAV). The task of drafting an official position paper fell to Stanford theologian Robert McAfee Brown, who eloquently summarized the year-old group's motivation. "A time comes when silence is betrayal," he began. "That time has come for us in relation to Vietnam."[1]

As Vietnam became an issue of public debate in the early 1960s, an emerging antiwar movement challenged the nation's foreign policy in a series of petitions, rallies, lobbying efforts, and teach-ins. Both the war and its organized opposition would continue for another decade. Among the war's opponents were members of America's churches and synagogues whose political activism demanded an outlet beyond the limitations of the existing ecclesiastical structures. In meeting that need, CALCAV emerged as the nation's largest religiously oriented, antiwar organization.

The emergence of two significant trends following World War II greatly facilitated the inclusion of the American religious community in this growing opposition to the war. The first was the ecumenical move-

---

A more comprehensive account of this subject appears in Hall's *Because of Their Faith: CALCAV and Religious Opposition to the Vietnam War* (New York: Columbia Univ. Press, 1990).

ment that produced in 1948 the World Council of Churches and later the National Council of Churches in the United States. The second trend built upon the civil rights movement in developing a stronger commitment to social involvement.

These changes occurred gradually and within certain boundaries. American religion was far from monolithic. The three largest religious groupings—Protestants, Catholics, and Jews—had only tenuous ties with each other and differed on both theological matters and social issues. Divisions also existed within these bodies.

Despite the differences within and among the leading American religions, the 1950s and 1960s provided years of greater movement toward unity and ecumenism. Within Protestantism, closer cooperation and even denominational mergers occurred. Interfaith cooperation grew out of the opening of Protestant-Catholic dialogues, the Vatican II declaration absolving Jews from special guilt in the death of Jesus Christ, and common support of the civil rights movement.[2]

The social criticism undertaken by politically active clergy in the 1960s developed in spite of strong constraints. The Cold War between the United States and the Soviet Union played a major role in limiting dissent. Many Americans who viewed their global antagonist as inherently evil turned the conflict into a moral crusade. So pervasive was this attitude that it encouraged the equation of U.S. strategies with godliness and in so doing blinded the nation to its own imperfections.

Conditions within the religious communities, together with these external pressures, contributed to the silence of the churches. A substantial segment of America's church and synagogue leadership traditionally avoided extensive participation in the political process. Theological liberals tended to be more inclined toward political activity than conservatives, but even mainstream denominations hesitated to advocate positions on controversial issues that might prove divisive. The clergy generally held more liberal social attitudes than the laity. Most of the latter felt the churches should stay out of political and social matters and disapproved of clerics who demonstrated for causes in those areas. These views, particularly in Protestant churches with strong congregational control over the selection of ministers, tended to mute social activism.[3]

The civil rights movement served as the catalyst for changing this situation. Martin Luther King, Jr., symbolized the leading role played by the clergy in the struggle. Predictably, this drive for equality drew charges of communist collusion, but when jolted into acknowledging the stark existence of racism, many religious leaders became less convinced of the existence of a monolithic communism and more sensitive to injustices that existed in the United States.[4]

Once committed to the idea that political issues could have moral implications, clergy searched for appropriate channels for their social witnessing. The growth of ecumenical and denominational bureaucracies freed many church executives from direct accountability to local opinion and allowed them to comment on political matters without fear of reprisal. Generally, those who took an active liberal position on racial issues took a similar stance on foreign affairs.[5]

As early as 1963, clerical and lay church leaders began moving outside established organizations to speak about the war in Vietnam. Buddhist demonstrations and self-immolations protesting the South Vietnamese government's religious persecution prodded some of America's leading theologians to challenge U.S. policy in Indochina. Sporadic reactions continued through the 1964 presidential campaign when several religious journals broke their tradition of not supporting particular candidates and endorsed the more moderate Lyndon Johnson over Barry Goldwater.[6]

Not until 1965 did visible religious opposition to the war occur on a regular basis. The initiation of a sustained bombing campaign over North Vietnam and the landing of American combat troops in the early months of 1965 indicated that the United States had adopted a more aggressive policy in Indochina. Groups such as the Fellowship of Reconciliation (FOR) and the ecumenical Interreligious Committee on Vietnam criticized this escalation, and by the end of the year other organizations, including the National Council of Churches (NCC), Catholic Peace Fellowship (CPF), and Union of American Hebrew Congregations (UAHC), had passed resolutions at least mildly critical of U.S. policies in Vietnam.[7]

This early dissent occurred in the face of widespread public support for the president's actions. Despite the growing activism within the religious community, most mainstream church organizations did not respond to the escalating conflict in Vietnam. In October, A. J. Muste, America's most respected pacifist and one of the leaders of the early antiwar coalitions, addressed this situation in a letter to John C. Bennett, president of New York's Union Theological Seminary: "It seems to me also that church forces—the National Council [of Churches], the denominational agencies, Christian, especially Protestant, leaders to whom we are in the habit of looking for initiative—are not saying or doing anything of real significance in relation to the problem. I have the feeling they are simply marking time and so contribute to the attitude of 'going along' with the Johnson administration, which is so widespread and, in my view, so dangerous."[8]

This passivity disturbed a number of prominent church leaders. Those who shared this perception looked initially to their local and denominational groups for support. Most found that local churches tended to ignore the war and that denominations, even if they could reach a consensus, moved painfully slowly. Frustrated by the failure of the institutional church to address the war, these individuals looked beyond religious barriers and bureaucracies for ways to express themselves.

Upon close inspection of the peace forces, antiwar activists within the religious community found few organizations which they could fit into comfortably. The major religious groups within the movement—FOR, American Friends Service Committee, and the Catholic Worker Movement—were predominantly pacifist. While this orientation did not preclude non-pacifists from working with them, the division between those who rejected all forms of violence and those who did not sometimes made it difficult to agree on methods and goals.

Prominent among secular peace groups, although they had a certain religious presence within them, were the War Resisters League (WRL) and the Committee for Nonviolent Action (CNVA). However, their acceptance of nonviolent civil disobedience, a position known as "radical pacifism," made them too radical for the vast majority of religious leaders in 1965. The National Committee for a Sane Nuclear Policy (SANE), a moderate peace organization, presented another possibility. SANE rejected nonviolent civil disobedience and refused to admit, or even associate with, members of the traditional Left. At this juncture, however, SANE concerned itself primarily with the long-term solutions to war and emphasized disarmament and nuclear test-ban treaties rather than the more immediate problem of Vietnam.[9]

The emerging New Left, which rejected rigid Marxist views of society but still advanced a radical critique of American society, provided another potential source of support. These groups lacked appeal to church leaders, however, because they were dominated by young, college-age people, whose critique of America went beyond what the religious community as a whole found itself willing to accept.

By late 1965 a significant number of religious leaders had concluded that the war in Vietnam was wrong and must be opposed. Acting as individuals or as members of ad hoc organizations, they became frustrated with their lack of influence and with the apparent neglect of the issue by denominational bodies that they normally turned to in times of crisis. Although established organizations already existed where they might pursue their concern about Vietnam, none seemed to meet fully the needs of those coming out of the dominant American religious traditions. The time had come for a new instrument that would make it possible for a common religious voice to speak out against the war. Clergy and Laymen Concerned About Vietnam would fill this gap.

If any single issue spurred the formation of the group that developed into CALCAV, it was the attempt to discredit the antiwar movement. James Reston of the *New York Times* claimed that antiwar demonstrations were "not promoting peace but postponing it."[10] A number of government officials sharply criticized nationwide protests in October 1965, including Attorney General Nicholas Katzenbach, who commented that "there were some communists involved in it. We may very well have to prosecute." Even President Lyndon Johnson expressed his "surprise that any one citizen would feel toward his country in a way that is not consistent with the national interest."[11]

In response to these attacks, an ad hoc group of about one hundred Protestant, Catholic, and Jewish clergymen from New York City organized an ecumenical forum to evaluate America's Asian policy. Spokesmen for the group held a news conference in the United Nations Church Center on 25 October 1965. Rev. Richard Neuhaus, pastor of the Lutheran Church of St. John the Evangelist, commented that "it concerns us that the president should be amazed by dissent." The clerics presented a declaration signed by more than one hundred New York clergy that supported the right to protest the government's conduct in Vietnam. It asserted that "to characterize every act of protest as communist-inspired or traitorous is to subvert the very democracy which loyal Americans seek to protect." Noting Jewish objections to the term *churchmen,* this group took the name Clergy Concerned About Vietnam.[12] In the years that followed, the maintenance of the American tradition of dissent would be one of its most notable successes.

Clergy Concerned was so heartened by its ability to rally support for its declaration that it formulated a program under the leadership of Neuhaus, Rabbi Abraham Heschel, a professor at Jewish Theological Seminary, and Daniel Berrigan, a Jesuit priest, to mobilize opposition to United States intervention in Southeast Asia. Over the next few months, this group of New York clergy sponsored rallies, demonstrations, vigils, picketing, and fasts.

Encouraged by their success in local activities, the leadership recognized the potential for a national organization that would encourage and facilitate religiously motivated efforts to end the war. To discuss the possibility of expanding the New York group nationwide, several clergy met in John C. Bennett's apartment on 11 January 1966. In addition to Bennett, Neuhaus, and Heschel, those present included Harold Bosley, minister of Christ United Methodist Church, Rabbi Maurice Eisendrath, president of UAHC, Rabbi Balfour Brickner who directed Interfaith Activities for the UAHC, and Dr. David Hunter, deputy general secretary of the NCC. They decided to ask clergy across the country to mobilize their congregations in support of an indefinite extension of the recent bombing pause and a negotiated settlement. They called themselves a National Emergency Committee of Clergy Concerned About Vietnam.[13]

Clergy Concerned anticipated pressure to escalate the war if Hanoi did not respond favorably to the pause within a few weeks. Careful to note its respect for the loyalty and courage of U.S. soldiers in Vietnam, the committee argued that, even if achieved, military victory could cause political and moral defeat by destroying the nation America was trying to defend and damaging Vietnam's capacity to maintain its independence from China.[14] They urged instead that the bombing halt over North Vietnam be maintained, that the president pursue a negotiated settlement that included the National Liberation Front (NLF), that he resist further escalation of the war, and that humanitarian aid be given priority over military spending.[15]

The points of view expressed in these statements identified Clergy Concerned as a moderate peace organization. By advocating a holding action, it avoided the extremes of immediate withdrawal and military escalation. Its tactics of petitioning and demonstrating, while offensive to some, continued long-established methods of expressing grievances. It was not deliberately antiadministration, as its support of any positive movement toward negotiations showed. By rejecting civil disobedience and expressing favorable regard for America's martial capabilities, the National Emergency Committee revealed the limits of its opposition as well as its commitment to reaching the American political center.

Working by telephone, Clergy Concerned organized nearly 165 small, temporary, local committees in a matter of weeks. Roughly half of those initiated some type of action within the first few months after formation of the National Emergency Committee. Their success owed, in part, to the fact that the Emergency Committee was correctly viewed as a complementary rather than a competing movement. As Robert McAfee Brown recalled, "All of us, in effect, had one foot in CALC and the other foot in our denominational or maybe sometimes even more secular activist groups." Many hoped that Clergy Concerned would prod denominations into action. [16]

The resumption of the bombing on 31 January 1966 jolted the National Emergency Committee's hopes. The steering committee of the national office then shifted its emphasis toward trying to stop further military escalation. Although "shocked by the intransigence of the Hanoi government," the committee was disturbed by the American government's refusal to talk with the NLF, its continued buildup of troops, and the self-righteous, misleading claim that northern aggression alone caused the war. The committee urged Americans to resist pressures to conform, stressing that true patriotism did not necessitate surrendering individual judgment and conscience.[17]

Through all of its criticisms of American policy in Indochina, Clergy Concerned emphasized that the antiwar position stood in the nation's best interest. "Do not let the hawks monopolize patriotism," Yale chaplain William Sloane Coffin wrote to the local groups. Distancing the committee from the tactic of direct action, he explained that "as a committee we cannot now call for withholding of income tax or other acts of civil disobedience, but should such acts take place our job should be not to condemn or necessarily condone, but rather to point again to the situation that produced them." [18]

The National Emergency Committee flourished during the first months of 1966. It put together an impressive list of prominent clergymen and organized local groups on a national scale. The moderate tone of its opposition to the war was unmistakable. Clergy Concerned claimed for itself a share of the patriotic label, supported President Johnson's peace initiatives, and upheld the traditional American right of dissent.

As the war escalated, other American religious groups responded in a variety of ways and at different speeds. Social action agencies were among the first to react. National organizations such as the Central Conference of American Rabbis and the NCC followed with objections to U.S. military escalation and calls for a bombing halt and negotiations.[19]

Individual denominations entered the arena more slowly and with less consistency. The American Baptists and United Presbyterians specifically condemned both the bombing and military escalation, and by more than two to one, the General Synod of the United Church of Christ approved selective conscientious objection.[20]

At this juncture, however, most official pronouncements from religious groups supported the administration. The National Conference of Catholic Bishops affirmed its acceptance of U.S. policies, while the American Baptists pushed for continued pursuit of a just and peaceful settlement. At its convention, the Lutheran Church in America passed a resolution opposing both escalation and unilateral withdrawal and warning against underestimating the threat of international communism.[21]

Although several churches still refused to take a stand on Vietnam, their conventions included major debates on the war. The Presbyterian Church of the United States affirmed its "loyalty to the government in this current conflict," but posed war-related questions for church study. Southern Baptists resolved to pray for world peace and a negotiated settlement in Vietnam. The Lutheran Church–Missouri Synod encouraged prayers, counsel, and study, without either endorsing or condemning the war. At their annual assembly, the Disciples of Christ reversed the previous year's decision and opposed selective conscientious objection.[22]

The statements that emerged from these bodies ranged from cautious to moderate. Credit for the good will of American leaders and impatience with antiwar protests mixed with dismay over the erosion of military restraint and affirmations of dissent. Tense floor debates often pitted liberal social action committees against conservative military chaplains, but few resentments lingered. Clergy Concerned kept abreast of these developments through its members who attended the conventions.[23]

Having abandoned its original purpose as a temporary lobbying group in favor of an ongoing commitment, the steering committee of Clergy Concerned hired Richard Fernandez as executive director in May 1966, about the same time it changed its name to Clergy and Laymen Concerned About Vietnam. Fernandez, a United Church of Christ minister and former campus minister at the University of Pennsylvania, spearheaded the drive to organize permanent chapters around the country. CALCAV grew steadily to a peak of about one hundred local groups in 1969 with a mailing list of over 40,000. With the onset of de-escalation, the number of chapters fluctuated, but stabilized at about fifty by the time of the Paris accords in January 1973.[24]

Diversity characterized CALCAV's grassroots network as chapters emerged at different times and pursued common goals in distinctive ways. Some developed a countercultural orientation and contained members who felt alienated from the major churches.[25] Nevertheless, certain common threads held them together. Each pursued a religious constituency that was generally moderate and middle class, opening the antiwar movement to people who would have otherwise had no outlet.

The New York office maintained its link to the field primarily through its funding of local staff and provision of resources, but also through mobilizations, correspondence, and coordinated programs.

Nevertheless, the ties remained loose. Local chapters hired their own staff, raised most of their own operating funds, and ran their own programs.

CALCAV maintained a cautious relationship with national antiwar coalitions. Concerned about its moderate image, CALCAV promoted most of its actions independently or with other religious groups. Particularly in its early years, CALCAV stressed its separation from radical, pacifist, or traditional peace organizations.[26] Moderates and liberals also recognized that participation in coalition movements exposed them to possible manipulation by the radical Left. Still, the fear of becoming too timid motivated several cooperative ventures with the larger antiwar movement. As Robert McAfee Brown admitted, however, "every now and then you get burned."[27]

Having chosen to remain formally independent of the antiwar coalition, CALCAV held its own annual mobilizations in Washington from 1967 to 1969. These national gatherings of the religious community gave CALCAV the opportunity to meet the heads of social action groups and to educate clergy in more effective methods of pressuring politicians and raising a significant protest against the war.[28] By ending what they saw as the silence of the churches, leaders hoped to spark further antiwar activity on the local level.

CALCAV's association with the American religious mainstream earned it increasing favor from liberal politicians of both major parties. The Johnson administration respected it more than most other groups in the antiwar movement,[29] and Senator Eugene McCarthy referred to its initial mobilization as "the most significant early protest" against the war because of its broad religious and geographical representation.[30] Senator Mark Hatfield's office solicited CALCAV's support for a bill to replace the Selective Service System with a volunteer military.[31]

In its first one and one-half years as a permanent organization, CALCAV made impressive strides. The success of its mobilization and the growing number of local chapters testified to its grassroots appeal. Clergy and Laymen Concerned continued to champion the preservation of dissent, de-escalation, and a negotiated settlement. Working within the religious community, it became an influential component of the antiwar movement. Its programs helped to stimulate some of the first important sources of Catholic opposition to the war, and with Martin Luther King, Jr., serving as a national co-chair, its visibility was enhanced by leaders who placed Vietnam in the larger context of American society. Encouraged and aided by CALCAV members, mainline Protestant churches examined the war more closely and increasingly adopted positions critical of government policy. The Johnson administration gave its watchful attention to the peace forces as consensus on the war eroded.

In the last one and one-half years of the Johnson administration, the frustration of having most policymakers ignore its arguments combined with a greater moral emphasis to produce a shift in CALCAV's approach to ending the war. The continuation of the war pushed many members to adopt various methods of civil disobedience. CALCAV also indicted American actions in Vietnam in a four-hundred-page book entitled *In the Name of America*. This study of American military conduct in Vietnam concluded that the United States consistently violated the rules of warfare and was guilty of war crimes. [32] These events, in addition to CALCAV's advocacy of unpopular positions, such as amnesty for war resisters, marked the first departures from the traditional liberal approach. The organization, however, remained firmly rooted in the religious community and diligently pursued moderate forms of dissent, particularly through electoral politics. [33]

The arguments that CALCAV advanced found an expanding audience during 1968. The Roman Catholic monthly, *U.S. Catholic*, called the Vietnam War "wrong, unjust and immoral." The Disciples of Christ, reversing themselves for the second time in two years, matched the support of the Lutheran Church in America for selective conscientious objection. American Baptists and the newly merged United Methodist Church upheld the rights of traditional conscientious objectors without endorsing that position over military service. The United Presbyterian assembly called for de-escalation and postwar relief for war victims. The more conservative Presbyterian Church of the United States commended the president for his negotiating efforts, and it too suggested postwar aid. United Methodists recommended negotiations by all South Vietnamese factions and the withdrawal of outside military forces. [34]

Whatever its ability to affect public opinion, CALCAV did not reflect the thinking of the majority of the churchgoing population at the beginning of 1968. In an admittedly unscientific poll, nine Protestant denominational magazines ran questionnaires before the Tet offensive. Sixty-three percent of the 34,000 respondents expressed dissatisfaction with President Johnson's handling of the war. A more revealing reaction however, was that 57 percent of the clergy wanted to stop the bombing of North Vietnam, while 60 percent of the laity opposed a halt. The United Church of Christ was the only American denomination that opposed a military solution and defended antiwar protest. "Officially the churches may coo like a dove but the majority of their members are flying with the hawks," the *Lutheran* observed.[35]

Though limited, the impact of mainline Protestants upon public opinion grew from not only their greater access to the media but also their control of most of the intellectually respectable journals, interdenominational bureaucracies, and prestigious seminaries. Conservative evangelicals consistently supported the war in the variety of journals, but the denominations officially remained silently neutral, fearing involvement in politics. [36]

The FBI first became interested in CALCAV in 1968. The bureau covered CALCAV's mobilizations and shared information with a wide variety of government and intelligence agencies but found no evidence of communist affiliation or violent tendencies. Reports on the organization described its activities as "dignified." Disregarding its own intelligence, however, the FBI placed CALCAV under Internal Security investigations from 1968 to 1973. [37]

By the end of 1968, CALCAV and its allies in the antiwar movement had battled to a draw with Lyndon Johnson. CALCAV continued to expand its audience and attract active supporters across the country. Much of its success derived from its adherence to issues and tactics that appealed to its religious, middle-class constituency. During the previous eighteen months, however, the line between attraction and irritation had sometimes become blurred. Not all who participated in prayerful witness appreciated even a peaceful, orderly demonstration; fewer still approved of civil disobedience. The sincere concern for the rights of draft resisters did not always transfer to acceptance of amnesty for military deserters. Not everyone who participated in electoral politics endorsed pressure against weapons producers, and many were troubled by accusations of American war crimes.

During the summer of 1969, CALCAV became more actively involved in prodding religious denominations to take positions on the war and related issues, such as amnesty and draft resistance. Workers at various conventions staffed information tables, spoke with delegates, and distributed literature in order to reach as many people as possible. CALCAV personnel, as outside observers or members of the particular denominations, also pressed for statements of church opinion. Working with progressive groups, usually a social action committee, they would sometimes suggest a particular issue or specific wording. The committee would then present a resolution to the entire gathering for debate and a floor vote. [38]

Despite CALCAV's more visible presence, in 1969 the churches seemed less concerned with Vietnam than with racial issues. President Richard M. Nixon was bringing U.S. troops home, and with de-escalation, the war appeared to be coming to an end. Nevertheless, several conventions dealt with the questions of war resistance.[39]

As American policy changed from escalation to gradual withdrawal in the late 1960s, more Americans saw Vietnam not as an aberration but as a reflection of a multitude of problems in their society, including race, poverty, and corporate power. This splintering of issues threatened to incapacitate the larger antiwar movement and challenged CALCAV's internal consensus. As the movement grew and permanent chapters sprang up around the country, CALCAV became more heterogeneous. Individuals in local chapters were not always guided by the same religious urgency, or sometimes failed to get that point of view across. The prolonged stay of Americans in Vietnam, now Nixon's war, accommodated the infiltration of radical rhetoric and ideas into CALCAV.

The organization entered the 1970s with more than an increasingly diverse constituency. CALCAV had struggled financially from its inception, but in August 1970 it received part of longtime supporter Daniel Bernstein's estate, which ultimately produced more than $1 million. Although this new income offered opportunities for greater creativity, because of legal complications and poor financial management CALCAV's monetary problems did not end.

The money did permit the development of new programs, however. From 1970 to 1974, CALCAV published *American Report,* a newspaper focused on the peace movement, and from late 1971 through late 1972 produced a radio news commentary program, "American Report Radio."[40]

CALCAV also distributed materials for a national advertising campaign known as "Unsell the War." The project produced a variety of ads for print, posters, television commercials, billboards, and radio spots, built around the theme of bringing U.S. troops home by the end of 1971.[41] A second phase of "Unsell" ads in 1972 emphasized the continuing air war.[42]

The "Unsell the War" project complemented another extensive effort. CALCAV and twenty-three other religious groups designed an ambitious program to pressure Congress and the president to withdraw all U.S. troops from Southeast Asia by 31 December 1971. The "Set the Date" campaign began in March 1971 to stimulate church and synagogue peace activities and lobby elected officials to back the concept and target date of the campaign.[43] The idea of a timetable for U.S. military withdrawal attracted support from individual denominations. National conventions of the United Presbyterians and American Baptists advocated withdrawal by the end of 1971; the United Church of Christ favored a more flexible deadline.[44]

CALCAV's most highly coordinated national project began in early 1972 when it established a program designed to pressure the Honeywell Corporation into stopping the manufacture of antipersonnel weapons. Demonstrations and stockholder challenges continued for over two years, until CALCAV ended funding for the Honeywell project in June 1974. Although CALCAV could claim limited successes, Honeywell never gave in to its demands: even as it phased out its weapons production, the corporation denied that CALCAV had any impact on that decision.[45] The campaign had less to do with Honeywell's decision than the war's de-escalation.

While CALCAV maintained its activism into the 1970s, other religious institutions moderated theirs noticeably. With the exception of the invasion of Cambodia during 1970, churches experienced relatively little debate, and by late 1971 several denominations began to shift their emphasis to other problems. United Presbyterians, the United Church of Christ, American Baptists, United Methodists, and the Disciples of Christ all established programs to aid returning servicemen in such areas as employment, education, drug rehabilitation, and counseling. The United Presbyterian Assembly labeled arguments for staying in Vietnam as immoral and recommended congressional limitations on presidential authority and church support for peaceful civil disobedience. At their annual convention, United Methodists called for an immediate bombing halt, release of all POWs, reparations, and the withdrawal of U.S. forces by the end of 1972; they rejected support for draft resistance, however. American Baptists advocated more government benefits for Vietnam veterans but defeated a resolution against the Vietnam War.[46]

These actions, although indicating that mainline churches continued their trend of opposition to American policy in Vietnam, also reflect the difficulty of maintaining a consistent position as convention representatives shifted from year to year. The focus on returning veterans, concern with presidential power, and POWs signified a belief in the imminent conclusion of the war and a desire to move on to other social issues.

In September 1972, CALCAV underwent its final name change. Clergy and Laity Concerned (CALC) reflected both an increased concern with issues beyond Vietnam and a greater sensitivity to the growing number of women in the organization.

The Paris accords of 1973, which marked the attainment of CALC's primary goal, served as a turning point for the organization. Surviving financial crises, a transition of leadership, and a period of decline in motivation and direction, CALC completed its transformation from a single-issue antiwar group to a multi-issue social justice organization by 1975. Having persevered during the trying years of the war's de-escalation, many veteran activists left to pursue new challenges. Others remained, hoping to direct the existing network in new directions. CALC survived and moved into the future, but its crusade against the Vietnam War became part of the past.

Perhaps CALC's most impressive achievement during the war years was its construction of an ecumenical organization against American policy in Vietnam. The common struggle in support of civil rights, reinforced by recent ecumenical advances, had established a strong precedent for interfaith social activism. CALC built upon that momentum, and the presence of Martin Luther King, Jr., gave it the most visible symbol linking the civil rights and antiwar movements. Churches with a history of social activism often addressed the war in Indochina, but many others, fearing this controversial issue, left their constituents with no outlet for their antiwar sentiment.

CALC appealed primarily to theological and social liberals from America's mainstream religious groups but attracted conservatives and radicals as well. If Protestant denominations provided the majority of its members, the organization also served as one of the first important channels for Jewish and Catholic peace activism. Jews initially formed a disproportionate percentage of CALC's leadership, not unusual for a reform movement, while the lack of a dissenting tradition and a greater reverence for state authority kept Catholics temporarily underrepresented. Time brought some notable changes. A significant number of Jews dropped out of the movement when Christians failed to give strong support to Israel during the 1967 Middle East war; many, too, departed because of Johnson's and Nixon's veiled threats to tie U.S. support for Israel to Jewish silence on Vietnam. Members of the Catholic hierarchy, increasingly convinced that Vietnam failed to meet the standards of a just war, joined the growing ranks of priests and laymen already active.

CALC's role in the antiwar movement also benefited American ecumenism. The war threatened formal ecumenical ventures, as fragile interfaith groups sometimes feared the divisive potential of a new controversy so soon after the civil rights campaign. Frustrated by the hesitancy of local councils of churches, socially concerned clergy and laity often turned to informal single-issue coalitions. CALC's antiwar focus provided an urgent moral cause that solidified the ecumenical cooperation nurtured by the civil rights movement. CALC found it easier to unite individuals than institutions, yet its close relationship with the NCC gave it legitimacy within religious circles.[47]

Mobilizing antiwar sentiment within the major churches was among CALC's most important and difficult challenges. The task of ending the Vietnam conflict invigorated some elements and infuriated others, as debates at denominational conventions clearly indicate. More than any other organization, however, CALC linked the diverse religious entities together and permitted them to speak out on the war with a united voice. This ability derived partly from its prominent membership: leaders of many of the largest and most influential denominations, ecumenical bodies, religious publications, and peace organizations in American religion. By external pressure and from within national church boards and agencies, CALC pushed various denominations to debate and formulate positions advocating a quicker end to the war or a more humanitarian solution to the problems that it left behind. It reinforced the idea that clerics could appropriately address social action as part of their ministry. For Christians and Jews who felt isolated within their own churches and synagogues, it provided a supportive outlet for their antiwar views and a platform from which to influence their local communities.

CALC and other peace activists mobilized millions of people, spent millions of dollars, and worked for ten years to end the war in Vietnam, yet overall they achieved only limited success in reversing the course of the war. Much of the reason lies in the antiwar movement's limited base. Public opinion analysts have identified a number of groups that tended to oppose the war: women, blacks, Jews, graduate students, students attending the nation's leading universities, and the lower socioeconomic classes.[48] Opposition to the war, however, did not necessarily imply participation in the antiwar movement. Blacks and working-class people did not join the movement in large numbers. Activists were generally upper-middle-class college students and professionals.[49] As a rule, the people who marched in demonstrations and actively opposed the war in their communities argued from a moral perspective that the United States had no right to intervene in Vietnamese affairs, to use excessive force, or to prop up a corrupt government against the will of the people. Passive antiwar sentiment reflected in the public opinion polls was largely pragmatic and influenced by specified events. Where activists saw the misguided application of Cold War policies, the general antiwar public saw only an isolated mistake.[50]

Passive opponents frequently disapproved of the movement's tactics and were offended by its moral analysis, its attacks on conformist patriotism, and its ties with the counterculture. They also shared much of the general public's aversion to the antiwar movement.[51] "Nobody in America," declared Balfour Brickner, "was prepared to learn or to hear that their president lied to them or that the authorities of their government were dissemblers, deceivers, masters of the coverup, and liars."[52] Because this was sometimes part of the movement's message, it brought the enmity that often goes to the messenger who carries bad news. Leslie Withers, a CALC worker in Greenville, South Carolina, in the early 1970s, recalled, "Active hostility was therefore something that I had to count on. We used to encounter hatred on a personal level when we demonstrated, leafletted, or conducted programs in churches."[53] National figures who took the opposite view exploited this hostility. "At best, dissenters in America are thought to be eccentrics," commented Leslie Gelb. "At worst, they are equated with the devil. The New American Puritans . . . had little difficulty convincing most Americans that those who opposed Vietnam policy were the enemy."[54]

Though managing to avoid some of the pitfalls of the larger antiwar movement, CALC encountered strong opposition despite its religious base and moderate approach. The public's habit of ignoring the differences between various antiwar groups diluted CALC's message. Government and media presented a misleading picture of the movement by focusing on the radicals and violent actions, thus tainting CALC and other moderate groups.

CALC may also be faulted for tactical errors. The violence that their nation committed and the silence that emanated from their churches shook the faith of many religious Americans. For some who found their trust in the government eroded or themselves estranged from organized religion, CALC served as a comfortable haven. When lobbying, petitions, and articles failed to prevent the war's expansion and government deception, activists responded with progressively stronger measures. This tactical and rhetorical escalation, however, did not always produce the desired results. Just as the institutional church's reluctance to challenge the war alienated dissidents, the actions of CALC sometimes antagonized the very people it tried to reach. Perhaps the organization would have been more effective if it had placed greater emphasis on reaching the apathetic majority within its constituency. In the end, CALC preached primarily to the converted. Its rhetorical abrasiveness towards the government and the military, its attacks on corporate irresponsibility, and its championing of unpopular causes may or may not have been morally sound, but they were ill-designed to capture the approval of a public less willing than CALC to leave the myths of American altruism and invincibility behind.

Although the hostility sometimes directed toward the U.S. government raised concerns about the antiwar movement's allegiance, attempts to portray CALC as disloyal are unsubstantiated. While the goals of independence and self-determination certainly attracted sympathy for the Vietnamese revolution, few held illusions about the beneficence of a communist regime. Moreover, CALC leaders, whatever their political views, frequently bore the brunt of overt hostility from the far Left and sought to maintain their distance. CALC remained neutral regarding the outcome of the Vietnam War, believing the Vietnamese should be the ones to determine their nation's fate. As George Webber remarked in 1974, "We do not support Thieu and we do not support Hanoi; as citizens our primary task is to address the evil wrought by our own government." [55]

Despite its limitations, the antiwar movement achieved certain successes. While Presidents Johnson and Nixon publicly disavowed that protests against the war influenced them, each remained concerned enough about the potential impact of dissent to go to great lengths to undermine the credibility of the antiwar movement. These efforts contributed to the fall from power of each. In addition, it is probable that the protests limited military options for prosecuting the war and restrained further escalations.[56]

Dissent against the war combined with the struggle for civil rights and the growth of the counterculture of the 1960s and early 1970s to create a period of domestic turbulence unparalleled in recent American history. The constant tensions of social disruption, threatening to split American society, contributed to a national weariness that eventually made it impossible for the government to continue the conflict in Vietnam.[57] If none of these actions was directly responsible for ending the conflict, they all certainly influenced that decision. "The Dissidents did not stop the war," observed historian Charles DeBenedetti, "but they made it stoppable." [58]

CALC played a significant role in the effectiveness of the larger movement. Its religious, ecumenical, and nonpacifist nature made it more resistant than most antiwar groups to the public's negative attitudes and allowed it to communicate with a moderate, middle-class constituency that would not listen to the radical Left. CALC cultivated the American mainstream. Many of its members, for example, made it a point to wear coats and ties during public demonstrations and rallies.

The government could not ignore CALC's influence with its constituency as it could most student and radical groups.[59] This legitimacy brought CALC access to government officials usually denied to most other antiwar organizations. Congressional doves supported CALC's efforts, and, in return, CALC provided a visible constituency for antiwar legislators to draw upon when confronting prowar forces in the halls of government. The personal effort and financial resources provided by antiwar activists helped elect to national office a number of doves who then played an essential role in changing U.S. policy in Indochina.

At the same time that CALC bridged the gap between activists and passive observers, it linked the extremes within the movement itself. Taking a position midway between exclusionary conservatives and radical ideologists, CALC served as a moderating force and tried to avoid the hardening of lines between Americans. Furthermore, its ability to pump money into coalition actions benefited organizations that typically existed on minimal levels of financial support.

CALC affected the larger society around it, but many members found belonging to the organization a very personal experience as well. CALC offered a new perspective for those discontented with organized religion, while others found their work against the war to be at the heart of their religious commitment. "It's very hard to convey . . . the fantastic feeling of fellowship and camaraderie and being together in a worthwhile struggle that had real spiritual dimensions to it," explained Harvey Cox.[60] Uncertain of what their impact might be, thousands of Americans felt compelled to act on their beliefs. "We've simply got to say something," stated Barbara Fuller, "because of who we are and because of our faith."[61]

The ability to influence American foreign policy is elusive for people without direct access to the levers of power. Even in a democratic system, expressing concern and hoping to be heard is sometimes all that can be done. In a time of national crisis, when silence would have been a betrayal of their religious faith, the people of CALC spoke up.

4

Pacifists and the Vietnam Antiwar Movement

DAVID McREYNOLDS

Pacifists played a significant role in the antiwar movement during America's involvement in Vietnam. Through their organizations and as individuals, they exercised leadership in the movement disproportionate to their numbers. There was, of course, no single pacifist approach to strategy and tactics. Their internecine conflicts, as well as their conflicts with other groups in antiwar coalitions, help to explain the successes and failures of the movement and offer lessons for future campaigns.

As a member of the War Resisters League (WRL) staff throughout this period and a member of the national council of the Fellowship of Reconciliation (FOR) for most of it, I found myself in a good position to observe the conflicts within the pacifist movement, as well as the Vietnam protests. And, not incidentally, I was on the national committee of the Socialist party (SP) until I resigned my membership and posts in protest of the party's less-than-dovish policy on the war. As someone who had joined the Left in 1951, I also had some sense of the political positions and tactics of the Communist party (CP) and the Trotskyist Socialist Workers party (SWP).

During the Vietnam War, I served as the primary WRL spokesperson and liaison between our group and the central committees of the mass mobilizations that began in 1965 and continued until the war's end. I also developed an international perspective from extensive work with the nonaligned peace movement in Europe and in Japan, and was in Vietnam twice during the war— at Saigon in 1966, and at Hanoi in 1971.

Pacifist strategy and tactics changed and deepened as the war dragged on. Being thirty-four years of age when the war began to escalate in 1963, I did not realize how profoundly it would radicalize me, particularly because I already thought of myself as a radical. Along with virtually everyone else in the movement, it never occurred to me that U.S. involvement in a war, which from its beginning was as irrational as it was cruel, would last for more than ten years. Part of our energy came from the belief that "this time will be the last time" we would need to demonstrate.

The climate of the time must be understood. When the war began, most of us had an "unexamined" view of America. We opposed racism but did not see it as central to our system. We had not read about the Spanish-American War or our suppression of the Filipino people. We did not know much about the U.S. role in Central America. We had never really examined the role of women in our country. And, when the Vietnam War began, we had been culturally trained to accept communism as the ultimate enemy. Our entire dialogue took place within clearly defined political parameters. The groups within which I worked had old quarrels with the Communists from the thirties and forties, which carried over into the sixties.

Had the war lasted only a year or two, I think we would have emerged from it politically intact—as we did, more or less, from the Korean War. But the war went on too long, exposed too much, and demanded that we rethink our history. It also precipitated conflicts within the pacifist movement.

The generally supportive view we held of our system meant that the terrible indictments that black nationalists, Communists, and Trotskyists made of our history struck us as shrill, at times hysteric. We had, for example, romanticized the winning of the West and the Frontier—without grasping the betrayal and near decimation this had meant for Native Americans. This Eurocentric view of our history unraveled even before the Vietnam War. If no history of the Vietnam antiwar movement is even partially complete without a hard look at the suffering of the Vietnamese; so, too, no examination of the essentially white, middle-class, antiwar movement is sound if it leaves out the events from 1955 on, when southern blacks, led by Martin Luther King, Jr., began to shake the foundations of American society. They introduced us to the concept of massive civil disobedience, gave nonviolence a living reality the pacifist movement lacked, and energized the whole of American society by challenging the fundamental assumptions of Jim Crow.

To grasp fully the position of the pacifists entails a review of their history. To understand the conflicts over strategy and tactics, as well as the intense urgency we felt about those issues, the nature of the times must kept in mind. The sixties, which actually began in the late fifties, were unique. No one examining the period should forget how much we had to learn when we began the Vietnam antiwar movement, or how long it took to learn some things, or why in our frenzy some pursued such dead ends as the Weather Underground.

When we speak of pacifist strategy and tactics toward Vietnam antiwar organizing, we should understand that pacifists as a whole participated in the same activities as many others. With very few exceptions, we all took part in educational processes such as the teach-ins. We wrote letters to Congress, sent delegations to meet with officials, voted in elections, and even ran candidates for office. We held vigils and played a vigorous part in all the legal mass demonstrations.

We also supported a variety of strategies, reflecting the disagreements within our own ranks. Proposals ranged from calling for a ceasefire, to calling for negotiations (or some combination of the two), to calling for unconditional withdrawal. Later I will discuss those disagreements over strategy that shook our ranks so hard. From the beginning, however, we differed from the broader opposition to the war in two key areas. First, we encouraged men to refuse service, either at the time of induction or by leaving (deserting if necessary) if they were already in the service and could not get released as conscientious objectors. Second, we believed in civil disobedience as a tactic to drive home our point. This might mean sitting in at a senator's office, or blocking an induction center, or trying to stop the shipment of weapons. Many of us also believed in withholding part or all of our federal tax, particularly on telephone bills, an easy means of resistance.

One more tactic, engaged in by only a few, yet so courageous, is worthy of a footnote in history. In 1963 a number of Buddhist monks and nuns startled and horrified the world by dousing their bodies with gasoline and then setting themselves afire—acts of self-immolation in protest of the Saigon dictatorship. The Buddhists, rather than showing support for the communists, were making a general appeal to the world. In the United States, self-immolation took at least eight lives, among them Norman Morrison, Alice Herz, and Roger LaPorte. Their actions, so alien to American experience, divided pacifists, some of whom saw self-immolation as an act of great violence. While not agreeing with the action, I had profound respect for it.

Pacifist strategy and tactics became a topic of internal debate, much of which has been documented in Guenter Lewy's *Peace and Revolution: The Moral Crisis of American Pacifism*.[1] I found Lewy's book inaccurate on the movement and a little off-target, as when he linked the Women's International League for Peace and Freedom with other pacifist organizations. But he accurately identified one central problem: the division within pacifist ranks over the issue of social revolution.

World War I saw the birth of the modern pacifist movement. FOR evolved in 1915, and the American Friends Service Committee (AFSC), the service arm of Quakerism, began in 1917. The WRL, which came into existence in 1923, consisted of men who had been in prison for refusing service and women, largely socialists, who had labored to prevent the war. The issue of war seemed fairly simple, both from a Christian point of view and also from the anarchist or socialist point of view, which deemed capitalism its cause. In general, young men who were radical enough to say they would go to prison or be shot rather than put on a uniform did not carry their resistance one step further and engage in disruption of the military effort.

Unlike World War I, World War II showed itself as much more of an ideological conflict than a "capitalist war." Looking back, it is impossible to not see the moral differences between the Allies and the Axis, although hindsight is always clearer. Nonetheless, why send a segregated army to fight racism in Europe? Why not desegregate the army and send it through Mississippi on the way to Europe, if fighting racism was the issue? And if democracy was the issue, how did that square with an alliance with the Soviets? When had they had a free election?

The anti-Semitism and unspeakable brutality of the Nazis were not a secret. Early on, the pacifist movement—and particularly the WRL, which had always had a number of Jews in its leadership—spoke out sharply against fascism and Hitler, urging that European Jews be allowed to enter the United States. Pacifists in World War II, numbering thousands of men jailed and sent to Civilian Public Service Camps or medical corps in the armed forces, preferred an Allied to an Axis victory (although they would have preferred almost any kind of peace given the millions who perished in the global conflict). Few pacifists tried to block the war effort, and fewer still encouraged desertion. To the degree we can say that in World War I no significant moral difference existed between the two sides, in World War II there was a difference, however blurred it became by war's end, with the fire bombings of Dresden and the nuclear bombings of Hiroshima and Nagasaki. In short, World War I necessitated no choice between the two sides, but in World War II, if a choice had to be made, then, for all its faults, one tended to choose the United States and its allies.[2]

The Vietnam War, however, exhibited a fundamental difference. When the war began in 1958, it was, as wars go, a cloud not much bigger than a man's hand on the political horizon. Few of us knew of Colonel Edward Lansdale. Few of us in fact knew much about the CIA, which then kept a profile as low as that currently maintained by the National Security Agency. And Vietnam comprised only one of a number of little brushfire conflicts. Another raged in Cuba under a romantic guerrilla leader named Castro. There were conflicts in Indonesia, in the Middle East, and in Africa. At home, reformers focused their attention on the civil rights movement. The peace movement concentrated on the testing of nuclear weapons; these were also the years of the great Aldermaston Marches in England and the Easter Marches here.

By 1961, however, Bertrand Russell had begun issuing harsh statements deploring the U.S. role in Vietnam. His hard, polemic style and charges which seemed too extreme to be true meant that his statements received scant attention. Within the United States, the SWP launched one of the first organized protests against the war and tried to force its way into the Easter Marches with slogans about this distant, obscure conflict.

Once the issue came into the open, it demonstrated the sort of moral elements (particularly the self-immolation of the Buddhist monks and nuns) that engaged pacifists. The WRL organized the first major peace demonstration on the Vietnam issue for 9 October 1963. In the summer of 1964, I drafted (with changes suggested by A. J. Muste) a "Memo on Vietnam," which pacifists in England and Canada soon reprinted. In this memo we called for the unconditional withdrawal of U.S. forces from Vietnam. The WRL newsletter from September/October of 1964 contains a photograph showing a demonstration of about two hundred people, organized by pacifist groups at the Democratic party's convention in Atlantic City. This was one of our first vigils of the war.

During that same year, I summarized WRL strategy on Vietnam in a statement "After the Election" (an election in which I ruefully admit urging a vote for Johnson): "According to figures made public by the U.S. military establishment (*New York Times*, 10.18.64), a total of 151,000 men, women and children have been killed or wounded or listed as missing since 1961. Of these, 88,000 are 'rebels.' The U.S. military estimated that at least 75% of the 88,000 Vietcong casualties were deaths.

In short, the U.S. role of organized murder in South Vietnam has now racked up a far higher score than the brutal Soviet action in Hungary. . . . *Our own position must now be absolutely clear. We are for negotiation. We are for neutralization. But first of all, and most of all, we are for the immediate withdrawal of all U.S. military forces and military aid. Not all peace groups have yet taken this position, but it is safe to predict they will be forced by events to follow the WRL's lead in this regard.*"[3]

In fact, a civil war had already broken out within the pacifist community. The disagreement did *not* involve whether or not to support the National Liberation Front (NLF). The key pacifist leadership in all groups never supported Hanoi or the NLF and always argued that a bad peace was better than a good victory. The division came over the point raised by Lewy: our attitudes toward social revolution. This question had come up during the world wars. Pacifists had been very clear they would not use violence, whether in wars or revolutions. I recall no statements any of us made about supplying military aid to Hanoi. But the key issue—and what made the Vietnam situation different—concerned what would happen if the United States simply withdrew. Would not the Communists win? The answer was, of course, that they would. Vietnam was going through a combined civil and revolutionary conflict and much as I, along with most pacifists, would have liked to see the Buddhists form a government, that appeared unlikely and we knew it. If the United States accepted the WRL's advice and unconditionally withdrew, the Communists would win—not Russian or Chinese Communists, who had very little control over Hanoi, but Vietnamese Communists. My own position, as someone very anti-Communist, was that we simply had no right to dictate the history of Vietnam, and that whether a left, right, or center government took over should be the decision of the Vietnamese. It became clear that the only aggressor in Vietnam was the United States. The Soviets and Chinese had not sent troops and were sending in relatively little military aid compared to us. We needed to get out of that country.

As pacifists we could not be neutral and say in effect, "Our conscience won't let us kill, but since the democracy we live in has decided to slaughter the Vietnamese, we will do nothing more than hold quiet vigils and pray." Democracy can be wrong, and if it is profoundly wrong (as when the Germans democratically gave Hitler a partial mandate in a free referendum), the majority must be opposed. In the case of Vietnam, given the lies and deceptions of the government, we had not even reached a decision, except by default. Congress had not approved the war. All one could say was that if the majority in Congress did not like it, they could cut off all funds. And anyone knowing how the U.S. political process works knows the courage required to call for ending "humanitarian aid" to a noncommunist government!

There had been no democratic decision. The United States had invaded a country 10,000 miles away with which we had no quarrel. We were killing their people at an alarming rate. The majority of pacifists felt we should use every nonviolent means at our command to end U.S. involvement.

Alfred Hassler, the hero in Lewy's book and the increasingly embattled (and finally, thanks in part to me, the deposed) executive secretary of FOR, took a position I never fully understood. He had as a staunch ally Robert Pickus, a hard-line anti-Communist on the West Coast. Hassler had been to Saigon. He had met and talked with the Buddhists, and they had deeply touched him. Hassler, who thought of himself as a socialist as well as a pacifist, was a man with considerable charm, real wit, and one terrible blind spot—Vietnam. I had a long talk with him on one occasion to try to understand his position. He said that if I was a pacifist I should support an immediate cease-fire by all sides. I did not think it likely that the NLF would agree. Such a cease-fire would have left the United States in charge of every major city, able to dictate the terms of peace. Even if the NLF wanted a cease-fire, it still seemed to me that we should get out. Hassler's position tended to be mixed. He argued, in part, that the NLF would be unlikely to accept a cease-fire when the growing movement in America threatened to so weaken the U.S. position that the NLF could gain more by waiting. While I understood why elements in the State Department favored a "cease-fire in place and then negotiations," I still could not see how Hassler himself did not realize that this position rewarded the invading army, or why the pacifist position could not simply be to demand that our military come home. Hassler's response was that we could not just walk away and leave those people: we had made such a mess out of Vietnam that we had an obligation to stay and help put things right.

The problem at a practical level became, How could we stay and "put things right" if a large segment of the population was trying to kill us? The deeper political question became, What had changed within our political and economic system that would compel the Johnson administration suddenly to work for or permit a neutral government to come to power? Socialists should never trust capitalist governments to carry out social revolutions! But to the end, Hassler, Pickus, and a very small minority within the pacifist community wanted U.S. troops to stay and back the Buddhist rise to power, thereby concluding a compromise settlement. It is an interesting position but it has nothing to do with pacifism.

Joseph Buttinger, author of *The Smaller Dragon,* a socialist who had originally hoped for a "third way," and a former chair of American Friends of Vietnam, a proadministration front, moved to the same position that Muste and I had taken, and became a financial supporter of the WRL.[4] By the late 1960s, that particular pacifist conflict was resolved. Resignations followed from the WRL Executive Committee, as well as the removal of Hassler as head of FOR.

Having finally agreed on a basic strategic position—the right of the Vietnamese to self-determination free of outside military forces—we confronted another hurdle. Pacifists did not work in coalition with groups they viewed as totalitarian. When I came to New York in 1956, pacifists often held demonstrations cosponsored by the WRL, SP, Libertarian League (an anarchist group), Catholic Workers, and sometimes FOR, but never the CP. After all, in the 1930s the CP had broken up SP meetings. During the war, it supported jailing the Trotskyist leadership and hinted that Norman Thomas should be silenced. From August 1939 to June 1941, the CP had been staunch antiwarriors during the period of the Hitler-Stalin Pact and then, within hours of the German attack on the Soviet Union, suddenly walked out of antiwar committees, often with the committees' mailing lists. Long before McCarthy, and for vastly different reasons, a deep animosity existed between the pacifist movement on the one hand and Marxist-Leninist groups on the other. Our first demonstrations against the Vietnam War were clearly exclusionary. I had put together the first international protest in December 1964, with sponsorship entirely from the pacifist and democratic radical community, ranging from Daniel Berrigan and Paul Goodman to Joan Baez, Norman Thomas, and A. Philip Randolph. The network we put into action was our own, primarily pacifist and nonaligned.

On 17 April 1965, leaders of the Students for a Democratic Society (SDS) broke the old patterns. They organized a demonstration in Washington that included among the supporting organizations the Labor Youth League, a front group of the CP. Neither Muste nor I felt happy about this development. On the eve of the demonstration, Muste signed a statement drawn up by Bayard Rustin deploring the "dangerous opening" SDS had given to nondemocratic groups. I would have joined in signing the statement had it been clear about unconditional U.S. withdrawal, but Rustin did not espouse such a radical statement. Thus, by accident I ended up on the right side. This marked the last time Muste would support exclusion. His position, and that of the movement, was about to change.

In early 1966, Norma Becker organized New York's powerful Fifth Avenue Peace Parade Committee. She felt that in order for the Second International Days of Protest to be successful, it had to have the widest possible support. Becker persuaded Muste that *every* group had to be invited. Thus, the CP, SP, SWP, and various splinters of these parties, along with trade unions, churches, pacifist groups, and local Democratic party clubs, received an invitation to participate. Nearing eighty, Muste played the crucial role of a person *everyone* trusted: both the Communists and the Trotskyists trusted him; SANE trusted him; FOR and WRL trusted him; labor trusted him; religious groups trusted him. He provided the remarkable seed around which, as with crystals, a structure began to form. Still so opposed to inclusion, I wanted to disband the committee after the 25 March rally; Becker and Muste wisely kept it alive. Within a short time the pattern emerged. For the duration of the war, the lions and the lambs would lie down together: Catholics, Jews, and Protestants would join forces with atheists; pacifists and nonpacifists would cooperate. The Trotskyists broke the pattern. Early in the seventies, they left the broader coalition and, having captured much of the student, but not the adult, movement formed the National Peace Action Coalition (NPAC). Their sole tactic became mass legal rallies and their sole demand "OUT NOW."

There were risks in this nonexclusionary strategy. A broad coalition not only opened the door to people who unwittingly caused trouble with extreme demands but also made it easier for government agents to penetrate the committees and try to provoke violent incidents with the police. But that exemplified the period in which we lived. At one point, a member of a group of ultramilitant veterans who rented space in the "peace building" at 339 Lafayette Street in Manhattan became involved in a bombing case as a witness for the government against another member of the group. Reliable sources told me that at the next meeting of the group, members looked around the room at each other and someone said, "You know, we don't know which of us or how many of us work for the government." Someone else said yes, that was true, and by general agreement the group dissolved on the spot.

A final area of growth and change for pacifists evolved. We had defended the right of anyone who objected to *all wars* to be exempt from military service. We knew that, in fact, most Quakers had not refused induction when drafted, and that many who had refused induction in World War II or the Korean War were not Quakers or even, in a formal sense, religious. Early in the 1960s we finally did win the right of exemption for agnostics who opposed *all* war.

Then large numbers of men emerged who were "selective objectors": that is, they would not fight in Vietnam or, more precisely, if in Vietnam, preferred to fight on the side of the Vietnamese rather than the Americans. We found ourselves defending, with no great legal success, the right to selective objection. We also found that for the first time in our history pacifist organizations had members of the military on their current and active lists.

Pacifists often came into conflict with the broader movement over tactics. Except for the most extreme part of the movement, which carried NLF flags and insisted on calling for victory to the NLF, the coalitions that developed were united around the concept of the right of Vietnamese self-determination. This meant pacifists and nonpacifists could unite in common actions. Many people, particularly younger people, supported the NLF. A picture of a Buddhist monk hung on my office wall. Many students flaunted posters of Ho Chi Minh on their dorm walls. Yet our nonviolence caught the mood of the times. While our generation comprised baby boomers, laced with pot and acid, tripping on wonderful music, it also framed Ho's portrait along with pictures of Martin Luther King, Jr., and Malcolm X. A great deal of confusion and anger existed, but not much venom.

Tension between the broader movement and the pacifists showed in two specific areas: service in the military and the role of civil disobedience. The Old Left, particularly the Trotskyists, was nervous about openly advocating illegal actions. The possibility of political trials, loss of jobs, subversive lists, and a host of other ills led this small subculture to act with caution. However, a conspiratorial approach to social change encourages the government to use conspiratorial methods in return; on balance, the case for being almost totally open in a democratic society is strong. Many who called for caution remembered the 1950s. One of my co-workers in the mass coalitions, Gil Green, who represented the CP, had originally gone underground after being indicted during the McCarthy period and later had surfaced and served a long prison term. He had not been targeted for advocating the overthrow of the government; the CP had not done that for decades. For him, being a leading member of the CP had in itself been defined as a crime.

We insisted on telling men of draft age that they should not serve in the military. We openly and vigorously encouraged men to refuse cooperation with conscription. We went a good deal further. At the Rome Triennial of War Resisters International (WRI) in 1966, I introduced a resolution, which subsequently passed, calling on all sections of the WRI to make it clear to Americans serving in the military that if they deserted, they could expect help. This differed significantly from World War II, when almost no one dreamed of encouraging troops in the Allied armies to desert. We addressed letters to servicemen and even tried to reach the ones in Vietnam. Furthermore, we succeeded. During the war, I always had a stack of correspondence on my desk from men serving in Vietnam, most of it friendly and supportive. Along with others, we also set up coffeehouses near military bases, places where the men could come and relax and, if they wanted, could talk. One result is that we had so many deserters that all of us on the staff had them staying at our homes. From that experience we discovered that men who had been drafted rarely deserted. They had obeyed orders, gone in, and stayed in. The men who had volunteered for duty left first. They had volunteered to fight communism and had the moral energy needed to "volunteer themselves out" when they found firsthand that the war was a fraud.

Our advocacy of desertion and draft resistance frightened moderates. In 1965, Congress passed a law making the burning of draft cards illegal. On 15 October, at the First International Days of Protest, David J. Miller burned his card near the Whitehall Induction Center in Manhattan and was arrested. The next month, five of us burned our draft cards at a rally in Union Square. Of the five in Union Square, I was the only one not arrested. The government insisted it could not find enough left of my card to be sure it was a draft card. I believe that my ineligibility for the draft at age thirty-six accounted for the government's reluctance to arrest me; one flawed case could have caused the loss of all five. Soon after this, in upstate New York, students wanted to launch a "provisional" draft-card burning. If approximately 10,000 students signed a pledge, on a certain date the pledge would be activated and everyone would turn in or burn his card. Ron Young, from FOR, and I flew up to meet with students and point out that their campaign would be much more powerful if a certain number would simply say: "On such and such a date I will burn my draft card; if you will join me, sign here and we'll let you know." But Ron and I lost. Most students, who were very conscious of security and deeply worried about prosecution, stuck with the provisional concept. Ultimately, the organizers attracted only a few hundred other students, but they had fired themselves up and decided to come down to Manhattan on 15 April 1967 for one of the first massive Vietnam protests.

The demonstration that included mass draft-card burnings was to gather in Sheep's Meadow in Central Park and then move through Manhattan. Moderates in the National Committee for a Sane Nuclear

Policy (SANE), as well as the Old Left opposed to illegal actions, expressed horror. The burning of draft cards! In Sheep's Meadow! The day of the March! My God! People might think the movement was serious about stopping the war! A struggle ensued over whether the draft-card burning would be part of the main event or entirely separate. When it became clear that the moderates would suffer heart attacks if we did not work out a compromise, we agreed that the draft-card burning would take place before the main rally started, and that it would be separated from the area of the main rally.

There was irony to this scenario, or even double irony. We certainly did not fool the FBI and the media by doing "the thing" ten minutes earlier and five hundred feet away from center stage. Furthermore, the students themselves were hesitant, with all the revolutionary clarity one might expect of the white middle class. They wanted to burn their cards, but they did not want anyone to arrest them. So Grace Paley and a number of the rest of us formed a human chain around the students and told people in Sheep's Meadow, "Sorry, you can't get any closer. These men are burning their draft cards and we are here to protect them."

This division of time and place became the formula for compromise between pacifists and nonpacifists. Sometimes an entire event would be in the hands of the pacifists, in which case the problem did not arise. We always made provision for a "legal vigil line" in addition to the area where civil disobedience was to occur. Although the 15 April action may have been confusing and clumsy, it was important. The Resistance, made up of draft-age men, began taking form that day and by October it called for the closing of induction centers. The movement had come a long way. From saying at first, "We won't go," it now said, "We won't go and they won't go—not our boys and not your boys—no one goes." Young and old joined in Oakland for the 16 October action that brought Joan Baez and a number of others lengthy jail terms. Later that week, the 21 October siege of the Pentagon began with one of those mass legal rallies in Washington that historians have all but forgotten. The nonviolent human wave that broke through fences and moved onto the Pentagon's home territory remains in the public mind, however, to this day.

By December 1967, the nonviolent approach had become so routine for the student leadership that when the Resistance called for an action to close the Manhattan Whitehall Induction Center, it yielded to the WRL, which had asked permission to organize the first day's activities. With a little luck, we hoped to set a tone that would keep the week from becoming bloody. The planning materials noted that the first day would be marked by "traditional nonviolent civil disobedience." "Traditional" civil disobedience!

Then, as now, I have never understood the opposition to civil disobedience from the Old Left, especially from the Trotskyists. They had no problem understanding the value of strikes. They had finally understood the force of the civil rights movement. How could people so perceptive on many political levels fail to understand that the government would not give way except under pressure, and that a series of large, legal rallies did not constitute sufficient pressure, but rather acted as a safety valve? Unions would still not be organized if workers had done nothing but hold legal rallies on Sundays, and the South would still be segregated if the racists knew the movement could be contained behind the barriers of a legal rally.

At the same time, I have also found myself impatient with those pacifists who, while rejecting the "macho" stereotype of American men, count arrests as a manly act, and feel that someone who has been arrested twenty times has more virtue than someone who has been arrested only once, and spent the rest of his or her time taking care of a family or volunteering in a Catholic Worker house. From my own perspective, serious movements use *every* means consistent with their ends, and while this rules out violence or lying, it includes just about everything else—from lobbying and vigils to refusing to pay taxes. For each of these tactics there is a time and a place. There is no virtue in a tactic as such.

In 1968 the police riot at the Democratic party convention in Chicago stands out, but the next major escalation in the struggle came in October 1969. It came not from the Old Left or from the pacifists, but from a group of bright young people that included David Hawk and Sam Brown. They set the date of 15 October, a Wednesday, for the Moratorium. The idea was simply to pause, to hold vigils, to gather quietly in town squares, to have meetings on campuses. A brilliant concept, it did an end run around all of us, locked into our slogans, clichés, and tactics. It was not a general strike, massive legal rally, or a "call to conscience to fill the jails." Quiet, massive, and with politics left vague, it gave every American a chance to be heard. The majority of Americans who did not support President Nixon, the Silent Majority, did not want to go to Washington, whether for a legal rally or an illegal one, but they were willing to go out onto town streets with candles. Several million Americans all over the country took part. In some ways, this was for us what the Salt March had been for Gandhi. It encouraged us to maintain the pressure, because we had the majority of people with us. Indeed, Nixon knew this, for in both of his election campaigns he did not run as a candidate who would press the war to victory, but in 1968 with a secret plan to end the war and in 1972 with Henry Kissinger's promise that "peace is at hand."

On 11 February 1967, Muste died, depriving pacifists of their clearest thinker and the one person whom all factions genuinely trusted. Dave Dellinger did his best to fill Muste's role, but the deepening crisis required greater consultation. I am indebted to Guenter Lewy for providing the date on which the National Action Group (NAG) formed—22 October 1968—though otherwise Lewy's reading of why it came into existence is very different from my recollection. Stewart Meacham, who worked for the AFSC, acted as convenor, but NAG never had officers, an office, or a fixed time or place of meeting. A "pacifist caucus" to help provide creative nonviolent approaches, NAG was partly responsible for the forty-hour-long March Against Death set to coincide with the second Moratorium and First Mobilization on 13–15 November 1969. Carrying the names of Americans who had died in Vietnam, 47,000 people holding candles marched past the White House. This profoundly moving experience took away the edge of violence that had hovered around the event (in part, because of the Nixon administration's attempt to scare people away from attending), and it provided a way to do something more meaningful than simply gathering for a few hours to listen to speeches.

The next year, 1970, witnessed the one time when almost the entire movement finally agreed to take part in civil disobedience, and then found it unnecessary or impossible. Thirty to forty members of the loose "central committee" of the antiwar movement gathered in Cora Weiss's home in upper Manhattan on 30 April to plan an all-day meeting to examine our situation as a movement. We did not seem to be ending the war! A wide representation of groups, it included the Communists, Trotskyists, Catholics, and pacifists. While we were meeting, word came that an invasion of Cambodia had begun—not a small invasion by South Vietnamese troops alone, but a major invasion by the Americans. Far from winding down, the war was expanding even as we met. We knew we had to act. The government had made it illegal for more than a small number of people to rally in Lafayette Park or to picket the White House. Someone suggested we round up all the people we could in a week's time, possibly as many as a thousand, and simply go to Layfayette Park and force a mass arrest of as many leading citizens as possible. This meant those frightful words: civil disobedience. As we went around the room asking people for their response, everyone said yes, including the CP representative, until we came to the Trotskyist, who predictably said he would have to check with his organization, which meant no.

But we had nearly unanimous agreement and left the meeting to rally our troops. Many citizens felt outraged over the invasion, but the worst was yet to come. On Wednesday, 4 May, national guardsmen at Kent State University opened fire on unarmed students, killing four. Although this did not mark the first time students had been shot and killed, to shoot white, middle-class students was to violate an unwritten social contract. Colleges throughout the nation went wild. Campus after campus closed down, freeing thousands of students to pursue political work and go to Lafayette Park. On Saturday, 9 May, 100,000—not 1,000—showed up. Nixon yielded to demands that he open the area immediately behind the White House for the rally, but civil disobedience remained virtually impossible. Our original target, Lafayette Park, was ringed wall-to-wall with buses. Entrance into the area around the White House, which I can guarantee had no visitors that day, would have required climbing over the buses or pushing them over, and doing pitched battle with the police. We had won a victory and did not know what to do with it.

That night, Nixon announced that all U.S. forces would be pulled out of Cambodia in thirty days. But the 100,000 people who had come expecting more than just a rally felt cheated. For weeks thereafter, the SWP, which had provided most of the marshals and had kept order, came under heavy attack within the movement for stifling the protest. For once I emphathized with the Trotskyists, who had done a good job and had shown responsibility.

A last look at the 1971 Maydays is important in order to understand the pacifist role during that time, and also because it marked the last major protest against the war. When Nixon withdrew the bulk of U.S. ground forces and fewer body bags came home, and when draft calls were lowered, much of our energy dissipated. Many smaller protests remained, a great deal of work had still to be done, and an unconscionable number of Indo-Chinese would yet die, but the movement's mass protests essentially ended in May 1971.

By 1971 the split between the primary coalition—which included the independents, pacifists, and religious groups, as well as the CP and the SWP—had been bitterly formalized. That is another history and an unhappy one. The coalition I consider primary, the People's Coalition for Peace and Justice (PCPJ), agreed to support a 24 April mass legal rally in Washington that the other coalition, the Trotskyist-organized NPAC, had called. But PCPJ also gave its support to what were being termed

Maydays, organized by Rennie Davis. The pacifists, through NAG, decided to bridge the long period between 24 April and 3 May, the first of the three days set aside for the Maydays. The Vietnam Veterans Against the War (VVAW) planned to act before the mass legal rally of 24 April, having set 19–23 April as Dewey Canyon III, a time for lobbying, guerrilla theatre, and returning combat medals. The veterans, with whom the pacifists had good relations, had been very careful to defuse the Washington police by handing out a special leaflet, "Open Letter to Our Brothers in Blue," at police stations before their actions began. Far from the fiery "off the pigs" rhetoric of the newly revolutionary white youth, the veterans effectively explained to the police just what they would be doing and why, and made it clear they viewed them as brothers. This approach helped cool the situation.

The pacifists decided that after the VVAW protest and the mass legal rally we would maintain nearly two weeks of People's Lobby actions during which we would block draft boards, the IRS center, and other targets in order to set a certain tone for the Maydays. Little came of this plan. I had become so worried about the impending violence of the Maydays that I hoped to be safely in jail before 3 May, but that did not happen. As the date for "closing down Washington" approached, so did my concerns about Rennie Davis. Abbie Hoffman I knew and trusted. Jerry Rubin I knew as being on a permanent ego trip, but not as an agent. Rennie, however, was very sharp and so reserved that I could not be sure what he really had in mind. Might he be a government agent planning to set us up for the kind of "Kent State magnified" that would scare the public into passivity? On the other hand, was it not possible Davis felt that a "Kent State writ wide" would galvanize the public? Gil Green shared my concerns, and at Gil's suggestion, I went to Brooklyn to talk to Dave Dellinger, who said he felt quite sure that Rennie would remain nonviolent. Pretty sure, but not absolutely sure.

Rennie held true to his word, at least on the level of not provoking a bloodbath. His dream of closing down Washington was a fantasy from the beginning. People who were always late to work arrived there early on 3 May so that no one would suspect them of being secret subversives. Traffic never became seriously delayed, except in one ironic case where those of us from the PCPJ contingent (the "older, more conservative elements" led by Dr. Benjamin Spock) who were supposed to be marching across the 14th Street Bridge on our way to the Pentagon (for civil disobedience, of course) found the Mayday Tribe had become confused and proceeded to close the bridge to all traffic. By the time our line of march reached the area of the bridge, we encountered clouds of tear gas and police with flying clubs, causing us to fall back, indirectly defeated by our own troops. The first day police arrested 7,000 people and enveloped much of downtown Washington in tear gas, while helicopters whirred like nasty insects back and forth over the heart of the city.

The second day we assembled to march on the Justice Department. The writer Dotson Rader arrived with his friend Tom Seligson. Wearing fashionable dark glasses, Rader looked around at the motley crowd and said, "David, where are all the celebrities?" "Dotson," I said, "they are all here, everywhere you look." To his and Tom's credit, they stayed for the day and landed in jail, two out of 3,500 more incarcerated that day. Those of us on the central committee had tried to stay out of jail until the end. On the third day, 5 May, the last 3,000 of us were arrested, many on the steps of Congress, while Congressman Ronald Dellums addressed us. So ended the Maydays, the largest, most sustained act of civil disobedience the Capitol had seen. The blacks in the District, normally indifferent to white folks who took off a day to come down and demonstrate (and often left behind angry police for the black community—a special gift from white liberals), stood and waved as buses hauled us off to detention. During the night they sent in fruit and chicken sandwiches, along with word that they thought we were crazy but they respected us.

Those long hours under detention were memorable—of the youths with all their energy, the sometimes risky dialogues in the sports arena where we were being held, the dialogues or confrontations with National Guard units and the police. When I think of Guenter Lewy and his heroes, I am sorry for them—I doubt that in their whole lives they have ever lived such a day. It was such a gift to have been there. And how symbolic that, as the last of our crew came in from the buses that carried us to detention, the very last two persons to come into the arena were the very old, very militant Anne Upshure and a young disabled man. The old and the disabled—on that day they too could take part. And that is one of the things nonviolence is about—the empowering of those not so brave, or not so strong, or not so young.

• • •

It was the struggle of the Vietnamese people that first created the Vietnam antiwar movement. Most of our movement comprised quite ordinary, nonradical Americans from the homes and churches and schools of America. It was a youthful movement and sometimes a very foolish movement—in the case of the Weather Underground, tragically foolish. That this nation could produce so vast a response to the crimes of the Vietnam War speaks well of the American people. No historian should minimize that broad aspect. Historians should also realize how important very small groups are. Each in its own way, the various Marxist-Leninist groups (and, in the case of the CP and the SWP, in two very different ways) and "Old Lefties" played a major role. So, too, did the pacifists. We were rarely seen on center stage, and, aside from Dellinger, we rarely provided a major speaker. But, being very good organizers and more free from old dogmas than some groups, we were better able to bend and shift with events, and to help keep things from becoming violent, which in my view is what would have damaged the movement most.

The disorder in the streets, which frightened people, provided one reason for Nixon's victories in 1968 and 1972. We needed that disorder and at the same time recognized the importance of keeping it nonviolent. When the mass demonstrations took on life of their own and seemed likely to get out of hand, Barbara Deming urged that we design a special tag. Mark Morris designed the brilliant square tag: a stylized dove of peace and the words "Practice Nonviolence" on it, with a brief blurb on the back for the WRL. That tag told police that we did not carry rocks. (It is easy to overlook the fact that the police are often fearful when they face a massive crowd.) That tag also told others in the crowd not to count on us for slogans of violence and hatred. Each person wearing the tag let others know that those who had come in a gentle, if determined, spirit comprised the majority. Perhaps that tag signified as much as anything we did. I know that, when police arrested me on 5 May 1971, most of the people in the sports arena were wearing the blue and yellow tags.

If our movement won, it also lost. For we did not change the course of American policy, which has continued to brutalize Central America, aid the rebuilding of the Khmer Rouge, tacitly support Israeli suppression of the Intifada, carry out dope deals in Afghanistan, and generally mess in everyone else's back yard. The Vietnam antiwar movement performed good work with good people. I am proud of every minute of it. But that work is still far from complete. While the Soviet Union tended to internalize its terror, American capitalism exports it. It is an export we must end.

5

"May Day" 1971

Civil Disobedience and the Vietnam Antiwar Movement

GEORGE W. HOPKINS

Let your life be a counter friction to stop the machine.
—Henry David Thoreau, 1849

There is a time when the operation of the machine becomes so odious, makes you so sick at heart that you can't take part; you can't even tacitly take part, and you've got to put your bodies upon the gears and upon the wheels, upon the levers, upon all the apparatus and you've got to make it stop.
—Mario Savio, 1964

To dislocate the functioning of a city without destroying it can be more effective than a riot because it can be longer-lasting, costly to the society but not wantonly destructive.
—Martin Luther King, Jr., 1967

If the government won't stop the war, we'll stop the government.
—May Day Tribe, 1971

On 3 May 1971, more than 15,000 anti-Vietnam War activists—many identifying themselves as members of the May Day Tribe—attempted to shut down the operation of the federal government in Washington to protest the continuation of the war. While previous antiwar demonstrations had often included civil disobedience as a component, this unprecedented protest differed in intensity, size, and purpose: mass civil disobedience was its goal. It would not be merely an offshoot of a larger march. The use of mass, nonviolent civil disobedience against what many perceived to be the illegitimate policy of an unresponsive government resulted in the largest mass arrest in American history: more than 7,200 people were incarcerated that day. More than 5,000 arrests followed at May Day actions during the next two days. Although the activists failed in their ultimate goal, controversy over the nature of the protests and the government's response (illegal dragnet arrests and preventive detention) polarized public opinion. Questions of citizens' rights, government repression, and civil liberties for radical demonstrators intensified the ongoing debate over American involvement in Indochina.[1]

Controversy over nonelectoral strategy and tactics continually agitated the multileader, multiorganization antiwar movement. From 1967 through 1970, the National Mobilization to End the War in Vietnam (Mobe) struggled to present a united front against the Indochina policies of the Johnson and Nixon administrations. Within the Mobe, those who advocated mass, legal demonstrations as the only appropriate tactic argued with proponents of civil disobedience; others debated whether a single-issue focus on the war had more effect than a multi-issue campaign that included racism, repression, and poverty. Ideological perspectives also fueled dissension, as liberals, radicals, socialists, communists, anarchists, pacifists, and others wrangled over issues.[2]

By the summer of 1970, many antiwar activists had become frustrated. After continual clashes over strategy and tactics, the antiwar movement's united front coalition was defunct. The Mobe dissolved in the wake of its 9 May Washington demonstration that it had called to protest the invasion of Cambodia and the Kent State killings. According to radical pacifist and demonstration co-marshal Bradford Lyttle, "about 120,000 morally outraged people were assembled at the Ellipse, at least 20,000 of whom were prepared for the risks of a determined civil disobedience action." But no call for such action came because of lack of consensus among the Mobe Steering Committee and disagreement among civil disobedience advocates about the type of action to undertake. The anticlimactic demonstration disillusioned many activists who criticized the Mobe's "spring picnic" as an insufficient response to further aggression abroad and deadly repression at home.[3]

As the Mobe dissolved, two new organizations emerged that reflected the divisions over strategy and tactics within the antiwar movement. On 21 June more than 1,500 activists committed to the single-issue, single-tactic approach met in Cleveland and established the National Peace Action Coalition (NPAC). A week later more than eight hundred advocates of the multi-issue, multi-tactic perspective met in Milwaukee to form what would become the National Coalition Against War, Racism, and Repression (NCAWRR). Partisans of both coalitions began immediately to snipe at each other. Many NCAWRR activists considered NPAC Trotskyist-dominated, and many NPAC members satirized NCAWRR as the "new coalition against everything."[4]

While the antiwar movement restructured itself, veteran pacifist, anarchist, and Chicago Eight defendant Dave Dellinger articulated the concerns of many activists dissatisfied with the limited choices of "endlessly repeated marches and rallies, on the one hand, or mindless, counter-productive violence, on the other." Dellinger argued that "there is a third non-electoral alternative—open, disciplined, carefully focused non-violent resistance." While "periodic marches and rallies" remained useful mass mobilizations, Dellinger believed that "such activities as work stoppages, draft-board disruptions, and other organized attempts to paralyze the war machine ... [would] add power and variety to the movement's assortment of tactics."[5]

What Dellinger advocated went beyond traditional concepts of civil disobedience. Proponents of Gandhian and Quaker methods wanted to bear witness to injustice, hoping to speak truth to power, confront the conscience of their opponents, and spark a conversion experience within the oppressor through deliberately unlawful, public acts of protest—performed conscientiously and nonviolently—including submission to arrest.[6] Dellinger argued for a more active, militant form of civil disobedience. He had less interest in converting opponents than in pressuring them to change or stop their unjust actions through the power of nonviolent mass disruption.[7]

Dellinger and others also found support for their advocacy of nontraditional civil disobedience from Dr. Martin Luther King, Jr. By 1967, King had come a long way from his 1963 "Letter from a Birmingham Jail." When he encountered persistent white opposition to his civil rights crusade in northern cities, King had threatened the use of mass civil disobedience to pressure (not convert) those communities as well as to provide an alternative to violence and rioting. King observed that "to dislocate the functioning of a city without destroying it can be more effective than a riot because it can be longer-lasting, costly to the society but not wantonly destructive."[8]

Veteran activist and Chicago Eight defendant Rennie Davis became convinced that this tactic had to be the antiwar movement's next step: "I decided we needed to do what Martin Luther King had done—take a mass mobilization to the civil disobedience level. The concept of shutting down the government was a more electrifying idea. I thought that mass civil disobedience was needed for its impact on this country and also on North Vietnam."[9] At the Milwaukee conference in June, Davis and Arthur Waskow had presented "A Proposal for the Formation of Liberation Collectives and Brigades and for the Disruption/Liberation of Washington," a prototype scenario of May Day actions that would be used to pressure the government to end the war or face massive civil disobedience. The conference deferred action on the proposal. In July, Davis and Waskow presented the idea to the pacifist National Action Group (NAG). Although Brad Lyttle and several others backed the plan, the majority opposed it.[10]

Davis also explored other avenues of support for the scenario. In August he presented a plan—which called for mass, nonviolent, disruptive actions in Washington if the government had not ended the war by 1 May—to the National Student Association (NSA) annual convention. In a close vote, 150-134, delegates defeated the proposal. However, NSA did approve another Davis proposal to send delegations to Saigon and Hanoi to negotiate a symbolic treaty of peace with Vietnamese student associations, a People's Peace Treaty. NSA would then sponsor a Student and Youth Conference on a People's Peace to ratify the treaty.[11] In September, NCAWRR's formal founding conference indicated strong support for the May Day proposal in principle, recommending the plan to its constituent groups.[12]

Armed with NSA's endorsement of the People's Peace Treaty idea and NCAWRR's sanction of the May Day actions, Davis went to colleges and universities in the fall of 1970 to build support for both projects. Many students responded favorably to his proposals. These politically and often culturally radical constituencies, quickly dubbed the "May Day Tribe," challenged the Student Mobilization Committees that dominated campus antiwar organizing. These student organizations mirrored the divisions between NPAC and NCAWRR within the larger antiwar movement. At the same time, the development of the May Day Tribe as "an independent youth force" provided Davis, Michael Lerner of the Seattle Eight, and others with an organizational base separate from, but related to, NCAWRR. Should coalition support waver, militant civil disobedience advocates now had an alternative network of support for May Day.[13]

The May actions soon became embroiled in internecine conflict between NPAC and NCAWRR. At an NPAC conference in Chicago on 4 December, NPAC and NCAWRR leaders quarreled over the dates for the spring actions. NCAWRR had already scheduled its own conference for early January to finalize plans for its April and May actions, including the well-publicized May Day scenario. NCAWRR leaders asked NPAC to postpone setting a date for its mass marches in Washington and San Francisco until after NCAWRR's January meeting. Then unified spring actions could be planned that would be linked to international protests expected in May. But NPAC delegates rejected the proposal and voted to hold their mass marches on 24 April. Each group saw the other in the worst possible light. To NPAC, NCAWRR appeared elitist and antidemocratic; to NCAWRR, NPAC appeared manipulative by knowingly setting the date for its mass action one week before the May action. To May Day organizer Michael Lerner, NPAC's action seemed to be a deliberate effort to undermine their plans: "The Trotskyists knew that it would be extremely difficult to convince people to stay in Washington for *two* consecutive weekends."[14]

The 8 January NCAWRR meeting was also contentious. After extensive discussion the conference took no position on NPAC's 24 April march. Furthermore, several hundred delegates argued over the nature of May Day. Davis and Dellinger spoke for the disruptive direct action proposal, while Ron Young of the Fellowship of Reconciliation and Cleveland activist Sid Peck advocated more traditional civil disobedience. The result was an ambiguous endorsement of a variety of "nonviolent and militant" antiwar protests during 1–8 May, "going beyond rallies and demonstrations, but also including them, into active struggle." For May Day organizers, the conference proved disappointing. It also confirmed their earlier decision to develop "an independent youth force committed to the May action."[15]

The People's Peace Treaty represented that youth force. Negotiated in late 1970 by a NSA delegation, the treaty called for an immediate cease-fire as soon as the U.S. announced "immediate and total withdrawal from Viet Nam, and publicly set the date by which all U.S. forces will be removed," as well as other provisions. Numerous peace and pacifist groups had endorsed the treaty concept, linking it to the Hatfield-McGovern proposal to set a date for U.S. withdrawal from Vietnam. Of particular importance to May Day, the document concluded: "As Americans ratifying this agreement, we pledge to take whatever actions are appropriate to implement the terms of this joint treaty of peace, and to ensure its acceptance by the government of the United States." By

February 1971 more than two hundred college and university student governments had endorsed the treaty.[16]

Formal ratification of the People's Peace Treaty occurred when two thousand delegates approved the document at the NSA's Student and Youth Conference on a People's Peace held 5–7 February at the University of Michigan in Ann Arbor. Debate then began over implementation of the treaty. As news reports of South Vietnamese and American troop buildups on the Laotian border heightened concern about an expanded war, Rennie Davis, Mike Lerner, and others forming the May Day Collective proposed giving the government until 1 May to ratify the treaty. If the government did not endorse the treaty, mass civil disobedience would disrupt the operation of the government until ratification occurred or all demonstrators were arrested. The conference adopted the May Day plan as an enforcement measure to implement the treaty. Socialist Workers party stalwart Fred Halstead, opposed to the May Day action, noted that "Rennie Davis finally had the vehicle he sought, dedicated to carrying out his tactic, and backed by the authority of a sizable national conference."[17]

Meanwhile, the National Coalition Against War, Racism, and Repression reconstituted itself as the People's Coalition for Peace and Justice (PCPJ). Its organizational membership, leadership, and perspective remained essentially unchanged, except for the inclusion of Students and Youth for a People's Peace—more commonly known as the May Day Tribe. At a joint press conference the day after the Ann Arbor conference, PCPJ spokesperson Dave Dellinger told reporters about the week of activities it would sponsor in Washington beginning 1 May: "We must move from expression of opinion to action. We have to move to the stage of force without violence." Rennie Davis, speaking for Students and Youth for a People's Peace, explained the May Day scenario: "Unless Nixon commits himself to withdrawal by May 1—that is, if he won't stop the war—we intend to stop the government." Davis was also one of several PCPJ national coordinators. With PCPJ endorsement, May Day gained additional momentum.[18]

The very day of the PCPJ–May Day Tribe press conference, South Vietnamese troops, supported by U.S. air power, invaded Laos. This widening of the war convinced many activists to join May Day. The poor performance and abrupt retreat of South Vietnamese troops increased antiwar opinion in the United States. By April a Gallup Poll showed that 73 percent of the American people wanted all U.S. troops withdrawn from Indochina by 31 December 1971. Yet the Nixon administration's refusal to set the date for such action, let alone order immediate withdrawal, fueled May Day militancy.[19]

PCPJ and NPAC continued to quarrel over antiwar activities. However, PCPJ asked NPAC to join it on Saturday, 1 May, to hold workshops and other legal activities followed by a legal, peaceful mass rally on 2 May, which PCPJ hoped would also build support for mass civil disobedience on 3 May. NPAC, while glad "that [PCPJ] now express[ed] a recognition of the need for mass action against the war, as distinct from civil disobedience," noted the confusion over 1 May and 3 May as dates for civil disobedience action, rejected the 2 May proposal, and urged PCPJ to join with them on 24 April. Reluctantly, PCPJ agreed to cosponsor the 24 April NPAC march and canceled its 2 May rally. PCPJ would also, on its own, project the demands of its civil- and welfare-rights groups on 24 April and publicize the May action. The two coalitions also agreed "to stay out of each other's way—no May Day civil disobedience on 24 April and no attempt by NPAC to interfere with it on the May Days." [20]

Feeling politically isolated and organizationally weak, PCPJ had arrived at this decision after David McReynolds of the War Resisters League and several other pacifists proposed that PCPJ teach nonviolent civil disobedience techniques to all May Day demonstrators between 25 April and 3 May. During the same week, PCPJ would also conduct a People's Lobby with Congress and federal employees about the war, publicize the People's Peace Treaty, and explain the 3 May actions. This plan wisely focused activists' energies on outreach and communication while also stressing self-discipline on the streets. In addition, the May Day Tribe's acceptance of the plan reassured many traditional pacifists within PCPJ who feared that the Tribe's nontraditional, confrontational, disruptive approach to civil disobedience might quickly degenerate into violence. Some May Day organizers, however, greatly resented PCPJ's cosponsorship of the 24 April march as bowing to Trotskyist pressure and viewed cancellation of the 2 May rally as "a severe blow to May Day." [21]

Meanwhile, in March, the Nixon administration began "extensive interdepartmental meetings" with federal and district agencies to plan its response to the upcoming demonstrations, especially May Day. President Nixon put Attorney General John Mitchell in charge of the project, reportedly telling him that the "demonstrators were to be allowed no semblance of a victory in tying up the government." According to one administration source, "Short of killing people, Nixon had given Mitchell a blank check." Mitchell in turn named Deputy Attorney General Richard Kleindienst to head the task force. The administration's new Intelligence Evaluation Committee considered preventive detention measures among its options.[22]

Even while the government made its plans, May Day organizing continued unabated. The Ann Arbor conference had decided that plans for May Day would be developed on a decentralized basis. This unprecedented strategy developed in reaction to the perceived top-down, hierarchical organization of other antiwar groups. The May Day Collective in Washington limited itself to "providing information, support, and coordination *only.*" The collective published and distributed the *Mayday Tactical Manual,* which told activists to make their own plans and decisions "within the discipline of nonviolent civil disobedience." The *Manual* did identify and number twenty-one targets, traffic circles and bridges, and assigned them to different regional groups. Several constituency groups (women, gay, and Third World activists) requested and received their own targets, but organization and tactics remained their own responsibility: "No 'National Office Organizer' will do it for you *(or to you)*." The only other caveat was to avoid disruptive actions near the District's black community.[23]

Organizers stressed their serious purpose: "The aim of the Mayday action is to raise the social cost of the war to a level unacceptable to America's rulers." The use of nonviolent civil disobedience would be combined "with our life culture to create Mayday in Washington." Fusing New Left activism with the counterculture projected the image of "Gandhi with a raised fist." The scenario envisioned "thousands of us with bamboo flutes, tamborines *[sic],* flowers and balloons moving out in the early light of morning to paralyze the traffic arteries of the American military repression government nerve center. Creativeness, joy, and life against bureaucracy and grim death. That's nonviolent civil disobedience; that's Mayday." [24]

More pragmatically, the *Manual* suggested tactics such as waves of ten to twenty-five people sitting down at a target until arrested, followed by additional waves of demonstrators. Street parties with music and dancing would disperse if gassed or charged but otherwise submit to arrest. Troop teach-ins would talk with GIs guarding targets and encourage them to join the demonstrators. The *Manual* also briefed demonstrators on likely police and military responses to planned traffic disruptions. Participants were told to expect to be arrested and jailed. Rumors of police brutality, extreme fines, or lengthy jail terms were to be ignored as disinformation designed to intimidate activists. The jailing of thousands of demonstrators "will make the choices painfully clear to America's rulers. End the war or face social chaos." [25]

The May Day Collective also produced *Time Is Running Out,* an emotionally powerful, thirty-minute film about "the Vietnamese people's centuries of struggle for independence." Folk singer Joni Mitchell narrated the film, which was shown on many campuses. Often Rennie Davis or Mike Lerner spoke afterward about how federal employees were "good Germans" just doing their jobs while the slaughter went on. May Day meant to disrupt and stop that business-as-usual attitude, while pressing for ratification of the People's Peace Treaty and an end to the war. The film and speakers, as well as distribution of copies of the People's Peace Treaty and literature about May Day, sparked widespread interest. But how many people would actually come to the capital remained problematic.[26]

The antiwar movement's Spring Offensive began on 19 April when more than one thousand members of Vietnam Veterans Against the War (VVAW) launched a five-day "limited incursion into the country of Congress" known as Operation Dewey Canyon III, a parody of the code name of the invasion of Laos. Dressed in fatigues, the veterans—many with long hair, some disabled—held memorial services for fallen comrades, conducted guerrilla theater search-and-destroy missions, and testified against the war before Congress. On 23 April, more than 700 VVAWs threw their medals over a fence in front of the Capitol as a final gesture. The next day, the NPAC-PCPJ March on Washington attracted between 200,000 and 500,000 participants, with an additional 150,000 marchers in San Francisco. Despite press reports of a generic antiwar march, it was an impressive mass mobilization drawn from a cross-section of the American public—by far the largest ever. Some May Day people viewed the march as "nothing but hors d'oeuvres for what's to come this week and next."[27]

During the week before May Day, Rennie Davis continued to predict that 50,000 demonstrators would take part. Pacifists and peace groups began training demonstrators in nonviolent civil disobedience in West Potomac Park.[28] PCPJ's People's Lobby urged Congress to end the war, while others staged traditional civil disobedience actions at the Selective Service headquarters, the Department of Justice, and the Department of Health, Education and Welfare. These actions resulted in almost eight hundred peaceful arrests.[29] Meanwhile, on 28 April, five members of the May Day Collective testified before the Senate Foreign Relations Committee to present the People's Peace Treaty and to urge committee members to sign it. They charged the Senate with abdicating its constitutional responsibility to declare war and challenged the committee to filibuster until the administration stopped the war. Much of the publicity value of this dialogue became overshadowed, however, by front-page news reports that May Day Collective member Leslie Bacon had been arrested as a material witness, alleged to have personal knowledge of the 1 March bombing of the Capitol. May Day organizers asserted that the timing of the arrest constituted "an attempt by the government to discredit" their planned protest. They also denounced FBI surveillance and phone taps.[30]

Government monitoring of May Day led to drastic action. When more than 50,000 people attended a "people's peace rock concert" on Saturday, 1 May, in West Potomac Park, federal officials became alarmed. Having predicted that only 20,000 would attend the concert and fearful that May Day organizers might recruit many new demonstrators, Deputy Attorney General Richard Kleindienst decided, contrary to the specifics of the permit agreement, to revoke the permit for the encampment without consulting May Day leaders. Eviction of the demonstrators from the park was a preemptive tactical move designed to eliminate the activists' staging ground for Monday's planned disruptions. At 6:30 on Sunday morning, 2 May, Chief Jerry Wilson and 750 police announced revocation of the permit to the 45,000 people still in the park and ordered them to leave by noon or face arrest. Caught off guard and resentful but nonviolent, all but 200 left by noon. The rest submitted peacefully to arrest.[31]

Many concertgoers and potential demonstrators left town, as government officials had hoped, but thousands of others regrouped at nearby universities, churches, and private residences. At a midafternoon press conference, Davis denounced the park eviction as "virtual martial law," while PCPJ spokesperson Sid Peck termed the police action "Vietnamization come home. The city has become Saigon West." May Day organizers reduced the number of targets from twenty-one to twelve as regional and constituency groups met hurriedly to revise their plans in light of the smaller contingent expected. Despite the confusion, the activists' determination was evident. One protester noted that the park eviction served at least one useful purpose: "We got rid of those who came just for the fun of it. The rest of us mean business."[32]

So did the government. Federal and district authorities had coordinated their resources. To contain the planned disruptions, Chief Wilson mobilized his entire police force of 5,100 as well as 500 park police and 1,500 District of Columbia National Guard personnel. An additional 10,000 army and marine troops stood on alert nearby—the largest number since the April 1968 civil disorders following the King assassination. Over the weekend, Commander-in-Chief Nixon phoned Wilson from San Clemente, commended him and his force, and told him to continue to deal "fairly but firmly with violators of the law." [33]

Each side began preparations early Monday morning, 3 May. At 1:38 A.M., "busloads of riot police" had parked, ready for action. An hour later, a large National Guard convoy arrived in the northwest sector of the city. By 4:30 A.M., Chief Wilson was patrolling the streets in Cruiser One. Bridge traffic grew heavy when 4,500 top-ranking officials and other key personnel reported to work early, as ordered. William D. Ruckelshaus, head of the Environmental Protection Agency, explained: "We were told to be in our offices at a quarter to five this morning so that no one could say that [the demonstrators] had stopped the executive process." Thus, May Day had already had a significant impact; as one employee on his way to the Pentagon observed, "If this isn't disruption, what is?" At police roll call shortly before 5 A.M., Chief Wilson radioed the president's commendation to the force, including Nixon's "desire that this city be open for business this week. Our responsibility is to insure that goal." Meanwhile, armed marine and army units were deployed at key bridges with police tow trucks positioned nearby.[34]

Before dawn more than 15,000 May Day demonstrators met in small groups across the northwest part of the city and on the Virginia side of several bridges. Many removed contact lenses and earrings, wrote lawyers' phone numbers in pen on their wrists, and tucked bail money inside their shoes. Many also put stickers saying "Practice Nonviolence" on their shirts. But when they hit the streets before 6 A.M., they found that the government would not allow them to perform mass, disciplined, nonviolent civil disobedience. As demonstrators sat down in rows or circles at intersections or near bridge entrances, police began spraying mace or lobbing tear gas cannisters to force them to disperse. Flying squads of officers on motor scooters roared through lines of demonstrators blocking streets. Other police began clubbing demonstrators. Instead of using the field arrest forms developed after the 1968 civil disorders to note the individual's name, address, charge, and circumstances of arrest, along with a Polaroid photo of the suspect, many police met nonviolence with violence.[35]

Forced to scatter because of the tear gas and clubs, May Day protesters quickly improvised with "mobile tactics," dashing into the street to halt cars and then running away when police charged. Some did not escape unscathed, as police continued to club protesters. At 6:19 A.M., an officer told a reporter that "it's the only way you're going to keep [traffic lanes] open." Occasional arrests were made, and some officers filled out field arrest forms. But at 6:25 A.M., as the number of demonstrators on the streets increased, Chief Wilson ordered normal field arrest procedures suspended. The police radio dispatcher was succinct: "Just load 'em on the bus and lock 'em up." Wilson essentially ordered indiscriminate dragnet arrests and illegal mass preventive detention to "sweep the streets" of demonstrators.[36]

For the next several hours, the streets of the capital in its northwest section resembled, as one commentator observed, "an extended, earnest game of hares and hounds." Protesters blocked traffic with their bodies, trash cans, cement blocks, tree limbs, and debris. Most fled when police approached. Some demonstrators lobbied with motorists to stall their cars; other activists apologized for inconveniencing drivers but told them the war had to end now. Demonstrators pulled small cars from parking spaces into the street, and even overturned a few. A small number of activists pulled distributor caps from vehicles or let air out of tires in an effort to cause a bigger traffic jam. Even fewer slashed tires or scattered nails in the street; only a handful threw rocks or bottles or swung sticks at the police. Press and police agreed that these were atypical incidents and that no looting or window-smashing had occurred.[37]

Many law enforcement personnel, however, did not restrain themselves as well as the demonstrators. Indiana activist Joseph "Jot" Kendall reported that "carloads of federal marshals in Civil Defense cars were jumping out with clubs and beating people. I didn't see them arrest anyone, just beat them. A Washington cop told me they were Maryland county sheriff's deputies, appointed as federal marshals for the occasion." Many police removed their badges to avoid identification as they joined in the fray. Journalists repeatedly witnessed police "swinging their long nightsticks freely at the milling demonstrators, young men and women alike." Tear gas also wafted through the streets as police dispersed groups, grabbed as many individuals as they could, and loaded them in vans or buses. Few had been informed of the charges against them. By 8 A.M., with the normal rush hour traffic increasing, more than 2,000 people were already in custody.[38]

The police dragnet swept up numerous bystanders, including six psychiatric patients and their attendants. Many clearly identifiable medical personnel called in to aid protesters were seized; police impounded two marked ambulances and destroyed medical supplies. Anyone questioning police about their tactics invited detainment. For many, matters quickly worsened; reporters noted that "the sight of District policemen jamming the butts of their sticks into the ribs and backs of prisoners, often shouting obscenities at the same time, has become commonplace." [39]

By 9:30 A.M., with the streets clear, Wilson claimed victory. Thirty minutes later, Attorney General John Mitchell declared, "The city is open. The traffic is flowing. The government is functioning." However, regular arrest procedures were not reinstituted until 2:10 P.M. Meanwhile, a spot-check of federal agencies revealed normal attendance levels of 90 to 95 percent. Presidential counsel John Dean updated the commander-in-chief every few hours on the "military" situation; Dean had also drafted an emergency declaration for the president should conditions require formal suspension of civil liberties. However, the administration's "military attack" on the protesters had won. The victorious government also had 7,200 "prisoners of war." [40]

While publicly delighted with the morning's results, the attorney general and other federal and district officials privately worried about the legality of their actions. Fearful of false-arrest suits, they summoned May Day attorney Philip J. Hirschkop to a meeting that afternoon. Speaking for the city, the police department's general counsel, Gerald M. Caplan, offered Hirschkop a deal: if May Day leaders cancelled further demonstrations, urged their followers to leave town, and helped provide buses for those leaving, the city would immediately drop all charges against those arrested without the standard field arrest forms and photographs, free those arrested properly on $10 collateral, not search detainees for drugs, and waive felony indictments of May Day leaders. Caplan gave Hirschkop a few hours to talk with May Day and PCPJ leaders and receive a response to the offer. [41]

Meanwhile, at a 3:30 P.M. press conference, Rennie Davis declared, "We want to make clear that we failed this morning to stop the U.S. government. Our biggest problem was not appreciating the extent to which the government would go to put people on the skids." He conceded that "we were taken by surprise at the closing of the [West Potomac] Park." He also noted that on Monday morning "many people arrived too early or forced themselves into situations, rather than letting things take their natural course." Undeterred, he announced a reduced schedule of targets for Tuesday morning's disruptive actions and a march to the Justice Department beginning at noon.[42]

After the press conference, Hirschkop presented the government offer to Davis and several other May Day and PCPJ leaders. They rejected the deal, Davis recalled, as preposterous. If they accepted it, their credibility with militant antiwar people would be destroyed. Moreover, the idea was impractical. Neither Davis nor any of the other leaders could "order" any of the demonstrators to leave. Despite prodigious intelligence efforts, the administration still did not understand the decentralized, autonomous nature of the May Day Tribe. Several moments later, before the government learned of the rejection, FBI agents arrested Davis on charges of conspiring to violate the civil rights of others and conspiring to interfere with federal workers.[43]

Meanwhile, thousands of demonstrators jammed District jail cells, the jail exercise yard, and the hastily commandeered, fenced-in practice field of the Washington Redskins across from RFK Stadium. The government was determined not to let May Day succeed, but, despite advance warning that thousands of protesters would be in town, it had not arranged adequate detention facilities. Overcrowded and unsanitary conditions, as well as lack of food and water, caused severe problems for the inmates of "Woodstockades." A judge later declared the conditions "cruel and unusual punishment." However, the mutual concern, sharing, and solidarity among those detained received widespread acknowledgement, especially by journalists caught up in the dragnet arrests and "Jailed With the Mayday Tribe," as one reporter titled his memoir.[44]

Undeterred by mass preventive detention, 700 demonstrators were legally arrested on Tuesday morning, 4 May, while trying to block traffic. Approximately 2,000 people were legally arrested that afternoon while practicing traditional civil disobedience at the Justice Department. On Wednesday afternoon, 1,200 people were peacefully arrested at the Capitol for unlawful assembly as four House members addressed them. On Thursday afternoon, Rennie Davis announced the end of May Day demonstrations as a "tactical retreat."[45]

• • •

The May Day actions provoked a storm of controversy. Columnist Mary McGrory summarized the general press reaction: "May Day, living up to all expectations, got the worst reviews of any demonstration in history. It was universally panned as the worst planned, worst executed, most slovenly, strident and obnoxious peace action ever committed." Mainstream pundits and politicians praised the respectable demonstrators of 24 April and bemoaned the "foolish and useless acts" of the alienated and egocentric May Day Tribe, "Leaderless Rabble" who "diverted public attention from the war issue to the issue of their own conduct." Worse still, critics charged that May Day had hurt, not helped, the antiwar effort.[46]

But others disagreed. A week after the protests, a Capitol Hill correspondent noted that "contrary to the fears of many Senate doves, however, who were quick to issue statements deploring the Mayday tactics, the demonstrations did not appear to have besmirched the antiwar movement in Congress." Public opinion had already shifted decisively against the war; the alleged excesses of May Day would not change that. Black columnist William Raspberry, ambivalent about May Day, noted that much of the criticism sounded embarrassingly familiar to civil rights advocates: "What it says is that I agree with your objectives but I believe your tactics are hurting the cause. I've heard that one too many times, and from too many wrong sources, to feel comfortable repeating it now."[47]

Nevertheless, the administration celebrated its victory. Attorney General Mitchell encouraged police throughout the country to emulate the tactics used in the capital: "I hope Washington's decisive opposition to mob rule will set an example for other communities." Mitchell declared that President Nixon shared this view.[48] In contrast, the American Civil Liberties Union decried the "Vietnamization of America [with] free-arrest zones [similar to] free-fire zones" in Vietnam.[49] When Nixon reiterated his support of the police actions, the ACLU expressed "shock that the President, sworn to uphold the Constitution, believes he can turn it on and off like a traffic light on the corner to keep the cars moving." Senator Edward Kennedy put it succinctly: "Lawlessness by the lawless does not justify lawlessness by the lawmen."[50]

The administration had at least three other options on 3 May. First, police could have permitted the nonviolent civil disobedience originally planned. Legal arrests could have been made, even at the cost of a traffic jam. In fact, that is what the government did on 4 May at the Justice Department, with resultant two-hour delays of traffic. Second, after using mace, gas, and clubs, police probably did not need to make 7,200 arrests on 3 May to keep traffic moving. Had they indeed found so many arrests necessary, they could have utilized military personnel to help with paperwork. Third, if police had been outnumbered, as Chief Wilson apparently believed, more personnel (such as nearby military on alert) could have been brought in to assist in legal arrests.[51]

Instead, the self-proclaimed law-and-order administration chose order, expediency, and punitive action over law. As Charles DeBenedetti concluded, the Nixon administration won the day, "but at a financial and constitutional cost."[52] Some demonstrators belatedly obtained a measure of justice in January 1975, when a Washington federal court awarded 1,200 victims of illegal arrest—those arrested Wednesday, 5 May, at the Capitol—approximately $10,000 each. That $12 million judgment represented the biggest civil rights monetary award in American legal history up to that date. The case also established a precedent for ordering damage payments paid directly to citizens whose constitutional rights had been violated.[53]

But May Day did more than precipitate legal and political crises within the system. May Day was an experiment in decentralized, autonomous antiwar organizing, focused on mass nonviolent civil disobedience in the nation's capital. More than 15,000 people did organize themselves for such an action. Under extreme provocation, and with few exceptions, they remained nonviolent. And they did perform civil disobedience, forced into mobile tactics on 3 May and allowed more traditional forms on 4 and 5 May. These actions showed discipline and commitment. May Day did not degenerate into gratuitous trashing, street fighting, or Weather-style Days of Rage. Even one of May Day's harshest critics within the antiwar movement, Trotskyist Fred Halstead, conceded that the "Mayday actions did . . . involve significant numbers, especially considering that they were civil disobedience demonstrations . . . and cannot be dismissed as isolated actions of a handful of ultralefts."[54]

May Day did disrupt Washington, but did not shut it down or stop the government. Nonetheless, Mike Lerner argued, "In terms of shaking people from their apathy, and stopping business-as-usual in the Capitol, the May demonstrations were clearly a success." Rennie Davis and others have noted that May Day, while irritating and angering many people, attracted support from a number of federal employees, especially civil service workers, National Guardsmen, and federal troops, as well as a surprising number of police, especially black officers. Support from the black community was also significant. David McReynolds commented that "it was the first time the Blacks had ever seen masses of whites get arrested and it changed a lot of attitudes." Brad Lyttle agreed, noting that "many members of Washington's black population were astonished by the militancy of the protest, and expressed exceptional friendliness toward antiwar activists for some weeks afterwards."[55]

May Day also had its downside. One participant noted that the May action "has been accused, with some justice, of being more like theatre than politics" because its goal was unrealistic. Moreover, "Mayday, like other spectacles on the left, relied heavily on the behavior of our uniformed adversaries and on the images which a predominately hostile media would convey. [Thus] Mayday made a lot of silly claims [about stopping the government] and set itself up for the media blitz which followed." In addition, with the focus on the capital, far fewer disruptive actions in other cities occurred in tandem with 3 May than originally envisioned. Structurally, May Day's decentralization sometimes led to disorganization and confusion. Most of its regional organizations and many of its local collectives did not survive long after May Day, although there were important exceptions. A network of protesters continued to organize new actions, although none came close to the scale of 3 May.[56]

But May Day also needed to be evaluated within the larger context of the antiwar movement and the debate on tactics. Paraphrasing John Reed, Dave Dellinger melodramatically declared that "from 24 April to Mayday (May 3) 1971, the antiwar movement produced ten days that shook Washington and were heard around the world."[57] Between 24 April and 3 May, the People's Lobby agitated. With the five-day "incursion" of the VVAW (19–23 April) and the two traditional civil disobedience actions following 3 May, added, the antiwar movement's Spring Offensive captivated the capital and the country for almost three weeks.

This sustained activity also revealed the sterility of the debate over tactics within the movement. May Day organizer Mike Lerner thought the 24 April march was "passive and meaningless." Many NPAC supporters claimed May Day would be a small "ultraleft" confrontation that would hurt the antiwar movement. Both views proved to be mistaken. Had either the 24 April mass legal march or the 3 May mass civil disobedience action occurred in isolation from other activities, the impact of each would have been lessened. Instead, in the context of the Spring Offensive, as independent radical James Weinstein observed, "the two were complementary means of applying pressure to end the war."[58]

Noam Chomsky also understood this interrelationship: "The [24 April] march provided evidence of majority opposition to the war; the Mayday action provided an implied threat that if the liberals in Congress do not act to end the war, future large-scale demonstrations may follow the path of Mayday, rather than 24 April." Chomsky noted that the first antiwar march in 1965 had attracted only fifteen to twenty thousand people, but that seven years later, hundreds of thousands attended the 24 April march "while more than 15,000 tried to disrupt the normal functioning of the government in protest against the continuing war." Chomsky wondered, "But is it impossible to imagine that in 197? hundreds of thousands will march on Washington prepared for some form of civil disobedience if the war still continues or is followed by some new horror?"[59]

The spring 1971 demonstrations, however, represented the last major sustained activities of the antiwar movement. Government repression of May Day intimidated or demoralized some protesters, while burnout and exhaustion took their toll on others. NPAC and PCPJ still quarreled; several May Day veterans planned a civil disobedience action for fall 1971, but it attracted only a few participants. Meanwhile, Vietnamization policies lowered U.S. casualties and draft calls, and the McGovern campaign siphoned off much activism into electoral politics. Protestors responded to the spring 1972 bombing and mining of North Vietnam, but antiwar militancy generally declined as peace seemed to be imminent. President Nixon won reelection in a landslide, increasing the antiwar movement's sense of isolation. Although the 1972 Christmas bombing of North Vietnam sparked outrage and renewed demonstrations, nothing on the scale of spring 1971 occurred. By January 1973, the peace treaty was signed and U.S. forces completed their withdrawal, although the war dragged on for more than two years.[60] May Day 1971 proved to be the peak of antiwar activity.

May Day drew inspiration from the civil rights movement. In following the later tactics of Martin Luther King, Jr., who eventually endorsed more disruptive and confrontational forms of civil disobedience, May Day played the role within the antiwar movement that Malcolm X had played within the civil rights movement. In both cases, the radical alternative and the specter of social chaos made liberals and their policies seem more moderate and acceptable to mainstream America. And the impact of May Day, like that of Malcolm X, remains controversial.

PART TWO

The Military and the Antiwar Movement

Introduction

Perhaps more than anyone else, the troops who served in Vietnam suffered most from the war and at the same time stood in a unique position to question—and eventually oppose—the American misadventure in Southeast Asia. The following four chapters paint a picture of the opposition to the Vietnam War in the military that formed and grew until it challenged the government's ability to prosecute the war effectively. All Vietnam-era veterans, the authors of these essays came to oppose U.S. involvement in Vietnam. Individually and collectively, they present a powerful account of the dimensions of dissent within the military during the period of the war.

In chapter 6, historian Terry H. Anderson carefully traces the origins, growth, and impact of the GI movement, which included protest over the war, disruption of the military, refusal to follow combat orders, and desertion. His main interest is the response of the brass to these activities, unprecedented in their scope. The generals and admirals tried through pressure, discipline, and courts-martial to stem the growth of opposition to the war within the ranks. However, as Anderson argues, by 1970 the U.S. armed forces had nearly stopped fighting in Vietnam. For him, the GI movement represents one of the more successful examples of social activism in the 1960s.

According to David Cortright, GI resistance to the war nearly brought U.S. armed forces to a halt, and mere survival, rather than concerted military action, became the norm. In chapter 7, expanding on his 1975 book, *Soldiers in Revolt,* Cortright combines his own antiwar experiences with extensive research to present a compelling account of dissent in the military. The widespread acts of resistance and rebellion in the ranks that ultimately affected one-third of the troops seriously compromised their effectiveness. The development of GI resistance paralleled the escalation of the war in Southeast Asia and the social and political rebellion at home. As Cortright argues, GI resistance, with the accompanying disintegration of morale and discipline, played a major role in the termination of the Vietnam tragedy.

The nature of the counterinsurgency in South Vietnam was a controversial issue for the grunts as well as for civilians back home. In chapter 8 historian Elliott L. Meyrowitz and political scientist Kenneth J. Campbell examine the war crimes hearings held in Washington (December 1970) and Detroit (February 1971). These hearings, which elicited graphic, powerful eyewitness accounts describing the searing brutality of the war, became an important element in the antiwar movement by challenging the legality and morality of the American position. Meyrowitz and Campbell contend that the war was not a "noble cause," but a political mistake and a military failure, and that its termination could be considered a small victory for international law.

Continuing this theme, historian William F. Crandell provides a personal account of the Vietnam Veterans Against the War (VVAW). In chapter 9, part memoir and part oral history, Crandell describes the organization and activities of VVAW and its chilling examination of atrocities through the Winter Soldier hearings. In addition, he analyzes the VVAW's highly successful April 1971 Washington protest that attracted the attention of millions of Americans and contributed significantly to the growth of antiwar sentiment.

These four chapters reveal important dimensions of the antiwar movement in the military. The troops, having sacrificed so much, deserve our careful attention.

6

The GI Movement and the Response from the Brass

TERRY H. ANDERSON

"If my soldiers began to think," said Frederick the Great, "not one would remain in the ranks." More than two centuries later, dissident American GIs published Frederick's statement in their underground newspapers as they fought an increasingly unpopular war in Vietnam. By 1969, U.S. troops proved Frederick right: many GIs were not only thinking, but also acting by protesting the war, disrupting military discipline, refusing combat orders, and even deserting the ranks. These dissidents became known as the GI movement.

An issue that scholars have thus far neglected is the rising number of these activists during the Vietnam War, their challenges to the armed forces, and the various ways in which their commanders—the brass—responded.[1] To generalize about the GI movement and the subsequent responses is, however, a precarious endeavor. Never well organized, the movement did not mount a systematic effort to disrupt the armed forces. Furthermore, because the military consisted of four services and hundreds of commands at home and abroad, commanders often responded in different ways. As a spokesperson for the Pentagon stated: "The varied responses our commanders make to the dissidents is going to keep them off balance. Whereas if our commanders always attacked at dawn they would know what to expect."[2] Generalizations also are dangerous because the nature of the GI movement changed considerably during the war. GI dissidents naturally reflected the American society from which they had been drafted. During the early years of the conflict, when there were few dissidents, rebels usually acted independently on their antiwar beliefs. After the Tet offensive in 1968, and especially after President Richard M. Nixon inaugurated his policy of Vietnamization in 1969, the GI movement expanded rapidly, became more organized, and had closer contacts with, and support from, the civilian movement.

GI dissidents had many similarities with their civilian counterparts. In the larger society, as in the military, dissidents always comprised a minority movement. When GI activists attempted to convince colleagues on one base to sign a statement that began, "We hold these truths to be self-evident," almost 75 percent refused to sign the preamble to the Declaration of Independence. In 1969, during a period when dissidence grew rapidly in the marines, only 10 percent of the corps received less-than-honorable discharges.

Yet activists claimed a disproportionate influence on society and the military. GI and civilian organizers who had attended college found military life irritating and spoke out more readily than the rank and file in their opposition to the Vietnam War. Like the student movement, the GI movement was transitory. Graduating, or being transferred or discharged, made organizing more difficult for activists and meant that after they had achieved some goals, coalitions or organizations often evaporated. The possibility of GI unionization, for example, which concerned the Pentagon in the early 1970s, no longer posed a threat a few years later.

The GI movement, as well as its civilian counterparts, claimed the moral high ground. Like blacks demonstrating for civil rights, or women advocating equality, GI activists were convinced that their movement attacked American hypocrisy and the wide gap between promises and practices. GI underground papers, or "undergrounds," stressed that military personnel should have the same rights as civilians. To support their contention, they quoted from the U.S. Constitution, the Declaration of Independence, or from great Americans. One of the latter ("It is a sin to remain silent when it is your duty to protest. Abraham Lincoln") appeared in the GI underground *Broken Arrow*. A sailor wrote in *Duck Power*, "My Country Right or Wrong. These could be the last words of a dying country. . . . Let the people question what they feel is wrong, and stand up for what they know is right."[3]

But the civilian and the GI movements attacked more than just the war and the armed forces. Both expanded their tactics and issues. By the early 1970s many military dissidents adopted a counterculture lifestyle as they opposed the war and advocated ending discrimination against black and female troops.

The first known GI to demonstrate, and the first response from the brass, occurred just six months after President Lyndon B. Johnson introduced combat troops in Vietnam. In November 1965, Lieutenant Henry Howe, stationed at Fort Bliss, Texas, participated in a small peace march in El Paso. He carried a placard that read, "End Johnson's Fascist Aggression." Although Howe marched out-of-uniform, his superiors later discovered his action. They reacted quickly and forcefully: in a court-martial they charged the junior officer with behavior insulting to his commander-in-chief and sentenced him to two years of hard labor. Howe's action and trial were not publicized.[4]

A more important act of defiance came in June 1966 after three privates stationed at Fort Hood, Texas, received orders for Vietnam. On the last day of that month, while on leave before transit to the war zone, James Johnson, Dennis Mora, and David Samas stunned the army by publicly announcing their intention to refuse the orders. They filed a suit against the government challenging the legality of the undeclared war and requested an injunction to bar the army from sending them to Vietnam. Although media coverage was skimpy, a few newspapers reported their defiance. Pentagon lawyers responded to the challenge by arguing that members of the armed forces who refused orders to Vietnam might be committing treason, and in extreme cases, could be sentenced to death. On 7 July, after the three soldiers had talked with peace organizations and while en route to present their case at a church in New York City, government officials intercepted and arrested them, and took them to Fort Dix, New Jersey, where they were held for "investigative detention." Because they had only declared their intent, were still on leave, and had not yet refused a direct order, the army did not file charges against them. A few days later, army officials separated the three, and on 14 July each one received orders to Vietnam. When they refused the orders, the brass placed them in solitary confinement in a stockade.

The Fort Hood Three demonstrated that just one year after the buildup in Vietnam, the military would have to fight not only the Vietcong, but also an enemy within its own ranks—soldiers who questioned the war. The three privates stated that their views reflected those held by a growing number of draft-age youths. In a joint statement, they explained that when "we entered the Army, Vietnam was for us only a newspaper box score of GI's and Viet Cong killed or wounded. We were all against it in one way or another, but were willing to 'go along with the program,' believing that we would not be sent to Vietnam." But the more they learned, the more they came to a decision: "We will not be a part of this unjust, immoral, and illegal war. We want no part of a war of extermination. We oppose the criminal waste of American lives and resources. We refuse to go to Vietnam!" [5]

This marked the beginning of the GI movement. The Fort Hood Three could have taken the easy way out by going AWOL before their plane left for Vietnam and accepting the usual military reprimand, fine, or reduction in rank, but to them "that would have been dishonorable." Instead, they challenged the establishment. Their action, which drew support from new antiwar organizations, forced the brass to respond. First, officers threatened the Fort Hood Three. That failed. Then government officials attempted bribes, informing Samas's parents that their son would receive an honorable discharge if he dropped the case. That also failed. Finally, the army relied on legal methods. In September, the brass held courts-martial, judged the men guilty, and sentenced them to three years imprisonment. The dissidents appealed but the Supreme Court refused to hear the case, and upon completion of their incarceration, the army awarded them dishonorable discharges.

The brass, then, fought the GI movement as they fought wars—based on action taken during the last one. Commanders responded to the first sign of dissent by relying on the court-martial, followed by imprisonment and some form of less-than-honorable discharge. This threat, always used rather successfully to control disrespect and maintain discipline, was applied again in October 1966 when the first officer, Captain Howard Levy, disobeyed a direct order. A physician, Levy had been a civil rights activist in college; he maintained that the war was wrong and that black soldiers should refuse service in Vietnam. He eventually refused to train Special Forces medics slated to serve in Vietnam because, he argued, the Green Berets were participating in war crimes that violated the Nuremberg Trial precedent. The army court-martialed him, and one month before his discharge date sentenced him to three years of hard labor. He sued, but the case did not reach the Supreme Court until 1974, when it ruled that while "members of the military are not excluded from the protection granted by the First Amendment, the different character of the military community and of the military mission requires a different application of those protections." [6]

During 1967, as many other young Americans began questioning the war, it soon became obvious that sending draftees to boot camp to make them military would not change the views of many civilians who became GIs. Most of the first dissidents, draftees who had attended college, carried their ideas from campus life into the military, a development reflected that year in the case of Private Andrew Stapp. As a college student, Stapp had been active in the antiwar movement and had burned his draft card. The army drafted him and stationed him at Fort Sill, Oklahoma, where he enraged his superiors by receiving antiwar literature and discussing his ideas with other soldiers. In May, Stapp's platoon leader appeared in the barracks to demand his antiwar material. The private said he would show but not surrender it without a guarantee that it would be returned. The lieutenant refused, left the barracks, and later returned with a sergeant, who broke into Stapp's locker with a pickax and confiscated the literature. The army then charged Stapp with refusing to obey a direct order and, ironically, having a broken locker. Stapp could have taken a minor penalty without contest, but he chose to publicize his views in a trial in order to mobilize antiwar support: he insisted on a court-martial.

The army charged that Stapp had refused to obey an order to hand over his antiwar literature. He and his lawyer claimed that the order was illegal since it infringed on his First Amendment rights. The military judges refused to listen to the defense and quickly declared the private guilty. To the bewilderment of courtroom officers, their verdict provoked an unprecedented response, as dissident GIs and a handful of civilian activists began chanting peace slogans in what probably constituted the first antiwar demonstration at an army fort. When Stapp broke his subsequent restriction to post, another court-martial resulted.[7]

Stapp's trial received national press coverage. In an attempt to keep the affair out of the headlines, the brass banned civilian activists from his second court-martial and asked cooperation from local police in the nearby town of Lawton, Oklahoma. Because most members of the community supported the nation's involvement in Vietnam, and because the city depended economically on the post, the police needed little encouragement. They arrested visiting peace activists in their rented motel room, charging them with trespassing on private property. Consequently, activists did not disrupt the second trial, but the charge against Stapp was so flimsy that the army prosecutor dismissed it. Shortly thereafter, Stapp and his civilian supporters organized the first national GI union, the American Servicemen's Union (ASU), and began publishing the first underground paper for GIs, *The Bond*. The trials also resulted in the formation by civilian activists of a new legal defense organization for dissident servicemen, the Committee for GI Rights.

For the military the question remained: what could be done with Stapp and a growing number of other antiwar GIs? Most of these men would refuse orders to the combat zone, and the ones who went might demoralize the troops. Imprisonment for a private exercising First Amendment rights seemed too severe. Stapp answered the question for the army when he began enlisting soldiers into his new union, which demanded an end to saluting, election of officers by enlisted men, collective bargaining, adoption of the federal minimum wage, and the right to refuse orders to Vietnam. Unwilling to tolerate such actions, the brass offered him a discharge. He refused it and forced them to grant him a hearing, which he again used as a forum to express antiwar ideas and to urge his colleagues to join the ASU. The army put the matter to rest in April 1968 by awarding Stapp an undesirable discharge.

In Stapp's case, and in others during the period from 1965 to 1968, when the majority of citizens supported the war effort, the brass responded to dissidence by employing traditional methods. Had the war ended in 1968, commanders would have implemented only minor changes in the armed forces. Yet that was not the case, and the war became more unpopular and as the antiwar movement spread, the brass had to consider major changes in regulations concerning dissident personnel. The tactic of court-martial and of less-than-honorable discharge had become less threatening by the late 1960s. On some college campuses, in fact, antiwar students often considered a dishonorable discharge a medal of honor.

Like the civilian antiwar movement, the GI movement expanded rapidly after Tet, and especially after the election of Nixon and the implementation of his policy of Vietnamization. Only three GI underground papers existed in 1967, but by March 1972 the Defense Department reported that about 245 had been published, and that issues of *Fatigue Press* and *Bragg Briefs* had circulations of 5,000. Active-duty servicemen published their views on ships at sea, on bases at home and overseas, in Vietnam, and even at the Pentagon.[8] The first GI movement organizations had been established in 1967. By 1971 there were at least fourteen, including two for officers. Academy graduates organized Concerned Graduates of the U.S. Military, Naval and Air Force Academies and boasted almost one hundred members. The ASU claimed 7,000 members by 1969, and off-base activists established about twenty GI coffeehouses, which provided antiwar literature and counseled servicemen on desertion and other topics aimed at disrupting the armed forces.

All the while, an expanding number of civilian antiwar activists aided the GI movement. Groups such as the Chicago Area Military

Project, the GI Office, Pacific Counseling Service, Vietnam Veterans Against the War, (VVAW), and the United States Servicemen's Fund (USSF) supplied information, organizational skills, equipment, and money. The USSF, for example, raised more than $150,000 in 1970 to help finance activities of the GI movement. Antiwar politicians and celebrities supported their cause; and actors such as Donald Sutherland and Jane Fonda staged FTA (Fuck the Army) Shows off base to counter proadministration Bob Hope Shows on base. The National Lawyers Guild, American Civil Liberties Union (ACLU), and other antiwar legal organizations donated free advice and defended GI dissidents in court. Churches played a role by granting sanctuary to deserters and AWOL servicemen.

As public opposition to the war increased, dissident behavior soared in the armed forces. During antiwar demonstrations in San Francisco in October 1968, Navy Lieutenant Sue Schnall dropped peace leaflets from a plane on local military installations and then marched in uniform with civilian demonstrators. In December soldiers in the Cleveland area held a "GI Teach-in, Speak-Out"; and in January 1969, twenty-seven inmates conducted the first stockade sit-down strike at the San Francisco Presidio. By June the movement had infiltrated the air force as airmen distributed antiwar leaflets on Wright-Patterson Air Force Base near Dayton, Ohio. Activists in and out of the service cooperated in planning the national Moratorium and Mobilization during the autumn. On 9 November the *GI Press Service* placed a full-page peace advertisement in the *New York Times,* signed by more than 1,300 active-duty GIs, including 190 stationed in Vietnam. Several hundred GIs marched in the front ranks of the massive 15 November demonstration in Washington. Some GIs even appeared on the speaker's platform to proclaim that Nixon was not just worried about "being the first president to lose a war, but to lose the Army," and others boasted that their "whole company went AWOL for the demonstration." A month later in California, over one thousand active-duty servicemen joined a group of citizens four times that number to march outside Camp Pendleton in a demonstration planned by a new organization, the Movement for a Democratic Military.[9]

Many of these GI demonstrations concerned the most serious issue the brass faced as the war became increasingly unpopular—freedom of speech for active-duty GIs. The most significant example of the brass's response to that demand came during the first half of 1969 at Fort Jackson, South Carolina. Activists had targeted the post because it was a training camp for Vietnam, had large numbers of minorities in its ranks, had an off-base coffeehouse, and had been the scene of the court-martial of Captain Levy. In January, eight soldiers, all members of GIs United, circulated a petition asking their commanding general, James Hollingsworth, for permission to hold an open meeting on base to "freely discuss legal and moral questions related to the war in Vietnam and the civil rights of American citizens within and outside the armed forces." Although three hundred soldiers signed the petition, Hollingsworth refused the request because "the Army does not recognize collective bargaining."[10] Then, on 20 March, as their flyer later proclaimed, "GIs United held our biggest, most successful meeting to date. It just happened. Guys gathered outside the barracks and began rapping about the Vietnam war to their buddies, most of whom were leaning out the windows.... No disturbances. Just a big rap session. The brass came around and they were scared. But there was nothing they could do except a little harassment of a few individuals. They knew they couldn't break up our meeting because the guys were just exercising their democratic constitutional right to free speech, so they just left."

General Hollingsworth responded by charging eight soldiers with breach of peace, inciting a riot, and disrespect to an officer. Activists quickly came to the aid of the Fort Jackson Eight. Prominent lawyers offered free counsel, students sent telegrams, actress and antiwar activist Jane Fonda traveled to the fort, and GIs from other bases sent petitions to Hollingsworth. A tough officer with a brilliant combat record in World War II, Korea, and Vietnam, Hollingsworth was given the command because his superiors knew that he would not back down from a difficult task. He later admitted that he was prepared to take a strong hand toward GI dissidents who he felt simply wanted to be disruptive to the armed forces. Such dissidents, he thought, had the support of "Communist elements in this country... the Jane Fondas and all the other types." After Hollingsworth announced that the case would not be open to the press, reporters pressured the Defense Department for a reversal of his order. When the department ordered an open court-martial, the general informed his superiors that either he would run the post his way or they could "send a new boy down here." The court remained closed, but the case drew more national attention after a reporter wrote an article in the *New York Times Magazine* entitled "Must the Citizen Give Up His Civil Liberties When He Joins the Army?" Under intense scrutiny, the army dropped most of the charges and disposed of the problem by giving the majority of the soldiers undesirable discharges.[11]

The Fort Jackson affair demonstrated the new aggressive tone of the GI revolt. After the trial, and with support from national antiwar organizations, ten Fort Jackson soldiers sued Hollingsworth and the secretary of the army for harassment and intimidation, and demanded the same freedom of speech and right to protest on post as civilians had elsewhere. Although Hollingsworth told his lawyer to "handle it and let me know the outcome, let me know when I'm supposed to go to jail with the Secretary of the Army," the Defense Department showed greater concern. A spokesperson described the suit as serious and "without parallel in American military history." Although the army eventually won the case and continued to restrict freedom of speech on posts, GIs, with the aid of their civilian allies, launched a legal attack that embroiled the Pentagon in a paper war stretching their resources to the limit.

The Fort Jackson affair also demonstrated that as military discipline degenerated, Pentagon brass became increasingly bewildered concerning the most appropriate response. For the short term, they assigned difficult commands to their finest—and toughest—officers, and then gave generals like Hollingsworth a free hand. The army also used undercover agents, GI spies, and local police to infiltrate what they considered possible conspiracies. Army Intelligence, knowing about the backgrounds of the Fort Jackson Eight, intentionally sent them to Hollingsworth's command. The general then worked closely with local authorities and the FBI, who planted informants among the eight and within the local GI movement. The brass also responded by shipping activists to other commands. The punitive transfer, the ACLU noted, became the "most widely used weapon against dissenting servicemembers." When a dozen soldiers at Fort Bliss established GIs for Peace in 1969 and began publishing *Gigline,* the paper's editor was shipped to Vietnam, another received orders to Germany, and within five months eight more had been transferred. One of the Fort Jackson Eight received a transfer to Fort Bragg, but when he organized GIs United on that base, the army transferred him again: "The Russians have Siberia," *GI Press Service* wrote, "and the U.S. Army has Alaska. That was the most obvious parallel . . . when the Army put Pvt. Joe Miles on a special one-man levy for a base inside the Arctic Circle."[12]

The Fort Jackson affair was the Pentagon's last frontal assault on the GI movement. Until 1969 the brass relied on punitive measures, but such tactics as transfers merely moved a problem from one base to another and concerned only one serviceman at a time when dissident behavior was expanding and disrupting numerous commands. Change became inevitable. On 27 May 1969, the Department of the Army issued a directive on dissent, modified during the summer by Secretary of

Defense Melvin Laird, and sent it to all commanders in September. The directive recognized that First Amendment rights applied to servicemen. Concerning GI undergrounds, it informed commanders that they could no longer prohibit their troops from having dissident literature on base: the "mere possession of unauthorized printed material may not be prohibited," even if the papers criticized government or military policy, unless they presented a "clear danger to the loyalty, discipline, or morale" of the troops. Nor could a commander punish a soldier who wrote for an underground as long as the author was off base and off duty. While commanders still could prohibit demonstrations or the distribution of antiwar literature on base, they had to be more careful of GI rights off base, after hours, and with out-of-uniform personnel.

Having the largest number of draftees and dissidents, the army issued more lenient and thoughtful directives. Its brass informed commanders that "freedom of expression is a fundamental right secured by the Constitution. . . . Severe disciplinary action in response to a relatively insignificant manifestation of dissent can have a counterproductive effect on other members of the command . . . and may stimulate further breaches of discipline." Officers must have "cogent reasons, with supporting evidence" to deny GI rights, such as distribution of publications critical of U.S. policy, or to bar attendance at coffeehouses, and they urged commanders to establish an open-door policy toward GI grievances and to not treat complaining personnel as "enemies of the system."[13] Although conservative congressmen pressured the Defense Department to toughen up these directives, they remained in force, demonstrating the effect of the GI movement on the armed forces. Faced with an unpopular war, the brass realized that they would have to become more flexible toward dissent.

Further evidence of that realization surfaced again in 1969 when the GI movement expanded to the war zone. In May the 101st Airborne Division attacked Hill 937, located northwest of Hue, close to the Laotian border. For ten days commanders ordered U.S. troops up the heavily fortified hill, which North Vietnamese Army (NVA) combat veterans defended. Entrenched in deep bunkers, the NVA repelled the American attacks. At one point, U.S. forces shelled enemy positions for thirty-six straight hours. Two U.S. battalions then conducted a frontal assault but again were repulsed. Even though the men grew tense and irritable, officers ordered another attack, until four battalions, taking heavy casualties, finally drove the enemy off the hill. American troops had been so bloodied, so ground up, that they named the affair "the battle of Hamburger Hill." After controlling the position for several days, the commanding officer ordered the troops to withdraw, stating that the "only significance of Hill 937 was the fact that there were North Vietnamese on it." Shortly thereafter, the NVA reoccupied Hamburger Hill.[14]

The sacrifice, and then the withdrawal, led to a political debate in Washington, enraged many troops, and bolstered the GI movement. The *GI Press Service* proclaimed that "Hamburger Hill is Nixon's 'secret plan' for ending the war." Activists at Ft. Lewis-McChord, Washington, wrote that the "Lifers, the Brass, are the true Enemy, not the enemy," and another GI underground advised readers: "Don't desert. Go to Vietnam and kill your commanding officer." In Vietnam dissident soldiers placed an advertisement in the division underground, offering a $10,000 bounty on the colonel who led the attack and on any other officer who would order future assaults. Numerous soldiers attempted to take the colonel's life before he was shipped back to the United States.[15]

"Another Hamburger Hill," stated one veteran combat officer at the time, "is definitely out."[16] Indeed, four months later, in August 1969, a lieutenant thirty miles south of Da Nang radioed his commander, "I'm sorry sir, but my men refused to go—we cannot move out." Company A, as it became known, had been ordered at dawn to move on a labyrinth of North Vietnamese bunkers and trench lines in the Songchang Valley. They had done so for five days. Each time they had been thrown back by an invisible enemy that waited until they advanced and then accurately picked them off. Company strength had been cut in half; most squad and platoon leaders had been killed or wounded. The commander ordered one of his trusted sergeants to fly to the scene and "give them a pep talk and a kick in the butt." The sergeant found sixty men lying in tall elephant grass, uniforms ripped and caked with dirt. They were exhausted; one was weeping. He asked them why they would not move, and it poured out of them—they were sick of the endless battle in torrid heat, with sudden firefights by day and constant mortar attacks by night. It was a nightmare. Sixty of their comrades had already perished, and they too would soon be annihilated. After a long talk and some cajoling, the sergeant started walking toward the ridge line. Slowly the men began to stir and follow.[17]

Although a few individual soldiers had refused orders in Vietnam, Company A's action marked the first sign of mutiny. Later that year soldiers in a unit of the 1st Air Cavalry Division flatly refused to advance down a dangerous trail, an act that CBS-TV aired, and in 1970 soldiers rejected about thirty orders to advance on the enemy. By that time there were so many cases of troop disobedience that the army developed an official euphemism, "combat refusal," for what in earlier wars had been tantamount to treason.[18]

Many reasons existed for combat refusal, including the nature of the war, the inability to tell friend from foe, the one-year tour of duty, fighting in an alien culture, and Nixon's policy of Vietnamization. The policy demonstrated that despite all the president's rhetoric, slow withdrawal meant that the U.S. no longer aimed to win the war for the hapless Saigon government. For many troops in the field, the policy meant that the hoax was up. Instead of fighting to win, the objective naturally became not fighting in order to stay alive. "What we're doing now," said one soldier in May 1970, "won't change the outcome at all." Instead of attempting to search and destroy the enemy, troops improvised, going out to "search and avoid." "CYA" became a common GI phrase: "Cover Your Ass and get home!" As Congressman Pete McCloskey of California stated, "We're asking a few individuals to make a tremendous sacrifice for the dubious goal of peace with honor. No one wants to be killed on the last day of a war." [19]

By the end of 1969, even more examples of dissent surfaced in the war zone. During the November Moratorium, fifteen members of a combat unit outside of Da Nang wore black armbands, and others wrote to underground papers back home that they were "overjoyed at the turnouts ... to protest the war. ... It's really a groovy feeling knowing that there's people back in the world who are trying to help us by giving us their active support." One hundred soldiers at Long Binh signed a petition in support of the demonstration. On Thanksgiving, 140 troops at the 71st Evacuation Hospital in Pleiku held an antiwar fast and gave the reason in a petition addressed to President Nixon: "American soldiers continue to fight and die in a senseless war that cannot be won." Soldiers at Qui Nhon who organized a chapter of ASU claimed that they were "holding large meetings on base." By 1971 soldiers signed petitions that activists circulated at antiwar marches. "We urge you to march for peace April 24," proclaimed members of the 1st Air Cavalry Division: "We'd do it ourselves, but we're in Vietnam." On 4 July over a thousand GIs at Chu Lai held an Independence Day Peace Rally, which became the "largest pot party in the history of the Army." As one Vietnam veteran in Minneapolis predicted, "If Nixon doesn't hurry up and bring the GIs home, they are going to come home by themselves." [20]

"The American Army of 1970 in Vietnam," a military historian later wrote, "was unraveling like the war around it, and morale and discipline were steadily deteriorating."[21] During that year the army virtually stopped fighting—and began surviving—in Vietnam. Forces eventually withdrew to coastal enclaves, and morale plummeted as units prepared to return to the United States. Drug use soared to more than 50 percent. Behavior became unruly; officers reported many more fights within the ranks and rude behavior toward the Vietnamese. Cases mounted in which soldiers refused combat orders, the most serious involving blacks who felt alienated fighting for freedom for the Vietnamese when they did not feel free at home. In one survey conducted in the Mekong Delta, 60 percent of black troops felt that black Americans should not have to fight in Vietnam, and in 1970 at least two predominantly black companies refused combat orders.[22]

In previous wars, refusing orders, one of the most serious offenses, could be punishable by death. But not in Vietnam. More tolerant toward troop concerns, field commanders did not even give reprimands to disgruntled black soldiers or to the men in Company A. Faced with demoralized troops, they threw out the rule book and adopted new combat procedures, improvised, and discussed orders, trying to work it out with their troops. "I've got to run a sort of carrot-and-stick operation," one platoon leader stated. "The idea I got in training was that I give an order and everyone would obey. But when I got out here, I realized things weren't that simple. I found I sort of had to negotiate things." Commanders realized that if they were too "gung ho" and made too many demands, soldiers might "frag" them—shoot them or throw a grenade into their tents. By 1970 many commanders who felt that their own troops could not be trusted began restricting access to explosives and rifles. In December 1972 the army acknowledged between eight hundred and one thousand actual or suspected fraggings, and that it could not account for the deaths of over fourteen hundred officers and NCOs. The army was at war with itself over the war in Vietnam.[23]

The brass responded to breakdowns in troop discipline in a number of ways. They increased the size of their military police force in Vietnam, and in two cases in September and October 1971, police task forces skirmished with field units in an effort to protect company commanders. At that same time, Military Assistance Command–Vietnam (MACV) launched its Drug Abuse Counteroffensive. MACV established drug treatment and rehabilitation centers in Vietnam and began drug-testing all units rotating back to the United States. For those soldiers who failed the test, the army erected a drug abuse holding center at Long Binh. The brass also began Operation Intercept, dispatching U.S. and

Vietnamese troops to destroy marijuana crops. To increase morale, they enlarged the rest and recreation program from seven days in Asian and Australian cities to two weeks, and included visits to the United States.[24]

As the troops came home, the returning veteran naturally proved to be the army's most serious morale problem. "I just work hard at surviving," one typical soldier stated in Vietnam, "so I can go home and protest all the killing." After a year in the war zone and experiencing looser codes of conduct in the wartime army, returnees had little interest in conforming to "Mickey Mouse regulations" on American bases. They had done their duty, wanted their honorable discharge, and often became an irritant to careerists. In 1970 a brigade commander ordered eight veterans to the stockade for disciplinary reasons at Fort Benning, Georgia. The Fort Benning Eight, as they became known, then filed the first class-action suit against the army. On behalf of the entire 3,700-man brigade, they charged their superiors with denial of equal protection under the law and cruel and unusual punishment. The brass responded by beginning the early discharge program so veterans would not spoil the morale of new draftees and taint them with their undisciplined behavior.

By the early 1970s the military was under siege. GI activism spread to the navy and air force, involving almost every American installation at home, abroad, and on the high seas. The number of GI undergrounds soared, with dozens publishing on ships and on bases in Germany, Japan, Korea, and Vietnam. Young officers joined the movement, organizing the Concerned Officers Movement (COM), which published *COMmon Sense* and distributed it to 3,000 junior officers throughout the services. When the navy attempted to give three COM organizers early honorable discharges, they launched a new tactic, charging that the navy was avoiding the issues of dissent and servicemen's rights. They refused the discharges and declared: "We won't go.... We won't give up the ship!" On the carrier U.S.S. *Hancock*, twenty officers demanded the right for an open discussion of the war, and twenty-seven others signed a letter to Secretary Laird demanding immediate withdrawal from Vietnam. When the Defense Department harassed these officers, COM filed a lawsuit against Laird with the purpose of ending "extra-legal actions by DOD against dissidents." By 1971 even the Pentagon had a COM chapter; authorities discovered the organizer, a navy physician, and in less than 48 hours awarded him the "fastest discharge in history." [25]

The GI movement in the army, which began to simmer as units withdrew from Vietnam, started to boil in the navy and air force as the president relied on naval and air power to obtain peace with honor. The first example of antiwar activity in the navy apparently occurred in May 1970, when someone aboard the destroyer U.S.S. *Richard E. Anderson* sabotaged the ship and delayed its war cruise for two months. In October 1971 sailors and civilians in San Diego initiated the S.O.S. movement—Stop Our Ship. Nine sailors refused to sail on the attack carrier, U.S.S. *Constellation,* as it began its sixth combat tour to Vietnam. The next month, S.O.S. expanded to the U.S.S. *Coral Sea,* where one-fourth of the crew signed an anticruise petition. Both ships sailed, but dissidence increased after three sailors were put in the brig for wearing cut-up American flags as headbands and one went on a hunger strike. These "flattop revolts" spread in 1972, especially when planes from the carriers conducted extensive raids against North Vietnam. Sailors signed petitions, disrupted operations, and conducted minor acts of sabotage on the *Kitty Hawk, Oriskany, Ticonderoga, America,* and *Enterprise* before they embarked for Vietnam. Sabotage on the *Ranger* and *Forrestal* prevented the carriers from leaving port for their regular tour to the war zone, and on the *Oriskany,* twenty-five sailors jumped ship. When asked what purpose the action served, one answered, "I'm not in Vietnam right now and I'm not killing anyone." Civilians joined in and formed people's blockades, employing rubber rafts or canoes in futile attempts to prevent ships from leaving port and to wish sailors a "non-voyage." [26]

By 1971 airmen had established ten underground papers, a number that tripled the next year. In January 1972 they conducted vigils for peace at the main gates of Travis, Mountain Home, and Wright-Patterson Air Force bases, protesting what they called the "stratolevel, technological genocide," and by the end of the year pilots and crews stationed in Thailand and Guam began to question the war openly. At the start of the 1972 Christmas bombing, Captain Dwight Evans, a fighter pilot, balked when ordered to strike North Vietnam, stating that he could no longer participate in the war. Even more sensationally, Captain Michael Heck, who had piloted 175 B-52 missions, refused to fly because "a man has to answer to himself first." When Nixon continued his secret bombing campaign in Cambodia in 1973 after the United States and North Vietnam had signed the Paris Peace Accords and after American POWs had returned home, more airmen protested. One crewman and three officers—one a pilot with 230 combat missions—shocked the Pentagon by filing a lawsuit, charging that the bombing was illegal. Others on Guam began a letter-writing campaign to their legislators. "Had I the courage of Captain Michael Heck or some of those whom the President and the Vice-President so vociferously condemn," an officer wrote to Senator

Edward M. Kennedy, "I would do more.... We do not sleep with our wives, we do not see our children. Instead, every hour we bloody our hands in this insane bombing. And we do not like it." [27]

Nor did dissidents at home. During the early 1970s the GI antiwar movement became the GI movement as dissidents in the military expanded the scope of their attack, just as the civilian movement had done. They advocated black power, counterculture lifestyles, and women's liberation, and they began to oppose businesses that discriminated against those in uniform.

The rise of black power was first reflected in the armed forces during the Detroit riot of July 1967, when two black marines at Camp Pendleton conducted a "bull session" and began questioning why the black man should fight the yellow man in Vietnam for the white man. Fourteen blacks then requested to discuss the question with their commander, who quickly demonstrated that the U.S. Marine Corps would not tolerate dissent and would enforce discipline harshly. Officers arrested the two leaders, charging them with insubordination and promoting disloyalty. For questioning policy in Vietnam, the base commander sentenced one marine to six years and the other to ten years imprisonment. Black power emerged quickly after the assassination of the Rev. Martin Luther King, Jr. Tensions between black and (especially southern) white troops soared, resulting in riots at installations in all services, including Camp Lejeune, Fort Benning, the Great Lakes, and Cam Ranh Bay. A September 1969 article in *Time* described black servicemen's demands that officers crack down on racism and become more aware of their problems and culture. GI undergrounds declared that the brass were "out and out RACISTS. The only hairstyle authorized for Black GIs is . . . a stinking skinhead. Try and enforce that one—there are too many brothers around who are going to wear Afros. Push it too far and the War's going to be brought right on home." [28]

Hair styles, as well as drugs, became an issue in the expanding civilian counterculture, the hippie movement. In 1967 the army investigated 3,600 soldiers for possible drug use, a figure that increased sixfold by 1970. At that time, over half the troops in Vietnam smoked marijuana. Naturally, they brought their habit home. Returning soldiers smoked enough dope to earn Fort Hood the underground name "Fort Head." Although in Vietnam drug offenders were punished only if they behaved violently, a different set of rules existed in the United States. Prosecution of the first drug case occurred in July 1968 at Fort Hood, where soldiers and antiwar civilians held a "love-in" at a local park. Military police arrested Pfc. Bruce Peterson, an editor of *Fatigue Press,* for possession of marijuana, although they found only seed residue of the drug in the lint of his trouser pockets. Authorities set his bail at $25,000, found him guilty, and sentenced him to eight years hard labor. He actually served two.[29] Tough sentences in military or civilian courts did not, however, inhibit the counterculture in the armed forces. By 1970 hippie dress became a common sight at reserve meetings. GI reserves formed the Reservists Committee to Stop the War, published the underground *Redline,* and began attending meetings with long hair and with antiwar slogans sewn on their uniforms.

GI hippies ridiculed the military establishment, mocked commanders and careerists in their underground papers, and developed a GI counterculture. Undergrounds carried "Lifer of the Month," or "Pig of the Week" series: "The subject is, just what the fuck is a lifer? Is it a fly, an animal or the missing link? . . . Maybe he's just a person that digs pushing people. You know, the skinny little kid on our block, comes into the service after getting his ass beat for ten years, and they give him a little gold bar on his collar, Now . . . he's gonna come around and start paying everybody back."[30] At the Great Lakes Naval Training Center, 150 recruits demanded any type of discharge. Two dozen of them irritated their petty officer by refusing to return meal trays and by playing the tune "Anchors Aweigh" on kazoos as they marched back to their barracks.

On the U.S.S. *Constellation* seventy sailors initiated the Peanut Butter Conspiracy, when for three days they constantly called the captain and tied up communication lines, demanding that "peanut butter be served at every meal." On the submarine tender U.S.S. *Huntley,* sailors published an underground paper, the *Huntley Hemorrhoid,* which informed officers: "We serve to preserve the pain in your ass." Hippies in the air force decided to take as much time as possible on all tasks, to "slow down the great and powerful Air Farce machine," and they even demanded a second opinion on haircuts. When an army band was ordered to perform a John Philip Sousa march to a crowd of military dignitaries in Manhattan, one clarinetist played the melody one and one-half octaves higher, sending a shrill oriental sound down Wall Street, which enraged officers and delighted local hippies. And when the army recruited two soldiers at Fort Bliss, Texas, to spy on antiwar GIs, they organized the base chapter of GIs for Peace and used army funds to fill its treasury. Officers realized something was amiss when half the troops under surveillance deserted and their two agents filed for conscientious-objector status. Nevertheless, the brass were relieved to grant the spies discharges after one of them claimed to be "on a continual trip," hearing sounds from the "heavenly hosts [and seeing] nursery rhymes." The man received a medical discharge because, as he claimed, "Someone injected LSD in my brain." [31]

GIs joined their civilian counterparts by expanding the attack to include business and sexism. After United Farm Workers president Cesar Chavez declared a lettuce boycott in 1970, GI undergrounds ran headlines "Lifers Eat Lettuce." At Sawyer Air Force Base near Marquette, Michigan, GIs complained that local "businessmen are happy to take the Airmen's money, but practice discrimination at the same time." Other undergrounds accused defense contractors of "Making War for Fun and Profit" and reprinted the words to Bob Dylan's song "Masters of War." In 1971 over one hundred Fort Hood soldiers started a boycott against Tyrrell's Jewelry, a national chain that sold diamond rings to homesick soldiers near military installations. The boycott spread to eleven bases, significantly reducing sales. The chain store ended the action by negotiating new sales procedures with GI organizations.

At the same time, a few servicewomen began forming support groups on bases, demanding the end to sexual double standards, and GI undergrounds began printing series like "Women's Rap" and articles such as "What It's Like For Women In The Navy." At Fort McClellan, Alabama, dissident male and female troops organized GIs and WACs Against the War and published *Left Face,* and in 1971 servicewomen on that post printed their own underground, *WHACK!*

The GI movement and the unpopular war had a disastrous effect on the military. Reenlistments in 1970 fell to the lowest on record, and ROTC enrollment dropped two-thirds from 1968 to 1972. Military manpower during those years declined 40 percent, while the number of young men filing for conscientious-objector status reached record levels. By 1972, the last year of the draft, there were more conscientious objectors than draftees. Withdrawing from Vietnam and cutting draft quotas only exacerbated manpower problems. By 1972 the reserves, earlier a haven for those desiring to avoid combat in Vietnam, witnessed a mass exodus and became understaffed by 45,000 men. "Recruiting," Chief of Naval Operations Elmo Zumwalt told Congress that year, constituted the "Navy's number one problem." Furthermore, young Americans were conducting an unprecedented revolt against the draft. The government reported that 15,000 men refused induction in 1971, 100,000 did not appear for their physicals, and local selective service offices sustained 190 attacks.

Desertion and AWOL rates reached to staggering levels. Although few men deserted in Vietnam, that was not the case at home. From 1966 to 1971, desertions increased nearly 400 percent in the army, reaching a rate three times higher than that during the Korean War. For every one hundred soldiers in 1971, seventeen went AWOL and seven deserted, the highest rates in army history. As President Nixon shifted from ground to air war, desertion and unauthorized absences soared on aircraft carriers and increased 300 percent in the air force, reaching the highest levels in 1972 and 1973 during the massive bombings of North Vietnam and Cambodia. In underground parlance, the armed forces were becoming the "armed farces."

Later on, in the 1980s, conservative politicians told the public that liberals during the war years never let American boys fight in Vietnam, and even went so far as to claim that U.S. troops were stabbed in the back by cowardly congressmen.[32] By entertaining this idea many Americans could point the finger at someone else and substitute another nationalistic myth for cruel fact. By 1970 most servicemen in the war zone had little desire to risk their lives. To them Vietnam represented not a noble cause, but a senseless one. No Rambos existed in the U.S. Army in Vietnam in 1970; that myth would be created after a decade of amnesia.

The brass knew the military was in trouble. "The Army's prestige is at the lowest ebb in memory," reported the commanding general of Fort Bragg in April 1971, "there's never been a more unpopular war and it's had its effect." The next month *Newsweek* reported on "Troubled Army Brass," and then Marine Colonel Robert Heinl published a stunning exposé in *Armed Forces Journal,* entitled "The Collapse of the Armed Forces." The military historian began with a salvo: "The morale, discipline and battleworthiness of the U.S. Armed Forces are, with few exceptions, lower and worse than at any time in this century and possibly in the history of the United States." Heinl, who had just returned from the war zone, reported that soldiers in Vietnam, "drug-ridden, . . . dispirited [and] near-mutinous," were refusing combat, and fragging their officers. "By every conceivable indicator," he summarized, "our army that now remains in Vietnam is in a state approaching collapse." A few months later, in the *Marine Corps Gazette,* Major H. L. Seay lamented the high AWOL rate, drug abuse, poor leadership, lack of motivation, and racial tension in the unpopular war. He concluded, "Unit leaders are faced with more problems today than ever before in the history of the Marine Corps."[33] By 1970 it was no longer a question of letting American boys fight in Vietnam; for most of them, the war was over.

The GI movement was one of the more successful examples of social activism during the 1960s. The aim of the GI activists had been to disrupt the military, to end business-as-usual on posts and in the war zone, and ultimately to reform the armed forces. By the early 1970s the brass admitted that an unpopular war, coupled with the GI movement, had poisoned morale, devastated discipline, and changed their beloved institution.

The brass's response changed significantly during the war. With a few cases of GI dissidence in the mid-sixties, commanders at that time adopted the traditional approach of considering the problem attitudinal and then attempted to intimidate malcontents to conform. They occasionally labeled antiwar GIs "commies" and warned that without honorable discharges they would never get a job. That threat might have been true during earlier wars, but it lacked relevancy as the Vietnam War became increasingly unpopular. While commanders attempted to stifle dissent, they also tried to suppress media accounts of antiwar activities in the armed forces. In October 1966 the first GI riot occurred at Fort Hood when a few infantry soldiers who felt that they had not been properly trained for combat decided that they would rather go to the stockade than leave the next day for Vietnam. Although the troops damaged $150,000 worth of government property, the authorities kept the episode quiet and the press away. The brass also employed spies for infiltration, ordered military police to raid GI coffeehouses, and charged dissidents with a violation of the Uniform Code of Military Justice. They sequestered dissidents from other personnel, and when the local community supported antiwar activities, the brass tried to change the venue of court-martials. For example, a seaman in the Bay Area who was charged with sabotage was tried in the Philippines. Ultimately, the brass placed offenders in stockades to crush dissent.

The punitive response had worked in earlier wars, but it became obvious that Vietnam was not a typical American war. The antiwar movement in and out of the military expanded rapidly, and the brass's response had to change with thousands of troops behind bars. By 1969 the prison population of the army alone swelled to over 7,000; stockades became another breeding ground for discontent and riots. With prisons overcrowded—80 percent of their inmates were jailed for being AWOL— the army established minimum security Special Processing Detachments and reformed separation procedures. The brass gave base commanders more flexibility concerning discharges. "For the good of the service" discharges were awarded only three hundred times in 1967; by 1972 the number had grown to more than 25,000. In 1970 the Pentagon allowed commanders to award "expeditious discharges" for soldiers with poor attitudes or "trainee discharges" to weed unmilitary personnel out of boot camp. This procedure meant, of course, that discharge rates given for administrative reasons soared, tripling for all services between 1968 and 1972. When the Pentagon began its "early out" program in 1971, granting honorable discharges to veterans with less than six months of duty remaining, thousands of potential dissidents went home.

The brass also demonstrated more flexibility toward troops who claimed they would refuse combat assignments because of moral or religious beliefs. The Pentagon began to grant many of them conscientious-objector status and assigned them to desk or hospital duty. In 1967 officials granted less than 30 percent of CO claims; by 1972 that figure reached almost 80 percent.

Commanders also became more concerned about the constitutional rights of their soldiers. Antiwar legal organizations bombarded the armed forces with lawsuits. In 1965 federal court decisions on military issues numbered 325. Four years later, that figure soared to almost two thousand, and some of those cases reached the U.S. Supreme Court. While the court had a difficult time balancing GI rights with military life, it did allow more due process for military personnel. In 1972 a Defense Department task force investigating how base commanders punished problem soldiers called for additional legal safeguards for personnel. Commanding officers, threatened by GI suits, could no longer consider bases their fiefdoms and realized that their orders might become the subject of a public forum during court litigation. The suits also contributed to a more flexible system of military justice. By 1973 the accused obtained expanded rights to counsel, and court-martials were restricted to cases involving only military discipline instead of all behavior while in uniform.[34]

Pentagon officials also became more responsive concerning the daily life of service personnel. In 1969 the brass issued more tolerant directives on dissent, which allowed for a more open atmosphere on the job. The next year the Defense Department appointed Elmo Zumwalt, the youngest admiral in history, as chief of naval operations. He later wrote, "I am certain that what finally decided Secretary of Defense Melvin Laird and Secretary of the Navy John Chafee to risk jumping me into the position . . . over the heads of thirty-three of my seniors was my advocacy of rapid and drastic changes in the way the Navy treated its uniformed men and women." Zumwalt immediately began humanizing the navy by sending out over a hundred "Z-grams" that not only admitted and then attacked racism and sexism, but also changed "Mickey Mouse regulations" and liberalized rules concerning liberty, dress, beards, and hair. Although the marines did not go that far, they did begin a leadership school that utilized group dynamics and role-playing in an attempt to train NCOs to deal with personnel problems.[35]

The army, too, began experimenting and easing regulations. In June 1970, Lieutenant General John J. Tolson II, commanding officer of the nation's largest military base, Fort Bragg, North Carolina, announced Operation Awareness. Tolson, the first commanding officer to admit that the army faced a serious drug problem, changed the classification of drug use from a criminal act to a medical problem. He granted amnesty if addicts voluntarily sought help at the newly established post clinic. During their rehabilitation, the general allowed a "crash pad [with] pulsating lights, acid rock stereo and Day-Glo," where patients smoked fake joints that tasted like marijuana or took methadone to aid withdrawal. By 1971, over 450 soldiers were receiving treatment, about one hundred of them in a special drug ward. Army Chief of Staff General William C. Westmoreland began relaxing base rules concerning reveille, bed checks, and travel; in December 1970 he even approved beer in barracks. On some bases, commanding officers permitted members of GIs United to hand out antiwar flyers at designated spots, and Westmoreland named Fort Carson, Colorado, an experimental installation. Troops there worked a shorter week, slept in private cubicles, and had an ombudsman to listen to grievances. The post commander even supplied dancers for the Enlisted Men's Club, stating that "If the soldiers want go-go girls, we'll give them go-go girls." [36]

Finally the brass responded to black and female activists in their ranks. Zumwalt appointed a black assistant who visited bases, evaluated race relations, and reported to him. The admiral then issued "Z-grams" that allowed more black pride, including modified Afro haircuts. Zumwalt increased the number of black midshipmen at the Naval Academy and established new reserve officer training programs at predominantly black high schools and colleges. After a race riot in 1971 that injured thirty and claimed one life at Travis Air Force Base, California, the Defense Department announced its effort to "eliminate and prevent racial tensions, unrest, and violence." The brass established a Race Relations Institute to train and educate personnel "to maintain racial harmony," and eventually all services became more sensitive not only toward blacks, but also toward servicewomen. In 1970 the air force offered coed ROTC classes on campuses; the navy and army followed suit two years later. Coed classes began graduating from officer candidate schools, war colleges, and the service academies. After reevaluating job stereotyping in 1972, the brass gave servicewomen new opportunities by allowing them to work in almost all noncombat categories. The double standard of punishing servicewomen more than men for adultery or other sexual relations was abandoned, and during the mid-1970s all services changed their regulations so that unmarried females no longer had to resign from the service if they became pregnant.[37]

The brass responded, of course, not just to the GI movement, but to the unpopular war in general. Besieged with a massive antiwar movement and soldiers unwilling to continue to fight in Vietnam, the commander-in-chief responded by calling for an end to the selective service and the establishment of all-volunteer armed forces. In a sense, the adoption of volunteer service marked the ultimate triumph of the GI movement. But it also meant that the dissidents went home and that the brass were left alone. "The danger is that the Old Guard leadership will temporize with beer in the barracks and other cosmetic issues until the pressure is off," commented Major Harry G. Summers, Jr., in 1971. "Then it'll be business as usual."[38]

Perhaps some reversion to the old ways occurred in the following years. However, many of the demands made by those GIs who, in the words of Frederick the Great, "began to think," forced the brass to make permanent changes in the armed forces—changes that have enabled the military to keep soldiers in the ranks since the end of the Vietnam War.

7

GI Resistance During the Vietnam War

DAVID CORTRIGHT

The internal rebellion that wracked the U.S. military during America's encounter with Vietnam marks one of the least-known but most important chapters during that period. From the Long Binh Jail in Vietnam, to Travis Air Force Base in California, to aircraft carriers in the South China Sea, the armed forces faced widespread resistance and unrest. Throughout the military, morale and discipline sank to all-time depths. Low-ranking GIs organized more than 250 antiwar committees and underground newspapers. Unauthorized absence rates soared to record levels, until in 1971 the army reported seventeen AWOLs and seven desertions for every one hundred soldiers.[1] Harsher forms of rebellion also occurred, including drug abuse, violent uprisings, refusals of orders, and even attacks against superiors. This resistance within the ranks resulted in a severe breakdown in military effectiveness and combat capability. By 1969 the army had ceased to function as an effective fighting force and it began to disintegrate rapidly. The very survival of the armed forces depended upon withdrawal from Indochina.

My book, *Soldiers in Revolt,* based on my own experiences as an antiwar GI activist at Fort Hamilton, New York, and Fort Bliss, Texas, chronicles and analyzes this rebellion. Enriched by interviews and correspondence with fellow GIs at dozens of bases, this book presents a comprehensive view of resistance throughout the military. While some critics have claimed that it exaggerates the rebellion within the ranks, reports produced in the early 1970s and afterwards confirm that the revolt was indeed widespread. If anything, *Soldiers in Revolt* may have downplayed the situation.

One of the most important retrospectives of the Vietnam era is a two-volume study of soldiers' dissent, prepared for army commanders in 1970 and 1971 by the Research Analysis Corporation. The two reports, *Determination of the Potential for Dissidence in the U.S. Army* and *Future Impact of Dissident Elements Within the Army*, were unavailable when I wrote *Soldiers in Revolt*. They provide new evidence of the startling dimensions of GI resistance, depicting a movement even more widespread than previously thought possible. The studies provide important data not only on the scale of the GI movement, but on the socioeconomic characteristics of those involved. They also offer valuable clues for understanding the potential for continued resistance within the volunteer force.[2]

Employing findings from a survey of 844 soldiers, the studies document the pervasiveness of resistance at five major army bases in the continental United States. Sociologists at the Research Analysis Corporation asked the GIs about their involvement in various forms of protest and classified the protests under two separate headings: dissidence and disobedience. Under dissidence they grouped activities such as attendance at a coffeehouse, publication of a GI newspaper, and participation in a demonstration; disobedience included insubordination, refusing orders, and individual sabotage. This categorization conforms to what GIs and their supporters, without the benefit of sociology degrees, long ago established as the distinction between the GI movement and GI resistance: the first category involves verbal and formal acts of opposition, while the second implies a more physical and immediate response. Middle-class "intellectuals" often practiced dissidence, which they aimed at the higher ranks—colonels, generals, and even the commander-in-chief; the resister or disobedient generally struck out at a more immediate target, the first sergeant or company commander.

The survey finds that during the height of the GI movement, one out of every four enlisted men participated in dissident activities and an equal percentage engaged in acts of disobedience. The combined results show a startling 37 percent of the soldiers engaged in some form of dissent or disobedience, with 32 percent involved in such acts more than once. The addition of frequent drug use as another form of resistance brought the combined percentage of soldiers involved in disobedience, dissidence, or drug use to an astonishing 55 percent. The army's own survey thus shows that more than half of all soldiers during 1970–71 became involved in some form of resistance activity—a remarkable and unprecedented level of disaffection.

Interestingly, the report notes that levels of dissent and disobedience were highest in Grade E-5 (sergeant), among those nearing the end of their first term of service. Twenty-five percent of those in Grades E-1 (private) to E-4 (corporal) engaged in dissent at least once, compared to 38 percent among first-term E-5's. These E-5's were almost certainly three-year volunteers (although often draft-induced), as few conscripts with a two-year term made it past the rank of E-4. The army's study seems to confirm what GI activists themselves noted: contrary to popular impressions, volunteer soldiers tended to oppose the war more often than draftees.

The findings about the social origins of resisters are also important. Dissidents and disobedients generally come from different social backgrounds, the former most often from the middle class, the latter from the working class. Analyzing personnel records of more than one thousand dissenters (gleaned from files of the army's Counter Intelligence Analysis Detachment), the Research Analysis Corporation reports portray the dissenter group as follows: More than half were volunteers (many draft-induced); they usually came from the Pacific states and from the eastern and north central regions; they tended to be well-educated and to come from suburban, middle-class backgrounds; they were more likely to have attended college than most GIs; and they scored significantly above average on Army Classification Battery Tests (with high scores on Verbal Reasoning, and slightly below average in mechanical categories such as Automotive Information).

While dissenters were apt to be above average in terms of class and educational achievement, those involved in disobedience tended to come from less advantaged situations. The educational levels and socioeconomic backgrounds of those inclined toward direct resistance matched those of the average volunteer soldier. The army report noted that "it may well be that the better educated do not engage in direct confrontations with individual superiors from whom they would presumably receive punishment, but they rather confine their dissidence to coffee house and protest meeting attendance, contributions to underground newspapers and other covert or non-punishable activities. This supports what we learned through interviews where the NCO's said it was not the college-types, but rather the ill-educated, undisciplined individual who causes them most of their troubles."[3]

It is important to understand this differentiation between the two types of opposition in order to understand the changed nature of resistance in the volunteer force. As the Pentagon reports confirm, the social composition of the all-volunteer force, significantly different from the mixed force of the Vietnam era, has changed in directions that make disobedience as a form of resistance more prevalent. With the enlisted ranks now almost totally lacking the suburban-reared, college-educated recruits who sparked the overt manifestations of the GI movement, the dissident component of resistance has virtually disappeared. The disobedience forms of resistance have continued, however, because the changed socioeconomic base of the volunteer forces reinforces the tendency toward direct resistance. Thus, as the percentage of poor and less-educated recruits has increased, levels of insubordination and disciplinary conflict have remained high, and in some cases have even increased. This is especially evident in the extraordinarily high rates of attrition and less-than-fully-honorable discharges that have prevailed in the volunteer force during the 1980s. [4]

When sociologists asked soldiers in the 1971 study to give a reason for their participation in dissenting activities, the soldiers interviewed cited the Vietnam War 58 percent of the time, and ending the war their primary motivation. The other major reason, "the way the Army treats the individual," was expressed 38 percent of the time. When the sociologists asked the soldiers to identify which army practices caused the greatest unrest, they most frequently cited "harassment of the troops and lack of personal freedom and dignity." The next most frequent complaint involved "unnecessary make-work duties and practices," followed by "personal appearance standards—hair regulations." This concern for dignity and individual freedom again helps to explain why disciplinary problems have continued in the all-volunteer force and why the potential for soldier resistance continues to this day.

African-Americans comprised the most militant and politically active group of soldier-resisters during the Vietnam era. Their resistance was a direct reaction to the pervasiveness of racial discrimination within the military. Although racism has always existed in the American military, as it has in the larger civilian society, in some respects the military has been more progressive. The armed forces instituted desegregation ahead of many civilian agencies, and military service has always provided potential advancement opportunities for African-Americans. In other respects, however, the military does not have a good record. The arbitrary nature of command authority can make life miserable for those who serve under prejudiced commanders, and soldiers victimized by military injustice often returned to civilian life embittered by experiences in the military.

The Department of Defense conducted one of the most thorough studies of the time and issued its own four-volume *Report of the Task Force on the Administration of Military Justice in the Armed Forces* in December 1972. According to the Pentagon report, "No command or installation . . . is entirely free from the effects of systematic discrimination against minority servicemen."[5] The Congressional Black Caucus also conducted a study of discrimination within the military in 1972 and produced similar findings, concluding that "racism has become institutionalized at all levels of the military."[6]

As evidence of the discriminatory nature of military justice, the Department of Defense task force reported that "a greater number of black enlisted men receive non-judicial punishment (25.5%) than their proportionate number."[7] Likewise, in general and special court-martials studied by the task force, 23.4 percent of African-Americans and only 16.9 percent of whites received a punitive discharge as part of their sentence.[8] The incidence of less-than-fully-honorable discharges reveals the same pattern. In 1971 one in every seven African-American GIs received less-than-honorable discharges, compared to only one out of every fourteen whites.[9] Given such conditions, it was not surprising that African-American soldiers played a leading role in the resistance movement.

For African-Americans, opposition to military authority was often expressed in cultural forms. Throughout the military, they gathered in informal study groups and cultural clubs to listen to music, to study and rap together, and to promote black pride and consciousness. Many of these groups became centers of resistance activity, as the connections between the war and racism spurred growing numbers into action. Often they would join together in collective defiance of military authority. From my own experience at Fort Bliss, Texas, I remember that "the brothers" roomed together in the same part of the barracks and engaged in behavior that was blatantly against regulations. Many had Afro haircuts that far exceeded allowable standards. A group of ten or more of the brothers, adorned with beads or African jewelry, would strut conspicuously across the quad between the barracks carrying "power sticks" (African walking sticks with a carved fist at the top). Wearing their army caps perched atop oversized Afros, sneakers rather than combat boots, and shirts untucked and unbuttoned, they affronted the military dress code. Nevertheless, they received no reprimand. The company sergeants and commanders, who already had more than enough trouble dealing with the existing level of dissent, had no intention of stirring up more trouble by challenging them.

• • •

As I detailed in *Soldiers in Revolt*, the development of the GI movement followed the evolution of the war itself. Resistance appeared first in the army and marine corps, which bore the brunt of the fighting in the early years, and spread to the air force and navy as those services assumed the primary combat role from 1970 to 1973, the last three years of American involvement in Vietnam.

During the initial stages of the GI movement, marines and soldiers staged numerous rebellions at stateside bases, often in the form of prison uprisings against mistreatment and oppressive conditions. Many dissident actions occurred while dozens of underground newspapers and GI organizing projects operated at stateside bases between 1968 and 1972.

GI resistance was even more widespread among American troops in Germany, especially among African-Americans. On 4 July 1970, one of the most remarkable groups in Germany, the Unsatisfied Black Soldiers, staged a Call for Justice rally at the University of Heidelberg, attended by nearly one thousand active-duty soldiers, most of them African-American. Not only in Germany but throughout the military, numerous acts of protest and resistance occurred at military bases. This mounting wave of resistance deepened the crisis for U.S. ground forces. Already reeling from the heavy combat losses and huge manpower commitments to Vietnam and confronted with mounting political opposition within the ranks and in society at large, the army faced perhaps the worst nightmare in its history.

A wounded combat veteran, Captain Shelby Stanton, offers a startling account of the crisis gripping the American military during the Vietnam era in his book, *The Rise and Fall of An American Army*. Drawing on unit archives and internal military reports that were unavailable to earlier authors, Stanton paints a picture of internal ruin even more bleak than that offered in *Soldiers in Revolt*. Some have claimed that the army fought with its hands tied during Vietnam. Stanton's account shows that, in fact, all the ground combat forces of the United States military had been fully committed during the peak years of the war. When General William C. Westmoreland, the commander in Vietnam, demanded additional combat units in the wake of the Tet offensive, he found the military cupboards "almost bare," in Stanton's words. Although the armed forces had been greatly expanded during the war and draft calls were extremely high, the United States had no additional combat units left to send to Vietnam, short of calling up the reserves.[10]

The ground forces faced problems other than those in Vietnam. With the bulk of the army and marine corps committed to Indochina, Stanton reminds us that during that time the United States needed troops at home to quell a near-insurrection. During the first nine months of 1967 alone, over 150 cities experienced major civil disorders, the largest in Newark and Detroit. Detroit required more than fifteen thousand federal and national guard troops to restore order, including lead battalions of the 82nd and 101st Airborne Divisions. Paratroopers who had faced burning cities and sniper fire in Vietnam were now experiencing the same at home. Calls also went out to army units to quell the Pentagon demonstration in October 1967 and the antiwar demonstrations at the Democratic Convention in Chicago the next year. The massive urban revolts in Washington, Chicago, and Baltimore, following the assassination of Dr. Martin Luther King, Jr., in April 1968, also required troop commitments, including the deployment of most of the regular army formations remaining in the United States at that time.

The picture that emerges from Stanton's account is of an army that had committed nearly every fighting man to service. Faced with a large-scale war in Indochina and massive civil disorder at home, the army and marine corps were extended beyond the limit.

The military faced a terrible nightmare in 1968, according to Stanton. Army units worldwide had been stripped to provide men for Vietnam. In Europe their condition was appalling: "By that year in Europe only 39% of the 465 reporting units had a personnel readiness equal to even their deliberately diminished assigned capability. Within the eight major combat units posted to Germany, rapid personnel turnover and shortages of experienced officers and sergeants prevented four divisions from meeting minimum combat standards.... Even more chilling was the secret December 31, 1968 announcement by United States Army Europe that none of its major combat units had met their operational training readiness commissions for the second straight year." [11]

In the United States itself, the situation was even worse: "In June of 1968 the Joint Chiefs of Staff were forced to flunk every division on the continent with the lowest rating possible in all categories—including personnel, training and logistics, with the exception of the 82nd Airborne Division (which had a brigade in Vietnam).... Army response had been stretched to the breaking point." [12]

That breaking point was reached in the wake of the Tet offensive and the siege of Khe Sanh in 1968, when the last remaining effective unit in the United States, the 82nd Airborne at Fort Bragg, North Carolina, was tapped for Vietnam duty. Because only one brigade (one-third of the division's full strength) could be mustered in the rush to deploy, the army ignored rules limiting soldiers to a single one-year tour of duty. Thousands of paratroopers who had just returned from Vietnam found themselves heading back to the jungle. Amidst vociferous complaints from the troops, the army backed off and offered those who had already served in Vietnam the option of returning home. Of the 3,650 Fort Bragg paratroopers sent to Vietnam, 2,513 rejected the inducement of a full month's leave if they would stay with their unit and returned to the United States. The army had no paratroopers remaining to replace them, and as a result, the 3rd Brigade of the 82nd dwindled to a light infantry unit, a mere shadow of its assigned capability. Ironically, many of the troops who elected to return home soon found themselves fighting in the streets of Washington, dodging sniper fire from burned-out buildings.

Within Vietnam itself, the disintegration of morale and discipline sapped the very heart of military capability. Here is how Stanton describes it: "Serious disciplinary problems resulted in disintegrating unit cohesion and operational slippages. In the field, friendly fire accidents became more prevalent as more short rounds and misplaced fire were caused by carelessness. There was an excessive number of accidental shootings and promiscuous throwing of grenades, some of which were deliberate fraggings aimed at unpopular officers, sergeants and fellow enlisted men." [13]

"Fragging," meaning an attack with fragmentation grenades, was a new word in the GI lexicon, coined from the experience of despair and resistance. According to the army's own statistics, 551 fragging incidents occurred from 1969 through 1972, resulting in 86 deaths and more than seven hundred injuries.[14] Approximately 80 percent of the victims were officers and noncommissioned officers. These statistics understate the actual number of attacks against superiors, for they do not include shootings with firearms. Whatever the exact numbers, the prevalence of fragging provided powerful evidence of an army at war with itself. Gung-ho officers, eager to push their men into battle, often became the victims of assault by their own men. Stanton confirms a story widely rumored at the time: After the bloody and senseless ten-day battle on Hamburger Hill in May 1969, embittered troops placed a notice in their underground newspaper offering a reward of $10,000 for the fragging of the officers in charge.[15]

Equally devastating to the army's effectiveness was what Stanton terms the "ugly stain of combat disobedience," that stage of ultimate breakdown when soldiers no longer obey orders to fight. In the latter part of the Vietnam War, such mutinies occurred often. Ten major incidents of combat refusal were documented in *Soldiers In Revolt;* military lawyers and fellow GIs indicated that many additional undocumented incidents also occurred. Stanton now confirms the prevalence of combat disobedience. In the elite 1st Cavalry Division alone, supposedly one of the army's premier units, thirty-five instances of refusals to fight occurred during 1970, several involving entire units.[16]

On some occasions, the breakdown in discipline became so severe that troops fought against each other. In a number of cases, military police served as assault troops against fellow GIs. At Whiskey Mountain in September 1971, fourteen soldiers of the 35th Engineer Group barricaded themselves in a bunker and held out with automatic weapons and machine guns. When a homemade explosive device went off, all fourteen were injured, then captured and sent to prison. A month later, at Praline Mountain near Dalat, military police were called in to quiet tensions in a company where fragging attacks against the company commander had occurred two nights in a row. The MPs patrolled the unit for a week in order to restore order. These and other findings in Stanton's book confirm the near-total collapse of army capability in the latter stages of the Vietnam War.[17]

The GI movement spread from the army and the marine corps to the air force and navy, as these services assumed the principal burden of continuing the American war effort. By 1972 resistance accelerated to such a degree that B-52 crews refused to fly; sabotage and internal rebellion crippled the navy's aircraft carriers.

As in the army and marine corps, African-American enlistees in the air force played a leading role in the GI movement. Faced with the same injustices experienced in the other services—unequal job assignments, a disproportionate number of disciplinary punishments, slow promotions—African-Americans joined together to defend their interests. As elsewhere in the military, they frequently formed discussion groups or cultural organizations. At the end of 1970, the *Air Force Times* admitted the existence of twenty-five such groups, many of them actively engaged in struggles against discrimination.[18]

The largest and most dramatic of all the uprisings and militant actions occurred at Travis Air Force Base in May 1971. A crucial center for the American war effort and the primary embarkation point for flights to Indochina, this important California base was crippled from 22 May through 25 May by perhaps the largest mass rebellion in the history of the air force. The conflict began with a fracas at the local enlisted men's club, and quickly spread into a generalized uprising throughout the base. Fighting began on a Saturday afternoon between African-Americans and the base security police. Resentment built through the weekend until it erupted in violence on Monday evening. More than two hundred enlisted people, including some whites who attempted to free a group of imprisoned airmen, were met by a force of three hundred military policemen and nearly eighty civilian officers called in from surrounding communities. A major brawl ensued, involving six hundred airmen. The officers' club was burned, several dozen people injured, and 135 GIs arrested, most of them African-American. Fighting continued into the next day, forcing armed guards to patrol the base and search all incoming traffic at the gate. For a few days, Travis remained in a virtual state of siege, with base activities disrupted and nearly all attention devoted to restoring order.[19]

In the wake of the Travis revolt, the Pentagon hurriedly dispatched special race-relations advisors to the base in an attempt to prevent further violence. Throughout the air force (and in the other services as well), racial harmony programs were established, including human relations councils and equal opportunity officers, as a means of stemming the growing internal rebellion. The new policies, designed primarily to channel grievances into controllable outlets, had little impact on the actual conditions in the service. These programs did little to alter the systematic injustice within the ranks, and, of course, did not even address the problem of the continuing war in Indochina.

The GI movement in the air force continued to grow until the end of direct U.S. involvement in 1973. By 1972 more than thirty active GI organizing projects and underground newspapers operated within the air force, not counting the substantial number of discussion groups and cultural clubs that African-Americans organized. With each new wave of bombing during the Nixon administration, protests and demonstrations erupted at bases throughout the world. The rising tide of antiwar resistance ultimately began to disrupt bombing operations and reached even the predominantly white officer-pilots. Morale among airmen and crew members at the combat bases in Thailand and Guam steadily dropped in 1972. In December of that year, two pilots stationed in Thailand, Captains Dwight D. Evans and Michael Heck, refused to fly any more combat missions.[20] In the spring of 1973, four B-52 crewmen stationed at Guam joined in a federal lawsuit filed by Congresswoman Elizabeth Holtzman to challenge the constitutionality of continued bombing.[21] Shortly thereafter, the Pentagon cut back on bombing missions and Congress finally severed funding, thereby starting to terminate America's longest war.

As in the air force, resistance within the navy increased dramatically when its giant aircraft carrier task groups assumed increased responsibility for the air war. By 1970 underground newspapers and protest actions began to appear at major naval bases and even aboard ships. One of the earliest GI movement groups in the navy was the Movement for a Democratic Military (MDM), a network of loosely connected radical groups that appeared at San Diego, Long Beach, and Alameda in California and at the navy's Great Lakes Naval Training Center near Chicago.

By 1971, as aircraft carriers left their California ports for combat duty in the South China Sea, protest demonstrations, rather than the traditional cheering crowds, greeted them. In October 1971 sailors and antiwar civilians in San Diego organized an informal election to decide whether the U.S.S. *Constitution* should sail for Vietnam. Thirty-five thousand San Diegoans voted in this unofficial referendum, including 6,900 active-duty men and women. Eighty-two percent of the civilians and 73 percent of the service people voted to keep the vessel home. A similar movement, initiated entirely by active-duty sailors, emerged at the same time aboard the carrier U.S.S. *Coral Sea* at Alameda. Twelve hundred sailors—one-fourth of the crew—signed a petition opposing the war in Indochina and urging that the ship stay home. Another below-decks movement emerged in opposition to the sailing of the U.S.S. *Kitty Hawk* a few months later. Each time one of these ships sailed, a small contingent of sailors declared that they could not in conscience participate in the war and publicly refused to go.

The Nixon administration's response to Hanoi's Easter offensive in 1972 placed even greater pressures on the already heavily committed navy. During the remainder of that year, as many as four carrier task groups remained on combat station in the Gulf of Tonkin. Normal operations were disrupted, as already overworked crew members faced greater hardships and morale plummeted. While many sailors expressed opposition through acts of political dissent, others resorted to more extreme measures of disobedience and obstruction.

Perhaps the most shocking manifestation of the disintegration of morale within the navy in 1972 was the growing problem of internal sabotage. In its 1972 report on navy disciplinary problems, the House Armed Services Committee disclosed "an alarming frequency of successful acts of sabotage and apparent sabotage on a wide variety of ships and stations," and reported "literally hundreds of incidences of damaged Naval property wherein sabotage is suspected." [22] The most dramatic and important of these internal acts of disruption occurred in July 1972 when, in the space of just three weeks, attacks from within put two of the navy's aircraft carriers out of commission. On 10 July 1972, a massive fire broke out aboard the U.S.S. *Forrestal* in Norfolk, causing $7 million in damage. This blaze, the single largest act of sabotage in U.S. naval history, was responsible for a two-month delay in the carrier's deployment. Three weeks later, another act of sabotage crippled the carrier U.S.S. *Ranger* as it was about to depart Alameda for Indochina. A paint scraper and two twelve-inch bolts had been inserted into the ship's reduction gears, causing nearly $1 million in damage and forcing a three-and-one-half-month delay for extensive repairs.

The sabotaging of the *Ranger* and *Forrestal* set the stage for one of the most violent internal uprisings in the history of the navy—the rebellion aboard the U.S.S. *Kitty Hawk*. In October 1972, after a grueling eight months at sea and constant bombing missions in the Gulf of Tonkin, the huge ship pulled into Subic Bay in the Philippines for a rest stop before returning home. There the crew received the unexpected news that they would be returning to combat operations in the South China Sea. According to the House Armed Services Committee report on the incident, "this rescheduling apparently was due to the incidents of sabotage aboard her sister ships U.S.S. *Ranger* and U.S.S. *Forrestal*."[23] With tensions already high among crew members due to declining morale and rising racial conflict, the order to return to Vietnam was the spark that ignited violence. On the evening of 12 October, as the ship arrived at Yankee Station off the coast of Indochina and resumed air operations, a riot broke out. Hundreds of African-American sailors clashed with armed marine guards in a brawl that left dozens injured and seriously disrupted ship operations.

A few weeks later, another major rebellion—this time nonviolent—occurred aboard the aircraft carrier U.S.S. *Constellation* in San Diego. Described by the *New York Times* as "the first mass mutiny in the history of the U.S. Navy," the rebellion aboard the *Constellation* grew out of the efforts of an organization on board known as the Black Fraction to resist repression and discrimination.[24] In early November more than one hundred sailors, mostly African-American, but including whites, staged a sit-in and dockside strike to protest racism and the threat of unfavorable discharges. Seeking to avert violence and prevent another incident like that on the *Kitty Hawk*, the captain allowed the dissident group to stay ashore as a beach detachment. Despite refusing a direct order to return to the ship, the rebels received light treatment. Although several were quietly discharged, most simply received reassignments to shore duty.

In the wake of the *Constellation* and the *Kitty Hawk* incidents, Admiral Elmo Zumwalt, chief of naval operations, called together eighty leading admirals and marine corps generals for an emergency meeting at the Pentagon to address the problem of race relations. The assembled commanders were urged to be more sensitive to the needs of enlisted sailors and to give greater attention to the human relations councils and other reforms that the Pentagon had recently introduced. In some places commanders responded by sponsoring educational programs on African-American history and culture, while also promoting sensitivity sessions and discussion groups. These attempts at reform, however, did little to address the structural injustices within the military. Moreover, as long as the war in Vietnam continued and American servicemen remained engaged in the military conflict, the GI movement and the internal rebellion within the armed forces continued. Not until 1973, when the U.S. combat role finally came to an end, did resistance within the ranks began to ease and military life slowly return to normal.

• • •

Although it is not widely known or understood, the GI resistance movement had a major part in the Vietnam experience. Never before in modern history had the American armed forces faced such widespread internal resistance and revolt. Often at great personal risk, hundreds of thousands of soldiers, marines, airmen, and sailors dissented and disobeyed military commanders, in order to speak out for justice and peace. Their struggle hastened American withdrawal from Indochina and played a major role in finally bringing that tragic war to an end.

8

Vietnam Veterans and War Crimes Hearings

ELLIOTT L. MEYROWITZ and KENNETH J. CAMPBELL

> "If certain acts and violations of treaties are crimes, they are crimes whether the United States does them or whether Germany does them. We are not prepared to lay down a rule of criminal conduct against others which we would not be willing to have invoked against us."
> —Mr. Justice Robert Jackson
> Chief Prosecutor for the United States
> at the Nuremberg Trials[1]

The Vietnam veterans' war crimes hearings represent an important, yet virtually unknown, chapter in the history of the Vietnam antiwar movement. These hearings suffered the same fate as the larger antiwar movement: they were relegated to the twilight existence of historical limbo when the nation, as a whole, decided in the mid-1970s, that the time had come to leave behind that bitterly divisive war. The issue of American war crimes in Vietnam was consigned to an even deeper level of obscurity, however, because of the intensely troubling questions it raised concerning the legality and morality of the American effort in Vietnam.

The war crimes issue raised dark questions about the personal responsibility of U.S. policymakers for the consequences of their policies in Vietnam, as well as doubts about their fundamental motives for prosecuting the war. It was one thing to debate the soundness of particular military strategies, or to argue the wisdom of choosing that particular corner of the globe in which to apply containment. Most political and historical analysts considered it quite another thing, however, especially at the height of neoconservative historical revisionism in the late 1970s and early 1980s, to raise questions about the justness and nobility of American policymakers' motives for waging the war against Vietnam. Consequently, the war crimes issue possessed the status of a "dirty secret," never to be discussed in front of women, children, or impressionable college students.

Nonetheless, the war crimes hearings deserve exposure, not only because they played an important part in the larger antiwar movement, but also because the American war in Vietnam cannot be understood properly without inclusion of the issue of war crimes. In fact, this issue may indeed provide the *key* to understanding the U.S. experience in Vietnam.

• • •

In November 1969 the unfolding story of the My Lai massacre shocked the United States and the world. A company of the Americal Division was accused of beating, raping, and murdering more than five hundred unarmed Vietnamese men, women, and children and burning down their homes in the hamlet of My Lai on 16 March 1968.[2] Around the world, comparisons were made between My Lai and Nazi war crimes at Lidice and Babi Yar.[3] The final defense of American policymakers had been that no matter how mistaken their strategy or how misapplied their tactics, at least their cause was just.

The revelations of the American military's brutal, methodical, and sadistic actions against unarmed, unresisting Vietnamese civilians at My Lai exploded this last myth. The message of My Lai came through loud and clear to many Americans—not only did their commitment of sons and tax dollars to Vietnam appear questionable, but also the very morality of the mission. My Lai caused some Americans to reevaluate the U.S. role in Vietnam, while others reacted by denying that it happened or by contending that the victims deserved the treatment. Some Americans even blamed the media for disclosing the massacre.[4]

The My Lai massacre also had a profound effect on U.S. policymakers. For them, it became imperative to demonstrate that the slaughter at My Lai represented an aberration rather than typical American behavior in South Vietnam. U.S. policymakers engaged in damage-control to try to keep the My Lai massacre from undermining the American public's will to remain in Vietnam until a solution acceptable to Washington could be worked out and the remaining American troops withdrawn. In a speech to the Association of the U.S. Army in the fall of 1969, the Army Chief of Staff, General William C. Westmoreland said,

"Recently, a few individuals involved in serious incidents have been highlighted in the news. Some would have these incidents reflect on the Army as a whole. They are, however, the actions of a pitiful few."[5] On 26 November 1969, White House press secretary Ronald Ziegler emphasized that My Lai constituted an unfortunate aberration.[6]

While U.S. policymakers sought to portray My Lai as just an isolated incident and an unfortunate excess of war not specific to Vietnam, other individuals expressed skepticism. After thorough research into the My Lai massacre, journalist Richard Hammer concluded that "the massacre at Son My [My Lai] was not unique, although it may have been the largest such incident of its kind in any one particular location and moment."[7] After his own investigation, journalist Seymour Hersh wrote: "What, perhaps, would happen inadvertently in the beginning became routine. Terry Reid of Fond Du Lac, Wisconsin, spent much of 1968 serving with the 11th Brigade of the Americal Division near Chu Lai, the division headquarters a few miles north of Quang Ngai City. The indiscriminate slaughter of Vietnamese women and children was commonplace in his unit."[8] Larry Colburn, who witnessed the My Lai massacre from a small observation helicopter, told Hersh: "I'd seen it happen before, but just not with that many people."[9] According to Hersh, reporters knew of similar incidents before the My Lai revelations, but either they hesitated to report them or their editors hesitated to publish them.

A group of Americans who sharply disagreed with the official depiction of My Lai as an aberration decided to challenge publicly the U.S. government's explanation. This group consisted of veterans of Vietnam, along with their legal advisers and supporters. Through two different organizations and two major conferences in late 1970 and early 1971, these veterans attempted to inform the American public and the rest of the world that My Lai was unique only in its size, and that similar cases of indiscriminate American military brutality occurred daily in Vietnam. Furthermore, they sought to demonstrate that these smaller-scale but frequent atrocities resulted from policies designed by American military and civilian leaders in Washington and Saigon.

The first conference, or "war crimes hearings" as they were referred to by the participants, took place at the Dupont Plaza Hotel in Washington, D.C., on 1–3 December 1970.[10] The National Veterans Inquiry into U.S. War Crimes in Vietnam was organized by the Citizens Commission of Inquiry (CCI), a group founded by lawyer Todd Ensign and antiwar organizer Jeremy Rifkin earlier that year. CCI relied on Vietnam veterans to help organize the national hearings and to provide firsthand accounts of American atrocities, ranging from the destruction of villages, to the torture of prisoners, to the deliberate killing of unarmed civilians.[11] The more than thirty veterans who testified at the hearings painted a picture of routinely brutal, criminal, and immoral U.S. policy in Vietnam.

Sergeant Mike McCusker, a combat correspondent for the 1st Marine Division, described an incident that occurred in October 1966 near Chu Lai when "a sniper killed a staff sergeant, so the skipper pulled us back and then ordered nape [napalm] on the village itself. When we went in later, after the fires burned down, there were many, many bodies of old women and men. But I think the worst was thirty dead children who had been laid out for us to see by the survivors."[12]

Lieutenant Michael J. Uhl, military intelligence officer with the Americal Division in 1968, "witnessed, not only in the interrogation section, which was located in the base camp, but also with the counterintelligence agents out in the field, the frequent use of electrical torture using the TA-312 field telephone, which is part of the organic equipment of any combat unit. How this was used—the wires coming from this telephone were bared and attached to the sensitive parts of the detainees' bodies. Electrical torture at the 11th Brigade base camp was used on a daily basis, on people who were generally classified as innocent civilians at the termination of the interrogation."[13]

Lieutenant Larry Rottman, information officer with the 25th Infantry Division at Cu Chi from June 1967 until March 1968, described that "some units have large scoreboards on which the body count is kept. The unit that reports the highest body count gets public commendation. The soldier who kills the most VC by himself often gets an in-country R & R (Rest and Recreation)."[14]

Kenneth Barton Osborn, area intelligence specialist with the Army's 525th Military Intelligence Group from September 1967 until December 1968, responded:

> with . . . the 3rd Marine Division, I went along twice when they would go up in helicopters which belonged to the marine division and take two detainees along. They used one as a scare mechanism for the other. If they wanted to interrogate detainee A, they would take someone along who was either in bad health or whom they had already written off as a loss—take both these Vietnamese along in the helicopter and they would say, they would start investigating Detainee B, the one they had no interest in, and they wouldn't get any information out of him and so they would threaten to throw him out of the helicopter. All the time, of course, the detainee they wanted information from was watching. And they would threaten and threaten and, finally, they would throw him out of the helicop-

ter. I was there when this happened twice and it was very effective, because, of course, at the time the step one was to throw the person out of the helicopter and step two was to say, "You're next." And that quite often broke them down, demoralized them, and at that point they would give whatever information.[15]

Twenty-eight other veterans testified at the CCI hearings to incidents of a similar nature; the significance was not that the crimes were unusual, but that they were all too common in Vietnam.

Two months later, from 31 January through 2 February 1971, the Vietnam Veterans Against the War (VVAW) held the Winter Soldier Investigation at the Holiday Inn in downtown Detroit. During those three days, more than one hundred Vietnam veterans testified to having witnessed or participated in a wide range of atrocities.[16] In his opening statement, former Lieutenant William Crandell of the Americal Division said: "We intend to demonstrate that My Lai was no unusual occurrence, other than, perhaps, the number of victims killed all in one place, all at one time, all by one platoon of us. We intend to show that the policies of Americal Division which inevitably resulted in My Lai were the policies of other Army and Marine divisions as well." [17]

For three days following Crandell's opening statement, more than one hundred veterans poured forth the gory details of everyday life in combat in Vietnam. Specialist 5th Class Nathan Hale, an interrogator with the Americal Division testified:

I arrived in Vietnam in December of '67. In January of '68 . . . I arrived at the base camp of the 1st of the 1st Cav which is Hill 29. When I arrived there, my S-2, a captain, told me that my job was to elicit information. This meant that I could elicit information in any means possible. He told me that I could use any technique I could think of and the idea is "Don't get caught," and what he meant was I could beat these people, I could cut 'em—I never shot anyone—just don't beat them in the presence of a non-unit member or person. That's someone like a visiting officer or perhaps the Red Cross. And I personally used clubs, rifle butts, pistols, knives, and this was always done at Hill 29. And in the field it even gets better.[18]

Pfc. Charles Stephens of the 101st Airborne Division, in Vietnam from December 1965 to February 1967, revealed that "they didn't believe our body counts. So we had to cut off the right ear of everybody we killed to prove our body count. I guess it was company SOP [Standard Operating Procedure], or battalion SOP, but nothing was ever said to you." [19]

Sp.4 Steve Noetzel of the 5th Special Forces Group, in Vietnam from May 1963 to May 1964, testified:

> At the B Team in Can Tho, . . . the headquarters of the Four Corps, they had an eight-foot python snake which was kept at the camp in a cage, supposedly for rat control. When we had prisoners or detainees who were brought to the B Team, they were immediately questioned, and if they balked at all or sounded like they weren't going to be cooperative, they were simply placed in a [detention] room overnight. . . . The door was locked, and this snake was thrown in there with them. Now the python is a constrictor, similar to a boa. It's not poisonous. It will snap at you but it's not poisonous, and it probably can't kill a full-grown American or a large male, but it sure terrified the Vietnamese. Two of them usually in a room overnight with the python snake, struggling with it most of the night, I guess, and we could hear them screaming. In fact, on one instance, they had to go in there and gag the prisoners, so they wouldn't keep everyone awake all night. In the morning they were usually more cooperative.[20]

Corporal John Geymann of the 3rd Marine Division, in Vietnam from June until December 1969, reported that "when somebody asks, 'Why do you do it to a gook, why do you do this to people?' your answer is, 'So what, they're just gooks, they're not people. It doesn't make any difference what you do to them; they're not human.' And this thing is built into you, it's thrust into your head from the moment you wake up in boot camp to the moment you wake up when you're a civilian."[21]

Sgt. Scott Camil of the 1st Marine Division, in Vietnam from March 1966 until November 1967, explained that

> the main thing was that if an operation was covered by the press there were certain things we weren't supposed to do, but if there was no press there, it was okay. I saw one case where a woman was shot by a sniper, one of our snipers. When we got up to her she was asking for water. And the lieutenant said to kill her. So he ripped off her clothes, they stabbed her in both breasts, they spread her eagle and shoved an E tool up her vagina, an entrenching tool, and she was still asking for water. And then they took that out and they used a tree limb and then she was shot.
>
> Moderator: Did the men in your outfit or when you witnessed these things, did they seem to think that it was all right to do anything to the Vietnamese?

VETERANS AND WAR CRIMES   135

>   Camil: It wasn't like they were humans. We were conditioned
> to believe that this was for the good of the nation, the good of our
> country, and anything we did was okay. And when you shot someone
> you didn't think you were shooting at a human. They were a gook or
> a Commie and it was okay.[22]

Although a few of these veterans at the Winter Soldier Investigation had also testified at the CCI hearings in December, the vast majority told their story for the first time.

Both hearings sought to demonstrate that, as a direct result of American military policies in Vietnam, American forces carried out actions usually considered illegal and immoral in war. These accusers—the sons of middle America sent to fight the war—proved far more credible than previous critics of American tactics. In many cases they had volunteered for service in Vietnam. Now they were saying that My Lai was neither an isolated incident nor a case of aberrant behavior. The veterans who helped organize and testified at these unofficial war crimes hearings contended that war crimes had become standard operating procedure for American troops in Vietnam.

The press covered these hearings sporadically at best. For the National Veterans Inquiry in Washington, the coverage in the mass media was extensive in some parts of the county, but superficial or nonexistent in many others. The mass media virtually ignored the Winter Soldier Investigation in Detroit, however, leaving publicity up to the movement's media.[23] A radical film collective, for example, produced a ninety-minute documentary entitled "The Winter Soldier Investigation," which the VVAW showed to community, church, and peace groups all over the nation.

The public expressed ambivalent reactions to veterans' allegations that My Lai only touched the tip of the iceberg in Vietnam. On the one hand, there seemed to be general acceptance of the veterans' veracity. On the other hand, many, if not most, Americans were reluctant to believe that brutal atrocities could be part of the routine in Vietnam.[24] A fable written by Larry Rottman, one of the veterans who testified at both the CCI and the VVAW hearings, perhaps best expresses the frustration that many veterans felt in trying to share their dark experiences in Vietnam with their fellow citizens.

>   APO 96225
>   A young man once went off to war in a far country. When he
>   had time, he wrote home and said, "Sure rains here a lot." But his

mother, reading between the lines, wrote "We're quite concerned. Tell us what it's really like." And the young man responded, "Wow, you ought to see the funny monkeys." To which the mother replied, "Don't hold back, how is it?" And the young man wrote, "The sunsets here are spectacular." In her next letter the mother wrote, "Son we want you to tell us everything." So the next time he wrote, "Today I killed a man. Yesterday I helped drop napalm on women and children. Tomorrow we are going to use gas."

And the father wrote, "Please don't write such depressing letters. You're upsetting your mother." So, after a while, the young man wrote, "Sure rains a lot here." [25]

The revisionist approach to the veterans' war crimes hearings was to ignore them. There was, however, one major attempt to examine and address the extremely sensitive political, legal, and moral issues the hearings raised. In *America in Vietnam,* Guenter Lewy described the hearings at some length but declared that they lacked credibility for several reasons.[26] First, he objected to the veterans' policy at both hearings of not naming individual officers and enlisted men alleged to have ordered or committed atrocities. Second, he pointed out that because several veterans testified at both sets of hearings, there was duplication of data. Third, he charged that several veterans at the Winter Soldier Investigation in Detroit were later found to be frauds. Finally, and what seemed to Lewy the most serious weakness of the war crimes hearings, the veterans were openly taking an antiwar stance and were, therefore, alleging war crimes for political reasons. Lewy maintained that the hearings failed to demonstrate either widespread American atrocities in Vietnam or any immoral or illegal actions.[27]

Lewy's first point—the fact that the veterans refused to identify lower-level troops and instead chose to focus responsibility on the higher military and civilian policy-making levels of government—does not, however, mean that the atrocities that the veterans described did not happen. Indeed, the strategy of focusing on command responsibility is entirely consistent with international law and the Nuremberg Principles.[28]

In his second point, Lewy is correct that some duplication in testimony occurred. But he failed to explain that of the thirty-two veterans who testified in Washington and the 117 who testified in Detroit, only seven testified at both. That means that 142 different veterans testified at the two hearings.[29]

As for Lewy's third point, he offers no evidence, other than Pentagon allegations, of "fake" veterans at the Winter Soldier hearings. Lewy never identified the "fakes"; given the Pentagon's record for playing fast and loose with the truth about Vietnam, one must wonder why Lewy accepted its evidence without question. Moreover, the Pentagon openly admitted it had no doubts that the veterans who testified at the CCI hearings were genuine.[30] Later attempts by the Nixon administration to question the authenticity of the veterans in the VVAW, the group that sponsored Winter Soldier, also backfired when the veterans produced copies of their discharge papers.[31]

Lewy's last point is correct. The veterans who testified at these war crimes hearings had ending the Vietnam War as their ultimate objective. But does this mean, therefore, that the atrocities described did not happen, or if they did happen, that they were not war crimes? These former infantrymen, pilots, artillery observers, and interrogators did not testify to witnessing or participating in atrocities in Vietnam because they opposed the war; rather, they opposed the war *because* they had witnessed or participated in atrocities. Lewy did not appreciate this crucial distinction.

In the final analysis, the number of veterans testifying about personal knowledge of American atrocities in Vietnam and the many independent sources corroborating their experiences in the war make the veterans' allegations of routine American war crimes in Vietnam extremely difficult, if not impossible, to dismiss.

• • •

The war crimes hearings served as an important transition between the veterans' role as warriors in the service of their nation and their new, albeit quite uncomfortable, role as public witnesses against their government's policies in Vietnam.[32] Many of the veterans who testified at these hearings viewed the larger antiwar movement as an alien force. Some viewed it with suspicion, resentment, and hostility. Nevertheless, the very process of confronting what they saw and did in Vietnam radicalized many of them.[33]

One of the other important functions of the hearings was to shift legitimacy from the U.S. government to the antiwar forces. Certainly, the much larger nonveteran portion of the antiwar movement had begun that process years before the hearings, but by 1970 there was still major public support for the government's gradualist approach towards withdrawal. Though many Americans suspected that serious mistakes had been made in Vietnam policy and that the conflict might end without a clear victory, few questioned the righteousness of the cause, the very foundation of the government's policy. The veterans gave the process of delegitimization new momentum by exposing the government's policy as not only less-than-noble, but actually immoral and criminal. In achieving this major objective, the organizers of the hearings contributed to the eventual unraveling of the government's most dependable segment of political support, the blue-collar working class.

In the huge political struggle then taking place in the United States, veterans had a special advantage that set them apart from typical antiwar protestors: they had actually "been there" and could speak about U.S. policy in Vietnam from dramatic, personal experience. During the national VVAW demonstration in Washington from 19 April to 23 April 1971, a member of the Daughters of the American Revolution commented that their demonstration eroded troop morale, whereupon a veteran responded, "Lady, we are the troops." [34] Mary McGrory, writing of the veterans' demonstration for the *Washington Evening Star,* observed that "the veterans looked like hippies. But these were hippies with combat infantry badges pinned below the knees of their blue jeans, and Purple Hearts swinging from their headbands. The Administration saw them differently, as a new and dangerous animal—anti-military, anti-war veterans who swapped atrocity stories and griped, not about the first sergeant, but about the commander in chief. . . . Middle America saw at once that this was not the usual hippie-authority clash." [35]

The conservative, blue-collar, flag-waving segment of the public had dismissed antiwar protesters as middle-class until the antiwar veterans started to speak out. But when the veterans, mostly members of the blue-collar segment themselves, became vocal, the government's last bastion of support for its policies began to crumble.

Finally, the hearings questioned the legal basis of the U.S. government's war in Vietnam. Before the hearings, the primary focus of any legal strategy stressed that the United States was waging a war of aggression. This approach proved too legalistic, however, to be an effective part of a larger political strategy to win masses of Americans over to the antiwar position. The public more easily recognizes atrocities as crimes, and the veterans' war crimes hearings helped the antiwar movement show the criminal nature of the Vietnam War, and to further delegitimatize it.

Of course, if this legal approach had been attempted in isolation from other tactics of the antiwar movement, it would not have had much impact; although simply demonstrating that the behavior of American troops in Vietnam violated the laws of war might have been embarrassing to policymakers, it would not have seriously undermined the war effort. But as part of a much larger and more complex antiwar strategy, this legal assault made an important contribution to ending the war.

The events in Vietnam have challenged the relevance of the law of armed conflict to modern warfare and highlighted the tension between legal restraints and military expediency. Even those for whom My Lai typified American war crimes in Vietnam have tended to overlook or ignore the larger legal implications of the issue. The Vietnam veterans, however, were compelled by their own experiences to consider the military's actions in the context of international law. The moral objections raised by the antiwar movement in regard to the American presence in Vietnam produced a climate conducive to an inquiry into the legal status of military policies. Yet, even in the face of these objections, many policymakers and citizens alike refused to confront the logical and inevitable consequences of American policies in Vietnam.

The testimony of Vietnam veterans concerning the methods and tactics that the United States relied upon to conduct counterinsurgent warfare in Vietnam provided the factual basis for the contention of many war critics that those methods and tactics violated international law. Furthermore, the veterans sought to impose primary responsibility upon those civilian and military leaders who devised, approved, and carried out the war policies establishing the methods and tactics that American troops employed in Vietnam. What most disturbed American troops about the tactics they were compelled to employ in Vietnam was that the entire civilian population became the enemy. Accordingly, the extent to which American military policies challenged the relevance of the laws of war to counterinsurgency operations became a central concern of the Vietnam veterans.

The grotesque realities that have tormented Vietnam veterans over the years can be attributed largely to the policymakers who devised the strategies that the soldiers had to implement each day in Vietnam. Nevertheless, the policymakers' continuing insistence that the war was simply a lost crusade, a political mistake, and a military failure makes it possible for them to be oblivious to the testimony of Vietnam veterans. How does one account for this anomaly? It is not because the information is unavailable, but because those same policymakers have removed it from the agenda of legitimate concerns. In numerous published accounts, policymakers failed to recognize the nature of the military policies in Vietnam that the veterans described.

Because the official interpretation is that the Vietnam War was simply a political mistake, political survival makes it essential that the policymakers discourage any revelations about the massive suffering that American military tactics imposed on the Vietnamese. The depraved realities of war crimes, which the testimony of veterans brought home to

Americans, could only undercut the credibility of counterinsurgency as one of the major implements of American foreign policy. Accordingly, the real tragedy of Vietnam is the extent to which it has been possible to hide or disguise the true nature of the war and to ignore and overlook those who courageously raised their voices in opposition to the policies that U.S. soldiers carried out in the name of America.

While the Nuremberg tradition makes it clear that those who commit war crimes should bear personal responsibility, it would be politically impractical to prosecute the policymakers who bear responsibility for the Vietnam War. It is not impractical, however, to educate the American public about the nature of the war by setting the historical record straight regarding the issue of war crimes in Vietnam. Moreover, the issue of war crimes is of political importance in evaluating whether the Vietnam War represented a "noble cause."

The war crimes hearings embodied certain moral impulses that serve Americans well, especially when there is a profound political crisis involving the use of military force. By participating in the hearings, veterans not only challenged governmental policy in Vietnam but sought to overcome widespread disillusionment about the capacity of international law to restrain the exercise of sovereign prerogative and claims of military necessity. Through their efforts these Vietnam veterans strengthened the belief among many citizens that international law should set the dominant standard for American conduct in foreign relations. Practical, not idealistic, motives caused Vietnam veterans to take international law seriously. Implicit in their actions was a belief that we would be more, rather than less, secure as a people had our governmental leaders oriented American foreign policy toward minimum obligations of international law.

9

They Moved the Town

Organizing Vietnam Veterans Against the War

WILLIAM F. CRANDELL

> God were we set up!
> Women, cheers, uniforms, decorations,
> parades, proud parents and
> the National Anthem!
> What a life! When we were seventeen.
>
> When we were eighteen
> in Vietnam
> only the ambulance showed up.
> And when we got back home
> somebody'd moved the town.
> — Steve Mason, "The Casualty"

The veterans of a divided nation's wars are different from those who knew "the thanks of a grateful nation." Oliver Wendell Holmes, speaking to his generation of Union veterans of the American Civil War, commented, "Through our great good fortune, in our youth our hearts were touched with fire." His was the only generation of Americans more divided by war than the one that fought—and fought *over*—the Vietnam War. As in the Civil War, even the warriors took opposing sides. The Vietnam Veterans Against the War (VVAW) represented the largest group of them to take public positions during the conflict.[1]

Johnny's Song, "The Casualty," copyright ©1986 by Steve Mason. Reprinted by permission of Simon & Schuster, Inc.

This is an organizer-historian's memoir and an oral history of organizing VVAW. It analyzes the organization's efforts from 1967 through 1975, from VVAW's birth to the end of the war. In addition to my own recollections, I have also made extensive use of personal archives, contemporary interviews (many of which were conducted in 1987 at the twentieth anniversary reunion of VVAW), and primary source materials that I helped gather as the senior scholar on the staff of the Winter Soldier Investigation, the first oral history of the Vietnam War.

Most members of VVAW were combat veterans who fought a second tour as citizen-soldiers in an effort to end an unjust war and bring their brothers and sisters home. Their activities began at the Spring Mobilization in New York City on 15 April 1967 when six veterans marched under a VVAW banner. VVAW's emblem was a grim parody of the crusaders' shield insignia of the U.S. Military Assistance Command–Vietnam (MACV). The official insignia had a red background, with an upright sword over a yellow wall. The sword represented "infiltration and aggression from beyond the embattled 'wall' " (i.e., resistance to Chinese aggression from beyond the Great Wall). Vietnam vets replaced the sword with a modern helmet atop a rifle stuck muzzle-down in the ground of a soldier's grave.[2]

An ad for VVAW in the *New Republic* during the 1968 Tet offensive drew a number of new members, mostly from the east coast. I was one of two new members pulled in from the entire midwest. An ex–rifle platoon leader cynical about victory, I still believed in the war until General William C. Westmoreland declared Tet a great American victory. His statement finally convinced me that our commanders lacked any understanding about the war, that we were thus doomed to lose, and that the lives lost would be wasted. Like most VVAW members, I had as my strongest motivations to keep faith with the men left in Vietnam and prevent their lives from being thrown away.

Dan Burdekin and I, both graduate students at Ohio State University (OSU), were given the grand title of "midwest coordinators." Through his contacts with the antiwar movement, we scheduled speeches at churches and universities. We also carried signs in demonstrations and at readings of the names of the war dead, bearing witness as Vietnam Veterans Against the War. We did not try, at that time, to establish a formal organization. We hoped that ending the war would not take that long.[3]

By the spring of 1970, I was the sole midwest coordinator, and I decided to organize a chapter of VVAW at OSU. The growth of VVAW on that campus typified the formation of local chapters in that period. A sign-up table drew a few other vets who had recently returned to campus. Two weeks later, on 29 April 1970, a student strike began at the university.

Colleagues planning the strike, upon hearing that a veterans' chapter was forming, asked us to serve as strike marshals. At an organizing meeting, we all agreed to the proposal. The six-week strike, which began over campus issues the day before President Richard M. Nixon ordered troops into Cambodia, became an organizing windfall for VVAW. After the Kent State shootings—conducted by the same frightened and leaderless Ohio National Guard we faced in Columbus—the war became a central focus of the strike, and our increasing visibility moved us into leadership positions. Vets who agreed with our position came out of isolation to join us.

Because of our ability as former soldiers to accept leadership and act together, we knew how to direct activities at several critical points. If a cadre of disciplined militants sought to stampede a large, amorphous crowd of student strikers into confrontations with armed and ill-led guardsmen, the vets' disciplined cohesion and experience tipped the scales away from violence.[4]

Like other new VVAW chapters that were springing up across the country, the one in Columbus decided to admit supportive veterans who had served in places other than Vietnam, although membership remained about 70 percent Vietnam vets. The OSU chapter grew as each action attracted more disaffected veterans. After twelve VVAW members demonstrated with a peace flag at Lockbourne Air Force Base on 21 June, they left without incident. In contrast, twenty-seven VVAW members who had received permission to march in the Upper Arlington Fourth of July parade were threatened with arrest by local police and denied permission to participate. We settled for leafletting and a local television appearance.

Our Buckeye Army of Liberation prepared itself better for Veterans Day 1970. After the American Legion denied us permission to march in the traditional parade, the vets obtained a court order allowing VVAW to march along the parade route thirty minutes ahead of the regular marchers. Columbus police wanted to charge us for the use of police overtime, but upon the discovery that the Legion had already paid for the period, sixty VVAW members marched free, performing guerrilla theater and passing out leaflets to the crowd. By that time we had become seasoned marchers.[5]

At the end of June 1970, the national office of VVAW announced plans to conduct its first national demonstration, Operation RAW (Rapid American Withdrawal), "a four-day search-and-destroy operation" in New

Jersey and Pennsylvania. The Columbus chapter (still the only one in Ohio, although others were beginning to form in the Midwest) offered its services as an organized platoon. Art Flesch, Joel Ann Todd, and I went to New York to help plan the march, set for Labor Day weekend of 1970. We arranged support services, reconnoitered the route, and wrote two leaflets to be used along the way.[6]

The FBI counted eighty-one Vietnam vets gathered on 4 September at George Washington's encampment in Morristown, New Jersey, for the four-day, eighty-six-mile march to Valley Forge, many drawn by a last-minute ad in the *Village Voice*.[7] At Valley Forge, 150 Vietnam vets with 110 Purple Hearts were on hand to complete the assembly. Virtually all wore old jungle fatigues with decorations, and most carried toy M-16 rifles. Buckeye Recon, the only organized contingent, was asked to lead the march and act as the demonstration platoon. Along the route, while veterans of other wars denounced our long hair and our message, we staged typical Vietnam War incidents with members of the Philadelphia Guerrilla Theater and Nurses for Peace. They played civilians whom we roughed up, rounded up, and took away. The leaflets left with the townspeople read:

> A Company of U.S. Infantry Just Came Through Here
> If you had been Vietnamese—
> We might have burned your house
> We might have shot your dog
> We might have shot you.
>
> Vietnam Veterans Against the War

We marched across the Delaware River at sleepy Stockton. During each of the three nights we camped out, local veterans groups threatened violence that never materialized, although police picked up a seventeen-year-old youth who had pointed a real rifle at us.

Many of us had our first experiences with flashbacks and post-traumatic stress disorder (PTSD) during this march. During one frightening moment we realized that an ex-marine who was using his old K-Bar knife to simulate torturing a prisoner had lost control and was not simulating any more. His brother vets calmed him down before he harmed anyone. Some of the "detainees" in our staged incidents were treated more roughly than we intended, and I remember very clearly my shock at how concerted an effort I had to make to keep my finger off the trigger of my dummy submachine gun. Most of us revisited Vietnam at some point during Operation RAW.

At Valley Forge the speakers—Vietnam naval hero John Kerry, Rev. James Bevel, Mark Lane, Donald Sutherland, and Jane Fonda—were joined by a small group of disabled Vietnam vets who broke out of the local Veterans Administration hospital after having been ordered to stay away from the rally. A group of menacing bikers shut off their engines when told who we were, and the rally ended with a formal parade-field drill in which we smashed our toy rifles.

Operation RAW, VVAW's first major demonstration, drew generous press coverage and new members. The sixteen members of Buckeye Recon who had led the march, including one planted by Army Intelligence, went back to OSU and Kent State prepared for more protests. We had already started organizing the Winter Soldier Investigation.[8]

The My Lai massacre, a shock to the American conscience, did not surprise many Vietnam veterans. Of a dozen vets gathered at OSU when the story broke in 1969, I had been the only one who did not have an atrocity story of my own to tell. And when I talked to one of the other platoon leaders from my old unit during the planning of Operation RAW and learned that he had been charged with shooting civilians on a specific date that was fresh in my memory, neither of us could say for sure whether he had shot anybody that day or not. The moral certainty common to both hawks and doves often eluded the footsoldiers in Vietnam.

The Winter Soldier Investigation (WSI) grew out of a project that VVAW co-founder Jan Crumb, attorney Mark Lane, and Jane Fonda had supported: the Citizens Commission of Inquiry (CCI). CCI attempted to link American policies to individual atrocity stories vets brought home. As veterans, we knew that everyone who participates in war crimes suffers, and we needed to tell our country that these horrible acts did not represent simply aberrations or psychotic episodes, but the inevitable outcomes of directions the soldiers had been given.

CCI had contacted VVAW in the hope that we could provide witnesses to link policies and atrocities. We could. But as the process played out, we decided that the public event emerging from the gathering of this testimony would have more credibility as a VVAW project.[9]

The name "Winter Soldier Investigation" came from Tom Paine's first "Crisis" paper, in which he wrote: "These are the times that try men's souls. The summer soldier and the sunshine patriot, will in this crisis, shrink from the service of their country; but he that stands it *now*, deserves the love and thanks of man and woman."[10] We saw ourselves as soldiers who continued to serve past our enlistments because we were needed even more then. The identification with Paine's pamphlet marked the beginning of VVAW's self-awareness that we played a revolutionary role, embracing the American tradition of revolution and not those of Lenin, Mao, or Castro.

VVAW had approximately 7,000 members by the opening of the WSI on 31 January 1971. Its membership had nearly doubled in the previous month because of the response to a full-page ad contributed by *Playboy*. Three leaders from the national office and three members from the growing list of chapters comprised the six-member WSI steering committee. One of the first decisions we made was to hold WSI in a midwestern city, Detroit, in order to make it easier for witnesses to get there.

With the help of Catholic antiwar activists Bill Pace and Carolyn Agosta, the steering committee set up a collective in a house on the industrial east side of the city. They moved into it along with Mark Lane and Jane Fonda, who contributed both their fund-raising talents and their perspectives as national celebrities who understood the media. Although the gathering of testimony had begun the previous summer, it took another six weeks of on-site planning to put the conference together.

The support of antiwar celebrities brought in essential funding. Jane Fonda and her agent, Steve Jaffe, produced a series of benefits, including "Acting in Concert for Peace," in which Fonda, Dick Gregory, Donald Sutherland, and Barbara Dane performed, and two musical concerts, one given by Graham Nash and David Crosby and the other by legendary folk singer Phil Ochs. In addition, Protestant, Jewish, and Catholic clergy arranged for housing for witnesses because, as one of them (Dr. John B. Forsyth, then Director of Missions for the Detroit Metropolitan Council of Churches) put it, "[It] is important that the public realize that American atrocities in Vietnam are an everyday occurrence." Attorney Dean Robb and his partner Ernest Goodman raised support among area lawyers. UAW secretary-treasurer Emil Mazey and Michigan secretary of state Richard Austin also endorsed the program and sought contributions for it.[11]

From 31 January through 2 February, 105 Vietnam vets appeared on nine panels, grouped with their past units in order to corroborate each other's testimony. Both vets and civilian experts who had been to Vietnam spoke on additional panels about weaponry, prisoners of war, and the medical effects of the war. There were also two long panels: the one on the first night, called "What We Are Doing to Vietnam," addressed the ecological and cultural damage caused by the war; for the one on the second night, called "What We Are Doing to Ourselves," I wrote and presented the opening statement.

The testimony was chilling. Veteran after veteran described the training and orders that led to the murder of civilians. Several vets admitted that they had tortured prisoners and had seen their comrades commit rape, arson, and other savage acts, all stemming from their commanders' policies. Dr. Bert Pfeiffer of the University of Montana presented the first public testimony at WSI on the toxic effect of Agent Orange.

WSI also broke the story—then classified—of the 3rd Marine Division's major border crossing into Laos, called Operation Dewey Canyon. Although the Pentagon immediately denied the story, its credibility was undermined by the timing of the testimony, which occurred the same day that marines publicly launched Operation Dewey Canyon II in support of South Vietnamese troops invading Laos.[12]

The Winter Soldier Investigation provided a turning point, but not the one we expected. We naively believed that the testimony of 105 American combat veterans on the criminal nature of the Vietnam War would simply end it—that an America already shocked by war crimes would demand an end to the slaughter of innocents and the waste of our brothers.

We had not expected the media to ignore the story. The local stringer for the *New York Times* forwarded little testimony, telling us that "this stuff happens in all wars." Although the story's potential electrified the CBS News crew attending WSI, they showed none of what they taped on network news. The less-than-mainstream Pacifica Radio had the best coverage. Although Senator Mark Hatfield did place a transcript of the testimony in the *Congressional Record,* we still had miles to go to reach the public.[13]

Nevertheless, WSI was very important for its effect on VVAW's growth into a nationwide mass organization. The search for testimony had led organizers like Mike Oliver, Jeremy Rifkin, and me to crisscross the country looking for anti–Vietnam War vets, contacting scattered members who had replied to the *Playboy* ad or other announcements. Oliver made it a point to organize chapters and appoint state coordinators wherever he went.

By the end of WSI, VVAW had become a national organization run by a steering committee composed of twenty-six regional coordinators. What had happened to the old midwestern region was typical. I had driven with Jeremy Rifkin (who was not a veteran) in September 1970 from Columbus to Minneapolis, organizing new chapters as he collected testimony for WSI. By February there were enough strong chapters and talented coordinators to allow me to cut my territory down to Ohio and Indiana, which I shared with Jim Pechin of Terre Haute.[14]

Our next operation, in April of 1971, involved a massive VVAW protest in Washington, named Dewey Canyon III, in ironic reference to the Pentagon deception we had exposed. Borrowing from the Nixon administration's description of the Laotian invasion, we announced that Operation Dewey Canyon III would be "a limited incursion into the country of Congress." The call went out to VVAW chapters, to the growing GI movement, and to antiwar and counterculture newspapers.

Dewey Canyon III grew out of Senator George McGovern's invitation to us at the end of the Winter Soldier Investigation to send a veteran to testify before the Senate Foreign Relations Committee. We selected John Kerry, a Silver Star winner and former navy swift-boat captain, one of our most articulate spokespersons. The demonstrations of Dewey Canyon III would support Kerry's testimony, give our members a chance to lobby their own representatives, and reveal to the nation Vietnam veterans' opposition to the war.

An important part of the planning revolved around our work with the District of Columbia police. The Pentagon had established a program that allowed troops serving in Vietnam to muster out early if they became law enforcement officers. The D.C. police had a heavy contingent of Vietnam vets in their ranks. Mike Oliver, Mike Phelan, and Jack Mallory spent several days leafletting the police with a piece Oliver had written, spelling out our opposition to the war, our pride in service, and our disinclination to engage in "pig-baiting." As the main contingent arrived, and members could demonstrate to inquisitive veterans on the police force that we were who we claimed to be—in many cases police and VVAW vets who had fought together and been reunited—we won the support of the local police. It would soon prove important.[15]

We began arriving on Sunday, 18 April, camping that night in West Potomac Park. Only nine hundred had registered. At the evening meeting of the national coordinators, we became concerned that we might not have enough participants to accomplish our several missions. The next morning, now 1,100 strong, we began marching to Arlington, where we were denied entry to the national cemetery—as if we would have desecrated it. With several Gold Star Mothers, we laid wreaths at the barred gates.

Then we marched back into the capital by foot, on crutches, and in wheelchairs, following a banner with our name and emblem on it, past the Lincoln Memorial, past the headquarters of the Daughters of the American Revolution, where a woman said, "Son, I don't think what you are doing is good for the troops," and a vet replied, "Lady, we *are* the troops." We marched in the sunlight, chanting "Bring 'em home—bring our brothers home." We marched past a brooding White House to the part of the Mall nearest the Capitol, and there we camped. That day the Washington District Court of Appeals lifted an injunction that the Justice Department had requested to keep us from camping on the Mall.

Some vets began lobbying their congressional delegates even before dropping their gear at the campsite. We were angry. Over a thousand vets who had fought in our country's latest crusade, we were treated as scum for speaking the truth, barred from paying tribute to our dead, and hounded by the government we had served. When the *Washington Evening Star* came out that afternoon and treated us honorably, a wave of relief swept our camp.[16]

The next day two hundred vets went to the Senate Foreign Relations Committee hearings, while others met with their senators and representatives. Another two hundred went back to Arlington National Cemetery, marching in single file across the Lincoln Memorial Bridge. This time they were permitted entry. Having led the guerrilla theater during Operation RAW, I was asked to do the same thing in the streets of D.C., again with Buckeye Recon and the Philadelphia Quaker troupe, now augmented by many other vets. We began that Tuesday afternoon, 20 April, on the steps of the Capitol.

That night, during a fund-raiser by Senators Claiborne Pell and Philip Hart, we learned that Chief Justice Warren Burger of the Supreme Court had reinstated the injunction against us, and had ordered us to leave the Mall by 4:30 the next afternoon. We continued to march, spending much of the day lobbying and doing guerrilla theater, while fifty vets went to the Pentagon and offered to turn themselves in as war criminals.[17]

Meanwhile, we prepared to face the injunction deadline. The national coordinators decided early that it would be the entire encampment's decision whether to stay and face arrest or to do something else. As part of preparing for an alternative, I was sent to the National Cathedral, where I negotiated successfully for permission to camp on the grounds there if we decided to leave the Mall.

That afternoon, 2,000 of us met to decide what to do next. Our lawyer, former U.S. attorney general Ramsey Clark, announced that the Supreme Court had met in special session and offered us an option: if we stayed awake, we would not be arrested. By a close vote, we decided to sleep on the Mall, risking arrest. After everyone agreed to abide by that decision, we wrote "POW" (for "prisoner of war") on our shirts as we waited for the arrests that never came. It turned out that while Senator Edward M. Kennedy waited with us, the head of the park police refused to "throw some guy in a wheelchair into the gutter in the middle of the night." After painstakingly obtaining its injunction, the administration proved unable to enforce it. The next day's Washington *Evening Star* bore the headline "Vets Overrule Supreme Court." A district court judge scolded the executive branch for its behavior, quashed the injunction, and dismissed a similar ban against the upcoming Mayday demonstrations.[18]

Throughout our stay, new members joined us—some still on active duty—as well as would-be infiltrators. It proved difficult to tell them apart because members of both groups had relatively short hair and new facial growth. The presence of several thousand legitimate vets, however, made it easy to challenge suspicious characters. Members would ask what unit the newcomer served with, find somebody from that unit, and make or break the suspect's story. Among those with phony stories who were recognized by men who had met them in Vietnam were a CIA agent and a Special Forces type who claimed to have served only in a regular infantry outfit. We became used to it. People continually approached me with offers to supply weapons or explosives. Assuming they were provocateurs or crazies or both, I gave them a speech on nonviolence.

Thursday, 22 April, was another busy day. In the morning a large group of vets, led by the Ohio chapters, marched to the steps of the Supreme Court—perhaps a bit tired and cranky—and demanded to know why the nation's highest court had not ruled on the unconstitutionality of the war. When they sang "God Bless America," an equally cranky Supreme Court had 150 vets arrested for disrupting court business. The veterans negotiated the terms of arrest with friendly police, who took them away one by one—with their hands on their heads, POW-style. They soon gained release on their own recognizance after Ramsey Clark worked out an arrangement whereby one test case would settle whether charges were dropped or the vets would all plead guilty. In the test case, a judge ruled that the veterans had not disrupted court business and threw out the charges.[19]

The charismatic and eloquent John Kerry testified for two hours that day before the Senate Foreign Relations Committee with a presentation that electrified the media and the public. "Where is the leadership?" he asked. "Where are they now that we, the men whom they sent off to war, have returned? These are commanders who have deserted their troops, and there is no more serious crime in the law of war.... [T]his Administration has done us the ultimate dishonor. They have attempted to disown us and the sacrifices we have made for this country. In their blindness and fear they have tried to deny that we are veterans or that we served in Nam. We do not need their testimony. Our own scars and stumps of limbs are witness enough for others and for ourselves." [20] That night we held a candlelight march past the White House.

Friday, 23 April, was our last day in Washington. While the House began hearings on distortion of news and information on the war and the Senate held hearings on atrocities that American soldiers committed in Vietnam, as many as 3,000 Vietnam veterans filed past the steps to the Capitol and one at a time threw away their medals in one of the most effective antiwar protests of the period. As press and electronic media recorded the emotional scene, a vet tossed the artificial leg he had been issued into the pile of Silver and Bronze Stars, Purple Hearts, army and navy commendation medals, and Vietnamese Gallantry Crosses. It was a cathartic experience for the vets: their faces became radiant as they dispelled their guilt and anger. The medals represented a burden of shame for heroic service in a corrupt and dirty war.[21]

By the summer of 1971, VVAW, like the rest of the antiwar movement, had spent much of its energy. For many Americans, Vietnamization, or the withdrawal of American ground troops and the stepping up of bombing to "change the color of the bodies," had taken the urgency out of ending the war. The public watched in dismay as some antiwar groups, frustrated at their apparent lack of success, turned to terrorism and sectarian infighting.

Although VVAW continued to grow—by that summer we had several hundred active-duty members in Vietnam and hundreds more awaiting discharge at army and marine camps in the United States—we, too, felt the pull of internal disputes. National policy was determined at meetings of the regional coordinators, usually held in the Midwest for logistical reasons, but in the interim the national office ran things. Conflicts ensued, especially in the early 1970s, when every movement organization became divided over the "correct line."

The growth of the regions decentralized VVAW. And, like much of the rest of the antiwar movement, we were also sinking into sectarian conflict. At a national coordinators' meeting in 1971, we had voted in the spirit of revolutionary solidarity to do at the national level what many chapters had done: admit members who were not Vietnam veterans. This reflected both the enthusiasm of other vets and the importance of nonveteran women—most, but not all, wives and girl friends—in the daily workings of chapters. We rechristened ourselves Vietnam Veterans Against the War/Winter Soldier Organization (VVAW/WSO) so that we could speak either as Vietnam vets or as the larger Winter Soldier Organization.

Almost immediately, we became aware that an organization called Revolutionary Union (RU) was attempting to take over VVAW/WSO in what seemed to be outside penetration by a disciplined cadre of leftists. For VVAW/WSO this was a period in which frustrated macho drives sometimes took the form of posturing to show who was the most revolutionary. RU appealed to a number of members impatient with our relative moderation.[22]

While that dispute raged, VVAW/WSO held a second march on Washington in the summer of 1974, called Dewey Canyon IV (even our powers of imagination seemed to be fading). It was not fun. The dying Nixon administration, perhaps grimly mindful that it had set up the self-destructive White House plumbers partly to deal with Daniel Ellsberg and the VVAW, became determined this time to enforce another injunction against sleeping on the Mall.[23] The few hundred vets, harassed and threatened constantly, found little rest. These tactics culminated in a confrontation at daybreak on our last day, when dozens of mounted police with clubs prepared to disperse us, breaking off only after we formed a defensive link to meet their charge. We had no intention of going peacefully, and they rode away into the dawn.

That fall, RU became the Revolutionary Communist party (RCP). VVAW/WSO members Barry Romo (who had testified at the Winter Soldier Investigation), Bill Davis, and Pete Zastrow numbered among the founders. Although initially cautious about attempting to take over VVAW/WSO because they had no mass base of their own, Davis, Zastrow, and Romo were elected to the national office. Their takeover resulted in the disintegration of the organization. By the fall of Saigon in May 1975, VVAW/WSO had become just another small left-wing splinter group.[24]

• • •

Vietnam Veterans Against the War grew from a handful of antiwar veterans to a national organization with thousands of members. During a war in which the specter of McCarthyism remained, and in a time of cultural revolution, the loyalty of war protesters was constantly impugned. VVAW members possessed credibility that could not be ignored or scared away. Our slogan was "What can they do to us—send us to Vietnam?"

The history of the antiwar movement in America is a story of courage, integrity, creativity, and diversity. Although VVAW worked within the broad, mostly middle-class, coalition, it may have been the most working-class, nonunion organization in the movement. Like much of the movement, our members tended to be college students, but VVAW was concentrated at public universities—and even those we could barely afford on the meager GI Bill that an ambivalent nation provided. Guilt feelings about our roots troubled us far less than they did many nonveterans at elite schools.

The guilt we faced was not handed down from our parents. We incurred it ourselves. Raised on the best images of valor from what may have been the most just war in human history, World War II, the soldiers of the Vietnam War entered combat in the mistaken belief that our democratic nation could never do anything as evil and destructive as what the Nazis or the communists had done. We went willingly, for the most part, to a war in which the collapse of the officer corps, the racism of our society, and an overzealous reaction to the fear of communism put incredible firepower into the hands of nineteen-year-old young men with far too little supervision. What we learned as a nation, thanks to the honesty of VVAW and the courage of a handful of war correspondents, is that atrocities result from unchecked power—not limited to dictatorships.

Protesting against policies that sent us into combat in Vietnam had a healing and cathartic effect on many of us. It is no wonder that the "rap groups" VVAW formed to handle the psychological scars we bore were the foundation of the vet centers, a whole new treatment modality, or that we played such a crucial role in identifying PTSD as a genuine psychological problem. Nor did it come as a surprise to learn, when Nixon's lawyers finally released a number of unclassified papers in 1987, that his White House, afraid to admit that the Vietnam War had been detrimental to its veterans, had scrapped Veterans Administration initiatives to deal with PTSD as a response to Dewey Canyon III.[25]

Being a member of VVAW was not easy. Members were wiretapped, beaten by police officers, shot by drug agents, and stabbed in jail cells.[26] But for many of us, no other choice existed. The high price our generation of veterans has paid in suicide, mental illness, and substance abuse testifies to the cost of remaining silent and alone. We were reviled as much as we were honored. But we also prolonged, for many years, that wonderful alchemical bonding and camaraderie that is known only by those who face great dangers together. In fact, because of VVAW activities, our members less often fell prey to the psychological traumas associated with coming home from Vietnam than did our other cohorts.

When we went into the service, we had taken an oath to defend the Constitution against all enemies, foreign and domestic. In VVAW we served a second hitch. We made it possible for a nation that hated the Vietnam War to honor its veterans. Our truth helped make America free again. In the face of a great national tragedy, ours remained a prophetic voice, summoning America to be true to its deepest beliefs. What we learned is that a prophet is never without honor, whether the state bestows it or not.

PART THREE

Women and the Antiwar Movement

Introduction

During the sixties and early seventies, millions of demonstrators flooded the nation's streets and campuses, not just from the antiwar movement, but also from civil and gay rights organizations, black and brown power movements, and environmental action groups, to name a few. Of all of the relationships between the various movements, those that involved the antiwar movement and the women's movement were the most complex. This section explores from three different perspectives the nature of those often very difficult relationships.

In chapter 10, historian Amy Swerdlow describes the philosophies and politics of the most effective women's antiwar organization, Women Strike for Peace (WSP). The middle-class, middle-aged mothers of WSP concentrated their efforts on draft resistance and counseling. Although WSPers participated in the great antiwar coalitions of the period, they maintained their separate motherist identity in part because of the gender discrimination they had experienced from the male-dominated leadership of the larger groups. A member of WSP herself, Swerdlow emphasizes the significance of the organization not only in the movement but also as an empowering experience for those who took part in its vigils, marches, and counseling sessions.

Alice Echols concentrates her attention on the development of the women's liberation movement (WLM) in chapter 11. She is especially interested in the ways the New Left and black freedom movements affected that movement and how the often uneasy relationship between the WLM and antiwar leaders helped to define radical feminist politics beyond the Vietnam War era. Echols, an historian, demonstrates how the doctrinal struggles between the New Left and the radical feminists, complicated by the pressing need to forge tactics to oppose American policies in Southeast Asia, ultimately impeded efforts to create a multicultural, multiclass, feminist movement.

In chapter 12, Nina S. Adams, another historian, analyzes the reasons why many women left the civil rights and antiwar movements to work within a movement of their own. She suggests that this break, which occurred more in sorrow than anger, was not complete in the sense that women of the WLM brought with them a wealth of constructive experiences from their earlier activities. The admirable roles of southern black women in the civil rights movement and the Vietnamese in their national liberation influenced the organizers of the WLM. That movement, however, adopted strategies and tactics different from those of the New and Old Left, particularly in their emphases on the individual and the personal.

Women and men worked together and separately to change their society during the Vietnam War era. Although the antiwar movement ended in the early seventies, it had a profound impact on the directions that leaders of the WLM had taken and would take in the future.

10

"Not My Son, Not Your Son, Not Their Sons"

Mothers Against the Vietnam Draft

AMY SWERDLOW

In the 1960s a movement of middle-aged, middle-class, white women, Women Strike for Peace (WSP), built on the postwar cultural construction of motherhood to organize a militant female opposition to the draft for Vietnam. Theirs was not an easy task, as the draft was a male institution in which only men were called upon to serve in the military forces or brave the risks and punishments of refusal to do so.[1] According to sociologist Barrie Thorne, who studied two Boston-area resistance groups in the late 1960s, the young female cohorts of the draft-age men who had joined the resistance because of their own commitment to end the war found that they could not be principal, or even significant, players. Leslie Cagan, still a leading peace activist today, recalls a discussion of a "We Won't Go" petition drive being planned by the Boston area resistance, in which the young women in the room were told that they would not be allowed to speak because women did not face conscription and therefore had no right to decide the tactics of resistance. Finding themselves confined to supportive and sexual roles characterized by the slogan "Gals Say 'Yes' To Guys Who Say 'No,'" a group of young women in the Boston area resistance left antidraft activity to form their own resistance to male domination.[2]

Why and how, given the stereotypical division of gender roles within the draft resistance movement, could the middle-aged, middle-class women of WSP find an effective and satisfying role for themselves, while the radical draft-age young women experienced a level of trivialization so denigrating that most of them left to form what they called "our own resistance"?

WSP, founded in 1961, had conducted a widely publicized and successful campaign for a ban on atmospheric nuclear testing.[3] At a time when Cold War dissenters were dismissed by the press, the public, and political leaders as either subversives or deviants, the respectable lady-next-door image projected by WSP women helped to legitimize radical criticism of the Cold War and U.S. militarism. The movement's defeat of an attempt by the House Committee on Un-American Activities to brand it as a communist front was accomplished through humor, evasion, irony, and scornful moral superiority—manifestations of the creativity, the playfulness, and the potential power of the politics of motherhood.[4]

By mid-decade, WSP had moved from antinuclear activism to militant protest against U. S. intervention in Vietnam. Early in 1964, WSP women began educating themselves on the Geneva Accords, the origins and extent of the "secret war," and the history of the puppet regime in the south. Everything the WSPers learned they shared with their communities, their congressional representatives, and newspaper editors. As the war in Vietnam escalated, and President Johnson ordered the bombing of the north, WSP escalated its campaign to halt the war. From 1966 until the end of the war, the women conducted an intense and consistent campaign: lobbying, demonstrations, sit-ins, maintaining information tables at supermarkets and at church doors, chainings to the White House fence, lawsuits, consumer boycotts, vigils at the homes of draft board members, public readings of the lists of the Vietnam dead, and draft counseling, as well as the overt aiding and abetting of resisters. Much of this action was not unique to WSP, and many times the protests were conducted in coalition with other peace groups. What made WSP's independent actions different, however, was that they were conducted exclusively by women in the name of outraged motherhood. An advertisement in the *New York Times* of 2 February 1966, announcing a "Mother's March on Capitol Hill to Stop the Killing," declared: "Stop! Don't Drench the Jungles of Asia With the Blood of Our Sons. Don't force our sons to kill women and children whose only crime is to live in a country ripped by civil war."[5]

The key women, many of whom were mothers of draft-age sons, and in touch with thousands of other mothers in the same predicament, sensed that undermining conscription, the weakest link in the interventionist chain, would undermine the war. They were also convinced that antidraft activity, particularly draft counseling, would be an ideal vehicle for attracting the much-sought-after "ordinary" women whose deep concern for the welfare of their sons would introduce them to the broader moral and political arguments against the war.

What distinguishing characteristics made it possible for the middle-aged women of WSP to achieve a sense of personal and social purpose, and also work effectively in a political culture not of their making? One answer is that the WSPers's socialization in the postsuffrage interwar years, and their coming to motherhood in the antifeminist late 1940s and 1950s, predisposed them to value self-sacrifice, both their own and that of the draft resisters, and to identify the needs of the sons as their own. They enjoyed acting as political mothers to the "brave young men who refused to kill or be killed in an immoral war."

In addition, the WSPers realized their unique position. Unlike the young unmarried female cohorts of the draft resisters, the middle-class married women of WSP had achieved social standing in the community, as well as access to discretionary funds. Thus they could provide much-needed and -appreciated material and financial resources, as well as social respectability and political influence. The response from the draft resisters to WSP support was appropriately filial and grateful—not sexual. It gave the WSPers the psychological, social, and political space to cross gender, age, race, and class barriers to counsel, and later to aid and abet, hundreds of thousands of young men unwilling to fight in Vietnam.

A letter to WSP from Gary Rader, a former marine who had become an antidraft organizer, communicated the sort of message WSPers found irresistible. Rader described himself as "woefully young and powerless . . . a 23 year-old facing eleven or so years in prison, working in my first movement ever, being trailed by the FBI and harassed by the police." He asked for support for those men who were "putting their lives on the line," and called on WSP to provide bail and legal defense funds, as well as living space and financial support for resistance organizers.[6] The *Sacramento Women for Peace Newsletter* responded to this kind of appeal by declaring: "It would seem that Women for Peace, if we are worthy of our name, should get behind this fine group of young idealists, working not for themselves but for the future of the race."[7]

A call to women in Oakland, California, to swell the ranks of a weekly WSP picket line at the local induction center stated: "We know that we are effective because we can see it; we often escort young men directly from the buses to Draft Help to be counseled before they enter the induction center—this in spite of the attempt by induction officials to herd them quickly into the building. We are often thanked for being there. We are even told we are beautiful."[8] To WSPers the word "beautiful" had no sexual connotation; it meant moral, brave, selfless, politically astute. The Los Angeles GI Civil Liberties Defense Committee, thanking the women for financial contributions and the provision of office space for GI resistance work, wrote to WSP: "The help that each of you has offered, and given us, in our day-to-day work has been beyond what anyone could really expect."[9] What WSP gave—money, space, time, and emotional support—was a familiar maternal service. Neither they, nor the young men, would have expected such services from the older male activists like Dave Dellinger, Dave McReynolds, and Sid Lens, from whom they expected leadership, not comfort.

Rarely consulted when national antidraft policies or tactics were formulated, WSPers experienced condescension, and even ridicule, when they disagreed with movement decisions. This disdain frustrated and angered some of the women, but it never drove them out of antidraft work. Their staying power can be attributed, in large measure, to the fact that their antidraft work was self-defined. They came to WSP from their own separate women's movement, where they felt appreciated and important, and in which they shaped their own policies. WSP decided on its own terms which issues, which groups, and what rhetoric and tactics it would initiate or support.

The Philadelphia WSP, for instance, "adopted" a number of young antidraft organizers and resisters and provided them with funds for housing and office expenses. They reported that they were not only encouraging the resisters, but *criticizing* as well as listening to them.[10] This prerogative to influence the sons, an ambiguous privilege of motherhood, mollified frustrations stemming from generational, cultural, and gender conflicts, even as it obfuscated WSP's real lack of power and influence in the decision-making bodies of the larger antiwar movement.

By late 1966, as Vietnam casualty figures rose, delegates to WSP's fifth national conference decided to make opposition to the draft a central focus of the movement's antiwar work.[11] This choice of direction meant developing a policy statement against the draft, devising a series of pressure tactics that could appeal to the mythical average woman, creating photogenic demonstrations that would dramatize the personal cost of the draft to sons and mothers, testifying at congressional and party platform hearings, and holding newsworthy mass lobbies against Congress for repeal of the draft and withdrawal from Vietnam. When Congress voted to renew the Universal Military Training Act in 1967 despite an active peace movement campaign for repeal, WSP determined to undermine the draft by counseling those who chose to evade it, and by supporting those who refused to be inducted. Although traditional pacifist groups were already offering draft counseling, the need had outgrown their resources. WSP joined the effort, establishing new centers and workshops for training counselors, and developing educational materials for movement activists and the community at large. While WSP conducted much of its draft-counseling activity in alliance with other groups, WSP women remained the mainstay of counseling centers, because they were usually free from full-time paid employment or the care of young children.

Very early in its campaign, WSP raised the slogan "Not Our Sons, Not Your Sons, Not Their Sons." Movement literature demonstrates, however, that the women realized that race and class inequities built into the Selective Service System benefited their own sons. The advantages for middle-class youths included student and teacher deferments as well as conscientious-objector status, granted only to those who had sufficient education to articulate their religious or ethical reservations in a manner acceptable to the draft boards. An article in the Los Angeles WSP newsletter, *LA WISP*, declared that counseling those who can avoid the draft is "simply a promulgation of the racism and dollar discrimination that has caused the war. . . . Who takes the place of the middle-class student with a 2-S deferment?, or the C.O., or the emigrant to another country who might come home in a coffin?"[12] A pamphlet, *Your Draft-Age Son: a Message for Peaceful Parents,* published by the Berkeley-Oakland WSP, pointed out that the draftee for Vietnam is "young, often working-class, often black; while his board . . . is overwhelmingly old, middle-class and white."[13]

WSP women took advantage of their roles as community leaders, PTA activists, and mothers of high-school students to pressure schools into providing seniors of all classes and races with alternative information on conscription, particularly at times when army and navy recruiters were present in the schools. The Los Angeles WSP filed suit against Selective Service Director Lewis Hershey and California educational authorities for failing to provide information about draft law alternatives in the high schools, as mandated by Selective Service regulations.[14] WSP also protested the spending of tax monies on ROTC and military assemblies while schools refused to provide peace assemblies or time for antiwar speakers.[15]

These appeals seldom proved successful. Failing to win their battles for draft counseling in most high schools, WSP, along with other peace groups, organized "End the Draft Caravans" that traveled into blue-collar and minority neighborhoods to counsel young men who would otherwise have no access to information on legal alternatives to the draft. Many WSPers worked full-time on these and other draft counseling projects.

On the upper West Side of New York City, WSP's draft-counseling service was housed in a storefront in a black and Puerto Rican urban renewal area that also contained new middle-income housing projects. This center advertised its services in a Spanish language newspaper and reported that it hoped to "train some black counselors to work 'in the streets.'"[16]

The extent of WSP draft counseling is revealed in the report from Nassau County, New York, where organizers of the service claimed that volunteers counseled 100,000 young men in an off-the-street facility. These volunteers often included doctors, lawyers, and psychiatrists, who were, for the most part, the husbands or male friends of WSP women. As a result of stories in the local press, word-of-mouth recommendations, and a sign on the headquarters advertising "Free Draft Counseling Sponsored by Women Strike for Peace," the Long Island service attracted blue-collar workers, black youths, school dropouts, and working-class apprentices. When questioned in a 1979 interview about a claim that the Long Island Draft Information and Counseling Service advised as many as 100,000 men, Irma Zigas, the WSP draft task force coordinator, insisted that her estimate was accurate.[17] She acknowledged that in the beginning WSP provided only ten counselors working twice a week from 7:00 P.M. until midnight, but that in the end thirty-five to forty counselors worked five days and nights a week, often until one or two in the morning. "At the height of the operation in 1968, '69 and '70," according to Zigas, "the center opened at 10:00 A.M. and was staffed by as many as 15 reception people."[18] Zigas recalled with pride that "not one person was paid, not even a receptionist." Assuming that the amount of time spent in counseling each individual totaled at least two hours with a cash value of ten dollars per hour, the WSP draft counselors in Nassau County alone contributed over $1 million in volunteer labor.

In the early stages of the Long Island draft counseling service, the majority of the counselors were men who were interviewed and appointed by WSP women. Zigas believes that the men in her center not only devoted as much time and effort as the women, but actually sacrificed more than the WSPers, giving many evenings while holding full-time positions of employment.

The number of male counselors declined when Zigas and Bernice Crane, another organizer of the service, insisted that no lawyers be allowed to serve as draft counselors lest they exploit the draftees to build their own practices. As a result, the women who ran the center had to acquaint themselves with draft law, which changed frequently as new regulations and court decisions came into effect. The nonprofessional women counselors addressed this problem by studying the *Selective Service Law Reporter*. Zigas maintains that the women became so well informed on the changes in the law that they had no problem in challenging lawyers, grilling them on the loopholes in the law and on their motivations for acting as counselors. In addition, WSP stipulated that counselors had to pass a political test. Only those who opposed the war could serve in the Long Island facility, a condition that angered the men. With a good deal of bitterness, Zigas recalled that many left because the women came on too strong. She intimated that it took much commitment for the men who stayed to do so "because most wanted the women to act as hostesses and secretaries; not to take charge or rock the boat."

After exhausting all legal avenues of appeal, young men who decided to refuse induction called on WSP for support. Women who might have been uneasy about civil disobedience in other circumstances felt that they could not let the young men down. They found themselves leaving home at dawn, driving long distances to induction centers, and standing in vigils with placards supporting, as Zigas put it, "the kid who was going to say, 'No' that day." The WSP newsletter in Nashville, Tennessee, urged women to go to induction refusals "because an adult on a picket line does wonders for young people and for their 'press image.'" Nashville WSPers were also urged to telephone or visit the parents of draft refusers because "a friendly call is a big help not only to their morale, but it usually affects the way the parents treat their sons." [19]

The next step for WSP entailed sitting in at arraignments and trials of resisters, with media representatives alongside them, to inhibit stiff sentences. Their presence demonstrated that respectable middle-class women believed that these young men were exemplary citizens upholding the best traditions of the nation. The WSP communications network also provided long lists of prisoners of conscience in jails and stockades all over the country so that women could write to them, especially during holiday seasons. Some WSPers even made trips to visit jailed draft resisters and GIs who refused to fight. They returned home saddened but strengthened in their commitment to fight the draft. One Los Angeles WSPer made weekly visits to fifteen young men in the federal prison at Lompoc. She reported in *LA WISP,* "We talk, drink coffee, read things I bring up, and laugh a lot for three hours. Then they go back to be stripped naked for searching, and I drive back to my family in Santa Monica." Through WSP funding, jail visitors were able to buy books and subscriptions to periodicals for the young prisoners.[20] WSP also picketed draft boards and the homes of board members, where the women read aloud the names of war dead in an attempt to remind officials that each draftee they dealt with represented a live human being too young to die.

Yet WSP as a group seems to have been intimidated by the antifeminism and antimomism of the 1940s and 1950s, which blamed assertive mothers for sissy sons, and ridiculed political women as dissatisfied, castrating neurotics. The women were therefore loath to speak on behalf of the sons, or to seem in control of them. On the other hand, as virtuous mothers, they took credit for proper moral upbringing. In October 1966, when Charlotte Keyes, a leading WSP activist from Champaign-Urbana, published an article in *McCall's* about her son's decision to resist the draft, she explained: "We have tried to find the seed of his present way of life and have more than once been taken aback to realize that we ourselves had planted some of them. . . . Well, we parents don't realize—do we—when we inculcate our moral standards, that the children may try to really live by them."[21] Keyes's conclusion that "we stand by our son and we learn from him" could have been the credo for WSP in relation to the draft resistance movement.

The pitfalls involved in directing a son's response to the draft are illustrated by the case of Evelyn Whitehorn of Palo Alto, California, described in press reports as a middle-class, graying, forty-seven-year-old devoted mother of four boys, who had never belonged to anything more controversial than the PTA and the Committee to Save Walden Pond. Whitehorn, who decided to seek a restraining order preventing the induction of her eighteen-year-old son Erik, contended that his pacifist convictions stemmed, in large part, from her efforts to bring him up with good moral character.

East Bay California Women for Peace saw the Whitehorn case as a conflict between the rights of mothers and the power of the state. As it turned out, it did not prove to be much of a contest. Erik was arrested, indicted, convicted, and eventually imprisoned for refusing to register. In court, the judge observed that Mrs. Whitehorn was five years older than her ex-husband, insinuating that there was something deviant about her life-style and family. Apparently Evelyn Whitehorn's action hit a responsive chord: hundreds of people wrote to her, supporting her stand, including many servicemen who wanted to "borrow her for a while."[22] *Plain Rapper,* the publication of the Palo Alto Resistance, reported that letters ran 500–14 in favor of the Whitehorn action. One boy taped his allowance of five pennies to a letter "to help because of my older brother." A grandmother in Long Island sent five dollar bills, one for each of her grandsons, and an air force reserve officer sent Erik his paycheck. However, *Plain Rapper* noted that governmental pressure produced growing tension between mother and son. "It is tough for an 18 year old male to let his mother stand up for him, even if that is the best legal strategy available," commented the male registers who edited *Plain Rapper*. "To make matters worse, mother and son are extremely articulate and sometimes find themselves competing." [23]

By the end of the summer of 1969, the Whitehorns had lost their case, confidence in their cause, and family unity. Erik eventually turned against his mother and decided to go into the army to get out of jail. Filled with anger and regret, Evelyn Whitehorn declared in a statement to the press that she had decided not to appeal her son's imprisonment because "the draft law doesn't give any consideration to the ... earnest desire of parents to interpose themselves between their offspring and injustice." She concluded that in the future, "Whatever I can do, or contribute, will be done only as 'me,' not with the use of any member of my family." [24] Whitehorn had been defeated not only by the law but by a gender ideology that found her too presumptuous and bossy.

WSP needed to find a way to join the resistance on its own terms, because it was reluctant to act in the name of the sons. In mid-1967 the National Consultative Committee composed a women's statement of conscience and complicity with draft resistance in defiance of the Selective Service Act. This decision to provoke retaliation from the government stemmed from the women's desire to act in their own names, to take risks, and to write their own scenario. But not all within WSP responded positively. Some women felt that they could not endanger an entire movement by undertaking illegal actions in its name. Others worried that the leaders might be imprisoned and the movement thus weakened. A sufficient number of women enthusiastically supported building a woman's resistance, however, and as WSP followed a do-everything policy, those who hoped to move the legal action away from long-haired youths to moral middle-class mothers won the day. Their goal was to tie up the courts, intensify the debate over the war, and escalate the struggle to end it. The WSP statement of complicity stressed the women's moral commitment to draft resistance: "We believe that it is not we, but those who send our sons to kill and be killed who are committing crimes. We do, however, recognize that there may be legal risks involved, but because we believe that these young men are courageous and morally justified in rejecting the war regardless of consequences, we can do no less."[25]

To publicize the Women's Statement of Conscience and launch a women's resistance, WSP organized the first adult, and the only women's, demonstration in support of draft refusal. It was planned as a triple-header: a rally, a march to the office of the director of the Selective Service System to deliver the complicity statement, and a picket line at the front gate of the White House to demand that the president stop listening to the generals and begin hearing the mothers.[26] After WSP had issued its call for the 20 September 1967 rally and march, the Department of the Interior announced a new ruling limiting to one hundred the number of persons permitted to picket at the White House gate. The WSP organizers, feeling that they could not accept this restriction on peaceful protest, refused to cancel their march. Despite WSP's appeal to sympathetic senators and representatives, the American Civil Liberties Union, and the president to have the order rescinded, it remained in place.

The rally and march to challenge the draft calls drew close to one thousand women from the eastern seaboard. After an emotional meeting addressed by two young male resisters, the women marched to the office of General Hershey carrying a coffin draped in a black shawl and bearing the slogan, "Not My Son, Not Your Son, Not Their Sons. Support Those Who Say 'No.'" The police proved particularly cooperative, allowing the women to march in the road, even though the organizers had applied only for a sidewalk permit. At 1600 Pennsylvania Avenue, however, the atmosphere changed abruptly. The marchers were met by a solid line of park police standing shoulder to shoulder behind a hastily erected fence that blocked their access to the White House. Incensed at the denial of their rights as mothers and citizens, the women—with no hesitation or consultation—pushed against the police line, crawled between the officers' legs, trampled the fence, and dashed into the road to reach the White House. Victory seemed within reach until another solid phalanx of club-brandishing police materialized.

The WSPers sat down in the road in front of the White House, continuing their protest. There they remained—singing and chanting, blocking traffic, and refusing to move despite threats of arrest. Finally, Bella Abzug, WSP's legislative representative, arranged a compromise with the police that would allow the women to picket at the gate, one hundred at a time. The women still refused, but Abzug and WSP spokesperson Dagmar Wilson finally convinced them that they had made their point, that their case would be taken to the courts, and that going to jail would be counterproductive because it would necessitate the cancellation of the national conference scheduled for the next day. At that point, the women reluctantly gave up the space they had usurped, claiming that they had, in effect, won their fight. They based this claim on the fact that all the women had managed to march at the White House in a revolving line. The police pretended that they were counting to see that only one hundred marched on the sidewalk at any one time, but they often looked the other way.

A front-page UPI story in the *New York Times* carried the headline "Women Fight Police Near White House." At the height of the fracas, according to the *Times,* about ten women were seen lying on the ground, one with blood on her head.[27] The *Baltimore Sun* carried a photo of a bedraggled woman pushing her head through a solid wall of police standing with arms locked. This wire service picture was disseminated across the country over the caption, "Coming Through—A Women Strike for Peace demonstrator maneuvers a blockade." The *Sun* reported that there were more police on the scene than women, but that the women failed to be intimidated. "The women screamed at the police and jeered at them," according to the *Sun,* "when they announced that the WSP picketing permit had been revoked."[28] At the convening of the national WSP conference that evening, it was noted that the two young resisters who had joined the women in the march were dragged several hundred feet, beaten, and arrested, thereby receiving much more brutal treatment than the women. This only affirmed the WSP conviction that middle-aged mothers could get away with more militancy than radical young men, and that WSP had to do more in its own name to end the war.

The confrontation with the police at the White House tarnished the ladylike image WSP had nurtured carefully for almost six years. For the first time, the *Washington Post* reproached WSP for its attempt to break through the police barricade by force. "Such conduct," the *Post* editorialized, "diminishes any influence the group might have."[29] WSP showed no contrition. A press release from the national conference declared that the women had broken through the police lines, strengthened by the conviction that they were fighting for the lives of their sons, the survival of the people of Vietnam, and the right to petition the president: "Neither billy clubs nor bruises will deter us. We will not be stopped."[30] WSP continued its struggle against the draft until after the United States withdrew from Vietnam. It was also one of the few organizations that insisted upon total amnesty for GI deserters, Canadian exiles, and other draft evaders as well as resisters.

Throughout the struggle, the WSP leadership displayed a high level of political acumen and a sense of the strategic moment for pressure, as well as talent for research, self-education, and public relations unprecedented for nonprofessional women. By testing themselves in battles with the Pentagon, learning the loopholes in the draft law, providing assistance to deserters in Canada, speaking at congressional hearings and public forums, confronting draft board officials and army officers at induction lines, and counseling working-class and minority sons and mothers, the women developed a strong sense of their own powers and a greater consciousness of the constraints under which they labored.

The history of WSP shows that women who build on traditional female culture to enter the political arena do not have to be trapped in that culture or bound to stereotypical gender roles. A separatist women's peace movement engaged in militant struggle against the patriarchal militarist institutions can develop a cadre of women who find themselves increasingly in opposition to the gendered division of political labor and power in the state and in the peace movement. When these women encounter a rising feminist consciousness, their possibilities for personal and social transformation are boundless. When the radical feminist declared that the personal is political, WSP women were ready to hear it: they already knew that political action could transform personal life.

11

"Women Power" and Women's Liberation

Exploring the Relationship Between the Antiwar Movement and the Women's Liberation Movement

ALICE ECHOLS

The uneasy relationship that existed between the Vietnam antiwar movement and the women's liberation movement is a topic that has provoked little scholarly inquiry.[1] But, then, most recent scholarship on sixties radicalism has paid scant attention to the women's liberation movement (WLM). For example, the authors of *Who Spoke Up? American Protest Against the War in Vietnam, 1963–1975* note the involvement of Women Strike for Peace in the antiwar movement but tell us nothing of antiwar rallies and marches sponsored by women's liberation groups or their participation in non-WLM demonstrations.[2]

Indeed, much of this scholarship mirrors the position of women in the male-dominated Movement—that is, the women's liberation movement remains on the periphery, far from the core of the narrative.[3] In fact, these scholars have often managed to marginalize women even more effectively than did the movements they study—women, of course, had succeeded in taking center stage by the end of the sixties. There are several reasons for the failure to integrate women's liberation into sixties scholarship, including, I suspect, a certain resistance to feminism. In addition, some feminist writers have tended to emphasize the disjunctures between the women's liberation movement and the larger male-dominated Movement, and to locate feminism's radicalism in its alleged repudiation of the New Left.[4]

Accordingly, I find it important to offer some correction to both the scholarship on the sixties and those feminist accounts that de-emphasize or deny the ideological and intellectual connections between the women's liberation movement and the male-dominated Movement from which it grew. The relationship between the fledgling women's liberation movement and both the antiwar movement and the larger Movement is complex. Although a study chronicling the contributions of women's liberation groups to the antiwar struggle would be valuable in its own right, that is not my focus here. Instead, I concentrate upon the contradictory ways in which the New Left and the black freedom movement contributed to the emergence of feminism and the turbulent relationship that developed between the antiwar movement and the women's liberation movement, with its consequences for the WLM.[5]

• • •

As the sixties began, no feminist movement of consequence existed. To the extent that women mobilized themselves politically as women, such activity centered around the issue of peace. By the middle of the decade, however, the contradiction between women's increased participation in the labor force and attendance at college, on the one hand, and the ideology of domesticity (what Betty Friedan called the "feminine mystique"), on the other, could no longer be contained. Just as important to the revival of feminism was the emergence of the black freedom movement and a revitalized Left, both of which challenged long-accepted social arrangements and conventions. The new feminism emerged from two different groups of educated, middle-class (and mostly white) women. Those who formed the National Organization for Women (NOW) with Betty Friedan were generally professional women and politically moderate. While many NOW members became doves over the course of the decade, they believed sex discrimination to be the major issue for NOW, not the Vietnam War. Like the NAACP, the group after which it was modeled, NOW took an integrationist and legalistic approach to gender inequality. The other group of women who organized the women's liberation movement were younger and considerably more radical, having come of age politically in the black freedom movement and the New Left.

Although radical women certainly encountered sexism in these movements, their experiences were not of unrelieved oppression. As Sara Evans demonstrates in her groundbreaking book, *Personal Politics,* it was here that they developed the skills, self-confidence, and political savvy to discern the disjuncture between the Movement's rhetoric of equality and their own subordination.[6] Important, as well, was their exposure during the civil rights struggle to black women—both the younger activists in the Student Non-Violent Coordinating Committee (SNCC) and older community leaders—whose self-reliance and assertiveness stood at odds with the feminine mystique.

The philosophical underpinnings of the Movement also contributed to the resurgence of feminist activism. For although the New Left lacked the Old Left's awareness of the "woman question," its conviction that "the personal is political"—that there is a political dimension to personal life—encouraged the development of feminist consciousness. By expanding political discourse to include the subject of personal relations, New Leftists unintentionally paved the way for women's liberationists to criticize marriage, the family, and normative heterosexuality. Moreover, the Movement's concern with achieving meaningful democracy (what was termed "participatory democracy") and building in the present the desired community of the future (termed "prefigurative politics" by sociologist Wini Breines)[7] encouraged challenges to any lingering inequalities within the Movement.

Many factors, of course, led women to discern the disjuncture between the Left's rhetoric of equality and their own subordination. The frenzied growth of Students for a Democratic Society (SDS), and the factionalism and competitiveness that accompanied this development, made the Movement a less hospitable place for women. Black power and the Vietnam War played a particular role in all this. Black power, which resulted in the expulsion of whites from SNCC by late 1966, forced white radicals to reconceptualize their role in the Movement. Writing several years after the fact, SDS leader Gregory Clavert maintained that black power, by "throwing us back upon ourselves, our own lives, our own situations . . . offered us the possibility of being sincerely radical, and not the liberal adjunct of the black movement."[8] White radicals came to believe that authentic radicalism entailed fighting one's own—not others'—battles; it meant confronting one's own oppression. This development and the intensification of the war inspired some white SNCC veterans to search for, in Staughton Lynd's words, "something white radicals could do which would have the same spirit, ask as much of us, and challenge the system as fundamentally as had our work in Mississippi."[9] They came up with the draft resistance movement. Unfortunately, this marginalized women even more, as heroic action became the exclusive domain of men. It further reduced women to the status of helpmates, or worse. One of the movement's most popular slogans claimed "Girls Say Yes to Guys Who Say No!"[10] Organizers of the GI coffeehouse movement were also initially guilty of using the tactic of employing women as sexual bait.

The idea that true radicalism involved struggling against one's own oppression also led SDS to refocus its organizing efforts on campus. But the movement for student power was barely under way when it began to lose credibility within the Movement. The Detroit and Newark riots in the summer of 1967, the promotion of armed resistance by some radical black leaders, and the resulting state-sponsored subversion of militant black groups led many white radicals once again to conceive of themselves as support troops for the black struggle. Indeed, to the Left, the idea that white, middle-class students were oppressed seemed increasingly preposterous when blacks were gunned down in the streets and Vietnamese peasants slaughtered as the Vietnam War escalated. The intensification of the war and the government's repression of the black movement fueled the delusion that America was on the brink of a revolutionary apocalypse. Unfortunately, this misperception discouraged radicals from pursuing the personal, prefigurative politics that had distinguished the Movement from the Old Left.

Black power gave radical women the ideological justification they needed to explore their own condition. But, again, as women began to invoke the idea that a revolutionary must first look at his or her own oppression, the concept was losing credibility. Women who demanded that the Movement face up to its male chauvinism were accused of diverting attention from the more important struggles of blacks, the Vietnamese, or the working class. Indeed, it is no coincidence that in the fall of 1967 radical women in Chicago and New York formed separate all-women's groups (usually numbering ten to fifty women) to discuss gender inequality. For it was at that very moment that the New Left was jettisoning the prefigurative, personal politics of the 1960s in favor of an orthodox and dogmatic version of Marxism.

However, their decision to meet apart from men did not signal an end to their relationship to the Left. Rather, the WLM's relationship to the Left remained a source of conflict within the fledgling movement, so much so that even the term "women's liberation" at first proved controversial, seeming too feminist to some.[11] It was not simply that meeting separately from their boyfriends and husbands (who were typically part of the Left) felt treacherous at times; it was instead that they, too, were radicals committed to ending the war and eliminating vestiges of racism.

But as radical women confronted a Left at turns indifferent, hostile, and patronizing to women's liberation, some women began to argue that the WLM should be independent, rather than an arm of the Left.[12]

This feeling, while a tactical response to male belligerence and intransigence, also grew out of a conviction that women's oppression would not be wiped away by socialist revolution, that male supremacy was not merely a byproduct of capitalism. These women, who would soon come to identify themselves as radical feminists, considered the primary purpose of the WLM to organize women to fight their own oppression rather than the war or the draft. Radical feminism developed first in New York City, aided by the splits in that city's Left and the fact that women's liberationists there were less organizationally embedded in the Left than women's liberationists elsewhere. For instance, Shulamith Firestone, Kathie Sarachild, Ellen Willis, Carol Hanisch, and Anne Koedt—all important early New York radical feminists—identified with the Left, but tended to occupy its organizational perimeters.

Those women called "politicos," who maintained that the new movement should be closely allied with the larger radical Movement, tended, by contrast, to be centrally involved with Left groups. The commitment of women such as Marilyn Webb, Heather Booth, and Charlotte Bunch to the organized Left followed in large measure from their conviction that capitalism caused women's oppression and that socialist revolution would liberate women. The politico-feminist fracture established the major fault line in the movement's early years and did much to determine the character of radical feminism. Of course, these positions were not monolithic or absolute, and over time shifting occurred, usually in the direction of radical feminism. Moreover, it was usually in large cities, where size facilitated polarization, that the schism resulted in separate groupings.

While the question of the WLM's relationship to the Left was already a source of some tension in the Chicago and New York groups by the fall of 1967, the fracture did not open until the 1968 Jeannette Rankin Brigade protest, the first all-women's antiwar action. The Jeannette Rankin Brigade (named after the first woman elected to Congress, and the only member to vote against U.S. intervention in both world wars) comprised a coalition of women's groups committed to mobilizing American women to petition Congress on its opening day, 15 January 1968, for the immediate withdrawal of U.S. troops from Vietnam. Although the Brigade's organizers tended to be older, liberal women with experience in peace organizations and church groups, they did approach younger, more radical women about participating in the protest. The mix proved explosive: the women planning the protest wanted to ensure that the demonstration would be peaceful, while the younger, leftist women felt that nonviolent protest had long since outlived its usefulness. In fact, they took issue with the Brigade's very premise that petitioning Congress constituted a politically useful act. Marilyn Webb, a New Leftist in Washington, D.C., asked what would be accomplished by petitioning a body that had not only proven itself impotent to end the war, but had "never even had the chance to vote on this war?" [13]

For radical women from New York and Chicago, the problem was not just the Brigade's liberalism but its assumption that women bore some special responsibility for ending the war. Women's liberationists rejected as sexist all culturally-received notions about women, and they found the Brigade's equation of femaleness with maternal selflessness especially repugnant. The Chicago women contended that "until women go beyond justifying themselves in terms of their wombs and breasts and housekeeping abilities, they will never be able to exert any political power." The New York women likewise criticized the Brigade for reinforcing dominant cultural assumptions about women and urged women to unite not as "passive supplicants" but as "a political force to be reckoned with." Interestingly, Betty Friedan, one of the protest's sponsors, also objected to the Brigade's equation of pacifism with femaleness and the notion that women should take it upon themselves to clean up the world. Friedan complained, "I don't think the fact that milk once flowed within my breast is the reason I'm against the war." [14] (Ironically, the idea that women are more pacific, an idea discredited in the WLM's early days, became almost commonplace in the women's movement by the 1980s.)

The Brigade did manage to turn out about five thousand women for its Capitol Hill protest. But its success ended there when Vice-President Hubert Humphrey prevented them from petitioning the legislators by invoking a long-standing precedent that barred Congress from conducting any business until the president delivered his State of the Union address. Thus the protestors found themselves stranded in the snow, singing "We Shall Overcome" with folksinger Judy Collins. Finally, the government allowed a small delegation, including Coretta Scott King and the eighty-seven-year-old Rankin herself, to enter the Capitol to present their petition to the House speaker and the Senate majority leader.

Having come to Washington fully believing in the uselessness of the protest, thirty to fifty radical women from New York, Chicago, Washington, and other cities spent most of the weekend meeting with each other to develop a program for women involved in the Movement. As a consequence of these meetings, Women's Liberation groups formed in Washington and Berkeley. The New York women also organized a separate demonstration—a funeral procession and burial of "Traditional Womanhood" in Arlington Cemetery. They urged women to stop "acquiescing to an order that indulges peaceful pleas / And writes them off as female logic / Saying peace is womanly." The protest marked the first use of the slogan "Sisterhood is Powerful," coined by Kathie Sarachild.[15]

Sisterhood, however, was sometimes in short supply those two days, and, by the close of the weekend, differences had become manifestly clear. The older Brigade planners were extremely nervous about this new thing—women's liberation—which they felt could divert attention from the struggle to end the war. Indeed, needing a speaker to represent younger women, the organizers turned to Charlotte Bunch, another New Leftist in D.C., because of her background in the University Christian Movement and her politico orientation. But many radical women felt apprehensive about women's liberation as well. Though they objected to the Brigade's assumption that women bore a special responsibility for ending the war, they still believed women should be protesting the war—albeit alongside men. Moreover, they doubted that women should be organizing solely to fight their own oppression. In fact, a number of D.C. women objected to the New York women's action, calling it apolitical. Shortly after the protest, Marilyn Webb suggested that the new women's groups focus on the issues of "corporate power, militarism, poverty, Vietnam and the 1968 election."[16] For Shulamith Firestone, who would play a major role in articulating radical feminism, the protest confirmed "our own worst suspicions that the job ahead of developing even a minimal consciousness among women will be staggering."[17]

The slick, New Left magazine, *Ramparts,* ran a feature story on the Jeannette Rankin Brigade shortly after the demonstration. The article proved enormously controversial, in large part because of the accompanying cover photograph.[18] In place of the usual photos of celebrated radicals, demonstrations, inner-city rioting, and campus takeovers, the editors of *Ramparts* ran a photo of a woman's torso, with her breasts very clearly the focal point. The faceless model—young and slender, yet well-endowed—wore a skin-tight black leotard with a "Jeannette Rankin for President" button just above her right nipple. Although the *Playboy*-like cover may have sold a lot of issues, it had very little to do with the accompanying article on the middle-aged, pacifist women of the Jeannette Rankin Brigade.

To the authors, Warren Hinckle (the president and editorial director of *Ramparts*) and his wife, Marianne, the Brigade portended the emergence of a major new force in American politics, the movement for "Women Power." What the Hinckles seemed to appreciate most about this new movement was its rejection of feminism and its embrace instead of what one might call "femininism," or the promotion of politicized femininity. In fact, they went to great pains to distinguish the Brigade women from the "narrow-minded bitches" who, they maintained, comprised the ranks of the woman suffrage movement. They also took care to distinguish the Brigade women from any contemporary manifestations of feminism. Thus they noted Betty Friedan's reservations about the essentialist assumptions of the Brigade protest, but only to assail her feminism: "[Friedan's] concept of women power, then, is assimilation to achieve a grey-flannel equality for the purpose of bettering women's estate in society by having them beat the hell out of—or at least tie—the men at the establishment game. William James called success the American 'Bitch-Goddess,' and Mrs. Friedan would have *our* women become the goddesses' acolytes." [19] The argument that feminism represented a capitulation rather than a challenge to the system became a common complaint on the Left in the late 1960s and early 1970s. It is worth mentioning that the same arguments were not raised against racial equality.

Of course, the feminist movement, not the Woman Power movement, became the major force in American politics. Nevertheless, *Ramparts* relegated the young women—who were by late 1967 beginning to organize a women's liberation movement and whose youth and style it could be argued that the magazine cover captured—to the end of the article and discussed them largely in terms of their good looks and colorful dress. The Hinckles's patronizing dismissal of them as the Left's "miniskirt caucus" angered many radical women. Letters (and at least one article by Chicago women's liberationists Evelyn Goldfield, Heather Booth, and Sue Munaker that went unpublished) poured into the *Ramparts* office. The cover prompted one woman to write, "If you had a cover on Black Power like your cover on Woman Power, it would have been a picture of a sharecropper with a harmonica in one hand and a piece of watermelon in the other." The Hinckles's treatment of the WLM was characteristic of the male-dominated Left, and, of course, not at all like that accorded to advocates of black power. Indeed, New Left men accepted black radicals' arguments for self-determination and the centrality of race. They balked only when women began applying the logic of black power to themselves. Over time, the Left's hostility towards women's liberation had the effect of pushing more and more women towards radical feminism.

By the fall of 1968, a year after its formation, New York Radical Women, the major women's liberation group in the city, was seriously divided along politico-feminist lines. What finally catalyzed New York radical feminists to organize apart from politicos was another antiwar action, the January 1969 Counter-Inaugural Protest, sponsored by the National Mobilization to End the War in Vietnam (Mobe) to oppose Nixon's inauguration.[20] Although the Mobe made a speaker's slot available for a women's liberation spokesperson, it was not a high priority for the antiwar coalition, which failed even to mention women's liberation in its ad in the *Guardian* announcing the protest.

The situation almost immediately rekindled old antagonisms between the New York women, who feared that the D.C. women would "sell out" women's liberation, and the D.C. women, who feared that the New York women would unnecessarily antagonize Movement men.[21] The New York women planned to use the slot on the program to "give back the vote." According to Ellen Willis of New York Radical Women, the action would demonstrate that suffragism—which they maintained had vitiated the first wave of feminism—was dead and that a new struggle for real liberation was underway.[22] However, when the New York women discovered that Marilyn Webb had arranged for men to be included in the action, they became furious. Convinced of the D.C. women's commitment to mollifying the men, the New York women ultimately decided that there should be two speakers, Marilyn Webb from D.C. and Shulamith Firestone from New York.

However, the expectation that Movement men could differentiate between the two speeches proved overly optimistic. Even Marilyn Webb's speech, which carefully assailed the system, not men, provoked a number of men in the crowd to yell, "Take it off!" and "Take her off the stage and fuck her!" Webb recalls that "it was like a riot was breaking out." Although she does claim that some men in the crowd opposed the hecklers, that is not what emerges from most accounts. The situation deteriorated further when Firestone started to speak. The hostility of the crowd and emcee Dave Dellinger's response—rather than to rebuke the crowd, as he had done earlier when individuals heckled one of the Fort Hood Three, he tried to get the women to leave the stage—made most women's liberationists furious. After the protest Ellen Willis wondered, "If radical men can so easily be provoked into acting like rednecks, what can we expect from others?"[23]

Although both the D.C. and New York women found the experience profoundly unsettling, they drew different conclusions from it. The D.C. women wanted to remain connected to the Left, but at least some in Washington's SDS chapter had decidedly different ideas. When Webb returned home after the protest, she received a phone call from a prominent SDS leader in D.C. who warned her that if she or anyone else "ever gives a speech like that again, we're going to beat the shit out of you wherever you are."[24] Webb found herself, as she put it, "cut out of" SDS in D.C., and as a consequence, both she and others in the local WLM were forced into a more independent stance. But some of the D.C. women's liberation activists, clinging to the idea that women's liberation groups should work with the Left, continued to work against the war.

In contrast, many of the New York women who had taken part in the Counter-Inaugural Protest concluded they should organize an independent radical feminist movement focused exclusively on women's issues. They did not object to women's remaining involved in the Movement as individuals; rather, they objected to the idea that women's liberation should remain an arm of the Left. In response to Webb's description of women's liberation as an arm of the Left, New York radical feminists asked, "Are we to be the 'arm' of a revolution, without asking who is the head?"[25]

Reuniting with the Left was possible, but only after women had established their own autonomous movement and men had come to acknowledge the seriousness of their claims. Soon after the action, Firestone wrote a letter to the *Guardian,* in which she declared: "We say to the left: in this past decade you have failed to live up to your rhetoric of revolution. You have not reached the people. And we won't hitch ourselves to your poor donkey. There are millions of women out there desperate enough to rise. Women's liberation is dynamite. And we have more important things to do than to try to get you to come around. You will come around when you have to, because you need us more than we need you. . . . The message being: Fuck off, left. You can examine your navel by yourself from now on. We're starting our own movement."[26]

And indeed they did. Shortly after returning to New York, Firestone and Willis formed the first explicitly radical feminist group, Redstockings. Within a year there would be several radical feminist groups in the city, and within two years the largest would number four hundred members. Women's liberation, as Firestone had predicted, had become dynamite.

• • •

Why was the Left so dismissive of women's liberation? Obviously, women's liberation hit male radicals where they lived. It demanded a restructuring of personal life and renunciation of male privilege. But the hostility is also inseparable from that particular overheated historical moment that felt to many like a revolutionary apocalypse. The relentlessness of the war, coupled with the government's repression of the black movement, led to a revolutionary nihilism in which almost anything short of "picking up the gun" seemed impotent. The personal, prefigurative politics of the early 1960s could not survive the war and the hardening that followed repression, nor could the assumption that one should organize around one's own oppression, as SDS struggled to transform itself into support troops for the black movement. In this climate of totalism, women's liberation seemed not merely trivial, but dangerously diversionary.

Murray Bookchin has argued that the war killed what was distinctively new about the New Left. Rather than providing the most important stimulus to the sixties phenomenon, as many have asserted, it actually "prevented sixties movements from developing slowly, organically, and indigenously into lasting, deeply rooted American phenomena." According to Bookchin, the war encouraged a return to "shopworn ideological dogmatism" and the embrace of an anti-imperialist politics that seemed more precisely anti-American.[27]

The war presented a paradox. Although it was a crucial stimulus to oppositional thinking and protest, its relentlessness helped discourage the personal, prefigurative politics that had fostered feminist consciousness and might have provided the possibility for a "feminist radicalism."[28] In helping to kill the distinctive newness of the New Left, the war contributed to the development of a women's liberation movement and radical feminism. While radical feminism's autonomy accounts for its tremendous originality and vitality, it also explains in large part its greatest weakness—the tendency of radical feminists to isolate male dominance from other forms of oppression. They saw themselves expanding rather than rejecting Left analysis. However, the Left's dismissal of women's liberation as bourgeois and its insistence upon class as the primary contradiction led feminists to develop their own litany, in which gender, not class or race, stood as the privileged category. And that litany, as much as anything, impeded feminist efforts to create a truly multicultural, multiclass feminist movement.

12

The Women Who Left Them Behind

NINA S. ADAMS

Three major social movements that dominated the 1960s—the civil rights movement, the antiwar movement, and the women's liberation movement—converged, then separated, as successive U.S. governments escalated the war in Vietnam. The war itself, usually seen as a young male experience, affected the lives of persons who were neither young, nor male, nor part of the military. The antiwar movement, usually portrayed as a creation of young white males, involved an equally diverse range of persons.

The three movements had more in common with each other than any of them had with previous social movements. Their demands ranged from reform to revolutionary transformation, and their models for activism occupied a continuum from respectable to outrageous. All three movements and their heirs and offshoots, as Barbara Epstein points out, "fail to fit paradigms of either traditional Marxism or conventional academic social science."[1] Groups other than the working class formed the core of each. Means and ends were connected in anarchist ways rather than separated as in socialist practice. The 1960s movements emphasized building community, secondary to achieving specific goals. Since then, direct action movements have extended their rejection of the individualist stances and politics of individualism of the antiwar movement.[2]

In retrospect, however, what distinguishes the feminist and civil rights movements from the antiwar movement is their success in changing the legal, social, and political worlds in which their participants operated. The antiwar movement, in contrast, created a powerful climate of dissent, unprecedented in any nation during wartime. It generated compelling critiques of North American imperialism, the war-making agencies, and the elites that exploited the poor and, particularly, people of color at home and in the Third World.

Although the intellectuals and militants in the antiwar movement included different colors and both sexes, the central issue remained the war. Once that had ended, the antiwar movement failed to sustain a push toward major changes in the assumptions and institutions of the national security state. It left discernible and valuable legacies, but it did not transform life in the United States to the same degree and with the same continuity that the civil rights and women's movements did.

The civil rights movement, however, made issues of racial justice and equality—and clashes between the two—central to both conventional and radical politics. Racism still dominates and buttresses the major institutions of North America, but evidence of its decline can be noted by academics, politicians, and ordinary people scrutinizing their daily lives. The women's movement—diffuse, splintered, sometimes diluted, and often chaotic—has put down roots and built supporting networks in unlikely corners of the nation and traditional institutions even as they resist feminist transformation.

During the Vietnam War, many thought the wave of revolution had arrived in the United States. The simplest prediction of the outcome—whether the war continued or the movement succeeded in bringing it to an end—was that radicalism would move to a central place on the political agenda as each wave of persons affected by the movement insisted that its ideas and programs be adopted. Few expected that any of the items on the agenda would appear under the rubric of feminism or that feminism itself might supplant earlier radical traditions.

Feminism has become a recognized, viable ideology that builds from and shapes social practice. The passage of time and increasing concern with women's lives and work has led to defining all issues as women's issues, not merely by asking what happens to women, but by placing feminist perspectives at the center of discussion. Poverty, for example, must be seen as a women's issue requiring a feminist perspective to examine it. That examination must lead to analyzing the structural causes of poverty, the uses of gender ordering, and, therefore, concern with the ideology and impact of the International Monetary Fund, the World Bank, the Agency for International Development, the United Nations agencies and other male-created and -dominated institutions that the Left has long criticized on a very different basis.

All issues are women's issues in consequence if not yet in formulation. When examining issues and movements, activists must reiterate Cynthia Enloe's question, "Where are the women?," and accept her argument "that women's lives are worth considering not only for the sake of detailing the impact of militarism and imperialism, but also for the sake of clarifying their basic underpinnings; how U.S. power locks into existing power relations within the countries it seeks to control."[3] The 1960s question, "What is the position of women in the movement?" (which Stokely Carmichael satirized and for which he then unjustly took the brunt of the blame),[4] has been replaced by Charlotte Bunch's question, "How does the feminist movement relate to Marxism or other social change movements?"[5]

The Vietnam War's effect on men in the black community, and the split within the civil rights movement that led some to active opposition of the war, have been written about extensively, but black women are seldom mentioned. The question of what it meant to be an African-American, male or female, was posed in increasingly deadly terms. Meanwhile, the war, opposition to the war, and the Vietnamese model of struggle pushed numbers of blacks into seeing themselves as oppressed Third World people, not just a minority in the United States. The same factors, plus the growing influence of the women's movement, led black women in the civil rights and antiwar movements to see themselves as doubly oppressed when black nationalism began to refashion patriarchal family systems as the ideal. White women were accused of losing sight of the larger class struggle and the need to oppose an imperialist war. Black women were pressured to stand by their men in order to avoid racist exploitation.

The flourishing of ideas about women's liberation and black liberation might have led to the creation of coalitions had it not been for the continuing existence of deeply embedded racism. Thus, the black antidraft movement and opposition to the Vietnam War operated separately from the white movement, which received most of the attention in historical accounts.

In an ideal world, those who opposed the war as an outgrowth of imperialist and "masculinist" power trips would have shared a common cause with those women who had to deal with the impact of the Vietnam War on men to whom they were connected by blood or affection. It is not surprising that this did not occur. As the war became increasingly unpopular, so did the radicals and demonstrators. The lines between doves and hawks, drawn by the media and emphasized by the politicians, did not soften. Antidraft slogans like "Girls say 'yes' to men who say 'no,' " left no door open to women whose men, because of race and class, had never been able to consider saying "no" to the Selective Service System or to duty in combat rather than in support units.[6]

The women, mostly white, who left the antiwar and civil rights movements for a movement of their own did so in search of theory and practice that further developed their values and power by including them. Politically sophisticated insights acquired within the civil rights and antiwar movements focused their feminism, which emerged in scattered letters and manifestos after 1965. It was further strengthened by the negative reaction of too many men on the Left, with their increasing emphasis on macho models and draft resistance, on political combat rather than political struggle. Women became increasingly conscious of the disparity between rhetoric about the liberation of others and oppression of and by themselves within the movements to which they committed themselves. Women's work as field directors, grassroots organizers, counselors, writers, and fund raisers was consistently disregarded or invalidated within the most prominent movement organizations. Men received credit for being the risk takers and the ones responsible for whatever the movements had achieved.[7] The phrase, "the extent of your resistance is a measure of my oppression," came into being after its reality had already been demonstrated.

Nonetheless, it is important to remember that the women did not leave either the civil rights or the antiwar movement for selfish reasons or in fits of pique over trivialities, although they have been accused of both. Women had reason to be grateful to the civil rights and antiwar movements for creating a space in which significant numbers of politically conscious women collaborated, exchanged ideas, and supported one another. Women had perfected skills in the public sphere by focusing on issues that both women and men regarded seriously.

Many women who left or distanced themselves from these movements did so more in sorrow than in anger. Rage is entirely absent from Casey Hayden's and Mary King's two catalytic pieces, writings that began the discussions and activities that formed the radical wing of the women's liberation movement. In her insider's account of the Student Non-Violent Coordinating Committee (SNCC), often overlooked, Mary King describes the slow process of reading and thinking that led her and her friend Casey to recognize pervasive sex discrimination and the historic devaluing of women. They began with Simone de Beauvoir and kept on reading. Their tentative analysis blossomed as they worked within rural southern communities where strong African-American women, as well as others, saw women as capable leaders, steadfast militants, and crucial organizers.[8]

Although Sara Evans's pioneering work, *Personal Politics,* made a rare error in stating otherwise,[9] King and Hayden were not reacting to a lack of status in the movement. They believed in the "beloved community" and in the SNCC work style that allowed every issue to be debated. The two women raised women's rights issues within that work-style just as it was disappearing, for reasons King outlines carefully in her book. Her disappointment at SNCC's reaction ran deeper than dismay that men had ridiculed the issue. She saw instead the demise of the approach that had challenged conventional definitions of power and leadership at the same time that SNCC confronted the terrifying institutions of segregation. She wrote: "Our second document was in part a call for a return to the fundamental values of the sit-ins and the early vision of SNCC, according to which any community should be free to define its own political agenda, spark its own local movement and raise up its own leaders."[10]

"A Kind of Memo from Casey Hayden and Mary King to a Number of Other Women in the Peace and Freedom Movements," dated 18 November 1965, summarizes "recurrent ideas or themes" and calls for discussion and analysis of male domination as a system that dictates women's roles in political work and personal lives. "The average white person," they wrote, "finds it difficult to understand why the Negro resented being called 'boy,' or being thought of as 'musical' and 'athletic' because the average white person doesn't realize that he assumes he is superior. And naturally he doesn't understand the problem of paternalism. So, too, the average SNCC worker finds it difficult to discuss the woman problem because of male superiority.... Assumptions of male superiority are as wide-spread and deep-rooted and every much as crippling to the woman as the assumptions of white supremacy are to the Negro."[11]

The memo identifies the need to criticize as well as to confirm basic institutions, including but not limited to marriage and child rearing. It then raises the question of men's reactions and the difficulty of discussing women's issues when men are present: "That [male] inability to see the whole issue as serious, as the straitjacketing of both sexes, and as scientifically determined, often shapes our own response so that we learn to think in their terms about ourselves and to feel silly rather than trust our inner feelings. The problems we're listing here, and what others have said about them, are largely drawn from conversations among women only—and that difficulty in establishing dialogue with men is a recurring theme among people we've talked to."[12]

Hayden and King drew some parallels between the treatment of women and people of color but saw "women who work in the movement caught up in a common-law caste system that operates subtly, forcing them to work around or outside hierarchical structures of power which may exclude them. Women seem to be placed in the same position of assumed subordination in personal situations, too."[13] They saw women as victims of a system, just as people then called Negroes found themselves victims.

Other women in the antiwar movement made a similarly subjective identification with the Vietnamese as victims of white male violence. Many North Americans turned against the Vietnam War in repugnance at the sight of the world's most technologically advanced country subjecting one of the world's poorest to the brunt of that technology. The older as well as the younger American women who traveled to Vietnam or met with Vietnamese delegations in Canada and Eastern or Western Europe received sympathy and support. For peace movement women from cities far from the New York–Washington axis of the women's liberation movement, the overseas meetings opened a new set of possibilities. In brief meetings, representatives of the National Liberation Front, the Provisional Revolutionary Government, and the Democratic Republic of Vietnam emphasized the role of women. They insisted not only that women be included in any delegations sent by North American peace organizations but also that there be women in specific women's delegations to meet with women from Indochina. The Vietnamese often asked that women speak first to overcome their socially conditioned reluctance to speak out.[14] Some American women, stunned but exhilarated, found this a transforming experience.

While respect for women as equals was less the norm in Vietnam itself than it appeared at international meetings, the consciousness-raising effect of these encounters was a crucial memory for several antiwar women. Upon their return, they were also struck by the disparity between the loving concern they had developed for individuals they met and the Vietnamese people in general and the more abstract style preferred by their white male colleagues. What later came to be termed "women's ways of knowing," the moving from experience to analysis without disconnecting feelings, the men rejected with impatience in favor of more "hard-headed" approaches to work in the peace movement.[15]

Students for a Democratic Society (SDS), which has received as much attention as if it were the antiwar movement itself rather than a small but articulate portion of it, was an organization of competitive, intellectual students with less progressive ideas about gender order than those of the Old Left. Its emphasis on combative argument was far from unique in the antiwar movement. Within the leadership, "from the beginning it was clear in SDS that the intellectual work was primarily a male task. No one said it in so many words, but then no one made a direct challenge to the shared cultural assumption."[16] The women who worked within SDS and other antiwar organizations recognized that men set the tone and that few women could demonstrate the verbal aggressiveness so highly prized. They did not yet have the feminist theory and research to analyze it; at the time, they merely reacted.

Mary Field Belenky and other feminist researchers have since described the ways in which approaches to learning and self-expression vary by gender. Presenting a challenge excites male competitiveness but discourages most women, who have been socialized to share and listen. Women learn more easily when they are asked to build on their own experience, to collaborate in solving problems, and to pause for reflection. Studies of patterns of female and male communication reveal other differences in mixed groups. Without outside intervention, men dominate in mixed groups unless they are overwhelmingly outnumbered. Men are quicker to speak and they interrupt more. They tend to speak to compete rather than to share in building a set of collective ideas. The more polite Vietnamese norms and a different presentation of masculinity made interaction with male Vietnamese easier for North American women than active debate with their colleagues in the North American peace movement.

The Vietnamese provided a significant model in other ways. The success of the National Liberation Front depended upon meticulous mobilization within every stratum and across class lines. Any group—peasants, women, or youth—was taught to become aware of its specific collective interactions with the Saigon government and the American war machine. For example, the demands made by mothers of political prisoners or widows with orphaned children—as well as the wider goals of the entire population—would be met if the revolution succeeded. If the Saigon government prevailed, these aspirations would be crushed, along with the people who held them.[17]

The revolutionary Vietnamese took seriously the notion that initially people had to organize themselves. Every struggle for social change had several components. Each area of struggle required a different style of organization and form of mobilization. Local people could mobilize when outsiders could not. The model of women organizing women meshed with one of the lessons whites had learned in the later years of the civil rights movement. With the rise of black power, non-African-Americans had been sent out of the black-led movement. When these white veterans of SNCC and related movements recovered from their pain at being expelled, they understood that their role was primarily to uncover and eradicate racism in their own communities. Although those defined as outsiders by color or class could assist in the process, local people remained the most effective organizers. African-Americans could develop organizations for their own struggle. So could women.

Black leaders who helped their communities to survive never believed that racism was purely a local problem or that it could be separated from issues created by national institutions with international as well as domestic interests. In order to cope with the external dimensions, however, communities had to be both united internally and joined together by common goals. Then they needed white allies to alter the power structure and to make their case in arenas from which blacks were still barred. Similarly, the Vietnamese had no need of an international brigade. They needed U.S. citizens to struggle with the Congress, the Selective Service, and Western media.

Vietnamese revolutionary organizing had followed a parallel path. Village people initially concerned only with their own safety and future eventually identified their local needs with the broader struggle for peace and justice. Nationalism and internationalism had ramifications that reached simultaneously down to the local village and out to the world. Nationalist leaders in Vietnam viewed colonialism and imperialism as related to internal feudalism. Vietnam was one place in which the actors gathered to resolve a set of struggles that started and ended far from, as well as within, Vietnam. In this same way, the women's movement began locally and personally, and then connected itself to themes and groups across classes, colors, borders, and languages.

In the antiwar movement, as in Vietnam, people working within their own communities organized most effectively. Most women who had direct contact with the Vietnamese were local organizers rather than nationally known speakers. The justification for struggling on behalf of one's gender and the belief that few will fight as hard for one's cause as one will oneself heralded a new Vietnamese approach.[18]

Not all of the white women who met with the Vietnamese switched their major focus from the peace movement, but many loosened their ties to male-dominated organizations and devoted time to women's issues.[19] The antiwar movement grew rapidly in the late 1960s. Small peace groups that might have been able to accommodate the sudden articulation of women's liberation issues grew too quickly to deal with the procedural problems that emerged when sexist practices came into question.[20] On the one hand, action-oriented groups grew uncomfortable with both the theory of interpersonal roles and the expression of personal feelings. On the other hand, intellectually oriented groups responded to tentative female initiatives about opening dialogues with requests for complete ideological analyses and critiques of current theory and practice, not realizing that the theoretical tools and polemical devices being used were themselves part of the problem. The confrontational either/or model that the Left had favored for decades and the preference for debate over sharing was inspired by white males (and found on the male Right as well). Emerging feminists rejected this model as male colleagues demanded that it be used. Most women could not yet document why the style made them so uncomfortable.[21] Neither could they yet collectively enforce an alternative style, even in nontraditional, nonhierarchical organizations.

Women of the civil rights movement knew of other ways to argue without being antagonistic. For white women with less exposure to alternate forms of collective decision making, the demand that they beat the men at their own game could only drive them from the white male Left. Feminism was an ideology in the process of becoming, not yet as complex and fully developed as socialist or anarchist theory. The second wave of feminists were explorers, retrieving past writings, going overseas for ideas, and proceeding on the basis of their exchanges with each other in small groups. The meaning of "the personal is political and vice versa" remained to be defined even as it attracted women to whom it offered what had been missing on the Left after the Marxists became the dominant wing of socialism. A handful of feminists, including Wilma Scott Heide, believed feminism to be a broader term than socialism, encompassing rather than competing with it. Most men and angry feminists could not agree with that formulation.

The women's liberation movement pioneered a method of organizing and mobilizing that contrasted directly with Leninism and even anarchism.[22] Mass meetings and workplace gatherings were few; the women's liberation movement organized small consciousness-raising groups, sometimes leaderless, sometimes not. When the eight to ten women gathered each week, they spoke in turn, without interruption, about the agreed-upon topic—adolescence, dating, self-image—focusing on socialization from their earliest memories to the present. Active listening, rather than debate, became the goal. Being listened to without interruption or challenge was an entirely new experience for almost every woman. Sessions concluded with discussion of the process as well as the conclusions that could be drawn from what had been said. Comparing experiences instead of reading texts made the issues real, allowing women the possibility of choosing to deal with them on a more abstract or activist level, or both.

Consciousness-raising groups differed enormously from traditional cells, although both comprised units of a movement. The groups built trust among strangers, allowing a safe place in which to deal with fears, biases, and ignorance before confronting an outside world disdainful of females and antagonistic to their increasing demands to be heard. Combining personal disclosure and group exploration of issues was a highly political act, for it dealt with the issues of power and subordination. But nothing further from the typical Old Left or New Left political meeting could be imagined.

These antiorganizational tendencies had been prefigured, most notably in Women Strike for Peace (WSP), whose communist members had found in it a gratifying contrast to party discipline.[23] WSP members insisted upon decentralization. They organized meetings to be informal enough so that real discussion could occur. Consensus rather than voting was the ideal; there was no line to which all had to adhere. Decentralization and consensus offered a substitute for the Communist party structure that had no place for women outside the paid workforce.[24]

Disclosing and analyzing one's past and one's socialization led to subjective, and later objective, understanding of the political implications of personal roles and the politics of male dominance. Earlier social change movements had emphasized release from subjectivity as one became conscious of being part of a class. Methods used to pursue the same objective—women becoming conscious of themselves as women while the working class became conscious of itself as a class—appeared anathema to white male intellectuals whose relationship to the male and female working class had always been problematic, more symbolic than real in the 1960s.

The small groups, circle techniques, and emphasis on process in the women's liberation movement turned out to be powerful tools for extending and strengthening the nascent movement. Women's consciousness of themselves as oppressed, dismissed, or scapegoated had been dormant for years. That consciousness—certainly as real as the proletarian consciousness Marx had posited—and the anger that came with it were waiting to be tapped; the proof is the speed with which the women's liberation movement organized itself. Formal and informal groups and chapters sprang up throughout the United States and Canada, sometimes on the basis of word of mouth, a small advertisement in a local newspaper, or a notice on the wall of a laundromat.[25]

The white male Left reacted with confusion, expressed as anger. White women demanded recognition of their issues, persons, theories, and potential, and men did not know how to respond constructively. Memory of a sense of betrayal is prevalent among women who moved from civil rights and antiwar groups to the women's liberation movement. Robin Morgan's "Goodbye to All That"[26] still springs from the page with the same vivid anger as when she wrote it. When men argued the triviality of women's issues, feminists responded by insisting that privilege, domination, and humiliation were the equivalent of war. These casualty figures seem convincing today, when a woman is beaten every fourteen seconds, and one is raped every ten minutes of every day in the United States. For the women feminists of the second wave to have again postponed working on the issue of women's rights would have been to accept the increasingly intolerable status of victim.

While true for the white women who left the men of the white male Left behind, the situation for women of color was quite different. African-American and Native American women began their feminist work from within identifiable and reasonably united communities that had already dealt with a range of practical and theoretical issues about personal and political power available to minorities or disenfranchised majorities. Outspoken women were respected, women working outside the home were the norm, and many of the psychological issues that white women faced for the first time had already been tackled by their African-American or Native American counterparts. Asian-American women raised similar issues in a different context.

While recognizing issues of sexism to be important, women of color were reluctant to frame the issue as one of gender apart from the racial context. Men of color, too, found their lives and their dignity imperiled by institutional racism. Women of color understood that for every point at which they and the white women's movement coincided in aims and ideology, half a dozen others existed where there was neither common language nor common cause.[27]

The developing women's liberation movement and the theory building that accompanied it soon posed a choice for white women. In 1965, Hayden and King had written: "Objectively the chances seem nil that we could start a movement based on anything as distant to general

American thought as a sex-caste system. Therefore, most of us will probably want to work full time on problems such as war, poverty and race."[28]

Their first supposition soon proved wrong. Their suggested course of action became increasingly untenable. White women would work with women's liberation—looking within themselves, their families, their relationships, and their communities—or remain within an intransigently male-dominated antiwar movement.

Their choice, however, was not between issues but between opposing political ways of life.[29] Feminists who began to study the system of patriarchy seldom understood at the start the complexity and resistance to change of that system. As the definition of what was political expanded to include what had been private or unimportant issues, all political and daily life had to be reconstructed.

A model existed for thinking through the issues: Virginia Woolf's *Three Guineas,* published in 1938 and reprinted at intervals since 1966. Woolf contemplated her possible responses to three appeals for her help in preserving world peace: donating money, donating ideas, and donating active work. She then considered the difficulty of contributing ideas when women had little chance to enter higher education and circles of policy making. Because men controlled the purse strings, even donating money seemed hard to envisage. And action meant working through male-dominated institutions in male-dominated public spheres, joining as a permanent junior with the aim of becoming like men.[30] As long as women remained outside of the public sphere, men would dominate that, too. The result was a hierarchical division of labor by sex that characterized the entire society in terms of masculine dominance and feminine subordination. This in turn encouraged the notion—and then the reality—of dictatorship and war as ordinary and acceptable. As Woolf looked for the best way to struggle against fascism and all it portended, particularly for women, she thought it impossible to prevent war without changing the gender order that admired it in England, as well as in Germany and Italy.[31] Her causal linkage—sexism, domination, war—was unpopular among the male antifascists of her time.[32]

One of Woolf's intellectual heirs, Cynthia Enloe, developed the analysis further in an attempt to account for the "militarized peacetime" of the 1970s and 1980s. Enloe documents how the U.S. military and the general militarization of society depend on rigid gender ordering. The military's psychological and political power rests on constructing definitions of masculinity and femininity that complement each other. Females must be protected and passive so that males can be made aggressive as their protectors. Men must abandon women to wage war, but women are vital to rationalizing and supporting war.[33]

The men who opposed the war machine and its logic were not ready to substitute a feminist vision for the establishment views they had discarded. More important, their activities mirrored those of their opponents in control of the state and its agencies. They held fast to a win/lose view of human affairs and placed a premium on militaristic language in expressing aggression toward opponents, even within their own circles. Things were to be "smashed" rather than altered and "soft" lines spurned. Personal issues, even when threatening, were to be disdained as trivial.

Women's liberation began with personal reactions to personal treatment and indoctrination that kept women in their place. Dealing with the issue of dominance and subordination in political and work settings was part of dealing with patterns that oppressed women in their personal lives, particularly when the three became so intensely connected within the political community.

But coming to terms with the issue of dominance and subordination meant that women began with the hardest, least abstract task: confronting those closest to them. It was more difficult to struggle with allies, family, friends, and lovers on one's own behalf than to storm the Pentagon, denouncing its warriors on behalf of the Vietnamese. Few precedents and no guides existed for the process. Confronting the war machine could mean physical pain inflicted by those from whom one expected only aggression. Confronting a loved one threatened the infliction of emotional pain that would take longer to be forgotten.

Few of those who broke away in the late sixties or early seventies retained their anger with male comrades or themselves. Most women chose to continue to work on issues of peace and justice with men as well as among themselves. But to this day, few of these women trust the white male Left except in limited coalitions and on particular issues. Many of those who joined the feminist movement have later never expressed any interest in discussing what feminism and the Left might have or do in common.

The antiwar movement had dissected what was then termed the "war machine," a set of institutions and imperatives rooted in issues of economics and power that extended their reach to wound and distort individual psyches. The women's liberation movement reversed the order of the dissection, beginning with the individual, and expanded the resulting analysis to a different set of ideas about primary and secondary causes. This analysis brought about a realization that the war machine incorporated a multitude of cousins, many of whom had been previously defined as neutral relatives or benign onlookers.

The debate around these differing analyses of the war machine continues. The need for redefinition took women away from the antiwar movement and into a politics and theory of their own. They were not the same when they returned to deal with global issues—but then neither were the myriad movements for peace, justice, and freedom that the antiwar movement left as its legacy.

PART FOUR

The Antiwar Movement in the Schools

Introduction

No area of American society was more affected by the antiwar movement than its educational system. Most of the leaders and foot soldiers of the movement were university-based; many of its major activities, from teach-ins to demonstrations, took place on university campuses. Students and their professors who opposed the war also protested against the Reserve Officers' Training Corps (ROTC) and classified research programs, and advocated sweeping curriculum and governance reforms. During this period of unprecedented turbulence, hundreds of colleges experienced massive boycotts and strikes and some even suffered the burning or "trashing" of buildings. The two chapters in this section involve several dimensions of the antiwar movement in the educational system.

In chapter 13, Kenneth J. Heineman examines campus politics at Kent State University during the sixties. The national media tended to concentrate their attention on protests and riots at more prestigious universities, such as Harvard, Yale, Columbia, Michigan, Stanford, and Berkeley. Thus, most Americans were surprised when Ohio National Guardsmen killed four students on 4 May 1970 at a rather obscure university not previously known for antiwar demonstrations. Heineman, an historian, reveals how an active New Left cadre developed at the university in the years before the tragedy. Moreover, he contends that its harassment and persecution by school administrators contributed significantly to conditions that led to the events of 4 May. He reminds us that beyond the Ivy League and the Big Ten, the antiwar movement and New Left dramatically affected hundreds of other campuses and their surrounding communities.

Not all the antiwar action in the educational system took place at the post-secondary level. In chapter 14, Charles F. Howlett, a specialist in peace history, explores the legal battles instigated by students and teachers who spoke out and organized against the war in public school systems. These battles frequently involved free speech, a fundamental issue that antiwar and religious dissenters raised during the First and Second World Wars. Howlett tracks the cases from the classrooms to the courts that ultimately expanded the boundaries of free speech and political activity in the schools. As with many university reforms, these cases demonstrate the lasting impact of the Vietnam antiwar movement on another important area of American society.

These chapters touch upon only some aspects of the antiwar movement in our schools and colleges. As the Vietnam generation assumes leadership positions during the present decade, its experiences on the campuses, as well as in Southeast Asia, are certain to shape American political and cultural life.

13

"Look Out Kid, You're Gonna Get Hit!"

Kent State and the Vietnam Antiwar Movement

KENNETH J. HEINEMAN

On 4 May 1970, the Ohio National Guard fired into a crowd on the campus of Kent State University, killing four young people and wounding nine others. In thirteen seconds of gunfire, Kent State became an international symbol of antiwar protest and government repression. As the wounded and dead lay upon the ground, the strike movement initiated to protest the American military invasion of Cambodia immediately increased: 4,350,000 students at 1,350 universities and colleges participated in demonstrations against the shootings and the escalation. In the aftermath of this unprecedented upheaval, which compelled President Richard M. Nixon to reconsider future escalations, Kent State administrators and faculty, as well as the national news media, made great efforts to convince the public that the university had always been a quiet place, untouched by student radicalism and antiwar protest. The shootings, they insisted, were an aberration in tranquil Kent, Ohio. The image they sought to project, however, was inaccurate.[1]

> The Kent State University Archives' May 4th Collection contains fragmentary materials on the university's SDS chapter. Most date from the fall of 1968, with the bulk pertaining to 1969 and, of course, 1970. There are no Kent Committee documents in the archives. Consequently, for the pre-1968 period, I have had to rely upon a few, sometimes flawed, secondary works; Sidney Jackson's papers in the archives; oral interviews; and the campus newspaper, the *Daily Kent Stater*. Although former activists may be biased, the campus newspaper is even more biased because its editors, until the fall of 1969, were ardently prowar and provided undercover agents to the local police. Hence, the newspaper either ignored or denounced the Kent Committee. Kent State president Robert White's papers have been sealed from the general public and scholarly viewing. We may never know exactly what was happening in the administration in the 1960s, although its actions spoke as clearly as secret memos.

During the post–World War II era, a dramatic expansion of higher education and a general acceptance of New Deal liberalism took place, even though anticommunism exercised a chilling effect upon universities, as well as upon government and private social reform initiatives. In Ohio, however, there was sustained resistance to funding higher education and an ingrained suspicion of liberalism. Most Ohio Republicans had vigorously resisted the New Deal and, after World War II, refused to reconcile themselves to the moderate-to-liberal sentiment in both national parties. In the early 1960s, while other midwestern states such as Illinois, Indiana, Michigan, and Wisconsin led the nation in appropriations for construction in institutions of higher education, Ohio lagged far behind. Dominated by conservative, rural interests, the Ohio legislature viewed universities as unnecessary expenses, as well as potential breeding grounds for communist (often meaning "liberal") subversion.

After Ohio State University physicist Byron Darling invoked the Fifth Amendment before the House Un-American Activities Committee (HUAC) in 1953, the legislature overwhelmingly passed a bill to dismiss any public employee or teacher affiliated with "a communist or subversive organization." Republican state auditor James Rhodes promised to withhold appropriations from Ohio State unless Darling was immediately fired. Ohio State promptly dismissed Darling, as well as other faculty, expelled "radical" students, and banned "communist" speakers from the campus. Furthermore, the Ohio Un-American Activities Committee, established in 1951 by the state legislature, held numerous hearings to investigate communism at the universities. Kent State, which did not knowingly hire potentially troublesome faculty, avoided the wrath of Rhodes and the Ohio Un-American Activities Committee in the 1950s.[2]

During that decade, Kent State students exemplified the label "The Quiet Generation" given to their peers at other schools. By the early 1960s, however, the forces of change had started to overcome the university's cultural inertia. Kent State's expanding student enrollment, from five thousand in 1954 to over twenty-one thousand by 1966 (the nation's twenty-seventh largest university), and the construction of more dormitories signalled Kent's transformation from a commuter and teacher's college to a residential and academically comprehensive institution. The only public university in the area until the mid-1960s, Kent drew students from the region who either could not afford to attend or could not gain admission to the more exclusive Oberlin College or Case Western Reserve University. Consequently, the sons and daughters of Akron, Cleveland, and Youngstown blue-collar workers and business people dominated the student body. As in most American universities, the majority of students in the 1960s were from Northern and Western European backgrounds. One-fifth of the student body, however, claimed Southern and Eastern European ancestry. This high proportion, compared to other land-grant colleges such as Michigan State and Penn State, underscored the humble class origins of many students. Less than 5 percent of the student body was Jewish, a number lower than at more prestigious universities.[3]

Standard works on the white student movement of the early 1960s assert that activists clustered at prestigious universities that had a large proportion of middle and upper-middle-class Protestant and Jewish students. Although Kent State seemed an unlikely place to have a student movement, one did develop there. Tony Walsh was its dynamo. The son of Irish Catholic immigrants, Walsh had been placed in a Cleveland orphanage at an early age and later taken in by an uncle who had served in the Irish Republican Army. Settling in Cleveland, Walsh's uncle had become involved in the struggle to unionize Republic Steel in the 1930s.[4]

After being drafted in 1958, Walsh was stationed at Fort Benning, Georgia, where he developed a distaste for Southern racial discrimination. Having spent his formative years in an orphanage and then with an activist uncle, he had acquired profound sympathies for the oppressed. His desire to further the causes of social justice and cultural diversity was realized when he enrolled at Kent State as an honors student. Along with several other members of the Cleveland NAACP at Kent State, Walsh founded a university chapter of the Congress of Racial Equality (CORE) in 1963. Although it claimed no more than twenty members, the organization began to disrupt the university community and become controversial. The president of the student government resigned in protest after his fellow representatives officially recognized the "communist-front" group. Kent State CORE activists initiated campaigns to integrate city swimming pools and, in the fall of 1963, formed an ad hoc committee on free speech that successfully challenged the university's ban on campus political activities. The organization also protested against university dress codes and the policy of *in loco parentis*. Walsh himself was elected to the student government. These activities took place months before the Berkeley Free Speech Movement that, according to conventional wisdom, marked the birth of white student activism.[5]

The university's student activists in 1963–1964 were an ideologically diverse and politically persecuted group. Not altogether facetiously, Walsh described himself as an "Irish Catholic Bolshi" who summed up his political philosophy in this advice to protestors: "If it feels good, do it." One of his opponents in the student government saw in that statement the seeds of anarchy and communism. Orthodox Marxists in the CORE chapter gravitated towards English instructor Bob Ehrlich, leader of the Young Socialist Alliance (YSA). A veteran of the Southern Freedom Rides, Ehrlich tended to be somewhat paranoid because his political activities could have led to his dismissal from the university. Hostile local newspaper publicity added to his sense of vulnerability. The *Record-Courier* made it a point, beginning in 1963, to print the home addresses of YSA members as well as to point out that the group was on the U.S. Attorney General's list of subversive organizations, an assertion that publisher Robert Dix, also chairman of the Kent State board of trustees, knew to be false.[6]

After a visit to Kent in the fall of 1964 by a State Department representative who defended President Lyndon B. Johnson's Indochina policy, Walsh and Ehrlich founded the Kent Committee to End the War in Vietnam. The committee had fewer than a dozen members, among whom was Joseph Jackson, the son of the group's faculty advisor, Sidney Jackson. In the early days of the Kent Committee, few faculty supported the peace group; many professors felt anxious lest they appear to be sympathetic to the organization. Indeed, as late as April 1967, Ehrlich could convince no more than thirty-five faculty members to sign an antiwar advertisement in the *Cleveland Plain Dealer*. This represented a mere 4 percent of the faculty, a strikingly low figure in comparison to the 25 percent of Michigan State's faculty endorsing a similar antiwar petition in February. Unlike many other universities, the Kent State campus peace movement was primarily student-led; the handful of antiwar faculty, particularly in the late 1960s, exerted only limited influence on activists.[7]

The Kent Committee's advisor, library science professor Sidney Jackson, had become radicalized in the 1930s while a student at Columbia University. Concerned with Hitler's rise to power, disillusioned with the New Deal's fundamental economic conservatism, and inspired by Stalin's efforts to build a socialist state, Jackson joined the Communist party. A Jew, he was also attracted to the party because of its strong stands against anti-Semitism. Sincerely believing that Americanism and communism were not incompatible, Jackson enthusiastically enlisted in the armed struggle against fascism. His ability to reconcile Stalin and George Washington did not impress the FBI, which after World War II made repeated calls to his home. Soon placed on an academic blacklist, he could not obtain a teaching position in New York.[8]

Desperately needing qualified faculty for its expanding library science program, Kent offered Jackson a position in 1959. Apparently impressed with his Ivy League credentials, the administration did not do a thorough background check. For five years Jackson seemed the epitome of the dedicated, relatively apolitical academic (he did, however, maintain a one-sided correspondence with President John F. Kennedy, chastising him for his Indochina policy). After Jackson received tenure in 1964 and with it some measure of job security, he set out to organize boycotts of segregated swimming pools in Kent, to coordinate civil rights protests, and to work closely with the Kent Committee. As a Marxist and a Jew, Jackson cooperated with Kent's other outsiders—blacks, Catholics, and Quakers—who did not fit the city's Protestant Republican mold. His son received a great deal of abuse from hawkish faculty; one history professor, for example, took pains to inform his class that there were "Stalinists in our midst."[9]

The Kent Committee launched its attack against American involvement in the Vietnam War in February 1965 as Walsh, YSA member Dave Edwards (the son of an Ohio labor union organizer), and ten other students participated in a campus peace picket. One hundred hawkish students mobbed the activists and threw YSA secretary Barbara Brock to the ground, kicking her in the face. Passions inflamed, the hawks "wrenched signs from the hands of the picketers" and confiscated and burned antiwar literature that the committee had brought to the demonstration. Shocked, one campus police officer, a friend of Walsh's, acted on his own to rope off the protestors in order to prevent further assaults. However, the crowd simply retreated a few dozen yards and then launched rocks and other projectiles at the terrified "communists." Kent State president Robert White, who had been teaching at the university since 1946 and looked fondly back upon an era when the school had been smaller and the students conformed to Cold War political and social mores, declined to take disciplinary action against the conservative assailants.[10]

The Kent Committee and the YSA nevertheless continued to demonstrate on the campus, while Walsh and Joseph Jackson doggedly spoke out against the war in the dining halls. Ehrlich fired off a great number of antiwar letters to the campus newspaper, the *Daily Kent Stater*, most of which never reached the printing press. Their efforts were not entirely unsuccessful. By April the Kent Committee's weekly peace vigils attracted up to twenty participants, as opposed to twelve, and thirty-six Kent State students attended the SDS-sponsored Washington demonstration on 17 April. Hawkish students continued to assault and ridicule the activists, but at least now there were a sufficient number of committed protestors to fend off random attacks. They also began to take the precaution of traveling in small groups rather than alone, both on and off the campus.[11]

The university community and the townspeople lashed out against them. In April, President White described the Kent Committee's organizers as publicity-seeking martyrs and argued that the YSA's goals "are distasteful to the overwhelming majority of us. Similarly, the mass of students within a true university process will come to see the shallowness of its arguments." Following the president's lead, the editors of the *Daily Kent Stater* taunted the committee and advised hawkish students to refrain from violence because enduring abuse only made the activists appear mature, respectable, and sympathetic. The campus newspaper, as well as the *Record-Courier*, featured numerous hawkish letters and in May publicized the Kent State Young Democrats' and Young Republicans' two-hundred-student prowar rally. In addition, many community residents and faculty expressed their feelings in hateful letters to Sidney Jackson. The professor responded to correspondents who signed their names.[12]

Throughout the summer and fall of 1965, antiwar and prowar campus demonstrations continued, the latter many times larger than the former. At the Kent Committee's protests against the war and ROTC that fall, right-wingers in the dormitories flew American flags from their windows as they blared "The Star-Spangled Banner" on their stereos, hoping to drown out antiwar chants. Kent Committee member Mike Van DeVere, a strong supporter of the Vietnam War until Walsh showed him the "error of his ways," sought in vain to reason with those "who attempt to crush criticism and apparently don't have any imagination and fear those who do."[13]

Weary of the unrelenting persecution the Kent Committee and the YSA faced at every protest, Barbara Brock organized a demonstration in February 1966 against the *Daily Kent Stater*'s biased and hostile coverage. Although this action had no affect on the campus newspaper's hawkish editors, it did impress a number of students and faculty who paused in front of Bowman Hall, an office building, to listen to Ehrlich's, Van DeVere's, and Walsh's pleas for fair play. Subsequently, on 10 April, faculty members from liberal arts and social science departments formed a committee on the draft and conscientious objection. Sensing a modest change in campus opinion, Walsh felt emboldened to participate in the Kent State spring parade. Transforming his "ratty '58 Dodge convertible" into an antiwar float, the committee followed the parade queen through Kent's streets. Brock passed out peace buttons and literature on napalm while Edwards and Roy Iglee, dressed in black and wearing gas masks, waved to the stunned spectators. Intrigued by the Kent Committee display, two hundred students attended a May antiwar rally on the Commons and loudly cheered the activists.[14]

Even though the Kent Committee began to attract sympathetic crowds, the number of committed activists remained small. Its ranks were depleted by Walsh's graduation and radical faculty member Barbara Gregorich's forced resignation in June as a result of her November 1965 arrest at a Cleveland Socialist Workers' party function that police had raided on the pretext that the radicals were serving liquor without a license. At the first peace vigil in the fall of 1966, a time of general quiescence in the movement nationally, only twenty people participated. The disappointing turnout did not deter Joseph Jackson from speaking at dormitory functions and maintaining an often lonely vigil at a Kent Committee literature table in Bowman Hall. His persistence began to pay off in October when a group of freshmen joined, reinvigorating the committee. Some wildly different undergraduate recruits soon played leading roles in the campus antiwar movement: Howie Emmer, the son of middle-class Ohio Communist party organizers; Rick Erickson, whose father, a former Democratic mayor of Akron, was still politically influential; Ruth Gibson, a lower-middle-class Methodist and hitherto apolitical student from West Virginia; and Jim Powrie, a working-class Irish Catholic from Indianapolis who came to Kent State on a football scholarship and had a brother in the SUNY-Buffalo Chapter of Students for a Democratic Society (SDS).[15]

The Kent Committee soon broadened the scope of its activities. During the fall of 1966, the activists brought Dr. Benjamin Spock to campus. Moreover, one student peace partisan and a professor, in cooperation with a former Kent Committee member, established an underground railroad to help draft resisters reach Canada. Peace activists also found an outlet for their energies in Kent's developing countercultural arena. The city's proximity to the Ohio Turnpike and other major highways made it a convenient way station from points east to Cleveland, Detroit, and Chicago. With the burgeoning resident student population, the city of Kent provided youth-oriented recreational establishments. Easy access and the youth market attracted rock 'n' roll and jazz bands from as far away as Chicago, who found in Kent's remarkable number of bars a place to work on their acts before breaking into the bigtime. Joe Walsh haunted Kent's taverns, developing his sound, and one of Lou Reed's cellophane-wrapped performers studied at Kent State, spending her summers with the Velvet Underground in New York. An iconoclastic musical subculture developed in conservative Kent when Kent Committee members Bob Lewis, a lower-middle-class Welsh Methodist, and Jerry

Casale, a working-class Italian Catholic, sought to fuse leftist politics with rock. Throughout the 1960s the fame of Kent's bar and musical scene spread throughout the Midwest, making the city a magnet for student revelers, teenage runaways, and activists. The city's residents, however, became increasingly torn between their desire to make a profit from their student "tourists" and their fear that "pot-smoking communists" would corrupt law and order.[16]

By the spring of 1967, the campus peace movement had made notable headway. One hundred fifty students journeyed to New York City for a massive April antiwar rally, and the Kent Committee had persuaded 240 undergraduate and graduate students to sign an antiwar advertisement. The Kent Committee's weekly campus peace vigils also began to bring out an average of thirty picketers. But the activists realized that there was still much work to be done. In a referendum on the Vietnam War sponsored by the student government in March, 727 of 1,185 students (61 percent) who cast ballots favored military escalation. Moreover, Ruth Gibson was beaten by community residents for wearing a peace button, and Joseph Jackson was roughly ejected from a bar for engaging in a debate on the war.[17]

In the fall the spirits of antiwar activists were dampened when Kent police began to come onto the campus to photograph picketers. Kent State security officer Donald Swartzmiller argued that it was vital to photograph Kent Committee members in order "to protect the university from professional demonstrators." Elaborating on this theme, Kent police chief Roy Thompson stated that the officers were searching for outside troublemakers, presumably nonstudent "tourists." The chief also informed city residents that "they got a lot of these people over on that campus who I don't suppose are plain communists, but an awful lot of them are pinkos." Campus security officer Leroy Peace also had been attending Kent Committee meetings to tape activists' conversations. Ruth Gibson decried political surveillance as "a form of intimidation and harassment." She also wryly observed that "it seems kind of ridiculous to look for professional demonstrators on this campus where there have never been any before." The activists soon learned that the Kent police had entered the campus at White's invitation as well as on the behest of the Cleveland field office of the FBI.[18]

Campus, city, and federal police agents began to pay attention to the Kent State antiwar movement because it had become larger and, therefore, more threatening to the anticommunist university president and board of trustees. Two hundred Kent State students, the largest contingent yet, marched on the Pentagon in October 1967 to "confront the warmakers." Jim Powrie and Howie Emmer came away from the Washington confrontation with significantly different perspectives. Powrie found the night he spent on the Pentagon grounds "romantic and terrifying." The burly Irishman, sympathetic towards the U.S. soldiers who surrounded the demonstrators, perceived that they were, like him, "scared working-class youth hoping to avoid violence." Education, not confrontation, Powrie believed, would end the war that continued to kill his relatives and hometown neighbors. Emmer, on the other hand, had vigorously charged into the soldiers that day and, in an exhilarated state thereafter, argued that students "have to be willing to engage in creative forms of disruption such as non-violently sitting in."[19]

While Emmer began to advocate confrontational tactics, Gibson maintained faith in peace education. The Kent Committee received encouragement in this endeavor from the campus Newman Club, which sponsored lectures by Catholic clergy on the "immorality of the Vietnam War"; from Rev. William Jacobs of the United Christian Fellowship, who counselled students on the draft; and from Rev. Peter Richardson of the Kent Unitarian-Universalist Church, who founded the Yellow Unicorn Coffeehouse, which featured antiwar speakers and folk music. Several young faculty recently recruited to the university—in particular, Ken Calkins, a former Lake Forest College SDS advisor—joined with the Kent Committee to promote the university's first Vietnam teach-in in November. The teach-in attracted two hundred students, a small number compared to similar events at other universities. It was a solid, albeit tardy, beginning: by this time teach-ins had become passé on most campuses. Moreover, the teach-in encouraged additional faculty to voice their opposition to the war publicly.[20]

As dissent seemed to catch on, and as respectable clergy and a few junior faculty identified themselves with the peace movement, greater numbers of students began to use the campus newspaper as a forum in which to criticize campus hawks. Overwhelmed by the volume of antiwar letters, prowar *Daily Kent Stater* editors felt compelled to publish more than what had been usual. Outraged, campus student government politico Frank Frisina warned that the newspaper and the Kent Committee were in league with the communists to undermine the Free World.[21]

Inured to campus criticism by this point, the committee went beyond peace vigils to active protest against military and corporate recruiters who came onto the campus. In November, seventy-five students spent two hours peacefully demonstrating against a Dow Chemical

Company representative who was conducting interviews in Stopher Hall. As Emmer read aloud the group's statement, which detailed the physical suffering that Dow-produced napalm inflicted upon the Vietnamese, spectators flung mud at the demonstrators and tore away and torched several of their "Dow Burns Babies" placards.[22]

The early months of 1968 were a time of both great success and great frustration for the Kent Committee. Antiwar education forums in the dormitories, as well as determined picketing, contributed to raising political consciousness on the campus. One thousand students participated in a campus memorial march for Rev. Martin Luther King, Jr., in April, and 240 canvassed in Indiana in May on behalf of Robert F. Kennedy's primary campaign. However, several activists, although encouraged by the fact that more students had at last become politically engaged, were not at all pleased that they had embraced a liberal-dovish, rather than a radical New Left, intellectual approach to the Vietnam War. Kent Committee members also took little comfort in the realization that while many students on campus opposed the use of napalm in Vietnam, only forty had chosen to brave harsh winter weather in February to picket Dow recruiters.[23]

Emmer, George Hoffman, and Vince Modugno, critical of the Kent Committee's leadership for clinging to ideological and tactical moderation, which, they contended, had so far failed to build a mass campus movement, established an action-oriented SDS chapter. As some of the Kent Committee members drifted into SDS, Gibson and Joseph Jackson attempted to increase the committee's visibility on the campus and to champion its moderate, pacifist principles. In late April they organized an antiwar rally on the Commons that featured local folk singers and dovish clergy speakers. While a few hundred students reclined on Blanket Hill, a recreational area near the Commons, hawkish "jocks" in Stopher Hall shot high-powered air rifles into the crowd, wounding both Rev. Peter Richardson and a Roman Catholic priest, the latter of whom required hospitalization.

After committee secretary Carol Carson complained to campus security officers, the administration had Gibson arrested for chalking a rally notice on the library. Charged with vandalism and violating White's decree against publicizing the rally on campus, she was taken to the Kent police station. Alone and frightened, the normally perky activist "broke down and cried." However, White made no effort to prosecute Stopher Hall's vigilantes once they had been identified. Campus radio director Bob Carpenter praised the hawkish students and White for turning the tables on the committee that for so long had infringed upon Dow's constitutional rights. He also claimed that Gibson had been impregnated by various campus subversives. Subsequently, SDSers pointed to Gibson's "feminine weakness," and to White's indirect encouragement of rightwing vigilantism as compelling arguments for a more militant and "masculine" campus radical organization.[24]

Seizing the initiative from the moderates in the rapidly fading Kent Committee, SDSers in May staged a dramatic protest against Vice-President Hubert Humphrey, who was speaking at the Memorial Gymnasium. On cue, 150 white and black students, the latter belonging to the recently established Black United Students (BUS), marched out of the gym. The vice-president, who angrily compared the demonstrators to the "racist Dixiecrats" who had walked out of the 1948 Democratic National Convention, then led the audience of 10,000 in a noisy booing and hissing session. Joseph Jackson, completely "turned off [by] SDS live theatre," was less concerned with the audience's ugly reaction than with the SDS-led heckling that had preceded the walkout. This denial of Humphrey's right to speak sent a "chill down [his] spine" and led Jackson to view the radicals as elitists dedicated to silencing those who did not "buy [their] line." Powrie, who had refrained from heckling, plaintively responded that the protest "was not to victimize Mr. Humphrey nor deny to him the right to speak. . . . It was, quite simply, an act of conscience [directed against] a supporter of an illegal and immoral war that continues to kill hundreds of people daily." Powrie, however, did not speak for SDS. Emmer and Erickson reasoned that imperialists like Humphrey had no right to free speech and, indeed, had to be silenced.[25]

Buoyed by the successful anti-Humphrey protest, Emmer and Erickson drove to Michigan State University to participate in the national SDS convention. At East Lansing they were attracted to Chicago activist Bernardine Dohrn, met with Michigan SDSers Bill Ayers and Jim Mellen, and re-established contact with Columbia radical Mark Rudd. (Erickson had become acquainted with Rudd while visiting Columbia during its celebrated spring student uprising.) Once they had purged the Ann Arbor SDS chapter of those opposed to "aggressive, confrontation politics," Ayers and Mellen created a network of Michigan-Ohio SDS travelers.

Excited by Emmer's accounts of the awakening white and black student movement at Kent and attracted to the town's flowering counterculture, Terry Robbins—a Kenyon College dropout who, Carl Oglesby observed, thought he was Butch Cassidy to Ayers's Sundance Kid—made the university his base of operations. Robbins and the wealthy Ayers donated a printing press that enabled Kent State and the Northeast Ohio SDS to publish their own newspaper, *Maggie's Farm*. Further assistance, in the form of a lease on a Cleveland office building for the Michigan-Ohio SDS travelers, came from Emmer and from activist Mark Lencl's parents, who were also former Ohio Communist party organizers. Armed with Black Panther and Third World revolutionary communist principles, as well as with the collected works of Bob Dylan, Emmer and Erickson set out in the fall of 1968 to intensify the struggle at Kent State. Interestingly, the Kent State SDS "house" where Erickson lived had been the model for the Bates Motel in Alfred Hitchcock's *Psycho*.[26]

To Emmer and Erickson's delight, 250 Kent State students came to SDS's first fall meeting. In many respects, the SDSers were atypical of the student body. While 17 percent of the student body claimed out-of-state residency, 41 percent of the SDSers came from outside Ohio. Furthermore, 51 percent of the SDSers resided in large cities such as Cleveland and New York, compared to 17 percent of the overall student body. Jewish students, comprising almost 20 percent of SDS at Kent, were disproportionately represented. Unlike other campus chapters, such as SUNY-Buffalo, Michigan State, and Penn State, Kent's SDS included a substantial number of Southern and Eastern European Catholics (18 percent), a reflection of the university's ethnic base. The defunct Kent Committee had fewer members from metropolitan areas (32 percent) and from out-of-state (28 percent). Also, the Kent Committee claimed nearly twice the proportion of graduate students and somewhat fewer females, though both organizations were dominated by undergraduate males.[27]

Only two dozen of the students who joined the Kent State SDS in the fall had been Kent Committee members. By far the majority had had little previous contact with the campus antiwar movement. Ken Hammond, a working-class suburban Cleveland undergraduate, did not associate with the activists until the spring of 1968, when he met Emmer and Modugno in a class. But it took the King and Kennedy assassinations, as well as the violent Democratic National Convention in Chicago, to make him angry enough to join SDS. Similarly, Alan Canfora, a sophomore whose father was a Barberton, Ohio, Democratic councilman and vice-president of his UAW local, became politically active only that fall. Even then, Canfora moved slowly into the SDS camp, while maintaining ties to the Kent State Young Democrats. His roommate after the first quarter of school, Tom Grace, a Syracuse, New York freshman, eventually followed

Canfora into SDS, but neither embraced, nor completely understood, New Left ideology.[28]

Grace and Canfora received their first exposure to SDS action tactics in October. Traveling with the Young Democrats to protest a Nixon appearance at the University of Akron, the two youths watched in awe as two hundred Kent State and Oberlin SDSers in the balcony of the hall shouted "Ho, Ho, Ho Chi Minh, NLF is Gonna Win." Canfora turned to Grace and, calling the rather staid Young Democrats "really lame," suggested that they move up to the balcony. Sensing that the "SDSers were more effective Nixon haters than the Young Democrats," Grace agreed. When the SDSers began to chant "Sieg Heil!" Nixon pointed to the balcony and vowed that decent Americans in November would "shout down the protestors." The audience wildly applauded and then, during a moment of silence before Nixon resumed speaking, an SDSer called back to the podium, "You fucking asshole!" Canfora and Grace accompanied SDS back to Kent—the former enormously impressed by the radicals, the latter far less enthusiastic. After all, it was difficult for a self-described "Cold War Democrat" and Irish Catholic parochial school graduate to identify readily with such a radical and indecorous movement.[29]

Having staged, according to *Time,* the "most successful disruption" of a Nixon speech since the beginning of the fall campaign, SDS began to expand its campus activities. Because Ayers, Dohrn and Robbins had decided that blacks represented the American "revolutionary vanguard," Emmer and Mark Real, a former Catholic seminarian, forged an alliance with BUS. In phrases that could have been written by Dohrn and Robbins (and probably were), Emmer described "the American empire [as] *institutionally* racist and violent" and argued that "the black community in America is in fact a colony within the mother country and is *excluded* as such." It was up to white students, Emmer continued, "to build a *white* radical movement," which, aligned with the Black Panthers, would overthrow the power structure. In order to accomplish this goal, he concluded, SDSers had "to get our white shit together."[30]

SDS got its "white shit together" in November, blockading the Placement Office to protest the presence of two Oakland, California, Police Department recruiters. Considering the Oakland police to be racists who persecuted Black Panthers, Emmer and 150 SDSers joined 150 BUS members in a five-hour sit-in. Real came to the Placement Office with a portable loudspeaker and vowed that any white student in the building who did not join the sit-in "would be considered a member of the Kent police force." Exactly what he meant by that statement required little imagination; Emmer and Erickson took the Viet Cong concept of revolutionary justice very seriously.[31]

President White, calling the SDS-BUS demonstration intolerable, filed legal charges against Emmer, Erickson, and eight other activists. Meanwhile, a few hundred hostile students gathered outside the office screaming, "Kill the nigger-lovers!" Gibson, uncomfortable with SDS's tactics but a sit-in participant nonetheless, asked several sympathetic faculty to escort demonstrators out of the building through the angry crowd. Their presence, however, did not deter several dozen counterprotestors, armed with motorcycle chains, from pursuing and severely whipping the activists. Campus police and administrators made no attempt to halt the beatings, and none of the hawks was charged with assault.[32]

Angered by the vigilante violence, as well as by the administration's actions, BUS leader Bob Pickett, a native of Perth Amboy, New Jersey, resigned his position as vice-president of the student government and convinced 250 black students to leave the campus. As all but a dozen black students marched off the campus to "political exile" in Akron, White and his subordinates issued press releases and circulated presidential bulletins among the faculty, accusing Pickett of physically coercing the majority of blacks into joining the walkout. SDS quickly organized a teach-in on racism and demanded that the university grant amnesty to the protestors.[33]

The majority of faculty, as well as the editors of the *Daily Kent Stater*, urged White to punish the SDS and BUS leaders. Only Sidney Jackson and sociologist Tom Lough openly praised the radicals for publicizing the issue of racism. In reply, many SDSers derided Jackson for his notion that activists could work successfully through "proper administration channels." Furthermore, they scorned his belief in the fundamental goodness of the American democratic political system, viewing his politics and religious observance as "bourgeois counter-revolutionary." SDSers were also annoyed with Jackson for accepting the word of the director of the campus Liquid Crystals Institute that the organization performed no military research at the university. Jackson's belief that one academic would not lie to another seemed incredibly naïve to the activists.[34]

Trying to stave off an investigation of his administration by the Ohio Civil Rights Commission, White decided within a week of the BUS walkout to drop all charges. SDSers were exultant, feeling that, in Ken Hammond's words, "a real victory had been won." Grace, who had declined to join Canfora in the sit-in, was duly impressed with the walkout, which convinced him that "if people joined together in numbers and stuck together," the forces of social change would triumph. Bob Pickett, however, came away from the November action with quite a different outlook. He had not been impressed by the SDS "actions" that had preceded the Oakland Police recruiting demonstration, including an invasion of a classroom in order to counter the teachings of a hawkish political scientist as well as an anti-ROTC protest in which activists ran alongside of cadets, screaming, "Kill, Kill, Kill!" The black student leader and his followers thought that SDS had used BUS as a shield to protect themselves from administration retribution and to further their own political agenda. They also came to the conclusion that Emmer and Erickson wanted "to live their fantasies out" and garner headlines for themselves. After BUS returned to campus, cooperation between the two groups diminished and Pickett soon became an outspoken antiwar liberal dove and critic of SDS.[35]

Powrie shared BUS's disenchantment with the SDS leadership. Although trained by Robbins to operate the SDS printing press, he did not identify himself with the Ayers-Dohrn "revolution now" or action faction. Strongly opposed to the potentially violent confrontations that Emmer, Erickson, and Robbins had staged—and planned to stage in the future—Powrie contended that the chapter should seek to recruit liberal doves and organize peace education forums such as an SDS Free University. Seeing merit in Powrie's ideas, Hammond coordinated dormitory draft counseling and antiwar information sessions. Gibson and Melissa Whitaker, wife of SDSer Bill Whitaker, also pleaded with Erickson to eschew violence and be more sensitive to gender issues. Erickson, who resented assertive women, pointedly ignored Gibson's entreaties, regarding her as "a pain in the ass." He also flippantly dismissed Whitaker's feminist concerns as nothing more than an insignificant "pots and pans revolution" when compared to the heroic anti-imperialist struggles of the Viet Cong and the Black Panthers. In the same vein, Emmer accused Powrie of being a timid liberal who would sell out to the Establishment "if he could find a good buyer."[36]

To underscore their commitment to action and "revolution," Emmer, Erickson, and Robbins organized a fifty-member SDS contingent that went to Washington in January to protest Nixon's inauguration. The Kent State activists gathered in Franklin Park, and, as the presidential procession approached, someone in the crowd threw a bottle at Nixon. Washington police charged into the demonstrators. Not anxious to be clubbed, Canfora and Grace broke into a run and wound up in the black ghetto that both considered "a much safer place to be than Pennsylvania Avenue." The police arrested four Kent State SDSers and severely clubbed a young woman who had crossed their path. Having witnessed this vicious and unjustified beating, Grace returned to Kent State even more opposed to the Establishment and the war.[37]

Canfora and Grace began to frequent SDS functions, including films, slide shows, and lectures. Both were stirred by SDS's Saturday morning "educational discussion on ROTC" and the links between "foreign imperialism abroad" and the domestic repression of the internal American "black colony." But they were far less impressed by the increasingly acrimonious debates between Powrie and Emmer. The friends also received an unexpected shock when, at one meeting, Jim Mellen contended that "we have to really get down to the serious business of developing a Young Communist movement in this country." Feeling the pull of their Catholic, anticommunist upbringings, Canfora and Grace left the meeting at the first possible moment and stayed away from SDS "for a week or two." But they had a change of heart, with Canfora arguing that "SDS was the only group on campus that was coming out with any concrete analysis of things, especially the war, and they weren't afraid of action."[38]

Emmer and Erickson began to formulate tactics that winter for the coming Spring Offensive at Kent State. While they intended to demand the abolition of ROTC, they also turned their attention to the research being done at the Liquid Crystals Institute. Established in 1965 with support from the U.S. Air Force and Army and the Department of Defense's Advanced Research Projects Agency, the Liquid Crystals Institute had received an $800,000 Project Themis grant in 1968 to develop liquid crystal detectors for the military. Prior to the university's acquisition of the Themis grant, the U.S. Department of Health, Education and Welfare had been Kent State's chief source of federal funding. After 1968 the Department of Defense became the university's major federal benefactor.[39]

Characterizing the Liquid Crystals Institute and ROTC as "institutions [of] genocide" that repressed "people of color all over the world who are struggling against exploitation and oppression by the American ruling class," three SDS representatives asked to meet with White on 8 April 1969. After he refused to talk to them, 250 SDSers marched to the administration building, where 700 hawkish students intercepted them. When fistfights between the hawks and the outnumbered radicals broke out, the president quickly ordered the arrest and suspension of Emmer and Erickson. He also banned SDS from the campus. A few days later, standing on top of an overturned trash can, Mellen warned jeering campus hawks "that the revolution has begun, [and] if you get in the way of that revolution, it's going to run right over you." Two hundred SDSers, insisting that Emmer and Erickson's closed suspension hearings be opened to the general public, then marched to the Music and Speech Building. There they clashed with 300 conservative students, some of whom were armed with baseball bats. Discovering an unlocked side entrance to the building, the SDSers proceeded to the third floor. Once they arrived at the hearing room, the activists learned that the university had stationed a large number of state police troopers in the basement of the building. Trapped and facing arrest, many SDSers were rescued by a sympathetic professor who led them to a service elevator that the police had overlooked.[40]

Making their escape, Canfora and Grace were relieved to have been extricated from White's entrapment. Fifty-nine not-so-fortunate activists, however, were arrested and later placed on trial, some facing sentences of up to three years for conspiracy, trespassing, and riot. The local chapter of the American Association of University Professors, a body committed to maintaining academic freedom, endorsed White's actions and castigated SDS. Faculty activist Ken Calkins also condemned the radicals. Even more galling to the activists was the discovery that university radio reporter Maggie Murvay, who had been covering SDS activities since the fall of 1968, had also been working as an undercover Kent police informant. Murvay and White both journeyed to Washington to testify on "communist subversion" at Kent State before the House Internal Security Subcommittee (formerly HUAC). During her testimony, the campus reporter named dozens of activists, focusing particularly on Jewish SDSers. The congressional committee shared Murvay's obsession with Jewish radicals and also commented on the ties Emmer and Mark Lencl, both Jewish, had to the Communist party through their parents. If it was any consolation to antiwar activists, three thousand hitherto inactive students, outraged by the administration's heavy-handed tactics as well as by hawkish student violence, rallied in support of SDS. Paradoxically, the FBI also helped out, persuading the telephone company to continue service to the Kent SDS house, which they had been bugging, even though the activists had failed to keep up with their bills.[41]

Affected by their campus experiences, Kent State activists made their presence felt at the June 1969 national SDS convention in Chicago, where Dohrn and Mellen announced their manifesto to the convention: "You don't need a weatherman to know which way the wind blows." The

Weatherman Manifesto, as it became known, condemned counterrevolutionary white working-class Americans, praised the Black Panthers, and exhorted SDSers to emulate the Viet Cong by waging guerrilla warfare in the United States. As three hundred Weathermen marched out of the convention, the majority of them from Michigan and Kent State, Michigan State SDSer Dick Oestreicher wryly observed that "in an organization [SDS] known for its crazies, Kent State SDS was in a class by itself."[42]

The Weathermen appointed Kent State SDSer "Corky" Benedict to its National Interim Council, while Emmer, Erickson, Lencl, Colin Nieburger, Real, and Robbins assumed national Weathermen leadership positions. Deciding to bring word of the revolution to Ohio's oppressed blacks, the Kent State Weathermen established communal houses in Akron, Athens, Cleveland, and Columbus. In the Columbus commune, under Emmer and Erickson's command, the Weathermen committed such revolutionary acts as "marching with an NLF flag through a local park" on Independence Day and spray-painting the walls of a high school with slogans such as, "Off the Pigs," "Viet Cong Will Win," and "Fuck U.S. Imperialism." Because the men in the house were busy with these activities as well as hanging out on street corners, "rapping about the revolution," one female SDSer had to obtain a job in a striptease club in order to pay the rent. The situation was the same in Akron, compelling Kent State SDSer Robin Marks, the daughter of a successful New York City writer, to obtain employment as a barmaid in a tavern. One night the Akron radicals urged everyone to get guns to fight the police. Appalled, Marks argued with the commune's leaders and then, when shouted down, fled. The Akron commune soon collapsed, and the Columbus Weathermen were driven from their house by their unresponsive, impoverished neighbors. Adding insult to injury, Columbus police authorities charged the Weathermen with having fanned the flames of the city's race riot on 21 July. A few months later, in October, Emmer and Benedict were arrested for their roles in the Days of Rage trashing of Chicago.[43]

Disturbed by the direction in which SDS was heading, Powrie spirited the chapter's printing press off to his brother in Buffalo so that it would not fall into Emmer's hands. He and his supporters also began to carry baseball bats in case of an attack by the Weathermen. A May attempt at reconciliation failed when Powrie and Hammond invited Emmer and the Weathermen to share ice cream and comradeship. Seizing upon the fact that Powrie had served vanilla instead of chocolate ice cream, Kent State Weatherwoman Bobbi Smith, who was white, denounced him as a racist. The irony of the Kent State Weathermen and anti-Weathermen relationship was further driven home with the 1970 trial and conviction of the activists for their roles in the 1969 Spring Offensive. Powrie, the advocate of education and nonviolence, received a one-year sentence to an institution for the criminally insane. Emmer and Erickson, the proponents of violent revolution, served no more than forty-five days of jail time and were released a few days before the burning of the Kent State ROTC building, which prompted the Ohio National Guard to occupy the campus. Powrie's father was a meter reader, Erickson's a former Akron mayor with influence in the Ohio Democratic party. [44]

With the beginning of the 1969 fall session, White discovered that his efforts to crush student activism had backfired. The cumulative impact of four years of escalating war, as well as university and community hostility towards even the most politically moderate activists, had outraged and mobilized a hitherto unthinkable number of students. Viet Cong flags were displayed in the windows of the Tri-Towers dormitory complex, and its halls became filled with marijuana smoke. Liberal dovish student government representatives, led by Craig Morgan, began to denounce the Vietnam War and President White. The new editors and reporters of the *Daily Kent Stater,* sickened by the role their journalist colleagues had played as police informants, followed Morgan's lead. Pickett and Hammond wrote special antiwar columns, and both eagerly cooperated with Morgan to organize a 15 October Moratorium peace march in Kent. Three thousand students demonstrated and five thousand boycotted classes to listen to Joe Walsh and The James Gang perform antiwar songs. [45]

Nevertheless, opposition to the campus antiwar movement remained vehement. In an April 1969 referendum sponsored by the student government, 4,745 students endorsed White's banning of SDS from the campus, while 3,012 students opposed it. Campus opinion continued to polarize into the fall. Hawkish student government president Frank Frisina distributed anti-SDS "scare circulars" on the campus, urged the Portage County prosecutor's office to clamp down on student radicals and "dope dealers," and accused Morgan of promoting communism at Kent State. White entered the fray, condemning SDSers and "bleeding heart" student liberals who gave comfort to the radical "culprits." The president also refused to cancel classes in recognition of the October Moratorium. Finally, community residents and student hawks continued to assault and denounce antiwar activists. [46]

As the campus antiwar movement coalesced, events were taking place in Columbus that would have serious ramifications for Kent State. Ohio legislators had drafted antistudent riot bills calling for investigations of antiwar activism at the state's universities. Major General Sylvester

Del Corso, commander of the National Guard, warned that the antiwar movement was part of "the international communist conspiracy" that sought to destroy America. More ominously, Governor James Rhodes, due to face the formidable Robert Taft, Jr., in the Republican Senate primary in the spring of 1970, was desperately searching for a popular campaign issue. Aware of mounting public reaction against campus activism and a desire for law and order, Rhodes decided to get tough with student demonstrators. In December 1969, after three black students at the University of Akron had staged a peaceful Black Power protest, Rhodes sent seven hundred National Guardsmen to occupy the campus. The Guardsmen provided the news media and the public with dramatic pictures that reflected Rhodes' decisive leadership and subsequently bolstered his popularity with the Ohio electorate. If any more campus disturbances developed, the governor let it be known that he was prepared to employ whatever force necessary to restore order.[47]

• • •

The final chapter of this tale unfolded on 4 May 1970. As thousands of students gathered on the Commons to protest the invasion of Cambodia, the National Guard, inspired by Governor Rhodes' earlier exhortation in Kent to punish the communist element, fired into the crowd. Alan Canfora, mourning the death of a hometown friend in Vietnam and angered by the soldiers' presence on the campus, defiantly waved a makeshift black flag. He took a bullet in the wrist. Tom Grace was shot in the foot. Loaded into an ambulance, he watched as medical attendants pulled a sheet over Sandy Scheuer's head. Almost as soon as the gunsmoke had cleared, the Portage County Grand Jury indicted twenty-four Kent State students and one professor, Tom Lough, for conspiracy to commit riot. Among those to stand trial were Ruth Gibson, who had not even been in Kent on 4 May, anti-Weathermen leader Ken Hammond, and newly elected student government president Craig Morgan. No Weathermen were indicted, only liberal doves and SDS advocates of political education. Tony Walsh, who had become an attorney, offered legal assistance to the Kent 25.[48]

For six years an antiwar movement had been painfully built at Kent State. Although initially a small movement—contrary to the image presented after the shootings by the media and particular faculty and administrators—antiwar protest had not been unknown at the university. Moreover, by 1968 the Kent antiwar movement had gained a significant presence on the campus, and the university's SDS chapter had begun to play a major role in the destruction of the New Left.

Through its hostility to peace activists and unwillingness to prosecute hawkish student vigilantes, the university administration had created an environment conducive to the escalation of violence. Moderate forces on the Kent Committee, unable to move the overwhelming majority of faculty to support the rights of minority dissenters, lost influence within the campus antiwar movement by 1968. The extremist faction that dominated Kent State's SDS chapter by 1968 was very much a creature of this environment of repression. The Weathermen may have been politically loathsome, but they represented an inverted image of the Kent community and President White.

Kent State's overwhelmingly conservative faculty, unlike their more liberal counterparts at schools such as Michigan State, eschewed their roles as mediators between students and administrators. They were content to remain silent on the great issues of the day or, if speaking out at all, to denounce antiwar activists as communist conspirators. White made few positive contributions to relations between students and the university. While most university presidents in the 1960s were vigorously anticommunist and opposed to student disruption, White stood out among his peers for his anachronistic administration of Kent State. One could be a sincere anticommunist university president and champion of law and order—such as Michigan State's John Hannah, a former assistant secretary of defense and Nixon's director of the Agency for International Development—while still promoting a measure of free speech and dissent on the campus. Hannah, like White, detested and spied upon peace activists, but he did not tolerate right-wing vigilante actions, and he was reluctant to summon police officers to the university.[49] White, in contrast, maintained a policy from 1964 to 1969 of doing nothing to stop hawkish students from beating peace activists. Through his actions, he proved right Howie Emmer's and Terry Robbins's contention that the American political system was repressive and unjust and that nonviolent protest would be met with crushing blows and hysterical denunciations.

White's failure as a leader must be seen against the background of the cold war history of Ohio and the political ambitions of James Rhodes. White could not be unresponsive to this historical and political reality. Lacking political influence in Columbus, the president also had no power over Kent Mayor LeRoy Satrom, who had summoned the National Guard to Kent State on 2 May 1970. In this sense, White was the ineffectual man in the middle, a victim of circumstances beyond his control. Had he made at least some effort to administer justice in an even-handed manner, or exhibit some kinship with the student body at large, whether in 1965, 1968, or 1970, an accommodation of sorts might have been reached. As it was, White most clearly revealed his interpretation of events before the Scranton Commission, pointing out that the state law that required all public universities to admit students with an Ohio high school diploma produced "a great deal of human debris on this campus that should never be here."[50]

Kent Committee and SDS members Bob Lewis and Jerry Casale may have given the best perspective on the 1960s and the shootings. As they hugged the ground, ducking bullets on 4 May, the two activists began to reflect on the peculiar nature of American Cold War politics and dissent. Both had been disgusted with the upper-middle-class Weathermen leaders who promoted violent confrontation, and both leftist musicians were shocked by the sight of middle-class students heaving spent tear gas canisters back towards *armed* Guardsmen. Lewis and Casale also expressed dismay at the system that had once produced "great leaders such as Franklin Roosevelt" but had since the onset of the Cold War put forth mediocre talents like Nixon and Rhodes. American society, they concluded, had regressed to the Dark Ages, and Kent State had witnessed the "devolution of a culture." Casale and Lewis founded a rock 'n' roll group, Devo, to express this idea to the public.[51]

14

Conscience and the Courts

Teachers and Students Against War and Militarism

CHARLES F. HOWLETT

> Events that occur in small towns sometimes have a way of raising large constitutional questions.
> —*Russo v. Central School District No. 1* [1972]

The nation's judicial landscape is seeded with scholarly articles and monographs discussing judicial review, due process, the first freedoms, and equality.[1] However, in the realm of free speech and conscience in the classroom, constitutional historians are just beginning to till the soil. In those issues involving education, many small-town events have raised large constitutional questions.

During the Vietnam War there were a number of court decisions affecting conscience and opposition to war in education. A discussion of legal cases that affected militarism in education, flag salutes, student and teacher protests, and use of school facilities for public meetings on world peace accentuates one aspect of the tumultuous history of academic freedom in twentieth-century America.

• • •

The judicial roller coaster ride in twentieth-century American education has been the direct result of unpopular ideas introduced in the classroom. The issue of free speech in public education has sent chills down the spines of school administrators and community leaders. In the early part of the twentieth century, improvements in the training of teachers allowed many teachers to exercise a considerable degree of freedom.

Along with this development, however, came the creation of an elaborate administrative bureaucracy making effective control of teachers possible. School leaders and powerful community groups who insisted that the business of the schools was to serve democracy constantly challenged classroom teachers interested in encouraging students' critical abilities. Not content to expect good citizenship as a result of having more informed and intellectually competent citizens, they felt it necessary to teach citizenship, democracy, and civic virtues. Thus, while it is true that the principle of freedom of speech "holds that the individual should be free from governmental threats, sanctions, or coercion directed toward prohibiting the individual from expressing himself or herself," it is also important to note that the American court system continues to accept a limited conception of academic freedom in public education.[2] Consequently, a unified theory of academic rights and responsibilities consistent with the unique institutional demands, social policies, and personal interests involved in the educational setting has never been developed.[3]

Although primarily interested in freedom in teaching as a social problem rather than as a natural right of the teacher, historian Howard K. Beale knew all too well the realities of wartime suppression of dissent. In 1936, in *Are American Teachers Free?*, he questioned the government's actions during World War I. His extensive survey concerning academic freedom led to one important finding: "The question of freedom and restraint of teachers vitally affects school children, the community, society itself, the future." Beale sadly observed that not only teachers who openly opposed the war or had formerly been known as pacifists, but "all who were suspected of not giving vigorous support to it, were subjected to local pressures, investigated, and made to give positive proof of their 'loyalty' to the war system."[4]

Intimidation and oppression characterized American education during World War I. Free speech in the classroom and respect for conscience suffered from the pressures of loyalty and conformity. The judicial system, at times ignoring the impact of these pressures, indicated reluctance to challenge restraints on classroom speech. Content with procedural regularity, courts remained relatively silent as both teachers and students fell victim to the discipline of Mars.

During World War II, judicial silence respecting loyalty and freedom of conscience continued. Though schoolteachers received little relief from the courts, a substantial breakthrough concerning student loyalty occurred in 1943. In the field of education law no case, excepting perhaps *Brown v. Board of Education*, has had a more wide-ranging impact than the flag salute ruling in *West Virginia v. Barnette*, which reversed the

Gobitis case. In the years before *Barnette,* in an 8-1 decision, the Court had declared that the state educational authority may require saluting of the flag, in the interest of "national feeling and unity," as a condition of school attendance.

The Court's dramatic turnaround was related to a West Virginia statute that required all schools to conduct courses of instruction for the purpose of teaching, fostering, and perpetuating the ideals of Americanism. A very subjective standard had been imposed on the schools. Ironically, the Parent-Teacher Association first raised objections to the salute as being too much like Hitler's. In Charleston, school officials expelled two sisters, Marie Barnett and Gath Barnett (the correct spelling of the last name), both Jehovah's Witnesses, after they refused to pledge allegiance to a picture of the flag at the front of the classroom. After the girls were called "traitors," "Nazis," "Japs," and "fifth Columnists," their father, Walter Barnett, a pipe fitter for Du Pont, petitioned the court.[5]

A change had occurred in the three years between *Gobitis* and *Barnette.* Two new justices had been appointed to the bench, and three had changed their minds, perhaps swayed by Justice Harlan F. Stone's dissent in *Gobitis.* By a 6-3 vote, the Court reversed *Gobitis* in *West Virginia v. Barnette.* Most significantly, the Court decided the case not as a free-exercise-of-religion case, but as a First Amendment, free speech (or freedom not to speak) case. The Court was slowly moving in the direction of greater protection of students' rights. Despite the serious objections of Justice Felix Frankfurter, the majority opinion, expressed by Justice Robert Jackson, has been cast in legal granite: "If there is any fixed star in our constitutional constellation, it is that no official, high or petty, can prescribe what shall be orthodox in politics, nationalism, religion, or other matters of opinion or force citizens to confess by word or act their faith therein. If there are any circumstances which permit an exception, they do not now occur to us."[6]

The *Barnette* decision addressed one basic right: free speech. However, as events would later show, the Court remained fragmented over proper accommodation between the school's authority to inculcate values and the right of students to freedom of mind and conscience.

In other matters governing conscience and the classroom, the court's latitude remained restrictive. In *Goodman v. Board of Education of San Francisco Unified School District et al.* [1941], the California Supreme Court dismissed Lillian Goodman's suit requesting an injunction against the school board for refusing to allow use of its auditorium for a speech by the Socialist party on the subject of peace. The court based its ruling on the premise that "any group that has as its object to overthrow the

United States Government shall not be granted use." The court failed, however, to establish guidelines for determining if the object of the group was to overthrow the government. Still, regarding the use of school property for outside functions, the courts have been consistent in their rulings, as later cases show.[7]

In the 1942 case of Rose K. Joyce, the superintendent of schools in Chicago suspended Joyce on charges of conduct unbecoming a schoolteacher. Joyce sued in court. Joyce had taught history at the Hyde Park High School in Chicago since 1933. The charges against her were twofold: "that she made un-American statements in her classroom derogatory to the United States Government" and "that she wrote a letter to a former student of hers who failed to register in accordance with the Selective Service Proclamation of the President of the United States, congratulating him on his 'courageous and idealistic stand.'"[8] The court upheld her suspension and ultimate dismissal.

Later, in *State ex rel., Schweitzer v. Turner et al.,* officials dismissed Edward O. Schweitzer for violating a Florida statute requiring educators to teach the "fundamental principles of patriotism." On July 23, 1943, with school out of session, Schweitzer made public his objection to war; his draft board had classified him as 4-E. The Board of Education argued that they considered his pacifist ideas "detrimental to the minds of the students in the public school system."[9]

• • •

Unquestionably, the Cold War era presented American educators with their greatest threat. The effects of McCarthyism accounted for the firings and silencings of many liberal and radical teachers from universities to public schools. Both official and private pressures brought to bear on American education were out of harmony "with traditional concepts of liberalism and academic freedom." Fear of communism, rather than opposition to war and conscientious objection, dictated the intensity of academic obedience. According to historian David Tyack; "In the past, the schools had often glorified patriotism in its military forms and had put the schools at the service of the war effort, but not until the cold war did the needs of a military-industrial complex assume lasting and great prominence in educational policy."[10]

Intimidated by McCarthyism, teachers and school systems "instead of being liberal intellectuals, alert to new ideas, became as a matter of professional survival conservative and careful in their thinking, and above all in their associations."[11] Faced with a hostile climate of opinion, few cases appeared before the courts pertaining to peace and militarism.

In terms of academic freedom, however, loyalty and oath-taking cases filled the dockets.

In Yonkers, New York, judges handed down decisions on two cases involving the use of school grounds for meetings on world peace. In both cases plaintiff and defendants were the same. In both cases the court, basing its decision on *Goodman v. San Francisco,* consistently held that "justifiable exclusion is not discrimination."[12]

The plaintiff, James R. Ellis, president of the Yonkers Committee for Peace, petitioned the court to allow his organization to use school facilities for the purpose of holding a forum on "peace and war." The Yonkers Board of Education refused the use of any of its public school buildings. The issue involved deprivation of the committee members' rights to freedom of speech, assembly, and equal protection of the laws under the First and Fourteenth Amendments. In both instances, the courts, reflecting the climate of opinion, upheld the right to withhold the use of school facilities by nonscholastic groups. Noting that previous meetings of the peace group had caused strife and dissension in the community, the courts found a convenient measure of excusability by applying the "clear and present danger" test. Ironically, the two cases failed to consider the educational importance of creating a dialogue regarding world peace. The schools remained bastions of patriotic fidelity and status quo formalism.[13]

By the 1960s, however, the courts could no longer sidestep the issue of conscience. The previous decade had presented grave problems surrounding the nature and meaning of the terms "loyalty" and "security," as well as the acceptance of legislation compatible with the prerogatives of free citizens. With the onslaught of the Vietnam War, marked by mounting protests at home, the courts "became increasingly generous toward the individual's constitutional claims as against those of a majoritarian society."[14]

Such an evolution demonstrated itself in American education. For the first time, both teachers and students found court relief not entirely contingent upon procedural due process. Although still limited in terms of academic freedom, courts acquiesced in matters of conscience that in no way materially disrupted daily school activities.

"Throughout American history," Howard K. Beale noted in 1941, "there has been a persistent purpose on the part of those supporting and controlling the schools to use the schools as a means of preserving the status quo and preventing unrest."[15] More than twenty years later, teachers and students could no longer be held in check. Legal experts, for instance, questioned the threat of student expulsion for criticizing American war involvement. Although antiwar actions on the part of college students were less subject to disciplinary action, public school students also found their own appropriate avenues of protest.[16] Public school officials looked on with dismay as legal decisions chipped away at their obligation to train obedient and faithful servants to the state.

In a series of rulings beginning in 1969, the veil of docility lifted. Most dramatically, the *Tinker* case illustrated "that the process of education in a democracy must be democratic."[17] It also became the first case examining students' free speech rights since the compulsory flag-salute case of 1943.[18]

The debate centered around a ban in the Des Moines public schools on wearing black armbands to protest the Vietnam War. Principals who heard that students planned to stage such a silent protest reacted swiftly. Any students wearing armbands to school would be asked to take them off. Should they refuse, they would be suspended until they removed them. "The schools are no place for demonstrations," one principal remarked. In the opinion of another administrator, "If the students don't like the way our elected officials are handling things, they should deliver their message through the ballot box and not in the halls of our public schools."[19]

John Tinker, his sister Mary Beth, and their friend Christopher Eckhardt knew the risks. They and their parents had met in the Eckhardt home to plan a silent "witness of armbands" from 16 December to 1 January. By wearing the armbands they would express their opposition to the American war effort in Vietnam—as well as their support for a truce.[20]

On 16 December 1965, Christopher and Mary Beth wore black armbands to school; the next day John wore his. The three, along with two other students, were suspended and sent home. Their fathers filed suit in federal district court requesting that the judge prohibit school authorities from suspending their children.

Few of the 18,000 students in Des Moines had worn armbands to school. Only five had been suspended. Outside the classroom, several students had verbally assaulted the armband wearers, upset by the protest that appeared to defame the memory of a recent high school graduate just killed in the war. But there had been no threats or acts of violence on school grounds. The school's daily routine had in no way been interrupted.[21]

The district's leaders desired to avoid dealing with the troublesome issue of antiwar sentiment. Interestingly, Des Moines school officials did not ban all political symbols. Some students had been allowed to wear political campaign buttons to school. Some had even worn the Iron Cross.

At first the federal district court dismissed the parents' complaint on the grounds that the school board had the power to implement such a regulation despite the absence of any finding of substantial interference with school conduct. The court ruled that this sort of symbolic protest might disturb school discipline. *In loco parentis* remained the court's guiding principle. When the next highest court, the United States Court of Appeals for the Eighth Circuit, divided equally, the lower court decision stood.[22]

The case finally reached the Supreme Court. On 24 February 1969, in a 7-2 ruling, the Court spelled out the free speech rights of students. Speaking for the majority, Justice Abe Fortas stated: "It can hardly be argued that either students or teachers shed their constitutional rights to freedom of speech or expression at the schoolhouse gate."[23] The disruption standard does not apply when such acts are designed to curtail a student's right to free speech. As the Tinker court observed: "In our system, state-operated schools may not be enclaves of totalitarianism. School officials do not possess absolute authority over their students. Students in school as well as out of school are 'persons' under our Constitution. . . . In our system, students may not be regarded as closed-circuit recipients of only that which the State wishes to communicate."[24]

The *Tinker* decision established the basic framework for deciding free speech issues in education. The case involved what might be termed political protest. But on what grounds did the Court reach its decision? In *U.S. v. O'Brien* [1968], the court established boundaries for the extent of First Amendment protection afforded to symbolic speech. David O'Brien, who had burned his selective service registration certificate on the steps of the South Boston Courthouse, was convicted in federal court for violating section 462(b) of the Universal Military Training and Service Act of 1948. In the course of these proceedings, the O'Brien court established a four-part test for determining when a government interest sufficiently justifies the regulation of expressive conduct. When applied to *Tinker*, it became obvious that part three of the O'Brien test did not apply: the regulation could not be shown to be unrelated to the suppression of free expression. Consequently, students received immunity from discipline unless school officials could establish that facts existed which could reasonably lead them to forecast substantial disruption of, or material interference with, school activities. The "clear and present danger" application (*Schenck v. U.S.* [1919]) had received its first modification as applied to public schooling.[25]

The *Tinker* victory did not imply that students became free to do whatever they pleased. The issue of whether the protections for symbolic speech encompass other school regulations, such as hair or skirt length or style of clothing, still remains divisive among lower courts. Free speech rights of students can be curtailed if the speech activity involves the "invasion of the rights of others." One should not forget that public schools have a significant interest in promoting respect for authority. Thus, while *Tinker* permitted the "wearing of black armbands in the classroom, it does not follow, for example, that a student may voice his opinion on the Vietnam War in the middle of a math class."[26]

Other students' rights cases followed the *Tinker* case. In *Zucker v. Panitz*, the court enjoined a New Rochelle, New York, high school principal from barring the publication of an advertisement expressing opposition to the Vietnam War because the student newspaper operated as a public forum and therefore had to remain open to free expression of ideas. The ad, which appeared in the *Huguenot Herald*, read: "The United States government is pursuing a policy in Viet Nam which is both repugnant to moral and international law and dangerous to the future of humanity. We can stop it. We must stop it." What is revealing in this case is the court's observation that the proper accommodation of students' First Amendment rights with the state's interests depends upon one's attitude toward minors: "This lawsuit arises at a time when many in the educational community oppose the tactics of the young in securing a political voice. It would be both incongruous and dangerous for this court to hold that students who wish to express their views on matters intimately related to them, through traditionally accepted nondisruptive modes of communication, may be precluded from doing so by that same adult community." Courts were beginning to recognize the free speech rights of minor students.[27]

In Dallas, Texas, a number of students decided to wear black armbands in school on 15 October 1969 in response to the Moratorium, which had issued "a manifesto to high school children elsewhere, among others, calling on them to boycott their classes that day, or attend them wearing black armbands as a symbol of protest." On the morning of 15 October, a group of students massed across the street from one of the schools, displaying a large banner reading "Try Peace." As the students proceeded to the school, the principal and assistant principals intercepted those wearing black armbands and charged them with unexcused absences. Although the school had a policy against wearing buttons, none of the school officials who testified expected the wearers of the armbands to initiate disruption. Thus, the court argued that schools have a duty to nurture constitutional rights, not extinguish them: "The use of the ancient symbol of mourning as a propagandistic device is clever precisely for the reason that it should put others differently minded on their best behavior. After all, over 44,000 Americans have died in Vietnam and all of us must mourn them. We differ only in what we think the President and Congress ought to do to end the war."[28]

Armband wearing had served as a symbolic act akin to pure speech. However, just as it appeared that the courts were moving in the direction of solidifying the free speech rights of students, a ruling in *Guzick v. Drebus et al.* suggested some backtracking. *Tinker* had established the free speech rights when matched against the disruption standard. The courts decided *Zucker* and *Butts* in the same spirit. Seventeen-year-old Thomas Guzick, an eleventh-grade student at Shaw High School in Cleveland, Ohio, claimed his First Amendment rights had been violated when he received orders to remove, while on school premises, a button soliciting participation in an antiwar demonstration in 1969. The court ruled otherwise.

Guzick's high school prohibited the wearing of buttons or insignia. A valid reason existed for this universally applied rule of long standing: with a student population 70 percent black and 30 percent white, both ethnic groups had been wearing racially inflammatory messages in school. The court applied the rule banning the wearing of all buttons to Guzick's button soliciting participation in a demonstration against the Vietnam War. "We must be aware in these contentious times," the court stated categorically, "that America's classrooms and their environs will lose their usefulness as places in which to educate our young people if pupils come to school wearing the badges of their respective disagreements, and provoke confrontations with their fellows and their teachers." No proof existed that this particular button might be the cause of disruption in the school. Because free speech is not an absolute right, however, the court used the disruption standard to limit political speech. In this instance, applying the *Tinker* standard correctly prevented Guzick from promoting an antiwar demonstration.[29]

• • •

Despite the *Guzick* ruling, students wishing to express their opposition to the Vietnam War had made significant gains. The courts, however, had been far more cautious regarding teachers' extramural speech. School became the *parens patriae,* "a substitute parent, to whom real parents delegated the task of education and the responsibility for discipline and training."[30] For that reason, school officials and the courts showed less tolerance of academic freedom for teachers: "Because students at the elementary and perhaps the secondary levels may be particularly susceptible to the influence of their teachers, serious harm may be done by a teacher who proselytizes in the classroom." [31] Yet, by the tumultuous sixties, even this view started to lose significance as schoolteachers began formulating their own strategies to protest American military action in Southeast Asia.

By this time, most teachers had been unionized and had developed a more elaborate legal structure protecting their tenured and nontenured membership. While the courts had always been vigilant regarding the protection of teachers' due process rights, the unionization movement of the late 1950s and early 1960s spelled them out more clearly. It had become far more difficult for school boards and school administrators to remove teachers for expressing unpopular ideas whether inside or outside school.

James v. Board of Education exemplified the shifting judicial interpretation from procedural regularity to safeguarding a teacher's conscience, barring no disruption of school routine.[32] Charles James, an eleventh-grade English teacher in the small village of Addison, New York, had been a minister before teaching. In November 1969 he went to a Quaker meetinghouse in nearby Elmira. Moved by the tragedies of the Vietnam War, the nontenured teacher desired to express his own moral disapprobation: "If my wearing it [black armband] could bring someone, anyone, to consider that some people do believe in the preciousness of life and dare to say so, then our world would have a better chance of surviving." [33]

James wore a black silk armband to school. He refused to obey the school board's rule that he not engage in political activities. The school district feared that his protest could result in student disruptions in school and divisiveness among the faculty. The district principal warned, "You are acting against the President of the United States, Mr. Nixon." Upon refusing to remove the armband, James was suspended and then fired in January 1970. He had few supporters. The Addison Teachers Association, the teachers' union, voted in favor of the suspension. Undaunted, James "just assumed that I had some kind of right to express my conscience." [34]

The New York branch of the American Civil Liberties Union (ACLU) came to his rescue. It initially appealed to Ewald Nyquist, Commissioner of Education, who ruled against James because he provided students with "only one point of view on an important public issue." Proselytizing in the classroom remained an anathema. The wearing of such an inflammatory symbol, Nyquist also reasoned, violated "sound educational principles" and was not "constitutionally protected."[35] James and the ACLU felt differently. "The irony of the situation," James's wife Neva pointed out, "is that quite likely Charles, for the first time in Addison, presented the other side of the issue on war and peace."[36]

James's vindication took three years and proved financially destructive for his family. Nyquist's rejection led them down a tortuous legal path. The federal district court dismissed James's complaint on grounds of insubordination. Wearing the armband in a classroom ignored state educational policy mandating "neutrality and objectivity" in dealing with issues such as the Vietnam War and protests against it.

Was a different criteria being applied to James than Tinker? The Second Circuit Court of Appeals thought so and ruled 3-0 in favor of James. The court applied two tests. First, it asked whether the wearing of the armband threatened to disrupt the classroom or the school. Here the court concluded the board made no showing whatsoever that the wearing of the armband posed any threat to the orderly operation of the school. Second, Justice Irving Kaufman asked if James's armband threatened to impair the school board's legitimate interests in regulating the curriculum. The court concluded it did not. The wearing of the armband did not interfere with his teaching of sixteen- and seventeen- year-old students.[37] The court also pointed out that another teacher in the same school "without incurring any disciplinary sanction prominently displayed the prowar slogan 'Peace with Honor' on a bulletin board in his classroom."[38] Clearly, the board had infringed on James's First Amendment right of free speech. In the words of Justice Kaufman: "The Board's actions ... indicate that its regulation against political activity in the classroom may be no more than the fulcrum to censor only that expression with which it disagrees."[39]

Although James's legal victory became assured, his ordeal with the Addison School District had not ended. Following a court-ordered reinstatement, James returned to work as a probationary teacher. Careful to obey all his superiors' directives, James still found himself without a job when his appointment failed to be renewed in June 1973. He again went to court and in July 1974 was awarded $27,000 in back pay and interest plus "reasonable legal fees." He filed another lawsuit against three school officials on the grounds that his due process rights had been violated. James and the board finally settled out of court. The $55,000 he received in return for not seeking reinstatement represented a moral, albeit costly, victory. James wore the armband "only as a symbol of conscience. I didn't do it so I would lose my job, or to hurt my family, or to be a martyr." If he had taken it off when so ordered, "I would have been without identity and self-respect. And if I hadn't fought on, I never would have felt free again."[40]

Another First Amendment case involved a probationary art teacher in New York who abstained from the recitation of the pledge of allegiance.[41] A school board policy, approved in September 1969, required the pledge by all students and teachers with a provision that "students who hold a sincere conviction giving rise to a conscientious objection to the Pledge of Allegiance shall establish this fact with a written statement indicating the reasons and rationale for such convictions. These written statements shall be signed by the student and his parents or those in parental relationship to him and shall be submitted to the principal of the school"[42]

Apparently, the board assumed that it had properly addressed the matter as ruled in *Barnette*. Susan Russo, a teacher at Sperry High School, near Rochester, New York, was dismissed in June 1970. She and another teacher, Catherine Adams, covered the same homeroom. When the pledge came over the public address system, Adams saluted the flag and recited the pledge. Russo did not, but "stood at respectful attention." Russo, dismayed by the Vietnam War, considered that her pledge would have been an act of hypocrisy: "liberty and justice" did not reflect her view of the quality of American ideals.[43]

A school investigation began in April 1970, after students and parents complained to the principal. Russo had always received excellent teaching evaluations. Subsequent evaluations, however, proved less than satisfactory. In court testimony, the principal admitted that the decision to dismiss Russo after the pledge issue came as an afterthought. Russo argued in court that her First and Fourteenth Amendment rights had been violated. Court testimony showed that Russo had in no way attempted to influence her students and no disruptions had occurred in the classroom because of her nonparticipatory action.[44]

Although Russo lost her case in federal district court, the Court of Appeals reversed the decision in 1973. She received an award of damages, the right to abstain from recitation of the pledge, and reinstatement. While the court acknowledged that schools do have a substantial interest in maintaining flag salute programs, it also made clear that "patriotism that is forced is false patriotism just as loyalty which is coerced is the very antithesis of loyalty." As Justice Kaufman concluded, "We ought not impugn the loyalty of a citizen—especially one whose convictions appear to be as genuine and conscientious as Mrs. Russo's—merely for refusing to pledge allegiance any more than we ought necessarily to praise the loyalty of a citizen who without conviction or meaning, and with mental reservation, recites the pledge by rote each morning. Surely patriotism and loyalty go deeper than that."[45]

Attempting to cause disruption in school, no matter how sincere one's convictions, is a different issue. During the first half of the the century, the courts dismissed the issue of conscience and ruled on procedural regularity. By the time of American involvement in Vietnam, conscience had been granted its day in court. Yet when conscience might lead to school disruption, the courts became far more restrictive in their rulings, as in the case of *Birdwell v. Hazelwood*.[46]

Probationary math teacher Beauregard F. Birdwell was dismissed from Hazelwood High School in rural Missouri because of an incident that occurred on 19 May 1971, when an administrator announced over the public address system that U. S. Army personnel would be in the building and invited students to speak with them. Birdwell became upset, arguing that military recruiters should have "a prior consensus of students and faculty in favor of inviting them to the school."[47] Birdwell, an army veteran who had become disillusioned about the Vietnam War, suggested to his algebra class that the students, "4,000 strong," could get the ROTC off campus. A year earlier, students at Washington University in St. Louis had burned down the ROTC building. Birdwell proceeded to confront the recruiters during a lunch break and demand that they leave. He also "encouraged students to throw apples at the army recruiters."[48]

After being dismissed, Birdwell took his case to court. Two facts worked against him. First, he disregarded an order to report to the principal's office after his confrontation with the recruiters, thus prompting a charge of insubordination. Second, student testimony in court supported the proposition that Birdwell's actions "led to disruptions of orderly and disciplined operation of the school." Significantly, the federal court took pains to point out that Birdwell's termination did not result from the exercise of his constitutionally protected right of free speech. In contrast to James, "the conduct of this probationary teacher in utilizing his algebra class as a forum from which to suggest, none too subtly, to young and immature minds that they employ measures of violence as a demonstrative device, presented a grave situation, with respect to which the Board was well authorized to exercise its implied authority."[49] Even though his actions represented an extension of his conscience, the court found justifiable cause of disruption to limit his academic freedom.

How much of a disruption did Birdwell cause, other than his own acts? Apparently, none. If so, why the difference in standard between

James and *Birdwell*? Perhaps, as the appellant's brief argued, "it is obvious that he [Birdwell] would not have been dismissed had he agreed with the school administration and told his class instead that he was in favor of having military recruiters on campus, even if some students in the class disagreed with him and voiced their objections."[50]

Although the academic freedom issue did not pose as much of a problem to college professors during the Vietnam War, one case bearing on a professor's antiwar actions deserves notice. Irving Stolberg, a former assistant professor of geography at Southern Connecticut State College, had been dismissed in 1968. In February of that year, as part of his participation in discussions regarding international political affairs, Stolberg sent fellow faculty members an invitation to support a peace program and memorial service in New Haven. The president of the college, Dr. Hilton C. Buley, considered Stolberg's views subversive. Court testimony revealed that the Board of Trustees questioned Stolberg "solely about his political and moral convictions. There was no discussion of his competency as a teacher." Justice M. Joseph Blaumenfeld found that Stolberg was discharged in retaliation for exercise of his First Amendment rights and directed the trustees to offer him reinstatement as a faculty member with tenure and no loss of seniority, and awarded him compensatory damages for wage loss. Though Stolberg accepted an appointment at another college, his case protected the right of college faculty members to send invitations to other faculty members to participate in peace programs.[51]

Since the Vietnam War, schools and campuses have remained relatively quiet. There have been cases, however, involving issues such as public forums and so-called "career days." The role of schools as public forums remains one area of judicial interpretation where the courts have been historically consistent.

In *Student Coalition for Peace v. Lower Marion School District,* a Pennsylvania court decided that a school district may exclude a student group access to its facilities if it has information that the student group intends to invite outsiders to the activity.[52] The Student Coalition for Peace (SCP) requested permission from the school board to use the athletic field for a peace fair. The peace fair was to be open to the public and include speakers on peace and nuclear disarmament, the distribution of literature, and entertainment. The school board did not want the school to become the "battleground of political ideas" and thus denied permission. SCP sought an injunction, claiming that denial violated their First Amendment rights and the federal Equal Access Act.[53]

The U.S. Court of Appeals for the Third Circuit held, however, that the athletic field was neither a traditional public forum, nor had it become a public forum by designation even though the school had from time to time let nonstudent groups use the field. In the court's opinion, "while a Bike Hike to benefit the mentally retarded may have an implicit political message, that message is plainly subsidiary to other aspects of the event, and could thus pose less of a threat either of disruption or of the appearance of favoritism. The Board is not required to delineate with absolute clarity the distinction between the political and the nonpolitical, as long as the line it does draw is reasonable and not a subterfuge for viewpoint discrimination. In particular, the Board could reasonably conclude the Memorial Day services do not create the same risk of partisan controversy as the Peace Fair."[54]

However, in *Searcey v. Harris,* the U.S. Court of Appeals for the Eleventh Circuit determined that restrictions placed upon a peace organization to participate in a school's career day were unduly restrictive and a violation of the First Amendment. In February 1983 the Atlanta Peace Alliance (APA) sent a letter to each of the Atlanta high-school principals, requesting permission to place literature in guidance counselors' offices, to place advertisements in school newspapers, and to appear at career days. In June 1983 the APA representatives met with then Superintendent of Schools Alonzo Crim, who agreed to distribute the materials to the guidance counselors and to allow the APA to set up a table at its career day.

On 4 October 1983 the school board reviewed Crim's decision and directed him to deny APA all access to the schools. APA took its case to court. After a lengthy court battle marked by numerous appeals, the U.S. court of appeals issued its decree on 21 November 1989, arguing "that the direct knowledge requirement and prohibition on criticism violated the APA's first amendment rights." The board's requirement that APA members possess "a present affiliation with the fields about which they speak" represented a direct challenge to open-mindness. Drawing upon *Brown v. Board of Education,* the court thus viewed school as "a principal instrument in awakening the child to cultural values, in preparing him for later professional training, and in helping him adjust normally to his environment."[55]

• • •

Whether American teachers are truly free remains a subject for speculation. There is considerable irony in this story. The issues involving teachers' and students' rights, the flag salute, and schools as public forums remain complicated, but a number of themes emerge. First, acknowledging a student's right to freedom of belief counters the long-held presumption that the main purpose of public schooling is to foster citizenship and respect for the basic political and social values of the nation.[56] In World War I no tolerance existed. In World War II *Barnette* opened the door. During the Vietnam War *Tinker* represented a major breakthrough, yet it had limitations. The threat, real and imagined, of possible disruption looms large in the minds of judges rendering opinions. The *Student Coalition for Peace* case, for example, is a recent reminder.

Second, courts have applied a different set of standards concerning academic freedom for college professors. Rarely have the courts been burdened with regulating a professor's views on war and peace. Though college professors endured hardships for their unpopular positions regarding war and loyalty, the courts have gradually recognized that freedom of inquiry and research and freedom of teaching are essential in the university setting—a setting devoted to the advancement of knowledge and the discovery of truth. Academic freedom in the public school context, however, is far more restrictive because it would have "the effect of frustrating the democratically elected school board's control of the message to be conveyed to the students and could have the further effect of authorizing each teacher to engage in his or her program of inculcation behind the closed doors of the classroom."[57] But how do we distinguish—in terms of mental, not chronological, maturity—between high school students and college students? Consider the rulings in *James, Zucker, Russo,* and *Searcey*.

Third, the courts have come a long way in protecting a teacher's right to speak out against war in the name of conscience. The evolution from procedural regularity to respect for conscience is most apparent, but there are limits to this academic freedom. Although the *James* and *Russo* cases are important, the *Birdwell* decision damps the enthusiasm of the advocates of free speech. The issue of disruption imposes its own standard of restriction of academic freedom for public school teachers. Because each state regulates its own educational program, courts have been subject to standards that remain vague and subjective at best. No universal application concerning academic freedom exists. The courts have traditionally been reluctant to intrude upon the domain of educational affairs largely out of respect for the autonomy of educational institutions. No consensus exists among the judiciary on the function of the public schools and the concept of education. Therein lies the dilemma.

The legal history of teachers and students against war and militarism deserves telling, but no final answers are available. Another war might possibly bring different court rulings. The interests of teachers and students in freedom from restraints on classroom speech, however, have received only limited legal recognition. No unified and universal theory of academic rights and responsibilities exists. Only when unpopular views are expressed do the courts entertain the commonly held belief that some measure of public regulation of classroom speech is inherent in the very provision of public education. Only then do small-town events raise large constitutional issues. For the present we are thus left with George Orwell's warning in *1984* that "Ideas . . . could only be named in very broad terms which lumped together and condemned whole groups of heresies without defining them in doing so."[58]

Notes
Selected Readings
Contributors
Index

Notes

1. The Counterculture and the Antiwar Movement

1. Ronald Fraser, ed., *1968* (New York: Pantheon, 1988), 116.

2. David Farber, *Chicago '68* (Chicago: Univ. of Chicago Press, 1988), 160. For insight into how some Americans melded together various strands of protest and resistance in the 1960s and early 1970s, see Robert Coles, *The Middle Americans* (Boston: Atlantic-Little, Brown, 1971).

3. Gurney Norman, interview by Ron Grele, 27 Sept. 1986, pp. 44–47, Columbia Oral History Project Research Office (COHP), Columbia University, New York.

4. Charles Perry, *The Haight-Ashbury: A History* (New York: Vintage, 1984), 26; Todd Gitlin, *The Sixties: Years of Hope, Days of Rage* (New York: Bantam, 1987), 209.

5. Leary tried to cut the difference between Kesey's acid dream of freaks freaking freely and Aldous Huxley's mid-1950s belief that hallucinogens should be reserved for a narrow elite capable of handling them. Leary obviously went public in a big way, but he also tried to spread the word of concern about scene and setting so as to heighten the possibilities of a good trip. But until early 1968, Leary always saw political activism as a dead-end road. For the best book on acid and the sixties, see Jay Stevens, *Storming Heaven* (New York: Harper & Row, 1988).

6. As Digger Emmett Grogan tells the story in his unreliable *Ringolevio* (Boston: Little, Brown, 1972), 279, the San Francisco *Oracle*, the ultimate psychedelic underground newspaper, which had originally asked Snyder for the poem, decided not to print it because it was " 'too hostile' to be compatible with their mild approach toward consciousness raising.' " So the Diggers, with Snyder's permission, spread the message. The *Digger Papers* appeared as a special edition of *The Realist*, Aug. 1967. Snyder's poem is in *Ringolevio*, 279–80; it is reprinted here courtesy of Little, Brown and Company.

7. Jane Kramer, "Paterfamilias—II," *New Yorker,* 24 Aug.1968, 40.

8. Fraser, *1968*, 116. The Diggers material comes from interviews the author conducted with Anonymous, Summer 1987, Honolulu, Hawaii. For more on the Diggers and the Haight-Ashbury see Perry, *Haight-Ashbury*.

9. Nancy Zaroulis and Gerald Sullivan, *Who Spoke Up? American Protest Against the War in Vietnam, 1963–1975* (Garden City, N.Y.: Doubleday, 1984), 55.

10. Ibid., 216.

11. Lew Jones, "Report on the Lake Villa Conference," 28 Mar. 1968, box 2, Fred Halstead Papers, State Historical Society of Wisconsin, Madison.

12. For Halstead's perceptive views of the antiwar movement, see his *Out Now! A Participant's Account of the American Movement Against the Vietnam War* (New York: Monad, 1978).

13. Carl Oglesby, interview by Bret Eynon, July 1978, p. 8, COHP.

14. Ibid., 13.

15. Richard Gid Powers, *Secrecy and Power: The Life of J. Edgar Hoover* (New York: Free Press, 1987), 428.

16. Abbie Hoffman, *Soon to Be a Major Motion Picture* (New York: Perigee, 1980), 200. Hoffman has an ax to grind, but his account is fair and is supported by my research for *Chicago '68*.

17. Tom Hayden, *Reunion: A Memoir* (New York: Random House, 1988), 204–5.

18. Gitlin, "What are We Doing to Dismantle the System and What to Decorate It?" Liberation News Service, 1968. For more on SDS members opposed to the counterculture and drug use see Fraser, *1968*, 117. And for more on Gitlin's sensitivity to American culture after his trip to Cuba, see Gitlin, *The Sixties*, 279. He makes no mention of his earlier comments on the counterculture.

19. Fraser, *1968*, 117, uses several excellent oral history excerpts to make this point. The oral histories used for the American sections of *1968* are available in the COHP.

20. Henry Anderson, "A Case Against Drug Culture," *Liberation*, Apr. 1967, 34–39; Allen Ginsberg, "Public Solitude," ibid., 33–35.

21. Kramer, "Paterfamilias," 40.

22. Kerry and Carol Berland, interview by Grele, 18 Dec. 1984, 27–28, 31, 47, COHP.

23. Carol Brightman, interview by Grele, 12 Dec. 1984, p. 104, COHP.

24. Anonymous, interview by G.H., Apr. 1990, author's files, 2.

25. Author's conversations with DoAn Sunim, June 1989, Honolulu, Hawaii.

26. Perry, *Haight-Ashbury*, 122.

27. Ibid.

28. Ibid., 128.

29. Grogan, *Ringolevio*, 275.

30. Perry, *Haight-Ashbury*, 120.

31. See Farber, *Chicago '68*, chap. 1.

32. *Mobilizer*, 1 Sept. 1967, 1.

33. See Zaroulis and Sullivan, *Who Spoke Up?*, 89–90, for Peck's background and 136–37 for Peck's reaction to Rubin's rhetoric and plans.

34. Ibid., 139.

35. Farber, *Chicago '68*, 88.

36. Ibid., 35.

37. Ibid., 89.

38. Abe Peck, *Uncovering the Sixties* (New York: Pantheon, 1985), 109.

39. Ibid., 108.

40. For a poignant analysis of this development, see Hoffman, *Soon to Be a Major Motion Picture*, 124. He calls Wenner "the Benedict Arnold of the sixties."

41. Up Against the Wall, Motherfuckers, "Self Defense," *Rat,* 9–22 Aug. 1968, 11.

42. The quotation comes from the 15 Sept. 1970 communiqué sent by the Weather Underground after they broke Timothy Leary out of prison. John Castellucci, *The Big Dance* (New York: Dodd, Mead, 1986), 124.

43. Up Against the Wall, Motherfuckers, "We are Outlaws," *Rat,* 6–19 Sept. 1968, 7.

44. Zaroulis and Sullivan, *Who Spoke Up?,* 249–301; Gitlin, *The Sixties.*

45. See Raymond Mungo, *Famous Long Ago* (Boston: Beacon, 1970).

46. Anonymous, interview by S.H., 26 Mar. 1990, 5, author's files.

47. It is critical to add that a number of young people who joined communes, particularly in Vermont, continued to be politically involved at the local level, setting up food co-ops, health clinics, and working on electoral campaigns. See Joyce Bressler, interview by Susan Halper, 18 Apr. 1990, author's file.

2. You Don't Need a Weatherman but a Postman Can Be Helpful

1. Letter to SDS National Office (NO), 23 Feb. 1966, reel 19, series 3, SDS Papers (SDSP). With the advice and insistence of this book's publisher, I have tried to maintain the anonymity of some of the SDS members whose unpublished letters I quote from the archives where they are deposited. I regret that this may make it more difficult for other scholars to track down the references I cite. One can only hope that the United States Congress will soon act to clarify the legal question of fair use of unpublished material, eliminating the need for such precautions.

2. When students were questioned as to political attitudes, rather than asking them to adopt labels with possibly negative connotations ("far left"), the potential radical constituency on campus loomed even larger. A full 75 percent of students questioned for a 1970 Harris poll believed that "basic changes in the system" were necessary in the United States, while 44 percent agreed that social progress was more likely to come from "radical pressure from outside the system" than through established procedures and institutions. For figures on the dimensions of campus radicalism, see Helen Lefkowitz Horowitz, "The 1960s and the Transformation of Campus Cultures," *History of Education Quarterly* 26 (Spring 1986): 12, 18; *The Report of the President's Commission on Campus Unrest* (Washington, D.C.: GPO, 1970), 18, 39, 48; Kirkpatrick Sale, *SDS* (New York: Random House, 1973), 636; *Guardian,* 16 Nov. 1968, 6.

3. Todd Gitlin, *The Sixties: Years of Hope, Days of Rage* (New York: Bantam, 1987); James Miller, *"Democracy Is in the Streets": From Port Huron to the Siege of Chicago* (New York: Simon & Schuster, 1987); Maurice Isserman, *If I Had a Hammer. . . : The Death of the Old Left and the Birth of the New Left* (New York: Basic Books, 1987); Richard Flacks, "What Happened to the New Left?" *Socialist Review* 19 (Jan./Mar. 1989): 96, 98–99. Wini Breines,

reviewing Gitlin, Miller, and Isserman, complained about their preoccupation with relatively few top (male) leaders of SDS at the expense of a broader consideration of New Left activism: "By focusing on the fate of SDS as an organization, these accounts diminish the mass movement after 1968"; Breines, "Whose New Left?" *Journal of American History* 75 (Sept. 1988): 531. Also see Paul Berman's review of Miller's book, in which he argues that it gives "an exaggerated idea of the significance of [Tom] Hayden's leadership, and of leaders in general [within SDS]." "Don't Follow Leaders," *New Republic,* 10 and 17 Aug. 1987, 28 .

4. Thomas Powers, *The War at Home: Vietnam and the American People, 1964–1968* (New York: Grossman, 1973), 82.

5. "Noon Caucus" statement, reel 20, series 3, SDSP.

6. Oglesby's comments appeared in the *Peacemaker* [1965?] reel 41, series 4-D, SDSP. Doug McAdam argues that rather than "three or four discrete movements in the Sixties," it was more useful to think of a "single, broad, activist community with its roots firmly in the Southern civil rights movement, and separate branches extending into various forms of activism (principally the black power, antiwar, student, and women's liberation movements)"; McAdam, *Freedom Summer* (New York: Oxford Univ. Press 1988), 6, 132. Also see Taylor Branch's comment on the "civil rights subculture" in *Parting the Waters: America in the King Years, 1954–63* (New York: Simon & Schuster, 1988), 718.

7. *Liberation,* 10 Mar. 1965, 46 (emphasis in original).

8. *Guardian,* 29 Apr. 1965, 6.

9. Clayborne Carson, *In Struggle: SNCC and the Black Awakening of the 1960s* (Cambridge, Mass.: Harvard Univ. Press, 1981), 93–95.

10. Lee Webb and Paul Booth, "The Anti-War Movement: From Protest to Radical Politics," reel 39, series 4B, SDSP. Old Guard veteran Robert Ross describes his own reaction to the proposal for the April 1965 march in his essay "Primary Groups in Social Movements: A Memoir and Interpretation," in *Toward a History of the New Left,* ed. R. David Myers (Brooklyn: Carlson Publishers, 1989), 161–62. Also see Norm Fruchter, "SDS: In and Out of Context," *Liberation,* Feb. 1972, 29.

11. Staughton Lynd, "The Movement: A New Beginning," *Liberation,* May 1969, 14.

12. Letter from Booth to Jeff Segal, Mel McDonald, and Dena Clamage, 20 July 1965, reel 6, SDSP.

13. Booth to Ira Sandperl and Joan Baez, 19 Sept. 1965, reel 19, series 3, SDSP.

14. Clamage to Booth, 14 Dec. 1965, ibid.

15. When Tom Hayden announced his plans to go to North Vietnam in late December 1965, FBI informants in Chicago reported to J. Edgar Hoover that Booth later remarked that the "National Administration Committee of SDS [National Interim Committee?] did not want Hayden to go but Hayden disagreed and told Booth he was going anyway and would disassociate himself from SDS." Chicago FBI to Director, 23 Dec. 1965, section 14, 100-439048-909, Weatherman Files, FBI.

16. Carl Davidson et al., "Our Fight is Here: Essays on Draft Resistance," reel 38, series 4B, SDSP.

17. David Arnold, "Vietnam: Symptom of a World Malaise," Peace Research Education Project (PREP), SDS, 1964. Donald McKelvey, assistant national secretary for SDS from 1962 through 1964, wrote in Dave Dellinger's *Liberation:* "[I]t is part of the genius of

pacifism to deny a dichotomy of personal and political life and to affirm that every act of an individual is a political act." McKelvey, "Pacifism, Politics and Non-Violence," *Liberation,* Aug. 1965, 22.

18. Bruce Dancis, a Cornell SDSer who helped spark the draft resistance movement and who served one and a half years in prison for burning his draft card, was the son of a World War II conscientious objector (CO). A pacifist background also crops up in less predictable places in SDS. Jeff Jones, one of three top leaders of Weather Underground, was also the son of a World War II CO. Jones, born in Philadelphia where his father had gone to work for the American Friends Service Committee after the war, later grew up in a community of Quakers in the San Fernando Valley. Jeff Jones, interview with author, 16 Sept. 1989.

19. Letter from University of Rhode Island SDS to NO, 1 Feb. 1966, reel 19, series 3, SDSP.

20. Letter to NO, 28 July 1967, ibid.

21. Letter to NO, 23 Nov. 1965, reel 21, series 3, SDSP.

22. Letter to NO, 25 Mar. 1966, reel 19, series 3, SDSP.

23. Press release from Wesleyan University SDS, received at NO, 19 Feb. 1966, ibid. The Wesleyan University SDS chapter was founded by John Strand, a graduate student and veteran of Mississippi Summer, in the fall of 1964. Strand to NO, 10 Dec. 1964, reel 7, series 2A, SDSP.

24. Steve Halliwell to Leo Haimson, 2 Aug. 1967, reel 19, series 3, SDSP. Halliwell wrote to another historian, Loren Baritz, soon afterwards: "Chicago is like an armed camp—the cops are carrying a nerve gas and sweeping the streets at night making mass arrests. We're at Madison and Ashland right on the edge of the West Side ghetto and are facing constant harassment. I only tell you all this because it seems that all of us careful academics are going to be sitting in our offices when the deal goes down if we don't watch what conditions are among the people that occupy the hearts of the cities." Halliwell to Baritz, 5 Aug. 1967, reel 19, series 3, SDSP.

25. Bill Sales, quoted in Jerry L. Avorn et al., *Up Against the Ivy Wall: A History of the Columbia Crisis* (New York: Atheneum, 1969), 48. Julius Lester's column appeared in the *Guardian,* 11 May 1968, 11.

26. Carson, *In Struggle,* 252-56, 274, 296.

27. Weissman's comments appeared in SDS's *National Vietnam Newsletter,* #2, 12 Aug. 1965. Lee Webb may have had Weissman's article in mind when he wrote in a working paper for the December 1965 SDS national conference: "SDS does not have a rich internal life. . . . The richness of publications, of drafts of SDS documents, of intense, regular chapter discussions, of conferences, of debates, is absent in SDS. Perhaps it was easier to have all this when we were smaller. SDS influences its membership to become more militant rather than more radical. At the same time as our intellectual life has declined, the calls to fight the draft, stop a troop train, burn a draft card, avoid all forms of liberalism, have become more vocal. Thus commitment, confrontation, martyrdom, anger become the substitute for intellectual analysis and understanding." Webb, "Conference Working Papers and Suggested Priorities for the NC," n.d. [ca. late 1965], reel 20, series 3, SDSP.

28. Webb, "Conference Working Papers."

29. Cornell, quoted in Nancy Zaroulis and Gerald Sullivan, *Who Spoke Up? American Protest Against the War in Vietnam 1963–1975* (Garden City, N.Y.: Doubleday, 1984), 344–45.

3. CALCAV and Religious Opposition to the Vietnam War

1. "The Religious Community and the War in Vietnam," Feb. 1967, series 4, box 1, Records of Clergy and Laity Concerned (RCALC), Swarthmore College Peace Collection (SCPC), Swarthmore, Pennsylvania.

2. Martin E. Marty, *Pilgrims in Their Own Land* (Boston: Little, Brown, 1984), esp. 403–26; and, *The Public Church* (New York: Crossroads, 1981), 70–93.

3. George W. Webber, "CALC: The Anti-War Years," *CALC Report*, Aug./Oct. 1985, 6; Jeffrey K. Hadden, *The Gathering Storm in the Churches* (Garden City, N.Y.: Doubleday, 1969), 123–36; George H. Gallup, *The Gallup Poll: Public Opinion 1935–1971*, (New York: Random House, 1972), 3:1933, 2120; Alfred O. Hero, Jr., *American Religious Groups View Foreign Policy: Trends in Rank-and-File Opinion, 1937–1969* (Durham, N.C.: Duke Univ. Press, 1973), 165–208.

4. See, for example, Richard Reinitz, *Irony and Consciousness* (Cranbury, N.J.: Associated Univ. Presses, 1980), 115–16.

5. Harvey G. Cox, "The 'New Breed' in American Churches: Sources of Social Activism in American Religion," *Daedalus* 96 (Winter 1967): 135–50; Webber, "CALC: The Anti-War Years," 4–6; Hero, *American Religious Groups*, 151–57, 207–8.

6. Seymour P. Lachman, "Barry Goldwater and the 1964 Religious Issue," *Journal of Church and State* 10 (Autumn 1968): 389–404.

7. *New York Times*, 4 Apr. 1965, E5; "Call to Vigil on Vietnam," *Christian Century*, 12 May 1965, 605; "Fifth General Synod Sets Forward Course," *United Church Herald*, 1 Aug. 1965, 12–18; "Weightly Unanimity," *Christian Century*, 22 Dec. 1965, 1564–65.

8. A. J. Muste to John C. Bennett, 15 Oct. 1965, box 52, A. J. Muste Papers, SCPC.

9. See Charles Chatfield, *For Peace and Justice: Pacifism in America, 1914–1941* (Knoxville: Univ. of Tennessee Press, 1971); Lawrence S. Wittner, *Rebels Against War: The American Peace Movement, 1933–1983* (Philadelphia: Temple University Press, 1984).

10. *New York Times*, 17 Oct. 1965, 9.

11. Ibid., 26 Oct. 1965, 4.

12. Bennett to Robert Bilheimer, 18 June 1966, series 2, box 1, RCALC.

13. William Sloane Coffin, Jr., *Once to Every Man: A Memoir* (New York: Atheneum, 1977), 216–17; Coffin to Fellow Clergy, 24 Jan. 1966, series 2, box 1, RCALC.

14. "National Emergency Committee of Clergy Concerned About Vietnam," 18 Jan. 1966, series 2, box 2, RCALC.

15. "Telegram to President Johnson," 11 Jan. 1966, series 2, box 2, RCALC; Coffin to Fellow Clergy, 24 Jan. 1966, series 2, box 1, RCALC.

16. Robert McAfee Brown, telephone interview with author, 12 Aug. 1985.

17. "Statement from the Steering Committee of The National Emergency Committee of Clergy Concerned About Vietnam," 1 Feb. 1966, series 2, box 2, RCALC.

18. Coffin to Fellow Clergy, 1 Feb. 1966, series 2, box 2, RCALC.

19. "Churchmen View Escalation in Vietnam," *Presbyterian Life*, 1 Aug. 1966, 28; "A Plea For Openness and Flexibility," *Presbyterian Life*, 15 Jan. 1967, 32–33.

20. "Excerpts From the Resolutions at Pittsburgh," *Crusader,* June 1967, 7; "A Declaration of Conscience," *Presbyterian Life,* 15 June 1967, 24–25; David F. Marshall, "'We Have Opened Another Door,'" *United Church Herald,* Aug. 1967, 12–19.

21. "Catholic Bishops Speak Out on Vietnam, Birth Control," *The Lutheran,* 21 Dec. 1966, 24–25; John C. Slemp, "Be Disciples . . . Make Disciples," *Missions,* June 1966, 15-18; "LCA 3rd Biennial Convention," *The Lutheran,* 20 July 1966, 6–9, 25–28, 44.

22. Frances Furlow, "General Assembly Highlights," *Presbyterian Survey,* Aug. 1967, 13–14, 16–17, 19–24; "Churches Continue to Call for Vietnam Peace," *The Lutheran,* 21 June 1967, 24; "When Compromise is Progress," *Lutheran Witness,* Aug. 1967, 6–7; "We Resolve," *The Christian,* 3 Dec. 1967, 11–13.

23. "Getting Close To Home," *Presbyterian Life,* 15 June 1967, 13–17; "The Assembly Views War, Peace, Justice At Home And Abroad," ibid., 25–27, 42.

24. "A History of Clergy and Laymen Concerned About Vietnam," 22 Aug. 1969, series 2, box 2, RCALC; Stephen C. Rose, "From Viet Nam to Empire," *Christianity and Crisis,* 3 Mar. 1969, 44; Report from New York, "Clergy and Laymen Concerned," 27 Apr. 1972, Files on Clergy and Laity Concerned (FBI), King Library Special Collections, University of Kentucky, Lexington.

25. "Givens, 1971—Pre–Ann Arbor," n.d., and "Report on Field Development and Honeywell Campaign Development since Ann Arbor Conference and Planning, 1971– September, 1972," 14 July 1972, series I, box 1, RCALC; Webber, "CALC: The Anti-War Years," 4–6; "CALCAV's Contributions to the Anti-War Efforts," *CALC Report,* Aug./Oct. 1985, 9-11; George W. Webber, telephone interview with author, 30 May 1985; Paul Kittlaus, telephone interview with author, 23 May 1985.

26. Richard Fernandez to William A. Slater, 3 May 1966, and Timothy Light to Philip Scharper, 6 Apr. 1966, series 2, box 1, RCALC.

27. Brown interview.

28. "Minutes of Executive Committee of CALCAV," 27 Sept. 1966, series I, box 1, RCALC.

29. William J. Jorden to Walt Rostow, 30 Jan. 1967, White House Central Files— subject file, Executive ND 19/CO312, Lyndon B. Johnson Library, Austin, Texas.

30. Michael Charlton and Anthony Moncrieff, *Many Reasons Why: The American Involvement in Vietnam* (New York: Hill & Wang, 1978), 164–65.

31. John C. Platt to Fernandez, 29 Oct. 1968, series 2, box 6, RCALC.

32. Clergy and Laymen Concerned About Vietnam, *In the Name of America* (Annandale, Va.: Turnpike Press, 1967), 1–11.

33. "Who's Right? Who's Wrong? on Vietnam," n.d., box 12, Records of Friends Committee on National Legislation, SCPC.

34. "Churchmen Welcome Pope Paul's New Year's Plea for Peace," *The Lutheran,* 17 Jan. 1968, 25–26; "Actions at Atlanta," *The Lutheran,* 17 July 1968, 5–8, 26–29; "Business—'Internal' and 'External,'" *The Christian,* 17 Nov. 1968, 7; "A Union . . . And Much More," *Together,* July 1968, 5–7, 9–16; "Vietnam Report: Looking Toward the Future," *Presbyterian Life,* 15 June 1968, 14–16; "Church & Society," *Presbyterian Survey,* Aug. 1968, 21–24.

35. "The Opinion Poll on Vietnam," *Presbyterian Life,* 1 Apr. 1968, 22–23; Albert P. Stauderman, "Editor's Opinion," *The Lutheran,* 27 Mar. 1968, 50; "Hawks in the Pews," *Christianity Today,* 12 Apr. 1968, 36.

36. Richard John Neuhaus, "The War, the Churches, and Civil Religion," *Annals of the American Academy of Political and Social Science* 387 (Jan. 1970): 128-40.

37. C. D. Brennan to W. C. Sullivan, 1 Feb. 1968; J. Edgar Hoover to Mr. Crowley, 7 May 1968; Cleveland to Director, 1 July 1968; "Protest Activity By Clergy and Laymen Concerned About Vietnam, Washington, D.C., 5–6 Feb. 1968," 6 Feb. 1968; J. Edgar Hoover to [censored], 2 Dec. 1968; "New York Office 'Clergy and Laity Concerned' Internal Security Activities," 9 Apr. 1973, FBI.

38. "Clergy and Laymen Concerned About Vietnam," 1969, series I, box 1, RCALC.

39. "Churches Asked to Provide Draft Counseling," *Presbyterian Life*, 15 June 1969, 14–15; "Church and Society Papers," *Presbyterian Survey*, June 1969, 19–24; "Issues at General Synod," *United Church Herald*, Aug. 1969, 10–11; "American Baptists at Seattle," *Crusader*, June 1969, 7; "The Business of the Christian Church," *The Christian*, 5 Oct. 1969, 14–15.

40. "American Report Radio," n.d., series 1, box 1, RCALC.

41. "Help Unsell the War," n.d., series 3, box 15, RCALC.

42. "Minutes of Communications Committee," 3 Nov. 1972, series 1, box 1, RCALC.

43. "Religious Groups Call for Withdrawal," *American Report*, 5 Mar. 1971, 1, 6.

44. "Vietnam Statement Causes Anguish," *Presbyterian Life*, 15 June–1 July 1971, 14–15; "Convention Roundup," *The American Baptist*, June 1971, 22; *United Church Herald*, Aug. 1971, 3, 30.

45. Kittlaus interview.

46. "Emergency Ministry Initiated for Services to Veterans," *Presbyterian Life*, 15 Feb. 1972, 42; "Presbyterian Group to Help Returning Vietnam Servicemen," *United Church Herald*, Apr. 1972, 12-13; "Face-Saving or Life-Saving," *Engage*, June 1972, 6–18; "A Message to United Presbyterians," *Presbyterian Life*, July 1972, 38-39; Frank A. Sharp, "Denver Wrap-Up," *The American Baptist*, June 1972, 14–17.

47. These sentiments are reflected in the author's telephone interviews with Richard Fernandez (10 Sept. 1988), Harvey Cox (22 Sept. 1988), Barbara Fuller (13 Sept. 1988), and Coffin (16 Sept. 1988).

48. William L. Lunch and Peter W. Sperlich, "American Public Opinion and the War in Vietnam, " *Western Political Quarterly* 32 (Mar. 1979): 21–44; Philip E. Converse and Howard Schuman, "'Silent Majorities' and the Vietnam War," *Scientific American*, June 1970, 17–25; Harlan Hahn, "Correlates of Public Sentiment About War: Local Referenda on the Vietnam Issue," *American Political Science Review* 64 (Dec. 1970): 1186–98; Sidney Verba et al., "Public Opinion and the War in Vietnam," *American Political Science Review* 61 (June 1967): 317–33.

49. James O'Brien, "The Anti-War Movement and the War," *Radical America* 8 (May/June 1974): 53-86; Michael Walzer, "The Peace Movement," *New Republic*, 10 Feb. 1973, 24–26; Milton S. Katz, "Peace Liberals and Vietnam: SANE and the Politics of 'Responsible' Protest," *Peace and Change* 9 (Summer 1983): 21–39.

50. Howard Schuman, "Two Sources of Antiwar Sentiment in America," *American Journal of Sociology* 78 (Nov. 1972): 513–36; Converse and Schuman, " 'Silent Majorities,' " 17–25; Michael Mandelbaum, "Vietnam: The Television War," *Daedalus* 111 (Fall 1982): 157-69; Katz, "Peace Liberals," 21–39.

51. Converse and Schuman, " 'Silent Majorities,' " 17–25; Walzer, "Peace Movement," 24–26; E. M. Schreiber, "Anti-War Demonstrations and American Public Opinion on the War in Vietnam," *British Journal of Sociology* 27 (June 1976): 225–36.

52. Balfour Brickner, telephone interview with author, 21–22 Aug. 1985.

53. "CALC Chapters and the National Office: Conflict or Symbiosis?" *CALC Report* 11 (Aug./Oct. 1985): 16.

54. Leslie H. Gelb, "Dissenting on Consensus," in *The Vietnam Legacy*, ed. Anthony Lake (New York: New York Univ. Press, 1976): 102–19.

55. "Webber to Martin: Our Country Fuels This Evil War," *American Report*, 15 Apr. 1974, 10.

56. Todd Gitlin, "Seizing History," *Mother Jones*, Nov. 1983, 33–38, 48; Melvin Small, *Johnson, Nixon, and the Doves* (New Brunswick, N.J.: Rutgers Univ. Press, 1988); Richard Nixon, *RN: The Memoirs of Richard Nixon* (New York: Warner, 1978), 434–41, 493–97, 616.

57. Ralph B. Levering, *The Public and American Foreign Policy, 1918–1978* (New York: Morrow, 1978), 130–36; Mandelbaum, "Vietnam: The Television War," 157–69; O'Brien, "The Anti-War Movement," 53–86.

58. Charles DeBenedetti, "On the Significance of Citizen Peace Activism: America, 1961–1975," *Peace and Change* 9 (Summer 1983): 14.

59. Brown interview; Brickner interview.

60. Cox interview.

61. Fuller interview.

4. Pacifists and the Vietnam Antiwar Movement

1. Guenter Lewy, *Peace and Revolution: The Moral Crisis of American Pacifism* (Grand Rapids, Mich.: Eerdman, 1988).

2. I omit the Korean War, noting only that it occurred quite suddenly, that it was marked by the crossing of an established, if temporary, boundary by large numbers of conventional forces, and that it occurred at the height of the Cold War when we tended not to be very critical of actions taken against communists.

3. David McReynolds, "After the Election," *WRL News*, Nov./Dec. 1964, emphasis added.

4. Joseph Buttinger, *The Smaller Dragon* (New York: Praeger, 1958).

5. "May Day" 1971

1. The author participated in the 3 May 1971 action. This event and the decentralized organizing effort supporting this specific nonviolent civil disobedience approach were both popularly known as "May Day." While the spelling of the term varied (May Day, MayDay, Mayday), proponents and opponents understood what was meant. In this essay May Day will refer to the 3 May event and approach instead of the traditional 1 May date associated with the term.

2. For an overview of these issues, see Thomas Powers, *The War At Home: Vietnam and the American People, 1964–1968* (New York: Grossman, 1973). Nancy Zaroulis and Gerald Sullivan, *Who Spoke Up? American Protest Against the War in Vietnam, 1963–1975* (Garden City, N.Y.: Doubleday, 1984); Melvin Small, *Johnson, Nixon, and the Doves* (New Brunswick, N.J.: Rutgers Univ. Press, 1988); George R. Vickers, "The Vietnam Antiwar Movement in Perspective," *Bulletin of Concerned Asian Scholars* 21 (Apr./Dec., 1989), 100–10; and Charles DeBenedetti with Charles Chatfield, *An American Ordeal: The Antiwar Movement of the Vietnam Era* (Syracuse: Syracuse Univ. Press, 1990).

3. For differing perspectives on the 9 May demonstration, see Bradford Lyttle, *May Ninth* (New York: Layfayette Service Company, 1970); David Dellinger, *More Power Than We Know: The People's Movement Toward Democracy* (Garden City, N.Y.: Doubleday, 1975), 136–43; Fred Halstead, *Out Now! A Participant's Account of the American Movement Against the Vietnam War* (New York: Monad, 1978), 536–56, 563; Michael P. Lerner, "May Day: Anatomy of a Movement," *Ramparts,* July 1971, 20; David Gelber, "Twilight of Demonstrations, Dawn of the General Strike?" *Village Voice,* 14 May 1970, 1, 10.

4. The Trotskyist organizations involved in NPAC included the Socialist Workers party (SWP), its youth affiliate, the Young Socialist Alliance (YSA), and the YSA-influenced Student Mobilization Committee (SMC). See G. Louis Heath, ed., *Mutiny Does Not Happen Lightly: The Literature of the American Resistance to the Vietnam War* (Metuchen, N.J.: Scarecrow Press, 1976), 301–8, 186–93, 180–85; Halstead, *Out Now!,* 566–69.

5. Dellinger, "Carrying It On: A Third Alternative," *Village Voice,* 4 June 1970, 12–13.

6. This definition of civil disobedience is drawn from extensive reading in the literature of civil disobedience, especially Carl Cohen, *Civil Disobedience: Conscience, Tactics and the Law* (New York: Columbia Univ. Press, 1971), 1–40; Elliott M. Zashin, *Civil Disobedience and Democracy* (New York: Free Press, 1972), 105–18; James F. Childress, *Civil Disobedience and Political Obligation* (New Haven, Conn.: Yale Univ. Press, 1971), 1–12.

7. Others, like Arthur Waskow, were also considering nontraditional civil disobedience. Waskow, an activist-scholar at the Institute for Policy Studies, had theorized in the mid-1960s about the use of nonviolent "creative disorder" and social disruption in the civil rights movement. Arthur I. Waskow, *From Race Riot to Sit-In, 1919 and the 1960s: A Study in the Connections Between Conflict and Violence* (Garden City, N.Y.: Doubleday, 1966), 243–46.

8. *New York Times,* 16 August 1967, 1, 29; cited hereinafter as *NYT.*

9. Zaroulis and Sullivan, *Who Spoke Up?,* 346.

10. Halstead, *Out Now!,* 568; DeBenedetti and Chatfield, *An American Ordeal,* 282.

11. Zaroulis and Sullivan, *Who Spoke Up?,* 340.

12. Heath, *Mutiny,* 187–93.

13. Lerner, "May Day," 21; Zaroulis and Sullivan, *Who Spoke Up?,* 340.

14. *The Militant,* 2 Apr. 1971, 8; Halstead, *Out Now!,* 583–87; Lerner, "May Day," 21 (emphasis in original).

15. *The Militant,* 22 Jan. 1971; Halstead, *Out Now!,* 588; Lerner, "May Day," 21; Zaroulis and Sullivan, *Who Spoke Up?,* 344.

16. The People's Peace Treaty essentially reflected the eight-point peace proposal put forward in Paris by Madame Nguyen Thi Binh, the representative of the Provisional Revolutionary Government (PRG) of South Vietnam, on 17 September 1970. Rennie Davis, Richard Falk, and Robert Greenblatt, "The Way to End the War: The Statement of Ngo Cong Duc," *New York Review of Books,* 5 Nov. 1970, 17–22.

17. NSA did not officially endorse May Day, although the conference it sponsored did. See Heath, *Mutiny,* 25–27, 234–48; *The Militant,* 19 Feb. 1971, 5; Lerner, "May Day," 21; Halstead, *Out Now!,* 591.

18. *The Militant,* 19 Feb. 1971, 5; Zaroulis and Sullivan, *Who Spoke Up?,* 345–46.

19. Zaroulis and Sullivan, *Who Spoke Up?,* 347–48.

20. PCPJ and NPAC statements reprinted in *The Militant,* 26 Feb. 1971, 9, 22; joint NPAC-PCPJ statement reprinted in *The Militant,* 12 Mar. 1971, 1, 24; Halstead, *Out Now!,* 598.

21. Zaroulis and Sullivan, *Who Spoke Up?*, 3, 348; DeBenedetti and Chatfield, *An American Ordeal*, 302–3; Halstead, *Out Now!*, 597; Lerner, "May Day," 21–23.

22. *Newsweek*, 17 May 1971, 24, 25D; *Washington Post*, cited hereafter as *WP*; 5 Sept. 1971, B1, B8, Jonathan Schell, *The Time of Illusion* (New York: Knopf, 1976), 150.

23. *Mayday Tactical Manual*, reprinted in Heath, *Mutiny*, 205, 212, 214.

24. Ibid., 206–8. Robin Reisig, "Gandhi with a raised fist," *Village Voice*, 13 May 1971, 9.

25. See Heath, *Mutiny*, 219–20, 229–30.

26. Reisig, "Gandhi," 9; *Time*, 10 May 1971, 14. *The Militant's* continued attacks on May Day, PCPJ, and the treaty further complicated organization. While YSA certainly had the right to criticize May Day, its pejorative assertions and actions only heightened conflict among activists; see *The Militant*, 30 April 1971, 9, 21.

27. *NYT*, 24 Apr. 1971, 1, 8; *WP*, 24 Apr. 1971, A1, A8; *WP*, 25 Apr. 1971, A1, A17; *WP*, 26 Apr. 1971, A16. More than one thousand protestors returning from the march shut down part of the New Jersey Turnpike for at least four hours by stopping their cars. Arrests exceeded one hundred. Although not sponsored by May Day, the incident provided a possible preview of 3 May; *WP*, 26 Apr. 1971, A1, A14.

28. More demonstrators began arriving and camping at West Potomac Park, dubbed "Algonquin Peace City" in honor of its original residents. Reporters noted that the park permit "put the government in the novel position of providing public ground for the launching of large scale lawbreaking." *WP*, 26 Apr. 1971, A1, A14.

29. *WP*, 27 Apr. 1971, A1, A10; *WP*, 28 Apr. 1971, A1, A6; *WP*, 29 Apr. 1971, A1, A8; *WP*, 30 Apr. 1971, A1, A8; *WP*, 1 May 1971, A1, A4.

30. The press played up Bacon's May Day connection while other features sensationalized reports of drug use, overdoses, thefts, and sexual activity at the May Day encampment. While May Day had problems with what some organizers referred to as adolescent "rock-concert lumpen," the representation of May Day as drugged out and prone to violence hurt the responsible, nonviolent image the group was trying to project. By Saturday, press coverage became more positive as reports of older, more serious protesters arrived to help offset negative publicity. *WP*, 27 Apr. 1971, A11; *WP*, 29 Apr. 1971, A1, A8; *WP*, 1 May 1971, A5; Lerner, "May Day," 24; *NYT*, 29 Apr. 1971, 6.

31. *WP*, 3 May 1971, A1, A16, A18; *WP*, 8 July 1971, A3; John Neary, "The Day Washington Did Not Shut Down," *Life*, 14 May 1971, 33–35.

32. *WP*, 3 May 1971, A1, A18; *NYT*, 3 May 1971, 1, 41.

33. *WP*, 3 May 1971, A18; *NYT*, 4 May 1971, 32; *Newsweek*, 17 May 1971, 24, 25D.

34. *WP*, 4 May 1971, A12, A14; *NYT*, 9 May 1971, sec. 4, p. 3; Neary, "The Day Washington Did Not Shut Down," 38.

35. *WP*, 4 May 1971, A14; *NYT*, 5 May 1971, 26. *Life* magazine published a photo of Deputy Chief Ted Zanders macing a Chicago group sitting down on 14th Street; Zanders satirically chanted "Ho, ho, here we go" as he sprayed. Neary, "The Day Washington Did Not Shut Down," 36.

PCPJ's separate planned march across the 14th Street Bridge to the Pentagon for traditional civil disobedience was also attacked. *WP*, 4 May 1971, A12, A14.

36. *WP*, 4 May 1971, A14; Neary, "The Day Washington Did Not Shut Down," 38. Wilson later explained that "if there had been 1,000 or 2,000 blocking the streets, we could have gone along with normal processes and processed them out on the street

without badly disrupting traffic." But Wilson also conceded knowing that there were at least ten thousand demonstrators in the city on Sunday night. *WP,* 30 June 1971, A8; Neary, "The Day Washington Did Not Shut Down," 38.

37. *WP,* 4 May 1971, A12, A14; *NYT,* 4 May 1971, 1, 32.

38. Kendall, quoted in Halstead, *Out Now!,* 619; *NYT,* 5 May 1971, 26; *WP,* 4 May 1971, A12.

39. *WP,* 4 May 1971, A13; *WP,* 5 May 1971, C1, C4; *NYT,* 5 May 1971, 26.

40. Neary, "The Day Washington Did Not Shut Down," 38; *WP,* 4 May 1971, A1, A12; *WP,* 4 June 1971, A15; Small, *Johnson, Nixon, and The Doves,* 217–18.

41. *WP,* 4 May 1971, A13; *WP,* 8 Aug. 1971, A1, A9.

42. *WP,* 4 May 1971, A12. PCPJ Coordinator Sid Peck was astounded at Davis's initial statement that May Day had failed to stop the government. He had always seen May Day as a symbolic action, not an actual effort to shut down the government. Quoted in Zaroulis and Sullivan, *Who Spoke Up?,* 362.

43. *WP,* 8 Aug. 1971, A9. The government offer had remained confidential until revealed in this issue of the *Post.*

44. *WP,* 5 May 1971, C1, C4; *Newsweek,* 17 May 1971, 26–27; John Mathews, "Jailed With the Mayday Tribe," *The Nation,* 24 May 1971, 646–48. Help arrived for some demonstrators when black community activists brought carloads of food to the Redskins' practice field. During the night, demonstrators were transferred from the open-air practice field and jail yard to the enclosed Washington Coliseum sports arena. *WP,* 4 May 1971, A14; *WP,* 5 May 1971, A1, A8, A11, A18.

45. *WP,* 5 May 1971, A1, A16, A18; *WP,* 6 May 1971, A1, A14; *WP,* 7 May 1971, A1, A12; *NYT,* 6 May 1971, 1, 38; *NYT,* 7 May 1971, 1, 45.

46. McGrory column quoted in Noam Chomsky, "Mayday: The Case for Civil Disobedience," *New York Review of Books,* 17 June 1971, 19; *Newsweek,* 17 May 1971, 24; *Time,* May 10, 1971, 13, 15; *WP,* 13 May 1971, A20; *NYT,* 5 May 1971, 47.

47. *NYT,* 9 May 1971, sec. 4, p. 3; *WP,* 6 May 1971, A19.

48. Mitchell then compared May Day demonstrators to Hitler's Brown Shirts in Weimar Germany. Other critics saw the clubbing and illegal mass arrests as more typical of Nazi tactics. The *New York Times* declared that the attorney general's polemic "evokes renewed dismay at Mr. Mitchell's unfitness to head what is supposed to be a Department of Justice." *NYT,* 11 May 1971, 1, 20; *NYT,* 12 May 1971, 42.

49. *WP,* 16 May 1971, D9. The Justice Department and District prosecutors had purposefully abused the legal system and the courts. Officials later conceded off the record to reporters that "up to 80 percent of last week's arrests were unconstitutional." Justice Department sources admitted their goal was to "keep people out of circulation" for at least twelve to twenty-four hours after arrest. *WP,* 6 May 1971, A11; *NYT,* 9 May 1971, sec. 4, p. 3; *NYT,* 16 May 1971, D1, D9.

50. *NYT,* 2 June 1971, 1, 24, 25; *WP,* 3 June 1971, A2; *WP,* 4 June 1971, A15. Court statistics supported the ACLU and Kennedy. Of the first two thousand May Day cases, *one* resulted in a conviction at trial. Hundreds of cases were dismissed for lack of evidence; charges were not even filed in hundreds of other cases. Dozens received acquittals. 584 pleaded no contest; only 3 pleaded guilty. By early June, of almost 13,000 arrests, nearly 6,000 were dropped. Thousands more would soon be dismissed, dropped, or forfeit collateral. *WP,* 19 May 1971, A8; *NYT,* 6 June 1971, sec. 4, p. 7.

51. My analysis here is shared in large part by Bob Kuttner, "Civil disobedience against the people," *Village Voice,* 27 May 1971, 1, 82–84.

52. Charles DeBenedetti, *The Peace Reform in American History* (Bloomington: Indiana Univ. Press, 1980), 189–90.

53. "Paying for Mayday," *Newsweek,* 27 Jan. 1975, 46.

54. Halstead, "Some Comments on the Mayday Actions," *International Socialist Review* (July/Aug. 1971): 9–10.

55. Lerner, "May Day," 41; *WP,* 9 May 1971, A17; McReynolds, quoted in Halstead, *Out Now!,* 622; Lyttle, *The Chicago Anti-Vietnam War Movement* (Chicago: Midwest Pacifist Center, 1988), 150.

56. Gelber, "The message of Mayday: types of disruption," *Village Voice,* 20 May 1971, 13–14; Lerner, "May Day," 41; Dellinger, "A New Stage of Struggle: Mayday and the Fall Offensive," *Liberation,* Sept. 1971, 12-22, 49; *WP,* 26 Oct. 1971, C1; *WP,* 27 Oct. 1971, A1, A8; *WP,* 28 Oct. 1971, B4.

57. Dellinger, *More Power,* 51.

58. Lerner, "May Day," 24; Halstead, "Some Comments," 8–10; James Weinstein, *Ambiguous Legacy: The Left in American Politics* (New York: New Viewpoints, 1975), 149.

59. "The Anti-War Movement" [editorial], *Socialist Revolution,* Jan./Feb., 1972, 76; Chomsky, "Mayday," 28.

60. Small, *Johnson, Nixon, and the Doves,* 218–21; Zaroulis and Sullivan, *Who Spoke Up?,* 369–420.

6. The GI Movement and the Response from the Brass

1. David Cortright, *Soldiers in Revolt: The American Military Today* (New York: Anchor/Doubleday, 1975) is the only account of the GI movement. Cortright was a GI dissident who sued the army, but his book is more balanced than Robert Sherrill, *Military Justice Is to Justice as Military Music Is to Music* (New York: Perennial Library, 1971). (Ret.) Colonel George Walton responds to Sherrill in his book, *The Tarnished Shield: A Report on Today's Army* (New York: Dodd, Mead, 1973). For a compilation of GI underground press articles, see Larry G. Waterhouse and Mariann G. Wizard, *Turning the Guns Around: Notes on the GI Movement* (New York: Praeger, 1971). Movement sources are not always reliable. Activists tended to exaggerate in their underground newspapers or flyers. As the Yippies often stated, "Be Realistic. Demand the Impossible." Consequently their statements are more important for relating the mood, rather than precise facts, about certain events.

2. Quoted in Sherrill, *Military Justice,* 65.

3. *Broken Arrow,* 1 Dec. 1969, 29 Jan. and 28 Feb. 1971, Underground Newspaper Collection (UNC), Bentley Library, University of Michigan, Ann Arbor; and *Duck Power,* 8 and 22 Oct. 1969, Social Protest Project (SPP), unprocessed, serials file drawers, Bancroft Library, University of California, Berkeley.

4. Cortright, *Soldiers in Revolt,* 52.

5. Alice Lynd, ed., *We Won't Go: Personal Accounts of War Objectors* (Boston: Beacon, 1968), 181–202; *NYT,* 3 July 1966, Ft. Hood Three Defense Committee flyers, undated, Social Action Vertical File (SAVF), box 19, State Historical Society of Wisconsin, Madison. For the growth of the antidraft movement see Michael Ferber and Staughton Lynd, *The Resistance* (Boston: Beacon, 1971).

6. *Parker v. Levy,* 417 U.S. 733 (1974). See also Sherrill, "Captain Levy and the Green Berets," *Nation,* 25 Aug. 1969, 133.

7. Committee for G.I. Rights folder, and F. O. Richardson, "The GI's Handbook on Military Injustice," 21 Nov. 1967, SAVF, box 12; *The Bond,* 13 May 1968; *Esquire,* Aug. 1968, 41–45; *Ramparts,* 15 June 1968, 16; Andy Stapp, *Up Against the Brass* (New York: Simon & Schuster, 1970).

8. For an annotated bibliography of GI undergrounds, see Cortright, *Soldiers in Revolt,* 283–302.

9. GI undergrounds reported and probably exaggerated these incidents. See *FTA* [Dec. 1968]; *The Alley,* Feb. 1969; *OM* [Dec. 1969], SPP; *Broken Arrow,* 1 Dec. 1969, UNC.

10. James Hollingsworth, interview with author, 16 June 1986, Texas A&M University Oral History Collection, College Station.

11. Antiwar activities, New York City folder, GIs United flyer, 22 Mar. 1969, and *The Fifth Estate,* 3 Apr. and 1–14 May 1969, SAVF box 3; Fred Halstead, "Antiwar GIs Speak Out: Interviews with Ft. Jackson GIs United Against the War," Nov. 1969, and Halstead, *GIs Speak Out Against the War: The Case of the Ft. Jackson 8* (New York: Pathfinder Press, 1970); *NYT,* 2 Apr. 1969; Hollingsworth interview; Sherrill, "Must the Citizen Give Up His Civil Liberties When He Joins the Army?" *NYT Magazine,* 18 May 1969, 25–27.

12. Hollingsworth interview; Robert S. Rivkin and Barton F. Stichman, *The Rights of Military Personnel: The Basic ACLU Guide of Military Personnel* (New York: Avon, 1977), 86–87; Cortright, *Soldiers in Revolt,* chap. 1; *GI Press Service,* 26 June 1969, SPP.

13. Army Circular No. 632-1, "Guidance on Dissent," 27 May 1969; this directive was published in GI undergrounds. See *GI Press Service,* 10, 24 July and 2 Oct. 1969, SPP, and Halstead, *GIs Speak Out,* 119–25. Also consult James B. Jacobs, "Legal Change Within the United States Armed Forces Since World War II," *Armed Forces and Society* 4 (Spring 1978): 391–421.

14. Shelby L. Stanton, *The Rise and Fall of an American Army: U.S. Ground Forces in Vietnam, 1965–1973* (Novato, Calif.: Presidio Press, 1985), 285–87.

15. *GI Press Service,* 26 June 1969, SPP. Disgruntled troops in Vietnam are quoted in Robert Heinl, "The Collapse of the Armed Forces," *Armed Forces Journal,* 7 June 1971, 31.

16. Heinl, "Collapse of the Armed Forces," 31.

17. *Time,* 5 Sept. 1969, 22–23; *Newsweek,* 8 Sept. 1969, 17; *Nation,* 8 Sept. 1969, 196.

18. Heinl, "Collapse of the Armed Forces." For numerous examples of combat refusals, see Richard Boyle, *Flower of the Dragon—The Breakdown of the U.S. Army in Vietnam* (New York: Ramparts, 1972).

19. *Newsweek,* 25 May 1970, 45; Pete McCloskey, quoted in *The* (London) *Observer,* 18 Apr. 1971. See also James Reston, "A Whiff of Mutiny in Vietnam," *NYT,* 27 Aug. 1969.

20. *GI Press Service,* 11 Dec. 1969, and box 18a, SPP; *The Fifth Estate,* 1–14 May 1969; National Peace Action Coalition flyer, SAVF, box 35; *The Observer,* 18 April 1971; *Minnesota Daily,* 18 Nov. 1969.

21. Stanton, *Rise and Fall of an American Army,* 331. See also Richard A. Gabriel and Paul L. Savage, *Crisis in Command: Mismanagement in the Army* (New York: Hill & Wang, 1978), chap. 2.

22. "Black Power in Viet Nam," *Time,* 19 Sept. 1969, 22-23; "Soul Alley," *Time,* 14 Dec. 1970, 39–40.

23. *Newsweek*, 25 May 1970, 45; Gabriel and Savage, *Crisis in Command*, chap. 2; Walton, *Tarnished Shield*, chap. 14.

24. Stanton, *Rise and Fall*, 331.

25. *Fatigue Press*, May 1970, and *COMmon Sense*, July 1971, SPP; *New York Post*, 13 July and 11 Nov. 1970; Cortright, *Soldiers in Revolt*, 108–10.

26. Cortright, *Soldiers in Revolt*, chap. 6.

27. *Fat Albert's Death Ship Times*, 30 Nov. 1972, SPP; *American Report*, 7 Apr. 1972 and 4 June 1973; *NYT*, 18 May 1973.

28. "Black Power in Vietnam," *Time*, 19 Sept. 1969, 22–23; *FTA*, June 1969, SPP. See also Bernard C. Nalty, *Strength for the Fight: A History of Black Americans in the Military* (New York: Free Press, 1986), chap. 19.

29. Cortright, *Soldiers in Revolt*, 19–23, 33, 57.

30. *Duck Power*, 10 July 1970, SPP.

31. *Navy Times Are Changin'*, June 1971, and *Fat Albert's Death Ship Times*, 30 Nov. 1972, SPP; Cortright, *Soldiers in Revolt*, 25–26.

32. See Jeffrey P. Kimball, "The Stab-in-the-Back Legend and the Vietnam War," *Armed Forces and Society* 14 (Spring 1988): 433–57. This idea was hardly original in the 1980s; see Charles C. Moskos, Jr., "Military Made Scapegoat for Vietnam," *Washington Post*, 30 Aug. 1970.

33. *The Observer*, 18 Apr. 1971; *Newsweek*, "Troubled Army Brass," 24 May 1971, 21–23; Heinl, "Collapse of the Armed Forces," 30–31; Major H. L. Seay, "Leadership Through Group Dynamics," *Marine Corps Gazette*, Sept. 1971, 27–32.

34. Jacobs, "Legal Change Within the United States Armed Forces, 409–12, and Jacobs, *Socio-Legal Foundations of Civil-Military Relations* (New Brunswick, N.J.: Transaction Books, 1986), chap. 1.

35. Elmo R. Zumwalt, Jr., *On Watch: A Memoir* (New York: New York Times Book Co., 1976), 167, chaps. 7–11; Seay, "Leadership Through Group Dynamics," 27–32.

36. *NYT*, 14 June 1970; *Newsweek*, 14 Dec. 1970, 51–52.

37. Nalty, *Strength For the Fight*, 314–17; Martin Binkin and Shirley J. Bach, *Women and the Military* (Washington: Brookings Institution, 1977); Jeanne Holm, *Women in the Military: An Unfinished Revolution* (Novato, Calif.: Presidio Press, 1982), chap. 19.

38. *Newsweek*, 24 May 1971, 23.

7. GI Resistance During the Vietnam War

1. David Cortright, *Soldiers in Revolt: The American Military Today* (New York: Anchor/Doubleday, 1975), 11–14.

2. R. William Rae, Stephen B. Forman and Howard Olson, *Future Impact of Dissident Elements Within the Army on the Enforcement of Discipline, Law and Order* (McLean, Va.: Research Analysis Corporation, Jan. 1972); Howard Olson and R. William Rae, *Determination of the Potential for Dissidents in the U.S. Army* (McLean, Va.: Research Analysis Corporation, Mar. 1971).

3. Rae, Forman, and Olson, *Future Impact*, 36.

4. According to figures from the Defense Manpower Data Center in Arlington, Virginia, less-than-fully-honorable discharge rates in the army rose to an all-time record of 26.6 percent in 1984. Attrition rates reached a record 40 percent in 1980 and remained above 20 percent for much of the decade.

5. Department of Defense, *Report of the Task Force on the Administration of Military Justice in the Armed Forces* (Washington: GPO, 1972), 1:19–20.

6. Congressional Black Caucus, *Racism in the Military: A New System for Rewards and Punishment* (Washington: GPO, 1972).

7. Department of Defense, *Report of the Task Force* 1:27–28.

8. Ibid. 1:30–31.

9. Ibid. 4:160.

10. Shelby L. Stanton, *The Rise and Fall of an American Army* (Novato, Calif.: Presidio Press, 1985).

11. Ibid., 366.

12. Ibid., 367.

13. Ibid., 357.

14. Cortright, *Soldiers in Revolt,* 43.

15. Stanton, *Rise and Fall,* 301.

16. Ibid., 349.

17. Ibid., 357.

18. *Air Force Times,* 16 Dec. 1970, 9.

19. Cortright, *Soldiers in Revolt,* 130.

20. *Washington Post,* 20 Jan. 1973, 4.

21. *New York Times,* 6 June 1973, 10; and 26 July 1973, 5.

22. House Armed Services Committee, *Report by the Special Subcommittee on Disciplinary Problems in the U.S. Navy of the Committee on Armed Services,* House of Representatives, 92d Cong., 2d sess., Serial 17670.

23. Ibid., Serial 17684.

24. Henry Leifermann, "A Sort of Mutiny: The Constellation Incident," *New York Times Magazine,* 18 Feb. 1973, 17.

8. Vietnam Veterans and War Crimes Hearings

1. Richard A. Falk, Gabriel Kolko, and Robert Jay Lifton, eds., *Crimes of War* (New York: Vintage, 1971), 222.

2. See Seymour M. Hersh, *My Lai 4* (New York: Random House, 1970); Richard Hammer, *One Morning in the War* (New York: Coward-McCann, 1970).

3. Hersh, *My Lai,* 138–39; Hammer, *One Morning,* 173–74.

4. Hammer, *One Morning,* xi; Hersh, *My Lai,* 151–55. A poll taken in St. Louis at the time of the My Lai disclosure indicated that only 12 percent of the respondents believed the story to be true; Frances Fitzgerald, *Fire in the Lake* (New York: Vintage, 1972), 504. A *Time* poll conducted in January 1970 showed that a majority of Americans felt that incidents like My Lai happened in all wars; see Hammer, *One Morning,* 176.

5. Hersh, *My Lai*, 132.

6. Ibid., 161.

7. Hammer, *One Morning*, 197.

8. Hersh, *My Lai*, 197.

9. Ibid., 141.

10. The complete transcript of these hearings can be found in James Simon Kunen, *Standard Operating Procedure* (New York: Avon, 1971).

11. Ibid., 22.

12. Ibid, 33–35.

13. Ibid, 80–81.

14. Ibid., 57.

15. Ibid., 211.

16. For the complete transcript of the Winter Soldier hearings, see the *Congressional Record*, 92d Cong., 1st sess., 1971, 17, pt. 8: 9947–10055. For excerpts from the hearings, see Vietnam Veterans Against the War (VVAW), *The Winter Soldier Investigation: An Inquiry into American War Crimes* (Boston: Beacon, 1972).

17. VVAW, *Winter Soldier*, 2.

18. Ibid., 120.

19. Ibid., 9.

20. Ibid., 104.

21. Ibid., 5.

22. Ibid., 14.

23. Kunen, *Standard Operating Procedure*, 27, 62–65. On 23 March 1971, the *New York Times Book Review* carried as its lead article Neil Sheehan's lengthy analysis of the issue of war crimes in Vietnam. That article was based on thirty-three books published at that time concerning the causes and consequences of American involvement in Vietnam.

24. Kunen, *Standard Operating Procedure*, 147–61.

25. Quoted in W. D. Ehrhart, ed., *Carrying the Darkness* (Lubbock: Texas Tech Univ. Press, 1989), 234–35.

26. Guenter Lewy, *America in Vietnam* (New York: Oxford Univ. Press, 1978).

27. Ibid., 313–24.

28. See especially Telford Taylor, *Nuremberg and Vietnam* (Chicago: Quandrangle, 1970).

29. See Kunen, *Standard Operating Procedure; Congressional Record* 17, pt. 8:9947–10055.

30. Citizens Commission of Inquiry, eds., *The Dellums Committee Hearings on War Crimes in Vietnam* (New York: Vintage, 1972), xii.

31. John Kerry, *The New Soldier* (New York: Collier, 1971) 24.

32. See Robert Jay Lifton, *Home From the War* (New York: Simon & Schuster, 1973), esp. chap. 8.

33. Kunen, *Standard Operating Procedure*, 28–31.

34. Kerry, *New Soldier*, 104.

35. *Washington Evening Star*, 23 Apr. 1971, A3.

9. They Moved the Town

1. A. D. Horne, ed., *The Wounded Generation: America after Vietnam* (Englewood Cliffs, N.J.: Prentice-Hall, 1981), 5-14; Oliver Wendell Holmes, "Memorial Day Address" [1884], in *The Occasional Speeches of Oliver Wendell Holmes*, ed. Mark Wolfe Howe (Cambridge: Harvard Univ. Press, 1962), 15.

2. "Shoulder Sleeve Insignia for the U.S. Military Assistance Command, Vietnam," memo, 10 Feb. 1966, Department of the Army Institute of Heraldry; Donald Smartt and Jan Crumb, " 'Vietnam Veterans Against the War' Speak," *Veterans News*, Jan./Feb. 1971, 20; Tim Wells, "That Was the War That Was," *VVA Veteran*, Mar. 1987, 23.

3. Arthur L. Flesch, "Brief History of Vietnam Veterans Against the War OSU Chapter," 1970, Vietnam Veterans Against the War Historical Collection (VVHC), New York State Vietnam Memorial Resource Center, Office of General Services, Albany; Smartt and Crumb, "VVAW," 20.

4. Flesch, "Brief History." Of twenty-eight student demands, three concerned Vietnam. One called for an end to ROTC credit and faculty status for its instructors, a second urged an end to war-related research, and the third simply asked that the university support its students in opposing the war; see *Our Choking Times*, 8 June 1970, VVHC. National Guard occupation continued from 29 April through 28 May; see Sandra Gurvis, "Diary of a Dilemma," *Ohio State University Monthly*, June 1970, 3-22.

5. Flesch, "Brief History"; Gurvis, "Diary of a Dilemma"; *VAW New World*, Nov. 1970. The Columbus VVAW chapter took the name "Veterans Against the War" (VAW) during the summer to reflect its inclusion of Vietnam-era vets.

6. Smartt and Crumb, "VVAW," 20; Flesch, "Brief History"; VVAW, "Operation RAW: Interim Report #1," 13 July 1970; "Operation RAW: Interim Report #2," 31 July 1970; and press release, 4 Sept. 1970, all in VVHC.

7. *Camden Courier-Post*, 12 Sept. 1970; ad in *Village Voice*, 20 Aug. 1970.

8. Smartt and Crumb, "VVAW," 20; *New York Times*, 5 and 8 Sept. 1970; *Philadelphia Inquirer*, 8 Sept. 1970; "Victory at Valley Forge," *World Magazine*, 19 Sept. 1970; "Bringing It Home," *GI Press Service*, 21 Sept. 1970; VVAW, "A Company of U.S. Infantry Just Came Through Here," 1970; "Ambushes Kill or Maim GIs in Vietnam Every Day," 1970; and Winterfilm Collective, *Different Sons* (film), 1970, all in VVHC.

9. National Committee for a Citizen's Commission of Inquiry on U.S. War Crimes in Vietnam, "What Are War Crimes?" 1970, and VVAW, "Call to the Winter Soldier Investigation," 1970, both in VVHC; author's interview with Mike Oliver, conducted at VVAW 20th Reunion, Chicago, 13 June 1987; Smartt and Crumb, "VVAW," 20. CCI had sponsored important testimony earlier on the use of torture and assassination in Operation Phoenix by former U.S. Army Intelligence agents Michael Uhl, Edward Murphy, and Robert Stemme.

10. Thomas Paine, "The Crisis," *The Writings of Thomas Paine*, vol. 1, ed. Moncure Daniel Conway (New York: AMS Press, 1967), 170.

11. Smartt and Crumb, "VVAW," 20-21; Oliver interview; Timothy C. Butz, telephone interview with author, 21 Jan. 1990; VVAW, "The Winter Soldier Investigation," 1971 and press release, 27 Jan. 1971, both in VVHC; Dean A. Robb, letter to colleagues, 19 Jan. 1971.

12. The complete transcript of the Winter Soldier Investigation testimony appears in the *Congressional Record*, 92nd Cong., 1st sess., 1971, 17, pt. 8: 9947-10055. This mate-

rial was followed by Rep. Jack Kemp speaking in behalf of his own resolution to name 30 April 1971 "Pledge of Allegiance to Our Flag Day," 10, 177; excerpts appeared in Vietnam Veterans Against the War, *The Winter Soldier Investigation: An Inquiry into American War Crimes* (Boston: Beacon, 1972), but are less cohesive and complete because of editing for polemic value. My opening statement incorporated a superb passage on the nature of war crimes, written by Jan Crumb.

See also Smartt and Crumb, "VVAW," 21; William Schmidt, "Five Ex-Marines Tell of 1969 Laos Invasion," *Detroit Free Press,* 1 Feb. 1971; Harry G. Summers, Jr., *Vietnam War Almanac* (New York: Facts on File, 1985).

13. Jerry M. Flint, "Veterans Assess Atrocity Blame," *New York Times,* 7 Feb. 1971. Even the *New Republic,* which took a month to cover WSI, began by stating, "The big news to emerge from the Vietnam Veterans Against the War Winter Soldier Investigation into American War Crimes—held here several weeks ago—was that Sen. George McGovern and Rep. John Conyers announced that they were calling for Congressional investigations based on the veterans' testimony." The story did note with derision that ABC News announced, five days after WSI's revelation and with no attribution to it, that American troops had been in Laos in 1969; see Peter Michaelson, "Bringing the War Home," *New Republic,* 27 Feb. 1971.

The Detroit papers, the *News* and the *Free Press,* gave excellent coverage. *Free Press* reporter William Schmidt, who initially raised the question of whether any WSI testimony could be verified, located three ex-marines on his own to corroborate the testimony presented in the hearings on Operation Dewey Canyon; see Schmidt, "Five Ex-Marines."

14. Smartt and Crumb, "VVAW," 21; Barry Romo, interview with author, VVAW 20th Reunion, Chicago, 13 June 1987; Oliver interview.

15. Smartt and Crumb, "VVAW," 21; Michaelson, "Bringing the War Home," 21; Sen. George McGovern, press release, 5 Feb. 1971, and Rep. John Conyers, Jr., press release, 5 Feb. 1971, VVHC; John Kerry and Vietnam Veterans Against the War, *The New Soldier* (New York: Macmillan, 1971), 26; Oliver interview.

16. Timothy Hutchens and William Holland, *Washington Evening Star,* 19 Apr. 1971.

17. Kerry and VVAW, *New Soldier,* 26–28, 104; *Washington Evening Star,* 19 April 1971; Irwin Silber, "3000 Vets March," *Guardian,* 5 May 1971.

18. Kerry and VVAW, *New Soldier,* 26–29, 76, 86, 88; Romo and Oliver interviews; Irwin Silber, "3000 Vets March"; *Washington Evening Star,* 21 Apr. 1971.

19. Author's telephone interview with Flesch, 29 Jan. 1990.

20. Kerry and VVAW, *New Soldier,* 22–24, 30–31; also see Wells, "That Was the War That Was," 22; Silber, "3000 Vets March."

21. Wells, "That Was the War That Was," 22; Flesch and Butz interviews; Kerry and VVAW, *New Soldier,* 31, 128–42; Silber, "3000 Vets March."

22. Author's interview with Pete Zastrow and Bill Davis, conducted at VVAW 20th Reunion, Chicago, 13 June 1987; Romo interview.

23. Watergate burglar James W. McCord, Jr., testified before the Ervin Committee on 18 May 1973 about the origins of the Plumbers. Also see Jan Barry, "Watergate and the VVAW," *The Drummer,* 12 June 1973, 1, 3, and 6.

24. In 1978, RCP split into RCP and "the Workers' Office," but by then Zastrow, Davis, and Romo had taken what remained of VVAW out of the organization; see Zastrow, Romo, and Davis interviews.

25. Arthur Egendorf, et al., *Legacies of Vietnam: Comparative Adjustment of Vietnam Veterans and Their Peers* (Washington: GPO, 1981), 28–29, 63–78; Louis Harris and Associates, *Myths and Realities: A Study of Attitudes Toward Vietnam Era Veterans* (Washington: GPO, 1980), 25–35, 51–77; Joel Osler Brende and Erwin Randolph Parson, *Vietnam Veterans: The Road to Recovery* (New York: Plenum, 1985), 188–89, 208–9.

26. For example, members of the Madison, Wisconsin, chapter told me during my 1970 visit that they had embarrassed local police by exposing to the press that their phones had been tapped when they used them to fake a drug sale. The next night, police beat members in the absence of reporters and lawyers. Mention of the shooting of Florida VVAW member Scott Camil and the stabbing of Detroit member Dewey Bartlett was made during the VVAW reunion in Chicago, 12–14 June 1987.

10. "Not My Son, Not Your Son, Not Their Sons"

1. For the political background of the women of WSP, see Elise Boulding, *Who Are These Women?* (Ann Arbor: Institute for Conflict Resolution, 1962).

2. Barrie Thorne, "Resisting the Draft: An Ethnography of the Draft Resistance Movement" (Ph.D. diss., Brandeis University, 1971); Leslie Cagan, "Women and the Anti-Draft Movement," *Radical America* 14 (Sept./Oct. 1980): 9. The famous slogan appeared in several different forms during the period.

3. Amy Swerdlow, "The Politics of Motherhood" (Ph.D. diss., Rutgers University, 1984.)

4. Jean Bethke Elshtain described the WSP encounter with HUAC this way: "The Women Strike for Peace didn't proclaim that the Emperor had no clothes; rather, it put him in a position where, to his own astonishment, he found he had disrobed himself with his own tactics and strategies"; Jean Bethke Elshtain and Sheila Tobias, eds., *Women, Militarism, and War: Essays in History, Politics, and Social Theory* (Savage, Md.: Rowman & Littlefield, 1990), 4.

5. *New York Times*, 2 Feb. 1966.

6. Gary Rader to *MEMO;* 10.

7. *Sacramento Women for Peace Newsletter,* July/Aug. 1969, 2, Women Strike for Peace Collection (WSPC), Swarthmore College Peace Collection.

8. Ibid.

9. Leo Frumkin, L.A. chairman, GI Civil Liberties Defense Committee to WSP, *LA Wisp,* Sept. 1969, 6, WSPC.

10. Philadelphia WSP *Newsletter,* Jan. 1968, 19, WSPC (emphasis added).

11. An antidraft resolution, which augmented the original policy statement of 1962, was agreed upon as a guide to action. It declared: "We are opposed to the U.S. policy of military intervention all over the world, and the reliance on military means for solving problems which are essentially social and political. We oppose the draft of young men for destruction and killing in Vietnam and anywhere in the world to further this policy of intervention. We oppose all conscription because we want a free society dedicated to the pursuit of human rights."

12. Veronica Sissons, "Who Buys that Dream?" *LA WISP,* Sept. 1969, 3, WSPC.

13. "Your Draft-Age Son: A Message for Peaceful Parents," Berkeley-Oakland Women for Peace, Berkeley, Calif., April 1968, 8, WSPC.

14. The suit named Long Beach Draft Board No. 25, Woodrow Wilson High School of Long Beach, Long Beach Unified School District, Los Angeles County Board of Education, and the State Board of Education. See *Los Angeles Times,* 16 Dec. 1969, and *Long Beach Press-Telegram,* 15 Dec. 1969.

15. *LA WISP,* Dec. 1969, 1, WSPC.

16. *WSP Newsletter, New York, New Jersey, Connecticut,* Oct. 1965, 2, WSPC.

17. Irma Zigas, interview with author, Merrick, N.Y., 26 June 1979.

18. Fearing that records might be stolen from the office or subpoenaed by the government, WSP kept no draft counseling records in Nassau County, so there is no way of knowing for certain how many young men WSP actually kept out of the army.

19. Nashville Tennessee Women for Peace and Social Justice *Newsletter,* n.d., WSPC.

20. *LA WISP,* June 1967, WSPC.

21. Charlotte E. Keyes, "Suppose They Gave a War and No One Came," *McCall's,* Oct. 1966, 26, 187–91.

22. *This Week,* 13 Apr. 1969; *Plain Rapper,* 10 Jan. 1969, 2.

23. *Plain Rapper,* 10 Jan. 1969, 1–2.

24. "Statement to the Press by Evelyn Whitehorn," 25 Aug. 1967, WSPC.

25. "Women's Statement of Conscience to be presented to General Hershey, nationwide director of Selective Service at a nationwide demonstration of women, Wednesday, Sept. 20, 1967," WSPC.

26. This WSP demonstration in support of draft resistance actually took place one month before a delegation of writers, college professors, and other professionals visited the attorney general's office to declare with more specificity than WSP had, that they would "counsel, aid, and abet draft resisters." See Denise Levertov, "The Intellectuals and the War Machine," *North American Review* 253 (Jan. 1968): 11.

27. *New York Times,* 21 Sept. 1967.

28. *Baltimore Sun,* 21 Sept. 1967.

29. *Washington Post,* 22 Sept. 1967, A24. WWDC, a local radio station, accused the "impatient women" of breaking the rules. "All the kicking and pushing was an outgrowth of this decision to defy the police and push through the barricade. Under the circumstances, WWDC rejects the tiresome cries of police brutality. To try to make the police the scapegoats for the misbehavior of these demonstrators does no credit to their cause." Transcript of WWDC Editorial #1 by Vice President Perry S. Samuels, 22 Sept. 1968, WSPC.

30. WSP press release, Washington, D.C., 22 Sept. 1967, WSPC.

11. "Women Power" and Women's Liberation

1. The essay's focus, however, is upon the relationship between the women's liberation movement and the *radical* wing of the antiwar movement, for with rare exceptions—such as the Jeannette Rankin Brigade protest described below—the WLM had little contact with the more mainstream antiwar movement.

2. Nancy Zaroulis and Gerald Sullivan, *Who Spoke Up? American Protest Against the War in Vietnam, 1963–1975* (Garden City, N.Y.: Doubleday, 1984).

3. The Movement refers to the overlapping protest movements of the 1960s—the antiwar movement, the black freedom movement, and the more self-consciously political New Left.

4. See Robin Morgan, "Rights of Passage," *Ms.*, Sept. 1975; Andrea Dworkin, *Letters from a War Zone* (New York: Dutton, 1989), 214–21; Jane Alpert, "Mother Right: A New Feminist Theory," *Ms.*, Aug. 1973; Kathleen Barry, *Female Sexual Slavery* (Englewood Cliffs, N.J.: Prentice-Hall, 1979), 118–36; and Leah Fritz, *Dreamers and Dealers: An Intimate Appraisal of the Women's Movement* (Boston: Beacon, 1979).

5. The material for this paper is drawn from Alice Echols, *Daring to Be Bad: Radical Feminism in America, 1967–1975* (Minneapolis: Univ. of Minnesota Press, 1989).

6. Sara Evans, *Personal Politics: The Roots of Women's Liberation in the Civil Rights Movement and the New Left* (New York: Knopf, 1979).

7. Wini Breines, *Community and Organization in the New Left: 1962–1968* (New York: Praeger, 1982).

8. Greg Calvert, "A Left Wing Alternative," *Liberation*, May 1969, 23.

9. Staughton Lynd, "The Movement: A New Beginning," ibid., 14.

10. Before singing at the SANE Emergency Rally on Vietnam in Madison Square Garden on 8 June 1965, folksinger Joan Baez gave a short speech, in which she said, "And if you young ladies think it is wrong to kill, and war is wrong, you can say yes to the young men who say no to the draft." Her remarks appeared in *Liberation*, Aug. 1965, 35.

11. Indeed, some politicos at first referred to themselves simply as radical women. By the summer of 1968, however, all factions embraced the term "women's liberation."

12. They did not, however, maintain that women as *individuals* should withdraw from the Left. In fact, many radical feminists continued to participate in Left activities.

13. Marilyn Webb, "Women: We Have a Common Enemy," *New Left Notes*, 10 June 1968, 15.

14. Quoted in Warren and Marianne Hinckle, "A History of the Rise of the Unusual Movement for Woman Power in the United States, 1961–1968," *Ramparts*, Feb. 1968.

15. See Echols, *Daring to be Bad*, 54–59, for an account of the protest.

16. Webb, "Call for a Spring Conference," *Voice of the Women's Liberation Movement*, March 1968.

17. Shulamith Firestone, "The Jeannette Rankin Brigade: Women Power?" in *Notes from the First Year: Women's Liberation*, ed. Shulamith Firestone, (New York: New York Radical Women, 1968).

18. Hinckle and Hinckle, "A History of the Rise of the Unusual Movement."

19. Ibid. (emphasis added).

20. See Echols, *Daring to be Bad*, for an account of the Mobe protest.

21. Space does not permit a discussion here, but other New York women's liberationists whose political orientation was politico attended.

22. Ellen Willis, "Women and the Left," *Guardian*, 15 Feb. 1969.

23. Willis, "Up From Radicalism: A Feminist Journal," *US* magazine, 1969.

24. Webb believes the caller was Cathy Wilkerson, an SDSer who became a Weatherman.

25. Ellen Willis et al., "New York Women Reply," *Voice of the Women's Liberation Movement* (1969), 1, 2.

26. Firestone, *Guardian*, 1 Feb. 1969.

27. Murray Bookchin, "Between the '30's and the '60's," in *The 60s, Without Apology*, ed. Sohnya Sayres et al. (Minneapolis: Univ. of Minnesota Press, 1984), 247–51.

28. See Willis, "Radical Feminism and Feminist Radicalism," in *The 60s, Without Apology*, 91–118.

12. The Women Who Left Them Behind

1. Barbara Epstein, "Rethinking Social Movement Theory," *Socialist Review* 90 (Feb. 1990): 35–66.

2. Ibid., 37.

3. Cynthia Enloe, "Bananas, Bases, and Patriarchy: Some Feminist Questions About the Militarization of Central America," *Radical America* 19 (July/Aug. 1985): 7–9.

4. Mary King, *Freedom Song: A Personal Story of the 1960s Civil Rights Movement* (New York: Morrow, 1987), 451–52.

5. Charlotte Bunch, *Passionate Politics: Feminist Theory in Action 1968–1986* (New York: St. Martin's, 1987), 269–77.

6. Barbara Omolade, "We Speak for the Planet," in *Rocking the Ship of State: Feminist Peace Politics,* ed. Adrienne Harris and Ynestra King (Boulder, Colo.: Westview, 1989): 171–90.

7. Barrie Thorne, "Gender Imagery and Issues of War and Peace: The Case of the Draft Movement in the 1960s," in *Role of Women in Peace and Conflict Resolution*, ed. Dorothy McGuigan (Ann Arbor, Mich.: Center for Continuing Education, 1977), 55–56.

8. King, *Freedom Song*, 139–43, 162, 280. The entire memo and its November 1964 predecessor are reprinted in full as Appendices 2 and 3.

9. Sara Evans, *Personal Politics: The Roots of Liberation in the Civil Rights Movement and the New Left* (New York: Knopf, 1979), 83.

10. King, *Freedom Song*, 460.

11. Ibid., 567–74.

12. Ibid., 572–73.

13. Ibid., 571.

14. Evans, *Personal Politics*, 188.

15. Mary Field Belenky et al., *Women's Ways of Knowing: The Development of Self, Voice, and Mind* (New York: Basic Books, 1986), introduction and chap. 1.

16. Evans, *Personal Politics*, 109.

17. The best accounts of organizing at the local level appear in David Hunt, "Organizing for Revolution in My Tho," *Radical America* 8 (Jan.–Apr. 1974): 3–181; Jeffrey Race, *War Comes to Long An* (Berkeley: Univ. of California Press, 1971); Arlene Bergman, *Women of Vietnam* (London: Zed Books, 1984).

18. For example, see Bunch, *Passionate Politics*, 274; Evans, *Personal Politics*, 188.

19. This paper rests in part on long conversations over the years with seven women who visited Vietnam during the war or met with Vietnamese delegations outside the United States. Two of the women became activists in women's liberation, five stayed closer to the peace movement, while two later worked only with women's peace groups.

20. Evans, *Personal Politics,* 170.

21. See Belenky et al., *Women's Ways of Knowing,* and articles in Charlotte Bunch et al., *Building Feminist Theory* (New York: Longman, 1979).

22. Temma Kaplan, "Other Scenarios: Women and Spanish Anarchism," in *Becoming Visible: Women in European History,* ed. Renate Bridenthal and Claudia Koonz (Boston: Houghton Mifflin, 1977): 416–19.

23. N.S. and C.K. (CP members and WSP activists), conversation with the author, 1989.

24. See Paul Lyons, *Philadelphia Communists* (Philadelphia: Temple Univ. Press, 1983), esp. chap. 3.

25. One of the better accounts, based on contemporary observation and later interviews, is found in Jo Freeman, *The Politics of Women's Liberation* (New York: McKay, 1975), esp. 103–46 and preface.

26. Robin Morgan, "Goodbye to All That," in *Voices From Women's Liberation,* ed. Leslie Tanner (New York: New American Library 1970).

27. For sophisticated discussions that bring together issues of race and class missing from many of the early writings by breakaway white women, see Bell Hooks, *Feminist Theory: From Margin to Center* (Boston: South End, 1984), chap. 5; Hooks, "Sisterhood: Political Solidarity Between Women," *Feminist Review* 23 (Summer 1986): 125–38; and Audre Lorde, *Sister, Outsider: Essays and Speeches* (Trumansburg, N.Y.: Crossing Press, 1984), especially her essays, "Age, Race, Class and Sex," "The Master's Tools will Never Dismantle the Master's House," "Learning from the '60s," and "The Transformation of Silence into Language and Action."

28. King, *Freedom Song,* 573.

29. Bunch, *Passionate Politics,* 275-77.

30. Marcia Yudkin, "Reflections on Woolf's *Three Guineas,*" in *Women and Men's Wars,* ed. Judith Stiehm (Oxford: Pergamon, 1983), 263–70.

31. Ruth Roach Pierson, "'Did Your Mother Wear Army Boots?' Feminist Theory and Women's Relation to War, Peace, and Revolution," in *Images of Women in Peace and War,* ed. Sharon MacDonald et al., (Madison: Univ. of Wisconsin Press, 1987), 218–19.

32. Lynne Hanley, "Her Story of War: Demilitarizing Literature and Literary Studies," *Radical America* 20 (Jan.–Feb. 1986): 17.

33. Cynthia Enloe, *Does Khaki Become You? The Militarization of Women's Lives* (London: Pluto Press, 1983).

13. "Look Out Kid, You're Gonna Get Hit!"

1. Tom Hayden, *Reunion: A Memoir* (New York: Random House, 1988), 501–5; Kirkpatrick Sale, *SDS* (New York: Random House, 1973), 479, 636; Ottavio Casale, letter to author, 2 Feb. 1988; Harris Dante, letter to author, 2 Feb. 1988; Dante, "The Kent State Tragedy: Lessons for Teachers," *Social Education* 35 (Apr. 1971): 357–61.

2. James T. Selcraig, *The Red Scare in the Midwest, 1945-1955: A State and Local Study* (Ann Arbor: University of Michigan Research Press, 1982), 33-36, 102, 124; Lionel S. Lewis, *Cold War on Campus: A Study of the Politics of Organizational Control* (New Brunswick, N.J.: Transaction Books, 1988), 83-84; Seymour E. Harris, *A Statistical Portrait of Higher Education* (New York: McGraw-Hill, 1972), 728.

3. Scott L. Bills, ed., *Kent State/May 4: Echoes Through a Decade* (Kent, Ohio: Kent State Univ. Press, 1982), introduction.

Because the Kent State University Office of the Registrar never responded to my inquiries concerning the sociodemographic characteristics of the student body in the 1960s (information readily provided by Michigan State and Penn State), I was forced to select at random a number of students and, using 1969 as a reference year, consulted the 1969-70 Kent State Student Directory. A random sampling of names (N=240) taken from the directory provided a profile of the overall student body. The directory provided residency; a careful analysis of surnames determined the ethnicity of the students sampled.

4. Tony Walsh, telephone interview with author, 14 Jan. 1989. For the emphasis on elite universities, see Richard Flacks, "The Liberated Generation," in *Youth in Modern Society*, ed. Shirley M. Clark and John P. Clark (New York: Holt, Rinehart & Winston, 1972), and Stanley Rothman and S. Robert Lichter, *Roots of Radicalism: Jews, Christians and the New Left* (New York: Oxford Univ. Press, 1982). For the author's revisionist look at this assumption, see Kenneth J. Heineman, "A Time of War and a Time of Peace: The Anti-Vietnam War Movement at Michigan State University, 1965-1970," *Peace and Change* 14 (July 1989): 285-323, and "To Undo the Heavy Burdens: The Anti-Vietnam War Movement at the Non-Elite State Universities" (Ph.D. diss., Univ. of Pittsburgh, 1990).

5. Walsh interview.

6. Walsh interview; Joseph Jackson, telephone interview with author, 24 Sept. 1989; *Daily Kent Stater,* 12 Jan. 1965, cited hereinafter as *DKS*.

7. Walsh interview; Joseph Jackson interview; Ruth Gibson, telephone interview with author, 4 Feb. 1989; *DKS*, 2 Mar. and 7 Apr. 1967; Michigan *State News*, 28 Feb. 1967; Michigan State University Faculty Antiwar Petition Addressed to President Lyndon B. Johnson, 27 Feb. 1967, Michigan State University Special Collections, East Lansing.

8. Miriam Jackson, interview with author, Kent, Ohio, 7 May 1989; Joseph Jackson interview; Tim Smith and Scott L. Bills, "My Perspective is Socialism: An Interview with Clara Jackson about the Life and Political Perspective of Sidney Jackson," *Left Review* 4 (Fall 1979): 1-7.

9. Miriam Jackson interview; Joseph Jackson interview; Jackson letter to Kennedy, 7 Jan. 1962, box 1, Sidney L. Jackson Papers (SJP), Kent State University Archives (KSUA).

10. Joseph Jackson interview; Walsh interview; *DKS,* 12 Feb. 1965.

11. Joseph Jackson interview; Walsh interview; *DKS,* 8, 14, 15, 20 Apr. and 19 May 1965.

12. Joseph Jackson interview; Walsh interview; Jackson letter to Mrs. Henry Lewis, 2 Apr. 1965, box 1, SJP; *DKS,* 6, 15 Apr. and 11, 12 May 1965.

13. Joseph Jackson interview; Walsh interview; *DKS,* 11, 16 Nov. 1965.

14. Joseph Jackson interview; Walsh interview; *DKS,* 24 Feb. and 8 Apr. 1966.

15. Joseph Jackson interview; Walsh interview; Gibson interview; *DKS,* 16 Nov. 1965.

16. Joseph Jackson interview; Gibson interview; Robert Lewis, interview with author, Kent, Ohio, 6 May 1989.

17. Joseph Jackson interview; Gibson interview; *DKS*, 1 Mar., 18 Apr., 25 May, and 2 June 1967.

18. Joseph Jackson interview; Gibson interview; Walsh interview; *DKS*, 27, 31 Oct. and 2 Nov. 1967; Joe Eszterhas and Michael D. Roberts, *13 Seconds: Confrontation at Kent State* (New York: College Notes and Texts, 1970), 34.

19. Howie Emmer and James Powrie, formal remarks made at the Kent State SDS Reunion, 5 May 1989, Kent, Ohio; *DKS*, 17, 20 Oct. and 2 Nov. 1967.

20. Gibson interview; Joseph Jackson interview; *DKS*, 17, 20, 27 Oct. and 9, 29 Nov. 1967, and 14 Feb. 1968; Kenneth Calkins, "The Frustrations of a Former Activist," in Bills, *Kent State, May 4*, 100–104.

21. *DKS*, 31 Oct. and 8, 14, 21 Nov. 1967.

22. *DKS*, 1, 2, 14 Nov. and 6, 7 Dec. 1967.

23. Joseph Jackson interview; Gibson interview; *DKS*, 17, 23 Jan., 22, 23 Feb., 30 Apr., and 7, 8 May 1968.

24. Joseph Jackson interview; Gibson interview; *DKS*, 17, 23 Jan., 22, 23 Feb., 30 Apr., and 7, 8 May 1968.

25. Joseph Jackson interview; Gibson interview; Miriam Jackson interview; *DKS*, 7, 8 May 1968.

26. Sale, *SDS*, 3, 490, 577-78; Todd Gitlin, *The Sixties: Years of Hope, Days of Rage* (New York: Bantam, 1987), 386-87; Gibson interview; Powrie and Emmer, SDS Reunion; Eszterhas and Roberts, *13 Seconds*, 58; James A. Michener, *Kent State: What Happened and Why* (New York: Ballantine Books, 1971), 76-77.

27. The Kent State SDS and the Kent Committee to End the War in Vietnam was determined by compiling data bases on both organizations, as well as on Kent State anti- and prowar students in general. KSU student directories were consulted.

28. Tom Grace, telephone interview with author, 3 Mar. 1989; Ken Hammond, "History Lesson: Kent State, A Participant's Memoir," Mar. 1974, box 21, May 4th Collection, KSUA; Eszterhas and Roberts, *13 Seconds*, 45-69; Milton Viorst, *Fire in the Streets: America in the 1960's* (New York: Simon & Schuster, 1979), 510.

29. Grace interview; Viorst, *Fire in the Streets*, 511-12.

30. *Maggie's Farm*, 12 Nov. 1968, box 20, KSUA.

31. Ibid.; *DKS*, 14 Nov. 1968.

32. Gibson interview; *DKS*, 14 Nov. 1968.

33. Kent State SDS circular, "I Read the News Today, Oh Boy: 250 Black Students Exiled from KSU," Nov. 1968, box 20; Kent State SDS circular, "Say Yes to Boycott! Say No to Business as Usual," Nov. 1968, box 21; Robert I. White, Special Bulletin to All Faculty and Staff, 18 Nov. 1968, box 20; Robert I. White, Kent State University Office of the President, Special Bulletin to All Faculty and Staff, 25 Nov. 1968, box 20; Robert E. Matson, Kent State University Dean of Students Office, press release, 18 Nov. 1968, box 20, all in KSUA.

34. Joseph Jackson interview; Andy Pyle, interview with author, Kent, Ohio, 5 May 1989; Kent State University, Statement by the University Committee of the University

Faculty Senate, 22 Nov. 1968, and Faculty Senate Minutes, 19 Dec. 1968, 12, both in box 20, KSUA; *DKS*, 14 Nov. 1968.

35. Hammond, "History Lesson"; Grace interview; Viorst, *Fire in the Streets*, 512–13; Eszterhas and Roberts, *13 Seconds*, 57; SDS National Office, *New Left Notes* (Chicago), 11 Dec. 1968; *DKS*, 1, 5, 21 Nov. 1968.

36. Grace interview; Powrie, SDS Reunion; Melissa Whitaker, interview with author, Kent, Ohio, 6 May 1989; Kent State SDS, "SDS Draft Committee," Dec. 1968 and Kent State SDS circular, "Kent Free University," n.d., [ca.1968 or early 1969], both in box 21, KSUA; Sale, *SDS*, 489; *DKS*, 8, 11 Oct. 1968.

37. Grace interview; Viorst, *Fire in the Streets*, 513–15; Sale, *SDS*, 517.

38. Grace interview; Viorst, *Fire in the Streets*, 515–16.

39. *DKS*, 3 Oct. 1967 and 23 Oct. 1968; *The Big US* (Cleveland, Ohio), 26 Apr. 1969; Bills, *Kent State, May 4*, 141–42.

40. Grace interview; Emmer and Powrie, SDS Reunion; Pyle interview; Gibson interview; Viorst, *Fire in the Streets*, 516–18; *The Big US*, 26 Apr. 1969; *DKS*, 6, 9, 10 Apr. 1969; Kent State SDS leaflet, "Liquid Crystals Chained Shut!" n.d. [ca. Spring 1969], box 21; Kent State SDS leaflet, "Abolish Liberalism!" n.d. [ca. Spring 1969], box 20; Kent State SDS leaflet, "Kent Thugs," n.d. [ca. Spring 1969], box 20; Kent State SDS position paper, "Now is the Time of the Furnaces, and Only Light Should Be Seen," n.d., [ca. Spring 1969], box 20; Kent State SDS leaflet, "Open it Up, or Shut it Down!" 15 Apr. 1969, box 21, all in KSUA.

41. Grace interview; Gibson interview; Pyle interview; Powrie and Emmer, SDS Reunion; *DKS*, 15, 16 May 1969; Hearings before the House Committee on Internal Security, *Investigation of Students for a Democratic Society, Part 2, Kent State University* (Washington: GPO, 1969), 475–642; Kenneth Calkins, "The Frustrations of a Former Activist," 100–104; Kent State SDS leaflet, "Mind F.U.C.K.*" n.d. [ca. Spring 1969]; Committee of the Concerned Citizens of Kent State leaflet, "Rally," n.d. [ca. Spring 1969]; Committee of the Concerned Citizens of Kent State leaflet, "Seek the Truth! Act on Your Conscience!" n.d. [Spring 1969]; Gene Wenninger, Memo to All Staff, 21 Apr. 1969; American Association of University Professors, Memo to Kent State University Community, 21 Apr. 1969, all in box 20, KSUA.

42. Powrie and Emmer, SDS Reunion; Richard Oestreicher, interview with author, Pittsburgh, Pa., 11 Jan. 1989; Sale, *SDS*, 558–74.

43. Sale, *SDS*, 576–83, 648; *DKS*, 10, 23 Oct. 1969; Penn State *Daily Collegian*, 14 Aug. 1969; Robin Marks, formal remarks made at Kent State SDS reunion, 6 May 1989, Kent.

44. Powrie, SDS Reunion; Pyle interview; Gibson interview; Hammond, "History Lesson"; Eszterhas and Roberts, *13 Seconds*, 68–69.

45. Pyle interview; *DKS*, 3, 8, 9, 10, 16, 31 Oct. and 12, 13, 14, 18 Nov. 1969.

46. *DKS*, 20 May, 14, 16 Oct., and 20 Nov. 1969, and 14 Jan. 1970; [Frank Frisina], anti-SDS scare leaflets, no title, n.d. [ca. 1969], box 21, KSUA; Eszterhas and Roberts, *13 Seconds*, 67; Gene Wenninger, Memo to All Staff, Graduate Assistants, etc., on Referendum, 24 Apr. 1969, box 20, KSUA.

47. SUNY-Buffalo *Spectrum*, 10 Dec. 1969; *DKS*, 15, 20 May 1969 and 14 Jan. 1970; Eszterhas and Roberts, *13 Seconds*, 100-03, 136–44.

48. Walsh interview; Gibson interview; Eszterhas and Roberts, *13 Seconds*, 143–44; Joan Morrison and Robert K. Morrison, *From Camelot to Kent State: The Sixties Experience in*

the Words of Those Who Lived It (New York: Time Books, 1987), 229–335; Bills, *Kent State, May 4*, 82–91; Viorst, *Fire in the Streets*, 528–39.

49. Heineman, "A Time of War and a Time of Peace," 285–323, and "To Undo the Heavy Burdens."

50. *Daily Collegian*, 20 Aug. 1970. See also *The Report of the President's Commission on Campus Unrest* [Scranton Commission] (Washington: GPO, 1970).

51. Lewis interview.

14. Conscience and the Courts

1. Works related to this issue include: John Brigham, *Civil Liberties and American Democracy* (Washington, D.C.: Congressional Quarterly Books, 1984); Robert F. Cushman, *Leading Constitutional Decisions* (Englewood Cliffs, N.J.: Prentice-Hall, 1982); Kermit L. Hall, *The Supreme Court and Judicial Review in American History* (Washington, D.C.: American Historical Association, 1985).

2. Richard Hofstadter, *Anti-Intellectualism in American Life* (New York: Vintage, 1962); Tyll Van Geel, *The Courts and American Education Law* (Buffalo, N.Y.: Prometheus Books, 1987), 211. Also consult Clark Spurlock, *Education and the Supreme Court* (Urbana: Univ. of Illinois Press, 1955); Perry A. Zirkel, *Digest of Supreme Court Decisions Affecting Education* (Bloomington, Ind.: Phi Delta Kappa, 1978).

3. "Developments—Academic Freedom," *Harvard Law Review* 81 (1968): 1050.

4. Howard K. Beale, *Are American Teachers Free?* (New York: Scribner, 1936), 17, 22.

5. *West Virginia State Board of Education v. Barnette*, 319 U.S. 624 (1943); Clarence Karier, *The Individual, Society and Education: A History of American Educational Ideas* (Urbana: Univ. of Illinois Press, 1986), 383-85; van Geel, *The Courts and American Education*, 187–89; *NYT*, 11 Sept. 1988, 1, 30; *Minersville School District v. Gobitis*, 310 U.S. 586 (1940); David Manwaring, *Render unto Caesar: The Flag Salute Controversy* (Chicago: Univ. of Chicago Press, 1962).

6. *West Virginia v. Barnette*, 642.

7. *Goodman v. Board of Education of San Francisco Unified School District et al.*, 48 Cal. App. 2d 731, 120 P.2d 665 (1941).

8. *Joyce v. Board of Education of City of Chicago*, 325 Ill. App. 543, 60 N.E. 2d 431 (1942).

9. *State ex rel., Schweitzer v. Turner et al., Member of the Board of Instruction*, 155 Fla. 270, 19 Southern Reporter 2d 832 (1944).

10. David B. Tyack, *The One Best System, A History of American Urban Education* (Cambridge, Mass.: Harvard Univ. Press, 1974) 275–76; Arthur A. Ekirch, Jr., *The Decline of American Liberalism* (New York: Atheneum, 1967), 356. The number of loyalty cases is extensive. For more information consult Walter P. Metzger, ed., *The American Concept of Academic Freedom in Formation* (New York: Arno, 1977); Nathaniel L. Nathanson, "The Communist Trial and the Clear-and-Present Danger Test," *Harvard Law Review* 63 (1950): 1167–75.

11. Ekirch, *Decline of American Liberalism*, 356. Representative works are David B. Davis, *The Fear of Conspiracy* (Ithaca, N.Y.: Cornell Univ. Press, 1971); John H. Scharr,

Loyalty in America (Berkeley: Univ. of California Press, 1957); Ellen W. Schrecker, *No Ivory Towers: McCarthyism and the Universities* (New York: Oxford Univ. Press, 1986).

12. *Ellis v. Dixon et al., Members of the Board of Education of the City of Yonkers,* 349 U.S. 458 (1954); *James R. Ellis, President of Yonkers Committee for Peace v. James E. Allen, Commissioner of Education of State of New York,* 165 NYS 2d 624 (1957).

13. Ibid., 462–64; Nathanson, "The Communist Trial," 1170–73. Moreover, in 1966, in *East Meadow Community Concerts Association v. Board of Education of Union Free School District No. 3,* County of Nassau 18 NY 2d 129 (1966), the court once again upheld the right of a school district to limit the use of its buildings.

14. Henry J. Abraham, *Freedom and the Court: Civil Rights and Civil Liberties in the United States* (New York: Oxford Univ. Press, 1972), 163–64.

15. Howard K. Beale, *A History of Freedom of Teaching in American Schools* (New York: Scribner, 1941), xii.

16. Karier, *The Individual, Society and Education,* 346; Patti McGill Peterson, "Student Organizations and the Antiwar Movement in America, 1900-1960," in *Peace Movements in America,* ed. Charles Chatfield (New York: Schocken, 1973), 116–32; Benjamin T. Harrison, "The Waning of the American Student Peace Movement of the Sixties," *Peace Research* 21 (Aug. 1989): 1–16.

17. "The Supreme Court, 1968 Term," *Harvard Law Review* 83 (1969): 159; *New York Times,* 5 and 26 Mar. 1969; *Tinker v. Des Moines,* 393 U.S. 503 (1969). It should be noted that in *Burnside v. Byars,* 363 F. 2d 744 (1966), the court had established precedence when it found in favor of civil rights activists in Booker T. Washington High School in Philadelphia, Mississippi. A high-school regulation prohibiting freedom buttons was viewed as an unreasonable infringement on a student's right of free speech.

18. Sheldon H. Nahmod, "Beyond 'Tinker': The High School as an Educational Public Forum," *Harvard Civil Rights Law Review* 5 (1970): 278–300.

19. Nat Hentoff, *The First Freedom: The Tumultuous History of Free Speech in America* (New York: Dell, 1980), 6–8.

20. *Tinker v. Des Moines,* 503–5.

21. Hentoff, *The First Freedom,* 6–8.

22. Ibid, 7–8.

23. *Tinker v. Des Moines,* 506.

24. Ibid., 511.

25. John E. Nowack, Ronald D. Rotunda, and J. Nelson Young, *Constitutional Law* (St. Paul, Minn.: West, 1986), 985–87; *U.S. v. O'Brien,* 391 U.S. 367, 88 S. Ct 1673.

26. Nahmod, "Beyond 'Tinker,'" 280; Casenote, *Harvard Law Review* 84 (1971): 1702.

27. *Zucker v. Panitz,* 299 F. Supp. 102 (S.D. NY 1969).

28. *Butts v. Dallas Independent School District & Nolan Estes,* 436 F. Supp. 728 (1970).

29. *Guzick v. Drebus,* 431 F.2d 594 (6th Cir. 1970).

30. Eva A. Rubin, *The Supreme Court and the American Family* (Westport, Conn.: Greenwood, 1986), 134–35.

31. "Developments—Academic Freedom," 106.

32. *New York Times*, 25, 26, 28 May and 5 Dec. 1972; *James v. Board of Education of Addison*, 461 F. 2d 566 (1972); Hentoff, *The First Freedom*, 46–53.

33. Hentoff, *The First Freedom*, 47. See also Richard Harris, *Freedom Spent: Tales of Tyranny in America* (Boston: Little, Brown, 1976), *passim*. Worthy of note is the fact that in contrast to World War I and World War II cases, where teachers with many years of experience were dismissed, the Vietnam War cases singled out only nontenured teachers.

34. Hentoff, The *First Freedom*, 47–48.

35. Ibid., 48.

36. Ibid., 48–51.

37. Van Geel, *The Courts and American Education Law*, 222–23.

38. *James v. Board of Education of Addison*, 566–76.

39. Ibid., 571–72.

40. This particular aspect is well documented in Harris, *Freedom Spent;* consult also Hentoff, *The First Freedom*, 52–54.

41. *Russo v. Central School District No. 1, Towns of Rush, et al., Monroe County*, 469 F.2d 623 (1972).

42. Hyman Kavett, "How Do We Stand with the Pledge of Allegiance Today?" *Social Education*, Mar. 1976, 135–40. In 1971 the New York Commissioner of Education, Ewald Nyquist, ordered the Boards of Education [Decision 8252, Matter of Bustin, 10 Ed. Dept. Rep. 168] of the towns of Rush, Henrietta, Pittsford, and Brighton, in Monroe County, to rescind their policy regarding the pledge of allegiance. According to Nyquist, a state legislature may mandate the performance of a daily pledge ceremony, but it is unconstitutional for it to require student and teacher participation.

43. *Russo v. Central School District*, 623–34.

44. Ibid.

45. Ibid., 634.

46. *Birdwell v. Hazelwood*, 491 F.2d 490 (1974).

47. Appellant's brief, filed by Daniel T. Rabbit for B. F. Birdwell, U.S. Court of Appeals, 8th Circuit, 1974; in author's possession.

48. *Birdwell v. Hazelwood*, 491 F.2d 491–92; (attorney) Richard O. Funsch, telephone interview with author, 5 Jan. 1988. Funsch reported that the judge, who came from rural Missouri, criticized Birdwell by pointing to the flag in the courtroom and reminding him of the many sacrifices men had made while serving flag and country.

49. *Birdwell v. Hazelwood*, 496.

50. Appellant's brief, 18; *Birdwell v. Hazelwood*, 490.

51. *Stolberg v. Board of Trustees*, 474 F.2d 485 (2d Cir. 1973).

52. *Student Coalition for Peace v. Lower Merion School District Board of Education*, 776 F.2d 431 (3d Cir. 1985).

53. Ibid., 431–42.

54. Ibid. Lawrence F. Russo, *The Equal Access Act Reaches the Courts: Student Coalition for Peace v. Lower Merion School District* (St. Paul, Minn: West Publishing Co., 1986).

55. *Searcy v. Harris*, 888 F.2d 1314 (11th Cir. 1989). In an earlier case, *San Diego Committee Against Registration and the Draft v. The Governing Board of the Grossmont Union High School*, the court of appeals held that the school board violated the First Amendment

when it excluded an antimilitary advertisement after having created a limited public forum by accepting military recruitment advertisements, and that the board violated the First Amendment even if the school newspapers represented a nonpublic forum. Consult *San Diego Committee v. Governing Bd.*, 790 F.2d 1471 (9th Cir. 1986).

56. Van Geel, *The Courts and American Education Law,* 212.

57. Ibid., 212–13.

58. George Orwell, *1984* (New York: New American Library, 1961), 254–55.

Selected Readings

Bibliographies and Documents

Burns, Richard Dean, and Milton Leitenberg, eds. *The Wars in Vietnam, Cambodia, and Laos, 1945–1982: A Bibliographic Guide.* Santa Barbara, Calif.: ABC Clio, 1983.

Clavir, Judith, et al., eds. *The Sixties Papers: Documents of a Rebellious Decade.* New York: Praeger, 1984.

Cohen, Mitchell, and Dennis Hale, eds. *The New Student Left.* Boston: Beacon, 1967.

Heath, G. Louis, ed. *Mutiny Does Not Happen Lightly: The Literature of the American Resistance to the Vietnam War.* Metuchen, N.J.: Scarecrow Press, 1976.

Levine, Mark L., et al., eds. *The Tales of Hoffman.* New York: Bantam, 1970.

Menashe, Louis, and Ronald Radosh, eds. *Teach-ins U.S.A.: Reports, Opinions, Documents.* New York: Praeger, 1967.

The Report of the President's Commission on Campus Unrest [Scranton Commission]. Washington, D.C.: GPO, 1970.

Taylor, Clyde, ed. *Vietnam and Black America: An Anthology of Protest and Resistance.* Garden City, N.Y.: Anchor/Doubleday, 1973.

Teodori, Massimo, ed. *The New Left: A Documentary History.* Indianapolis, Ind.: Bobbs-Merrill, 1969.

Thorne, David and George Butler, eds. *The New Soldier.* New York: Macmillan, 1971.

Vietnam Veterans Against the War. *The Winter Soldier Investigation: An Inquiry into American War Crimes.* Boston: Beacon, 1972.

Walker, Daniel. *Rights in Conflict: A Report Submitted by Daniel Walker, Director of the Chicago Study Team to the National Commission on the Causes and Prevention of Violence.* New York: Bantam, 1968.

Memoirs

Baez, Joan. *And a Voice to Sing With: A Memoir.* New York: Summit, 1987.
Berrigan, Daniel. *The Trial of the Catonsville Nine.* Boston: Beacon, 1970.
Coffin, William Sloane. *Once to Every Man: A Memoir.* New York: Atheneum, 1977.
Dellinger, David. *More Power Than We Know: The People's Movement Toward Democracy.* Garden City, N.Y.: Doubleday, 1975.
Duncan, Donald. *The New Legions.* New York: Random House, 1967.
Halstead, Fred. *Out Now! A Participant's Account of the American Movement Against the Vietnam War.* New York: Monad, 1978.
Harris, David. *Dreams Die Hard.* New York: St. Martin's, 1982.
Hayden, Tom. *Reunion: A Memoir.* New York: Random House, 1988.
Hoffman, Abbie. *Soon to be a Major Motion Picture.* New York: Putnam, 1980.
Hurwitz, Ken. *Marching Nowhere.* New York: Norton, 1971.
Johnson, Lyndon Baines. *The Vantage Point: Perspectives of the President, 1963–1969.* New York: Holt, Rinehart, 1971.
Kelman, Steve. *Push Comes to Shove.* Boston: Houghton Mifflin, 1970.
Kissinger, Henry. *White House Years.* Boston: Little, Brown, 1979.
Kovic, Ron. *Born on the Fouth of July.* New York: McGraw-Hill, 1976.
Lens, Sidney. *Unrepentant Radical: An American Activist's Account of Five Turbulent Decades.* Boston: Beacon, 1980.
Lynd, Alice, ed. *We Won't Go: Personal Accounts of War Objectors.* Boston: Beacon, 1968.
Mailer, Norman, *The Armies of the Night: History as a Novel, the Novel as History.* New York: New American Library, 1968.
McCarthy, Eugene S. *The Year of the People.* Garden City, N.Y.: Doubleday, 1969.
McGovern, George. *Grassroots: The Autobiography of George McGovern.* New York: Random House, 1987.
Nixon, Richard. *RN: The Memoirs of Richard Nixon.* New York: Warner, 1978.
Rader, Dotson. *"I Ain't Marchin' Any More!"* New York: McKay, 1969.
Rubin, Jerry. *Growing (Up) at 37.* New York: Evans, 1976.
Stavis, Ben. *We Were the Campaign: New Hampshire to Chicago for McCarthy.* Boston: Beacon, 1970.

Secondary Accounts

Andrews, Bruce. *Public Constraint and American Policy in Vietnam.* Beverly Hills: Sage, 1976.
Bannan, John F., and Rosemary Bannan. *Law, Morality and Vietnam: The Peace Militants and the Courts.* Bloomington: Indiana Univ. Press, 1974.
Baskir, Lawrence M., and William A. Strauss. *Chance and Circumstance: The Draft, the War, and the Vietnam Generation.* New York: Knopf, 1978.
Berman, William C. *J. William Fulbright and the Vietnam War: The Dissent of a Political Realist.* Kent, Ohio: Kent State Univ. Press, 1988.

Bills, Scott L., ed. *Kent State/May 4: Echoes Through a Decade.* Kent, Ohio: Kent State Univ. Press, 1982.
Bloom, Lynn Z. *Doctor Spock: Biography of a Conservative Radical.* Indianapolis, Ind.: Bobbs-Merrill, 1972.
Breines, Wini. *The Great Refusal: Community and Organization in the New Left: 1962–1969.* New York: Praeger, 1982.
Brown, Eugene. *J. William Fulbright: Advice and Dissent.* Iowa City: Univ. of Iowa Press, 1985.
Caute, David J. *Sixty-Eight: The Year of the Barricades.* London: Hamish Hamilton, 1988.
Cortright, David. *Soldiers in Revolt: The American Military Today.* Garden City, N.Y.: Anchor/Doubleday, 1975.
DeBenedetti, Charles, with Charles Chatfield. *An American Ordeal: The Antiwar Movement of the Vietnam Era.* Syracuse, N.Y.: Syracuse Univ. Press, 1990.
DeBenedetti, Charles. *The Peace Reform in American History.* Bloomington: Indiana Univ. Press, 1980.
Dickstein, Morris. *Gates of Eden: American Culture in the Sixties.* New York: Harcourt, 1973.
Donner, Frank. *The Age of Surveillance: The Aims and Methods of America's Intelligence System.* New York: Knopf, 1980.
Echols, Alice. *Daring to Be Bad: Radical Feminism in America, 1967–1975.* Minneapolis: Univ. of Minnesota Press, 1990.
Evans, Sara. *Personal Politics: The Roots of Women's Liberation in the Civil Rights Movement and the New Left.* New York: Knopf, 1979.
Farber, David. *Chicago '68.* Chicago: Univ. of Chicago Press, 1988.
Ferber, Michael, and Staughton Lynd. *The Resistance.* Boston: Beacon, 1971.
Garrow, David J. *Bearing the Cross: Martin Luther King, Jr., and the Southern Christian Leadership Conference.* New York: Morrow, 1986.
Gioglio, Gerald. *Days of Decision: An Oral History of Conscientious Objectors in the Military During the Vietnam War.* Trenton, N.J.: Broken Rifle Press, 1989.
Gitlin, Todd. *The Sixties: Years of Hope, Days of Rage.* New York: Bantam, 1987.
———. *The Whole World Is Watching: Mass Media in the Making and Unmaking of the New Left.* Berkeley: Univ. of California Press, 1980.
Hall, Mitchell K. *Because of Their Faith: CALCAV and Religious Opposition to the Vietnam War.* New York: Columbia Univ. Press, 1990.
Halloran, James D., et al. *Demonstrations and Communication: A Case Study.* Hammondsworth, U.K.: Penguin, 1970.
Hoffman, Abbie. *Revolution for the Hell of It.* New York: Dial, 1968.
Hoffman, Paul. *Moratorium: An American Protest.* New York: Tower, 1970.
Horowitz, Irving Louis. *The Struggle is the Message: The Origin and Ideology of the Antiwar Movement.* Berkeley, Calif.: Glendessary, 1972.
Isserman, Maurice. *If I Had a Hammer...: The Death of the Old Left and the Birth of the New Left.* New York: Basic, 1987.
Jacobs, Paul, and Saul Landau. *The New Radicals: A Report with Documents.* New York: Vintage, 1966.

Katz, Milton. *Ban the Bomb: A History of SANE, the Committee for a Sane Nuclear Policy.* Westport, Conn.: Greenwood, 1986.

Keniston, Kenneth, ed. *Young Radicals: Notes on Committed Youth.* New York: Harcourt, 1971.

Koning, Hans. *Nineteen Sixty-Eight: A Personal Report.* New York: Norton, 1987.

Larner, Jeremy. *Nobody Knows: Reflections on the McCarthy Campaign of 1968.* New York: Macmillan, 1978.

Lyttle, Bradford. *The Chicago Anti-Vietnam War Movement.* Chicago: Midwest Pacifist Center, 1988.

McGill, William J. *The Year of the Monkey: Revolt on Campus, 1968–69.* New York, McGraw-Hill, 1982.

Meconis, Charles A. *With Clumsy Grace: The American Catholic Left, 1961–1977.* New York: Seabury, 1979.

Miller, James. *"Democracy Is in the Streets": From Port Huron to the Seige of Chicago.* New York: Simon & Schuster, 1987.

Morison, Samuel Eliot, et al. *Dissent in Three American Wars.* Cambridge: Harvard Univ. Press, 1970.

Mueller, John E. *War, Presidents, and Public Opinion.* New York: Wiley, 1973.

Newfield, Jack. *A Prophetic Minority.* New York: New American Library, 1966.

O'Rourke, William. *The Harrisburg 7 and the New Catholic Left.* New York: Crowell, 1972.

Peterson, Richard E. *The Scope of Organized Student Protest in 1964–1965.* Princeton, N.J.: Educational Testing Service, 1966.

Powers, Thomas. *The War at Home: Vietnam and the American People, 1964–1968.* New York: Grossman, 1973.

Rapoport, Roger, and Laurence J. Kirshbaum. *Is the Library Burning?* New York: Random House, 1969.

Robinson, Jo Ann. *Abraham Went Out: A Biography of A. J. Muste.* Philadelphia: Temple Univ. Press, 1981.

Rorabaugh, William J. *Berkeley at War: The 1960s.* New York: Oxford Univ. Press, 1989.

Rosenberg, Milton J., et al. *Vietnam and the Silent Majority: A Dove's Guide.* New York: Harper & Row, 1970.

Rubin, Jerry. *Do It! Scenarios of the Revolution.* New York: Ballantine, 1970.

Sale, Kirkpatrick. *SDS.* New York: Random House, 1973.

Schandler, Herbert Y. *The Unmaking of a President.* Princeton, N.J.: Princeton Univ. Press, 1977.

Schlesinger, Arthur M., Jr. *Robert Kennedy and His Times.* Boston: Houghton Mifflin, 1978.

Skolnick, Jerome H. *The Politics of Protest.* New York: Ballantine, 1969.

Small, Melvin. *Johnson, Nixon, and the Doves.* New Brunswick, N.J.: Rutgers Univ. Press, 1988.

Surrey, David S. *Choice of Conscience: Vietnam Era Military and Draft Resisters in Canada.* New York: Praeger, 1972.

Theoharis, Athan. *Spying on Americans: Political Surveillance from Hoover to the Huston Plan.* Philadelphia: Temple Univ. Press, 1978.
Turner, Kathleen J. *Lyndon Johnson's Dual War: Vietnam and the Press.* Chicago: Univ. of Chicago Press, 1985.
Unger, Irwin. *The Movement: A History of the American New Left, 1959–1972.* New York: Dodd, Mead, 1974.
Useem, Michael. *Conscription, Protest, and Social Conflict: The Life and Death of a Draft Resistance Movement.* New York: Wiley, 1973.
Vickers, George R. *The Formation of the New Left: The Early Years.* Lexington, Mass.: Lexington Books, 1975.
Viorst, Milton. *Fire in the Streets: America in the 1960's.* New York: Simon & Schuster, 1979.
Vogelgesang, Sandy. *The Long Dark Night of the Soul: The American Intellectual Left and the Vietnam War.* New York: Harper & Row, 1974.
Wittner, Lawrence. *Rebels Against War: The American Peace Movement, 1933–1983.* Philadelphia: Temple Univ. Press, 1984.
Young, Nigel. *An Infantile Disorder? The Crisis and Decline of the New Left.* London: Routledge & Kegan Paul, 1977.
Zaroulis, Nancy, and Gerald Sullivan. *Who Spoke Up? American Protest Against the War in Vietnam, 1963–1975.* Garden City, N.Y.: Doubleday, 1984.

Articles

Armor, David J., et al. "Professors' Attitudes Towards the Vietnam War." *Public Opinion Quarterly* 31 (Summer 1967): 159–75.
Beisner, Robert L. "1898 and 1968: The Anti-Imperialists and the Doves." *Political Science Quarterly* 85 (June 1970): 187–216.
Berkowitz, William. "The Impact of Anti-Vietnam Demonstrations Upon National Public Opinion and Military Indicators." *Social Science Research* 2 (March 1973): 1–14.
Brown, Sam. "The Defeat of the Antiwar Movement." In *The Vietnam Legacy: The War, American Society and the Future of American Foreign Policy,* edited by Anthony Lake, 120–27. New York: New York Univ. Press, 1976.
Burstein, Paul, and William Freudenberg. "Changing Public Policy: The Impact of Public Opinion, Antiwar Demonstrations, and War Costs on Senate Voting on Vietnam War Motions." *American Journal of Sociology* 84 (July 1978): 99–122.
Burton, Michael G. "Elite Disunity and Collective Protest: The Vietnam Case." *Journal of Military and Political Sociology* 5 (Fall 1977): 169–83.
DeBenedetti, Charles. "A CIA Analysis of the Anti-Vietnam War Movement, October, 1967." *Peace and Change* 9 (Spring 1983): 31–42.
———. "Lyndon Johnson and the Antiwar Opposition." In *The Johnson Years,* edited by Robert A. Devine, 2: 23–53. Lawrence: Univ. Press of Kansas, 1987.

———. "On the Significance of Peace Activism: America, 1961–1975." *Peace and Change* 9 (Summer 1983): 6–20.

Fairclough, Adam. "Martin Luther King, Jr., and the War in Vietnam." *Phylon* 45 (March 1984): 19–39.

Hahn, Harlan. "Correlates of Public Sentiment About War: Local Referenda on the Vietnam Issue." *American Political Science Review* 64 (Dec. 1970): 1186–98.

Hixon, William B. "Nixon, the War and the Opposition: The First Year." *Journal of American Culture* 4 (Summer 1981): 58–82.

LaFeber, Walter. "The Last War, the Next War, and the New Revisionism." *Democracy* 1 (Jan. 1981): 272–82.

Lipsky, Michael. "Protest as a Political Resource." *American Political Science Review* 62 (Dec. 1968): 1144–59.

Lunch, William L., and Peter W. Sperlich. "American Public Opinion and the War in Vietnam." *Western Political Quarterly* 32 (March 1979): 21–44.

Miller, Frederick D. "The End of SDS and the Emergence of Weathermen: Demise Through Success." In *Social Movements of the Sixties and Seventies*, edited by Jo Freeman, 279–97. New York: Longman, 1983.

Morse, Stanley I., and Stanton Peele. "A Study of Participants in an Anti-Vietnam War Demonstration." *Journal of Social Issues* 27 (1971): 113–36.

Mueller, John E. "Reflections on the Vietnam Antiwar Movement and on the Curious Calm at the War's End." In *Vietnam as History: Ten Years After the Paris Peace Accords*, edited by Peter Braestrup, 151–60. Washington, D.C.: Univ. Press of America, 1984.

O'Brien, James. "The Antiwar Movement and the War." *Radical America* 8 (May/June 1974): 53–86.

Rader, Dotson. "The Day the Movement Died." *Esquire* 99 (June 1983): 304–20.

Robinson, John P. "Public Reaction to Political Protest: Chicago 1968." *Public Opinion Quarterly* 34 (Spring 1970): 1–9.

Roche, John P. "The Impact of Dissent on Foreign Policy: Past and Future." In *The Vietnam Legacy*, edited by Anthony Lake, 128–38.

Schreiber, E. M. "Anti-War Demonstrations and American Public Opinion on the War in Vietnam." *British Journal of Sociology* 27 (June 1976): 225–36.

Schuman, Howard. "Two Sources of Antiwar Sentiment in America." *American Journal of Sociology* 78 (Nov. 1972): 513–36.

Shapiro, Herbert. "The Vietnam War and the American Civil Rights Movement." *Journal of Ethnic Studies* 16 (Winter 1989): 117–41.

Singer, Benjamin D. "Violence, Protest, and War in Television News: The US and Canada Compared." *Public Opinion Quarterly* 34 (Winter 1970–71): 612–16.

Small, Melvin. "The Impact of the Antiwar Movement on Lyndon Johnson: A Preliminary Report." *Peace and Change* 10 (Spring 1984): 1–22.

———. "Influencing the Decisionmakers: The Vietnam Experience." *Journal of Peace Research* 24 (1987): 185–98.

———. "The New York Times and the Toronto Globe and Mail View Anti-Vietnam War Demonstrations." *Peace and Change* 14 (July 1989): 324–49.

———. "Public Opinion on Foreign Policy: The View from the Johnson and Nixon White Houses." *Politica* 16 (1984): 184–200.

Smith, Robert B. "Campus Protests and the Vietnam War." In *Collective Violence*, edited by James Short and Marvin Wolfgang, 250–77. Chicago: Aldine, 1972.

Walum, Laurel. "Sociologists as Signers: Some Characteristics of Protestors of Vietnam War Policy." *American Sociologist* 5 (May 1970): 161–64.

Contributors

NINA S. ADAMS teaches history and women's studies at Sangamon State University. Coeditor of *Laos: War and Revolution* (1971), she has published articles on the Vietnam War in the *Bulletin of Concerned Asian Scholars* and the *New York Review of Books*.

TERRY H. ANDERSON, a Vietnam veteran, is an associate professor of history at Texas A&M University. He has written many articles about the Vietnam War and the 1960s. Author of *The United States, Great Britain, and the Cold War, 1944–1947* (1981) and coauthor of *A Flying Tiger's Diary* (1984), he is currently writing *The Movement and the Sixties*.

KENNETH J. CAMPBELL is assistant professor of political science and international relations at the University of Delaware and teaches in the honors program. He served as artillery forward observer with the First Marine Division in Vietnam from 1968 to 1969.

DAVID CORTRIGHT is a visiting fellow at the Institute for International Peace Studies at the University of Notre Dame, where he is finishing a book on the peace movement during the 1980s. He is the author of *Soldiers in Revolt* (1975) and *Left Face* (1991).

WILLIAM F. CRANDELL served as a rifle platoon leader in Vietnam (1966–1967) and became a national organizer for Vietnam Veterans Against the War (1968–1973). He completed a doctorate in American history at the Ohio State University in 1983 and is currently the director of the New York State Vietnam Memorial in Albany.

CONTRIBUTORS

ALICE ECHOLS is author of *Daring to Be Bad: Radical Feminism in America, 1967–75* (1989). She is currently a visiting lecturer in the history department at the University of Michigan.

DAVID FARBER is assistant professor of history at Barnard College. He is author of *Chicago '68* (1988) and editor of *The 1960s: From Memory to History* (forthcoming).

MITCHELL K. HALL, associate professor of history at Central Michigan University, teaches courses on recent America and the Vietnam War. He is the author of *Because of Their Faith* (1990).

KENNETH J. HEINEMAN, of Ohio University, Lancaster received the Ph.D. in history from the University of Pittsburgh in 1990, with a dissertation on the Vietnam antiwar movement at non-elite state universities. He has published articles on aspects of twentieth century United States political history in *Peace and Change, The Historian, and Pittsburgh History*.

WILLIAM D. HOOVER, professor of history and chairman of the department at The University of Toledo, specializes in modern Japan. He has published articles on Japanese diplomacy, internationalism, and entrepreneurship and served as the Asian editor for the *Biographical Dictionary of Modern Peace Leaders* (1985).

GEORGE W. HOPKINS, associate professor of history at the College of Charleston, teaches courses on modern America, including the Vietnam War. He also serves as coordinator of American Studies and director of Urban Studies. He is completing a study of *The Miners for Democracy: Insurgency and Reform in the United Mine Workers of America, 1970–1978*.

CHARLES F. HOWLETT is an administrator in the Amityville (N.Y.) Public School System. He is author of *Troubled Philosopher: John Dewey and the Struggle for World Peace* (1977), and *The American Peace Movement: References and Resources* (1991) and is coauthor of the American Historical Association pamphlet *The American Peace Movement: History and Historiography* (1985).

MAURICE ISSERMAN, who teaches history at Hamilton College, is author of *Which Side Were You On? The American Communist Party During the Second World War* (1982) and *If I Had a Hammer...: The Death of the Old Left and the Birth of the New Left* (1987) and coauthor of *Dorothy Healey Remembers: A Life in the American Communist Party* (1990).

DAVID McREYNOLDS has been a prominent peace activist during much of the Cold War era. A longtime leader of the War Resisters League, he also served as chairman of the War Resisters International.

CONTRIBUTORS

ELLIOTT L. MEYROWITZ received a J.D. from Rutgers University Law School—Newark (in 1979) and a Ph.D. in history from the University of Pennsylvania in 1982. A practicing attorney in Michigan and adjunct associate professor of law at the Detroit College of Law, he served as a paratrooper in Vietnam from 1965 to 1966. He is author of *Prohibition of Nuclear Weapons: The Relevance of International Law* (1990).

MELVIN SMALL is the president of the Council on Peace Research in History. A professor at Wayne State University, he has written *Was War Necessary?* (1980) and *Johnson, Nixon, and the Doves* (1988).

AMY SWERDLOW is professor of history and director of the Women's Studies Program at Sarah Lawrence College. She is coeditor of *Class, Race and Sex: The Dynamics of Control* (1981) and *Families in Flux* (1989) and author of *Women Strike for Peace: Militant Mothers of the 1960s* (forthcoming).

Index

Abzug, Bella, 168
Adams, Catherine, 234
Addison School District, 233
Addison Teachers Association, 232
Advanced Research Projects Agency, 216
Agency for International Development, 183
Agent Orange, 147
Agosta, Carolyn, 146
Air Force Times, 124
Alpert, Richard, 15
America in Vietnam (Lewy), 136
Americal Division, 130, 131, 132, 133
American Association of University Professors, 217
American Baptists, 41, 44, 46, 47
American Civil Liberties Union (ACLU), 85, 99, 101, 168, 232–33
American Friends of Vietnam, 60
American Friends Service Committee (AFSC), 38, 56, 66
American Legion, 143
American Report (Clergy and Laymen Concerned About Vietnam), 46
"American Report Radio," 46
American Servicemen's Union (ASU), 97, 98, 104
amnesty for war resisters, 44, 45, 169. *See also* pacifist movement
Anderson, Henry, 13

Ann Arbor, Mich., 11, 76, 78, 211
antiwar demonstrations: Clergy and Laymen Concerned About Vietnam and, 43; GIs and, 95, 97, 99; march on Washington (April 1965), 12, 25, 205 (*see also* Students for a Democratic Society [SDS]); New York City (April 1967), 208; pacifists and, 57, 60, 63–64. *See also* Chicago Democratic Convention, International Days of Protest, Jeannette Rankin Brigade protest, Kent State University, March Against Death, May Day, Mobilization, Moratorium, Operation Dewey Canyon III, Operation RAW, Spring Offensive
antiwar movement: achievements of, 51, 69–70; alliance between counterculture and, 8, 11–12, 14–15, 16–17, 20–21, 51; divisions within, 72–74; effect of Vietnamese on women in, 187–89; effect of war crimes hearings on, 138; and electoral politics, 18–19, 44; influence of civil rights movement on, 24, 48, 54, 73; pacifists in, 62–63; public opinion of, 49–50; in response to escalation of war, 27–28; students in, 11, 14, 49, 98 (*see also* counterculture, Kent State University, National Student Association [NSA], Students for a Democratic Society [SDS]; support for

GIs in, 98–99, 100–1, 107, 126). *See also* Clergy and Laymen Concerned About Vietnam (CALCAV), May Day
Are American Teachers Free? (Beale), 224
Arlington National Cemetery, 148, 149, 177
Armed Forces Journal, 111
Army Intelligence, 101, 145
Association of the U.S. Army, 130
Atlanta Peace Alliance (APA), 237
Austin, Richard, 146
Ayers, Bill, 211–12, 213, 215

Bacon, Leslie, 80
Baez, Joan, 27, 29, 60, 264n. 10
Baltimore Sun, 169
Barnett, Gath, 225
Barnett, Marie, 225
Barnett, Walter, 225
Barnette. *See West Virginia v. Barnette*
Beale, Howard K., 224, 227
Becker, Norma, 10–11, 20, 61
be-in, 15
Belenky, Mary Field, 188
Benedict, "Corky," 218
Bennett, John C., 37, 40
Berkeley, University of California at, 10, 15, 16, 163, 176, 199, 203
Berkeley Free Speech Movement, 203
Bernstein, Daniel, 46
Berrigan, Daniel, 39, 60
Bevel, James, 145
Birdwell, Beauregard F., 235
Birdwell v. Hazelwood, 235, 236, 238
black community: opposition to war, 184; response to antiwar activists, 69, 78, 86
Black Fraction, 127
Black Panthers, 213, 215, 218
Black Power protest, 220
Black United Students (BUS), 211, 214
Blaumenfeld, M. Joseph, 236
Bob Hope Shows, 99
Bond, The, 97
Bookchin, Murray, 181
Booth, Heather, 175, 178
Booth, Paul, 26, 27, 28
Bosley, Harold, 40

Bragg Briefs, 98
Breines, Wini, 173
Brickner, Balfour, 40, 50
Brightman, Carol, 14
Brock, Barbara, 205, 206
Broken Arrow, 94
Brown, H. Rap, 33
Brown, Robert McAfee, 35, 40, 43
Brown, Sam, 19, 65
Brown v. Board of Education, 224, 237
Buckeye Army of Liberation, 143
Buckeye Recon, 144, 145, 149
Buddhists, 37, 55, 59, 60
Buhle, Paul, 7, 14
Buley, Hilton C., 236
Bunch, Charlotte, 175, 177, 184
Burdekin, Dan, 142
Burger, Warren, 149
Buttinger, Joseph, 60
Butts, 231

Cagan, Leslie, 159
Calkins, Ken, 209, 217
Cambodia: invasion of, 15, 47, 66, 67, 72, 107, 143, 201, 220
Camil, Scott, 134
Camp Lejeune, 108
Camp Pendleton, 99, 108
Cam Rahn, 108
Canfora, Alan, 212–13, 215, 216, 217, 220
Can Tho, 134
Caplan, Gerald M., 83
Carmichael, Stokely, 32, 184
Carpenter, Bob, 210
Carson, Carol, 210
Casale, Jerry, 208, 222
Catholic Peace Fellowship (CPF), 37
Catholic Worker Movement, 38
Catholic Workers, 60
CBS News, 103, 147
Central Conference of American Rabbis, 41
Central Intelligence Agency (CIA), 150
Chafee, John, 113
Chavez, Cesar, 110
Chicago Area Draft Resisters (CADRE), 13–14

Chicago Area Military Project, 98–99
Chicago Democratic Convention (1968), 10, 17, 65, 122, 212
Chicago Eight, 73, 74
Chicago Tribune, 17
Chomsky, Noam, 87
Chu Lai, 131, 132
Citizens Commission of Inquiry (CCI): hearings in Washington, 131–33, 145. *See also* war crimes hearings
civil disobedience: civil rights movement and, 33, 54; and Clergy and Laymen Concerned About Vietnam, 44, 45; and Committee for Nonviolent Action, National Committee for a Sane Nuclear Policy, War Resisters League, 38; and May Day, 69, 72, 73, 74, 76. *See also* Old Left, pacifist movement, radical pacifists, Women Strike for Peace (WSP)
Civil Rights Commission (Ohio), 214
civil rights movement, 51, 183, 189, 190; effect on antiwar movement, 25, 29, 32, 36, 48. *See also* Clergy and Laymen Concerned About Vietnam (CALCAV), May Day, pacifist movement, Students for a Democratic Society (SDS)
Clamage, Dena, 28
Clark, Ramsey, 149, 150
Clavert, Gregory, 173
Clergy and Laity Concerned (CALC): achievements of, 48–50, 51–52; difficulties of, 50–51; social activism of, 47–48. *See also* Clergy and Laymen Concerned About Vietnam (CALCAV)
Clergy and Laymen Concerned About Vietnam (CALCAV), 4; activism of, 44–45; beginnings of, 38–40; diversity within, 42–43; influence of civil rights movement on, 36–37; influence of ecumenical movement on, 35–36; programs of 46–47; relationship to antiwar movement, 39, 42, 43–44, 45, 48–49, 50–51. *See also* Clergy and Laity Concerned (CALC), Clergy Concerned About Vietnam, Federal Bureau of Investigation (FBI), National Emergency Committee of Clergy Concerned About Vietnam
Clergy Concerned About Vietnam, 39–41. *See also* Clergy and Laymen Concerned About Vietnam (CALCAV)
Cleveland Plain Dealer, 204
Coffin, William Sloane, 41
Cohen, Allen, 15
Colburn, Larry, 131
Cold War, 36, 49
Collins, Judy, 176
Columbia University, 31, 32, 199, 204, 211
Committee for GI Rights, 97
Committee for Nonviolent Action (CNVA), 30, 38
COMmon Sense, 106
communism, charges of: against Clergy and Laymen Concerned About Vietnam, 36, 39, 45; against Kent State University, 208, 209, 217, 220, 221
Communist party (CP), 53, 60, 61, 62, 67, 70, 191
Concerned Graduates of the U.S. Military, Naval and Air Force Academies, 98
Concerned Officers Movement (COM), 106
Conference on International Law and World Order, 30
Congressional Black Caucus, 120
Congressional Record, 147
Congress of Racial Equality (CORE), 26, 203, 204
conscientious objection, 41, 42, 44, 55. 61–62, 110, 206
constitutional rights: for demonstrators, 72, 83, 85–86; for GIs, 97, 98, 99, 101, 102. *See also* schools
Cornell, Tom, 30, 34
Cortright, David, 116
Council on Peace Research in History, xvi, 285
counterculture: differences between antiwar movement and, 8–11, 12–14, 15–18, 19–20, 50; in military, 94, 108, 109; students and, 10, 18, 27. *See also*

antiwar movement, Kent State University
Counter-Inaugural Protest (January 1969), 179, 180, 215
Counter Intelligence Analysis Detachment, 118
court decisions. *See* schools
courts-martial, 91, 95, 96, 97
Cox, Harvey, 52
Crandell, William, 133
Crane, Bernice, 164
Crazies, 19
Crim, Alonzo, 237
Crosby, David, 146
Crumb, Jan, 145
Cu Chi, 132

Daily Kent Stater, 206, 209, 219
Daley, Richard J., 7
Da Nang, 103
Dane, Barbara, 146
Darling, Byron, 202
Daughters of the American Revolution, 138
Davidson, Carl, 29
Davis, Bill, 152
Davis, Rennie: and May Day, 68, 79, 80, 83, 86; views on civil disobedience, 74, 75, 76
Days of Rage, 86, 218
Dean, John, 83
de Beauvoir, Simone, 185
DeBenedetti, Charles, xvi, 51, 85
Defense Department, 100, 101, 102, 113, 114
Del Corso, Sylvester, 220
Dellinger, Dave: and May Day, 68, 87; and pacifists, 29, 66, 70; and the Mobe, 13, 16, 17, 18; views on civil disobedience, 73, 75, 76; and the women's movement, 162, 179
Dellums, Ronald, 69
Deming, Barbara, 70
Democratic National Convention. *See* Chicago Democratic Convention (1968)
Democratic Republic of Vietnam, 187
desertion, 63, 110

Determination of the Potential for Dissidence in the U.S. Army (Research Analysis Corporation), 117
Devo, 222
Dewey Canyon III. *See* Operation Dewey Canyon III
Digger Papers, 10, 243
Diggers, 9–10, 243n. 6, n. 8
Disciples of Christ, 42, 44, 47
dishonorable discharges, 94, 96
Dix, Robert, 204
Dohrn, Bernardine, 211, 213, 215, 217
Dow Chemical Company, 210, 211
draft card burning, 63–64, 97, 229
draft counseling, 215. *See also* Women Strike for Peace (WSP)
Draft Help, 161
draft resistance: Chicago Area Draft Resisters and, 13; Clergy and Laymen Concerned About Vietnam and, 45, 47, 63; at Kent State University, 207. *See also* Women Strike for Peace (WSP)
draft resistance movement, 27, 162, 173–74
Drug Abuse Counteroffensive. *See* Military Assistance Command–Vietnam (MACV)
Duck Power, 94
Dylan, Bob, 34, 110

East Bay California Women for Peace, 166
Eckhardt, Christopher, 228
Economic Research and Action Projects (ERAP), 26
ecumenical movement, 35, 48–49
Edwards, Dave, 205, 206
Ehrlich, Bob, 204, 205, 206
Eisendrath, Maurice, 40
Ellis, James R., 227
Ellsberg, Daniel, 152
Emmer, Howie, 207, 209, 221; and Students for a Democratic Society, 210, 211, 212, 213–14, 215–17; and Weathermen, 218–19
"End the Draft Caravans," 163
enlisted men's club, 114, 125
Enloe, Cynthia, 184, 193

INDEX

Ensign, Todd, 131
Epstein, Barbara, 182
Equal Access Act, 236
Erickson, Rick, 207, 211, 212, 214, 215, 216–17, 218–19
Evans, Dwight, 107, 125
Evans, Sara, 172, 186

Fatigue Press, 98, 108
Federal Bureau of Investigation (FBI): and Clergy and Laymen Concerned About Vietnam, 45, 64, 80, 101, 144; and Kent State University, 204, 208, 217; and Women Strike for Peace, 161
Fellowship of Reconciliation (FOR), 30, 53, 59, 60, 61, 75; pacifism and, 37, 38, 56
Fernandez, Richard, 42
Fifth Amendment rights. *See* constitutional rights
Fifth Avenue Peace Parade Committee, 10–11, 17, 61
Firestone, Shulamith, 175, 177, 179
First Amendment rights. *See* constitutional rights
First International Days of Protest, 63
Five Beekman Street, 29
Flacks, Richard, 23
Flesch, Art, 144
Fonda, Jane, 99, 145, 146
Forsyth, John B., 146
Fortas, Abe, 229
Fort Benning Eight, 106
Fort Bliss, Tex.: resistance at, 95, 101, 109, 116, 120
Fort Hood, Tex., 95, 108, 110
Fort Hood Three, 95, 96, 179
Fort Jackson affair, 99, 101
Fort Jackson Eight, 100, 101
Fort McClellan, Ala., 110
Frankfurter, Felix, 225
freedom of speech. *See* constitutional rights
Freedom Rides, 26
Free Students for America, 31
Friedan, Betty, 172, 176
Frisina, Frank, 209, 219
Fuck the Army (FTA) Shows, 99

Fuller, Barbara, 52
Future Impact of Dissident Elements Within the Army (Research Analysis Corporation), 117

Gandhi, Mohandas, 65, 73, 78
Gelb, Leslie, 50
General Synod of the United Church of Christ, 41
Geymann, John, 134
GI Bill, 153
Gibson, Ruth, 207, 208, 210, 211, 214, 215, 220
GI Civil Liberties Defense Committee, 162
GI coffeehouses: 13, 63, 98, 99, 102, 112, 117
Gigline, 101
GI movement: in the air force, 106–8, 114, 125; beginning of, 96; college students and, 96–97; effect on military of, 104–5, 110–15; expansion of, 98, 102–5, 106, 108–10; lawsuits against military by, 96, 106–8, 113, 125; in the navy, 106–7, 108, 109, 113, 126; as reflection of civilian movements, 93–95; underground newspapers (undergrounds) of, 94, 97, 99, 102, 104, 108, 109, 117, 121, 123, 126
Ginsberg, Allen, 13, 19
GI Office, 99
GI Press Service, 99, 101, 103
GI resistance: in the air force, 125–26; combat refusal, 95–96, 103–4, 124; in contrast to GI movement, 117; desertion/away without leave, 110–11, 112; effect of, 128; expansion of, 124; fraggings, 123, 124; media coverage of, 95, 97, 100, 103, 112; in the navy, 126–27; tactics of, 123
GIs: African-American, 119–20, 125; antiwar activities of, 100, 104; drug use by, 105–6, 114; morale problems of, 123, 126–27; racial problems of, 108, 114–15; statistics on dissidence and disobedience by, 117–19, 258n. 4; shortage of, 121–22. *See also* military
GIs and WACs Against the War, 110
GIs for Peace, 101, 109

GIs United, 100, 101, 114
Gitlin, Todd, 12, 23
Gobitis. 225
Goldfield, Evelyn, 178
Gold Star Mothers, 148
Goldwater, Barry, 37
"Goodbye to All That" (Morgan), 192
Goodman, Ernest, 146
Goodman, Lillian, 225
Goodman, Paul, 60
Goodman v. Board of Education of San Francisco Unified School District et al. [1941], 225, 227
Grace, Tom, 212, 213, 214, 215–16, 217
Great Lakes Naval Training Center, 108, 109
Green, Gil, 62, 68
Green Berets, 96
Gregorich, Barbara, 207
Gregory, Dick, 146
Grogan, Emmett, 15, 243n. 6
Guardian, 32, 180
Gulf of Tonkin, 126
Guzick, Thomas, 231
Guzick v. Drebus et al., 231

Haimson, Leo, 32
Hale, Nathan, 133
Halliwell, Steve, 32
Halstead, Fred, 11, 76, 86
Hamburger Hill (Hill 937), 102–3, 123
Hammer, Richard, 131
Hammond, Ken, 212–14, 215, 218–19
Hanisch, Carol, 175
Hannah, John, 221
Hanoi's Easter offensive, 126
Hart, Philip, 149
Hassler, Alfred, 59, 60
Hatfield, Mark, 43
Hatfield-McGovern proposal, 75
Hawk, David, 19, 65
Hayden, Casey, 185–86, 187, 192
Hayden, Tom, 12
Health, Education and Welfare, Department of, 79, 216
Heck, Michael, 107, 125
Heide, Wilma Scott, 190

Heinl, Robert, 111
Hersh, Seymour, 131
Hershey, Lewis, 163, 168
Herz, Alice, 55
Heschel, Abraham, 39, 40
Hinckle, Marianne, 177–78
Hinckle, Warren, 177–78
Hirschkop, Philip J., 83
Ho Chi Minh, 62
Hoffman, Abbie, 17, 18, 19, 68
Hoffman, George, 210
Hollingsworth, James, 100, 101
Holmes, Oliver Wendell, 141
Honeywell project, 47
Hoover, J. Edgar, 12
House Armed Services Committee, 126, 127
House Internal Security Subcommittee, 217
House Un-American Activities Committee (HUAC), 202
Howe, Henry, 95
Huguenot Herald, 230
Humphrey, Hubert, 176, 211
Hunter, David, 40
Huxley, Aldous, 9, 243n. 5

Iglee, Roy, 206
Independence Day Peace Rally, 104
Intelligence Evaluation Committee, 78
International Days of Protest, 61, 63
International Monetary Fund, 183
international [peace] brigade proposal, 27–28, 246n. 15. *See also* Students for a Democratic Society (SDS)
Interreligious Committee on Vietnam, 37
In the Name of America (Clergy and Laymen Concerned About Vietnam), 44

Jackson, Joseph, 204, 207, 208, 210, 211
Jackson, Robert, 129, 225
Jackson, Sidney, 204–5, 214
Jacobs, William, 209
Jaffe, Steve, 146

James, Charles, 232
James, Neva, 233
James, William, 178
James Gang, The, 219
James v. Board of Education, 232, 236, 238
Jeannette Rankin Brigade protest, 175–78. *See also* women's liberation movement (WLM)
Jehovah's Witnesses, 225
Johnson, James, 95
Johnson, Lyndon, 24, 45, 48, 95; attention to antiwar protests by, 43, 44, 51; against policies of, 38, 72, 160; quoted, 39; support for policies of, 37, 41, 204
Joint Chiefs of Staff, 122
Joyce, Rose K., 226
Justice Department: May Day demonstration at, 69, 79, 83, 85, 149

Katzenbach, Nicholas, 39
Kaufman, Irving, 233, 234
Kendall, Joseph "Jot," 82
Kennedy, Edward, 85, 108, 150
Kennedy, John, 205, 212
Kennedy, Robert, 19, 210
Kent Committee to End the War in Vietnam (Kent Committee): antiwar activities of, 205–8, 209, 210; growth of, 208–9; membership in, 204–5. *See also* Kent State University
Kent State University: activities of Students for a Democratic Society at, 210, 211–12, 213–14, 215–16, 217–18, 218–19; counterculture at, 207, 211; effect of antiwar movement at, 220–22; prowar activities at, 205, 206, 208, 210–11, 214–15, 216–17, 219–20; reaction to killings at, 67, 68, 72, 143, 201, 220; student population at, 202–4, 212–13. *See also* Federal Bureau of Investigation (FBI), Kent Committee to End the War in Vietnam, National Guard, New Left, police
Kent State Young Democrats, 212, 213
Kerry, John, 145, 148, 150
Kesey, Ken, 8, 9, 243n. 5

Keyes, Charlotte, 166
Khe Sanh, 122
King, Coretta Scott, 176
King, Martin Luther, Jr., 108, 122, 210; and antiwar movement, 43, 48, 62; and civil disobedience, 73–74, 88; and civil rights movement, 25–26, 36, 54; quoted, 71
King, Mary, 185–86, 187, 192
Kissinger, Henry, 66
Kleindienst, Richard, 78, 80
Koedt, Anne, 175

Labor Youth League, 60
Lafayette Park, 67
Laird, Melvin, 102, 113
Lane, Mark, 145, 146
Lansdale, Colonel Edward, 57
Laos: invasion of, 76, 148
LaPorte, Roger, 55
LA WISP, 163, 165
Lawson, Arthur, 30
Leary, Timothy, 9, 15, 243n. 5
Left, the, 29, 38, 183, 190; and women's liberation movement (WLM), 172, 173, 175, 178, 179–80, 181, 192, 194
Left Face, 110
Lencl, Mark, 212, 217, 218
Leninism, 190
Lens, Sid, 20, 162
Lerner, Michael, 74, 75, 76, 79, 86, 87
"Letter from a Birmingham Jail" (King), 73
Levy, Howard, 96, 100
Lewis, Bob, 207, 222
Lewis, John, 26
Lewy, Guenter, 56, 58, 66, 69, 136
Liberation, 13, 29
Liberation News Service, 12, 20
Libertarian League, 60
Liquid Crystals Institute, 214, 216
Long Island Draft Information and Counseling Service, 164
Lough, Tom, 214, 220
Lutheran, 44
Lutheran Church, 42, 44
Lutheran Church–Missouri Synod, 42

Lynd, Staughton, 27, 28, 173
Lyttle, Bradford, 72, 74, 86

McCall's, 166
McCarthy, Eugene, 19, 43
McCarthyism, 152, 226
McCloskey, Congressman Pete, 104
McCusker, Mike, 132
McGovern, George, 88, 148
McGrory, Mary, 84, 138
McReynolds, David, 77, 86, 162
Maggie's Farm, 212
Malcolm X, 26, 62, 88
Mallory, Jack, 148
March Against Death, 66
Marine Corps Gazette, 111
Marks, Robin, 218
Marxism, 29, 190, 204
Marxism-Leninism, 24, 34, 60, 70
Mason, Steve, 141
May Day: and antiwar movement, 87–88; conflicts in planning of, 75, 76, 77; effect of, 86–87; goal of, 71–72; government response to, 77–78, 80–84, 85–86, 254n. 36; influence of civil rights movement on, 88; media and, 82–85, 253n. 30; support for, 74; tactics of, 78–80. *See also* National Coalition Against War, Racism, and Repression (NCAWRR), National Guard, National Peace Action Coalition (NPAC), New Left, People's Coalition for Peace and Justice (PCPJ), police
Maydays, 67–69, 150. *See also* May Day
Mayday Tactical Manual, 78
May Day Tribe (or Collective), 68, 71, 76–77, 78, 79–80, 84
Mazey, Emil, 146
Meacham, Stewart, 66
media coverage of war, 8, 50, 64, 184, 189. *See also* May Day, war crimes hearings, Winter Soldier Investigation, Women Strike for Peace (WSP)
Mellen, Jim, 211, 216, 217
"Memo on Vietnam," 57
Merry Pranksters, 9
Michigan, University of, 199, 284
Miles, Joe, 101

military: response to antiwar activities of GIs, 96, 97–98, 99–100, 101–2, 105–6; response to drug problems, 105, 114; response to racial problems, 125, 128. *See also* GI movement, GI resistance, GIs
Military Assistance Command—Vietnam (MACV), 105, 142
military police, 105, 124, 125
Miller, David J., 63
Miller, James, 23
Missions for the Detroit Metropolitan Council of Churches, 146
Mississippi Freedom Democratic Party (MFDP), 30
Mississippi Freedom Summer Project, 26–27, 28, 33
Mitchell, John, 77, 83, 85
Mitchell, Joni, 79
Mobe. *See* National Mobilization to End the War in Vietnam
Mobilization, 66, 99
Mobilizer, 16
Modugno, Vince, 210, 212
Mora, Dennis, 95
Moratorium, 19, 20, 65–66, 99, 219, 230
Morgan, Craig, 219, 220
Morgan, Robin, 192
Morris, Mark, 70
Morrison, Norman, 55
Moses, Bob, 28
Mountain Home, 107
Movement for a Democratic Military (MDM), 99, 126
Munaker, Sue, 178
Murvay, Maggie, 217
Muste, A. J., 37, 57, 60, 66
My Lai massacre, 130, 133, 135, 145, 258n. 4. *See also* war crimes hearings

Nash, Graham, 146
National Action Group (NAG), 66, 68, 74
National Association for the Advancement of Colored People (NAACP), 172
National Cathedral, 149
National Coalition Against War, Racism, and Repression (NCAWRR), 73, 74,

75, 76. *See also* May Day
National Committee for a Sane Nuclear Policy (SANE), 11, 30, 38, 61, 63–64
National Conference of Catholic Bishops, 41
National Consultative Committee, 167
National Council of Churches (NCC), 36, 37, 41
National Emergency Committee of Clergy Concerned About Vietnam, 39–41. *See also* Clergy and Laymen Concerned About Vietnam
National Guard, 122; and Kent State University, 143, 201, 219, 220, 221, 222; and May Day, 80, 81, 86
National Lawyers Guild, 99
National Liberation Front (NLF), 62, 187, 188; and Clergy Concerned, 40, 41; and pacifists. 58, 59; and Students for a Democratic Society, 27
National Mobilization to End the War in Vietnam (Mobe), 13, 17, 72; March on Washington (October 1967), 16, 122, 209. *See also* Counter-Inaugural Protest
National Organization for Women (NOW), 172
National Peace Action Coalition (NPAC), 67, 73, 87; March on Washington (April 1971), 75, 77, 79, 84, 104. *See also* May Day
National Student Association (NSA): People's Peace Treaty, 74, 75, 76, 77, 79, 252n. 16; Student and Youth Conference on a People's Peace, 74, 76
National Veterans Inquiry into U.S. War Crimes in Vietnam, 131
National Vietnam Newsletter, 33
Naval Academy, 114
Neuhaus, Richard, 39, 40
New Left, 3, 12, 38; at Kent State University, 210, 213, 220; and May Day, 78; and Students for a Democratic Society, 22, 23, 24, 25, 29, 31, 32, 34, 246n. 3; and women's liberation movement, 172, 173, 174, 177, 181, 191; and Women Strike for Peace, 171–72
New Left Notes, 23, 28

Newman Club, 209
New Republic, 142
Newsweek, 111
New York Radical Women, 179
New York Times, 39, 57, 99, 127, 147, 160, 169
New York Times Magazine, 100
Nieburger, Colin, 218
1984 (Orwell), 239
Nixon, Richard M., 48, 137, 213, 222; and antiwar protests, 51, 66, 152; and escalation of war, 15, 46, 107, 111, 126, 143, 201; and GI resistance, 99, 125, 153; and reelection, 70, 88, 179; and Vietnamization, 45, 67, 94, 98, 104
Noetzel, Steve, 134
Norman, Gurney, 9
North Vietnamese Army (NVA), 102–3
Nuremberg Principles, 136, 140
Nurses for Peace, 144
Nyquist, Ewald, 232

O'Brien, David, 229
Ochs, Phil, 146
Oestreicher, Dick, 218
Oglesby, Carl, 11, 25, 211
Ohio State University (OSU), 142, 145
Old Guard, 24, 26, 31
Old Left, 3: and antiwar movement, 11, 29, 70; opposition to civil disobedience, 62, 64, 65; and women's liberation movement, 173, 174, 188, 191
Oliver, Mike, 147, 148
One Flew Over the Cuckoo's Nest (Kesey), 8
Operation Awareness, 114
Operation Dewey Canyon, 147
Operation Dewey Canyon II, 147
Operation Dewey Canyon III, 68, 79, 148–51, 153
Operation Dewey Canyon IV (1974), 152
Operation Intercept, 105
Operation RAW (Rapid American Withdrawal), 143–45, 149
Oracle, 15
Orwell, George, 239
Osborn, Kenneth Barton, 132

Pace, Bill, 146
Pacifica Radio, 147
Pacific Counseling Service, 99
pacifist movement: background of, 56–58; civil disobedience and, 63–65, 66–67; influence of civil rights movement on, 54–55; and Maydays, 67–69; members of, 60–61, 62; refusal of military service and, 62–63, 163; strategies of, 55–56, 58–60, 61–62. *See also* Jeannette Rankin Brigade protest, National Action Group (NAG), Students for a Democratic Society (SDS), War Resisters League (WRL)
pacifists, 226; and antiwar movement, 53; at Kent State University, 210; and May Day, 77, 79
Paley, Grace, 64
Palo Alto Resistance, 166–67
Paris accords, 48, 107
Peace, Leroy, 208
Peace and Revolution: The Moral Crisis of American Pacifism (Lewy), 56
Peacemakers, 29
Pechin, Jim, 148
Peck, Abe, 17–18, 19
Peck, Sidney, 16, 20, 75, 80
Pell, Claiborne, 149
Pentagon, 68, 170, 194; GI resistance and, 98, 101, 107, 112, 113, 118–19, 126, 128, 148; and veterans, 136–37, 147, 148, 149
People's Coalition for Peace and Justice (PCPJ), 67, 68; and May Day, 76, 77, 83, 87; People's Lobby, 68, 79, 87. *See also* May Day
People's Peace Treaty. *See* National Student Association (NSA)
Personal Politics (Evans), 172, 186
Peterson, Bruce, 108
Pfeiffer, Bert, 147
Phelan, Mike, 148
Philadelphia Guerrilla Theater, 144
Philadelphia Quaker troupe, 149
Pickett, Bob, 214, 215, 219
Pickus, Robert, 59
Plain Rapper, 166–67
Playboy, 146, 147
police: and Dewey Canyon IV, 152; and GIs, 101; and Kent State University, 205, 208, 210, 214, 215, 217, 218, 219; and May Day, 80, 81, 82, 85, 86; and Operation Dewey Canyon III, 148, 150; and Women Strike for Peace, 161, 168–69
Port Huron, Mich., 23
post-traumatic stress disorder (PTSD), 144, 153
Potter, Paul, 25
Powers, Thomas, 24
Powrie, Jim, 207, 209, 211, 215, 216, 219
Prairie Power, 24
Praline Mountain, 124
Presbyterian Church of the United States, 42, 44
Progressive Labor party (PLP), 24, 25
Project Themis, 216
Protestants, 36, 43, 45, 48, 61
Provisional Revolutionary Government, 187
public opinion: about Vietnam War, 44, 49–50, 54, 65–66, 76–77, 85, 97, 98, 130, 187

Quakers, 61, 73. *See also* American Friends Service Committee (AFSC)

Race Relations Institute, 114
Rader, Dotson, 69
Rader, Gary, 161
radical feminism, 175, 177, 180, 183, 185. *See also* women's liberation movement (WLM)
radicalism, 15, 17, 28, 184
radical Left, 43, 51
radical pacifists, 29, 34
radical politics, 12, 31
Ramparts, 177–78
Randolph, A. Philip, 60
Rankin, Jeannette, 176
Raspberry, William, 85
Real, Mark, 213, 218
Record-Courier, 204, 206
Redline, 109
Redstockings, 180
Reed, John, 87

Reed, Lou, 207
religious community: attitudes about war, 35–38, 41–42, 44–46, 47, 48, 50, 209; support of GI dissidents, 98–99. *See also* Clergy and Laymen Concerned About Vietnam (CALCAV)
Report of the Task Force on the Administration of Military Justice in the Armed Forces (Department of Defense), 120
Reserve Officers' Training Corps (ROTC), 110, 114, 163, 206, 215, 216, 219
Reservists Committee to Stop the War, 109
Reston, James, 39
Revolutionary Communist Party (RCP), 152
Revolutionary Union (RU), 152
Revolutionary Youth Movement (RYM), 24
Rhodes, James, 202, 220, 221, 222
Richardson, Peter, 209, 210
Rifkin, Jeremy, 131, 147
Right, the, 190
Rise and Fall of An American Army, The (Stanton), 121
Robb, Dean, 146
Robbins, Terry, 211–12, 213, 215, 218, 221
Rolling Stone, 18
Romo, Barry, 152
Rosa Parks Society, 30
Rottman, Larry, 132, 135
Rubin, Jerry, 15–16, 17, 18, 19, 68
Ruckelshaus, William D., 81
Rudd, Mark, 211
Russell, Bertrand, 57
Russo, Susan, 234
Russo v. Central School District No. 1 [1972], 223, 238
Rustin, Bayard, 60

Sacramento Women for Peace Newsletter, 161
Samas, David, 95
Sandperl, Ira, 27
SANE. *See* National Committee for a Sane Nuclear Policy (SANE)
Satrom, LeRoy, 221
Savio, Mario, 71

Sawyer Air Force Base, Mich., 110
Schenck v. U.S. [1919], 229
Scheuer, Sandy, 220
schools: effect of court actions on constitutional rights in, 237–39; right of public forums in, 225–26, 227–28, 236–37, 273n. 55; rights of professors in, 236; rights of students in, 228–31; rights of teachers in, 224–25, 226–27, 231–36
Schweitzer, Edward O., 226
Scranton Commission, 222
SDS Free University, 215
SDS Papers, 22, 29, 32, 34, 245n. 1
Searcey v. Harris, 237, 238
Seay, H. L., 111
Seed, 17
Selective Service Act, 167
Selective Service Law Reporter, 165
Selective Service System, 43, 163, 185, 189; demonstration at, 79, 168
self-immolation, 55
Senate Foreign Relations Committee, 79, 148, 149, 150
"Set the Date," 46
Sinclair, John, 10, 19
Sklencar, Marge, 19
Smaller Dragon, The, 60
Smith, Bobbi, 218
Snyder, Gary, 9, 243n. 6
social activism, 36, 42, 45, 48, 49, 111
Socialist party (SP), 53, 60, 61, 225
Socialist Workers party (SWP), 11, 16, 53, 61, 70, 76, 207
Soldiers in Revolt (Cortright), 116–17, 124
S.O.S. Movement—Stop Our Ship, 107
Southern Baptists, 42
Southern Christian Leadership Conference (SCLC), 26
Southern Freedom Rides, 204
Special Forces, 96, 150
Special Processing Detachments, 112
Spock, Benjamin, 68, 207
Spring Mobilization (April 1967), 142
Spring Offensive, 79, 87, 138, 216, 219. *See also* May Day, Vietnam Veterans Against the War (VVAW)
Stanton, Shelby, 121–22, 123, 124
Stapp, Andrew, 97, 98

State Department, 59, 204
State ex rel. Schweitzer v. Turner et al., 226
State of the Union address, 176
Stephens, Charles, 133
Stolberg, Irving, 236
Student Coalition for Peace (SCP), 236
Student Coalition for Peace v. Lower Marion School District, 236, 238
Student Mobilization Committees, 74
Student Non-Violent Coordinating Committee (SNCC), 25, 26, 33, 173, 185–86, 189
students: 7, 10, 38, 96–97; antiwar attitudes of, 11, 14, 49, 62, 65, 98; and Women Strike for Peace, 163, 166–67. *See also* draft-card burning, GI movement, Kent State University, National Student Association (NSA), schools, Students for a Democratic Society, (SDS)
Students' Afro-American Society (SAS), 32
Students and Youth for a People's Peace. *See* May Day Tribe (or Collective)
Students for a Democratic Society (SDS), 4, 11–12, 20, 60, 173, 174; influence of civil rights movement on, 25–28, 32–33, 246n. 6; influence of pacifist movement on, 29–32, 34, 247n. 18; membership in, 22–23, 245n. 2; militancy of, 31–32, 33–34, 247n. 27; political radicalism of, 31; split between leadership and rank-and-file members, 23, 24–25, 246n. 3; and women's liberation movement, 173, 179–80, 181, 188. *See also* international [peace] brigade proposal, Kent State University, New Left
Sullivan, Gerald, 16
Summers, Harry G., Jr., 115
Sutherland, Donald, 99, 145, 146
Swartzmiller, Donald, 208

Taft, Robert, 220
teach-ins, 8, 31, 35, 55, 78, 99, 209, 214
Tet offensive, 44, 94, 98, 121, 123, 142
Thomas, Norman, 60
Thoreau, Henry David, 71
Thorne, Barrie, 159

Three Guineas, (Woolf), 193
Time, 108, 213
Time Is Running Out (May Day Collective), 79
Tinker, 228, 229, 230, 231, 238
Tinker, John, 228, 233
Tinker, Mary Beth, 228, 233
Todd, Joel Ann, 144
Tolson, John J., II, 114
Travis Air Force Base, Calif., 107, 116, 124
Triennial of War Resisters International, 62
Trotskyists, 11, 61, 62, 65, 66, 67; and National Peace Action Coalition, 73, 77
Tyack, David, 226

Uhl, Michael J., 132
Un-American Activities Committee (Ohio), 202
undercover agents, 101
underground papers. *See* GI movement
Uniform Code of Military Justice, 112
Union of American Hebrew Congregations (UAHC), 37, 40
Unitarian-Universalist Church, 209
United Auto Workers (UAW), 146
United Christian Fellowship, 209
United Church of Christ, 44, 47
United Methodist Church, 44, 47
United Nations, 183
United Presbyterians, 41, 44, 46, 47
United States Servicemen's Fund (USSF), 99
Universal Military Training and Service Act, 162, 229
University Christian Movement, 177
Unsatisfied Black Soldiers: Call for Justice rally of, 121
"Unsell the War," 46
Up Against the Wall Motherfuckers, 19
Upshure, Anne, 69
U.S. Army, 101, 235
U.S. Capitol: antiwar demonstrations at, 69, 79, 84, 85, 149, 151, 176
U.S. Catholic, 44
U.S. Congress, 46, 69, 175, 189
U.S. Court of Appeals, 229, 233, 234, 237

INDEX

U.S.S. *America,* 107
U.S.S. *Constellation,* 107, 109, 127, 128
U.S.S. *Constitution,* 126
U.S.S. *Coral Sea,* 107, 126
U.S.S. *Enterprise,* 107
U.S.S. *Forrestal,* 107, 127
U.S.S. *Hancock,* 106
U.S.S. *Huntley,* 109
U.S.S. *Kitty Hawk,* 107, 126, 127, 128
U.S.S. *Oriskany,* 107
U.S.S. *Ranger,* 107, 127
U.S.S. *Richard E. Anderson,* 107
U.S.S. *Ticonderoga,* 107
U.S. Supreme Court, 96, 113, 150; school rulings of, 225, 229
U.S. v. O'Brien, [1968], 229

Van DeVere, Mike, 206
Velvet Underground, 207
Veterans Administration, 153
Viet Cong, 95, 215, 218
Vietnam Day Committee, 15
Vietnamese: self-determination of, 51, 60, 62
Vietnamization, 45, 67, 88, 94, 98, 104, 151
Vietnam Veterans Against the War (VVAW), 68, 99, 137; cathartic effect on veterans, 153–54, 262n. 26; growth of, 147–48; origin of, 142–43; split within, 151–52. *See also* Operation Dewey Canyon III, Operation Dewey Canyon IV (1974), Operation RAW (Rapid American Withdrawal), Spring Mobilization (April 1967), Winter Soldier Investigation (WSI)
Vietnam Veterans Against the War/Winter Soldier Organization (VVAW/WSO), 152
Vietnam War: air strikes in, 111; beginning of, 95; dissent among GIs serving in, 103–8, 123–25; escalation of, 27, 37, 41, 160, 174, 182; overview of, 54, 57, 58–59, 181; withdrawal from, 46, 47, 75, 88, 125–26, 128. *See also* Cambodia, Hamburger Hill, Hanoi's Easter offensive, Laos, My Lai massacre, Tet offensive

Viet-Report, 14
Village Voice, 144

Walsh, Joe, 207, 219
Walsh, Tony, 203, 204, 205, 206, 207, 220
war crimes: allegations of, 44, 45, 96, 147
war crimes hearings: effect on public of, 135, 137–38; media coverage of, 131, 134, 135, 147; policymaker response to, 130–31, 139–40; questions about violations of international law, 139, 140; revisionist approach to, 136–37. *See also* Citizens Commission of Inquiry (CCI), Winter Soldier Investigation (WSI)
War Resisters International (WRI), 62–63
War Resisters League (WRL), 11, 29, 38, 53, 56, 61; antiwar position of, 57, 58, 60, 64, 70, 77
Washington District Court of Appeals, 149
Washington Evening Star, 138, 149, 150
Washington Post, 169
Waskow, Arthur, 74
Weatherman Manifesto, 218
Weathermen, 25, 218, 220, 221, 222
Weather Underground, 19, 69, 245n. 42
Webb, Lee, 26
Webb, Marilyn, 175, 176, 177, 179
Webber, George, 51
Weinberger, Eric, 17
Weinstein, James, 87
Weiss, Cora, 66
Weissman, Steve, 33
Wenner, Jann, 18
Westmoreland, William C., 114, 121, 130, 142
West Virginia v. Barnette, 224, 234, 238
WHACK, 110
Whiskey Mountain, 124
Whitaker, Bill, 215
Whitaker, Melissa, 215
White, Robert, 219, 221; against antiwar demonstrators, 205, 208, 210–11, 214, 216, 217; quoted, 206, 222
Whitehorn, Erik, 166–67
Whitehorn, Evelyn, 166–67
White House, 151, 169

White Panthers, 19
Who Spoke Up? American Protest Against the War in Vietnam, 1963–1975 (Zaroulis and Sullivan), 16, 171
Willis, Ellen, 175, 179
Wilson, Dagmar, 168
Wilson, Jerry, 80–81, 82, 83, 85
Winter Soldier Investigation (WSI), 133–35, 136, 142, 145–47, 148, 261n. 13. *See also* war crimes hearings
"Winter Soldier Investigation, The" (Winter Soldier Investigation), 135
Withers, Leslie, 50
Women's International League for Peace and Freedom, 11, 56
women's liberation movement (WLM): beginning of, 172–74; consciousness-raising within, 190–92; effect of civil rights movement on, 189–90; establishment of radical feminism in, 180–81; evolution of, 189–90, 192–94; minority women and, 186, 189, 192; politico-feminist split in, 174–75, 178–80, 264n. 11; relationship to antiwar movement, 194–95; relationship to other movements, 183–87. *See also* Jeannette Rankin Brigade, New Left
Women's Statement of Conscience, 168
Women Strike for Peace (WSP), 11, 16; antidraft demonstration by, 168–69; and civil disobedience, 165–66; draft counseling services of, 163–65; draft resistance on behalf of mothers, 167–68; draft resistance on behalf of sons, 166–67; effectiveness of, 170; independence of, 167–68, 191; media coverage of, 169; tactics of, 160–61, 162–63, 262n. 11; unique position of, 161–62. *See also* Federal Bureau of Investigation (FBI), New Left, police
"Woodstockades," 84, 254n. 44
Woolf, Virginia, 193
World Bank, 183
World Council of Churches, 36
Wright-Patterson Air Force Base, Ohio, 99, 107

Yellow Unicorn Coffeehouse, 209
Yippies, 7, 17–18, 19
Yonkers Committee for Peace, 227
Young, Ron, 30, 75
Young Socialist Alliance (YSA), 11, 204, 206
Your Draft-Age Son: A Message for Peaceful Parents (Women Strike for Peace), 163

Zaroulis, Nancy, 16
Zastrow, Pete, 152
Ziegler, Ronald, 131
Zigas, Irma, 164–65
Zucker v. Panitz, 230, 231, 238
Zumwalt, Elmo, 110, 113, 128

Give Peace A Chance

was composed in 10 on 12 Baskerville on a Linotronic 300
with display type in Americana
by Partners Composition;
printed by sheet-fed offset on 50-pound, acid-free Antique Cream,
Smyth-sewn and bound over binder's boards in Holliston Roxite B and notch bound
by Maple-Vail Book Manufacturing Group, Inc.;
with paper covers printed in 2 colors
by Johnson City Publishing Co. Inc.;
and published by

Syracuse University Press
Syracuse, New York 13244–5160

Syracuse Studies on Peace and Conflict Resolution
Harriet Hyman Alonso, Charles Chatfield, and Louis Kriesberg,
    Series Editors

A series devoted to readable books on the history of peace movements, the lives of peace advocates, and the search for ways to mitigate conflict, both domestic and international. At a time when profound and exciting political and social developments are happening around the world, this series seeks to stimulate a wider awareness and appreciation of the search for peaceful resolution to strife in all its forms and to promote linkages among theorists, practitioners, social scientists, and humanists engaged in this work throughout the world.
    Other titles in the series include:

An American Ordeal: The Antiwar Movement of the Vietnam Era. Charles DeBenedetti; with
    assistance of Charles Chatfield
Building a Global Civic Culture: Education for an Interdependent World. Elise Boulding
The Eagle and the Dove: The American Peace Movement and U.S. Foreign Policy, 1900–1922.
    John Chambers
From Warfare to Party Politics: The Critical Transition to Civilian Control. Ralph M. Goldman
Intractable Conflicts and Their Transformation. Louis Kriesberg, Terrell A. Northrup, and
    Stuart J. Thorson, eds.
Israeli Pacifist: The Life of Joseph Abileah. Anthony Bing
The Road to Greenham Common: Feminism and Anti-Militarism in Britain since 1820.
    Jill Liddington
Timing the De-escalation of International Conflicts. Louis Kriesberg and Stuart Thorson, eds.
Virginia Woolf and War: Fiction, Reality, and Myth. Mark Hussey, ed.